T3-BOF-629

Language Acquisition

SECOND LANGUAGE ACQUISITION
Series Editor: Professor David Singleton, *Trinity College, Dublin, Ireland*

This new series will bring together titles dealing with a variety of aspects of language acquisition and processing in situations where a language or languages other than the native language is involved. Second language will thus be interpreted in its broadest possible sense. The volumes included in the series will all in their different ways offer, on the one hand, exposition and discussion of empirical findings and, on the other, some degree of theoretical reflection. In this latter connection, no particular theoretical stance will be privileged in the series; nor will any relevant perspective – sociolinguistic, psycholinguistic, neurolinguistic, etc. – be deemed out of place. The intended readership of the series will be final-year undergraduates working on second language acquisition projects, postgraduate students involved in second language acquisition research, and researchers and teachers in general whose interests include a second language acquisition component.

Other Books in the Series
Portraits of the L2 User
  Vivian Cook (ed.)
Learning to Request in a Second Language: A Study of Child Interlanguage Pragmatics
  Machiko Achiba
Effects of Second Language on the First
  Vivian Cook (ed.)
Age and the Acquisition of English as a Foreign Language
  María del Pilar García Mayo and Maria Luisa García Lecumberri (eds)
Fossilization in Adult Second Language Acquisition
  ZhaoHong Han
Silence in Second Language Learning: A Psychoanalytic Reading
  Colette A. Granger
Age, Accent and Experience in Second Language Acquisition
  Alene Moyer
Studying Speaking to Inform Second Language Learning
  Diana Boxer and Andrew D. Cohen (eds)
Focus on French as a Foreign Language: Multidisciplinary Approaches
  Jean-Marc Dewaele (ed.)

Other Books of Interest
Audible Difference: ESL and Social Identity in Schools
  Jennifer Miller
Bilingual Children's Language and Literacy Development
  Roger Barnard and Ted Glynn (eds)
Developing in Two Languages: Korean Children in America
  Sarah J. Shin
How Different Are We? Spoken Discourse in Intercultural Communication
  Helen Fitzgerald

For more details of these or any other of our publications, please contact:
Multilingual Matters, Frankfurt Lodge, Clevedon Hall,
Victoria Road, Clevedon, BS21 7HH, England
http://www.multilingual-matters.com

SECOND LANGUAGE ACQUISITION 9
Series Editor: David Singleton, *Trinity College, Dublin, Ireland*

Language Acquisition: The Age Factor
2nd edition

David Singleton and Lisa Ryan

P
11 8.65
.S56
2004

MULTILINGUAL MATTERS LTD
Clevedon • Buffalo • Toronto

This book is dedicated to Mary Coward,
whose great courage in the face of recent adversity
totally belies her name.

Library of Congress Cataloging in Publication Data
Singleton, D.M. (David Michael)
Language Acquisition: The Age Factor/David Singleton and Lisa Ryan, 2nd ed.
Second Language Acquisition: 9
Includes bibliographical references and index.
1. Language acquisition–Age factors. I. Ryan, Lisa. II. Title. III. Series.
P118.65.S56 2004
401'.93–dc22   2004002819

British Library Cataloguing in Publication Data
A catalogue entry for this book is available from the British Library.

ISBN 1-85359-758-9 (hbk)
ISBN 1-85359-757-0? (pbk)

Multilingual Matters Ltd
UK: Frankfurt Lodge, Clevedon Hall, Victoria Road, Clevedon BS21 7HH.
USA: UTP, 2250 Military Road, Tonawanda, NY 14150, USA.
Canada: UTP, 5201 Dufferin Street, North York, Ontario M3H 5T8, Canada.

Copyright © 2004 David Singleton and Lisa Ryan

All rights reserved. No part of this work may be reproduced in any form or by any
means without permission in writing from the publisher.

Typeset by Archetype-IT Ltd (http://www.archetype-it.com).
Printed and bound in Great Britain by the Cromwell Press Ltd.

Contents

Foreword

This book started life as *CLCS Occasional Paper* No. 3 – entitled *The Age Factor in Second Language Acquisition* – and the original aim of the first edition of the book, which appeared in 1989, was simply to update and extend the paper in question. However, the product which emerged was in fact new in most respects. It was significantly longer than its predecessor, differently structured and considerably broader in scope. In particular, although the principal focus of the volume was on second language aspects of the age factor question, the sections dealing with the first language aspects were greatly expanded. With regard to the present edition of the book, again this started out as an attempt to update the earlier material, but it has again ended up as in many ways a new creation. A second author, Lisa Ryan, was recruited to revise the first language dimensions of the discussion – especially Chapters 2 and 3 and the neurology-focused section of Chapter 5, which, in consequence, have been significantly re-shaped – and there has been so much research activity around the age factor in second language acquisition since 1989 that revision in this connection too has had to go a long way beyond the mere insertion of more recent references. On the other hand, the overall structure of the 1989 volume has been retained and broadly the same kinds of conclusions emerge from the discussion.

The purpose of the book also remains true to that of the 1989 edition. The volume seeks to provide an overview of research and thinking on age-related aspects of language acquisition which will be of service to anyone likely to be in need of such a resource – notably students of linguistics / applied linguistics undertaking projects in this area, researchers in adjacent areas seeking to contextualise their research questions, and educationalists concerned with language / languages in the curriculum. The book is not in a strict sense introductory. Readers coming to it with absolutely no prior experience of linguistics or language acquisition research will find the going hard in places. However, even readers in this category should – with a little perseverance – find the text accessible in all essential respects.

Our thanks are due to a number of institutions and individuals without whose support and assistance the book would never have appeared:

- to Trinity College Dublin for granting the first author a number of leaves of absence to pursue research into the age factor in language acquisition;

- to a number of universities which generously provided the first author with a base and facilities during the leaves of absence in question – notably the University of Southampton, Université Stendhal (Grenoble), the Adam Mickiewicz University (Poznań), the Jagiellonian University (Kraków), the University of Silesia and the Max Planck Institute for Psycholinguistics, Nijmegen;
- to the Speech & Language Therapy Department, the General Manager of Community Services Area 7 and other colleagues of the second author at the Northern Area Health Board for their support and encouragement;
- to the East Dorset Health Authority Library Services for permission to use the library of the Poole General Hospital Postgraduate Centre;
- to the staff of all the libraries we had occasion to use – those of the institutions mentioned above plus the library of Instititiúid Teangeolaíochta Éireann – for their patience and ready help;
- to the Trinity College Dublin Arts / ESS Benefactions Fund, The Royal Irish Academy and the Polish Academy of Sciences for generous financial support;
- to a countless array of colleagues and students, who, through their support and encouragement, through their comments on the earlier edition and on papers which fed into the second edition, and / or by giving of their time on various occasions to discuss the relevant issues, have made invaluable contributions to the evolution of the book – in particular (in roughly chronological order) David Little, Sean Devitt, Chris Brumfit, Rose Maclaran, John Saeed, Louise Dabène, Christiane Bourgignon, Mike Long, Vivian Cook, Jennifer Ridley, Eric Kellerman, Janusz Arabski, Kenneth Hyltenstam, Suzanne Flynn, Jim Flege, Theo Bongaerts, Ellen Bialystok, Dawn Duffin, Christine Dimroth, Niclas Abrahamsson, Carmen Muñoz, Jasone Cenoz, Peter Skehan, Anna Cieślicka, Danuta Gabryś, Anna Niżegorodcew, Robert DeKeyser, Clive Perdue, Clothra Ní Cholmain, Paula Bradley, Max Hills, Susan Lawson and David Birdsong;
- to Eithne Healy for invaluable assistance in the preparation of the manuscript;
- and, last but by no means least, to everyone at Multilingual Matters, including the late Derrick Sharpe, who was a a source of excellent guidance and unfailing encouragement during the preparation of the first edition.

We are all too conscious that, despite the best efforts of those who have given us the benefits of their insights and advice, the book has many weaknesses. For these, of course, we alone are responsible.

David Singleton
Lisa Ryan

Dublin, October 2003

Chapter 1

Introduction

The topic of this book is not only one of the few truly perennial issues in discussion of language acquisition[1], it is also one of the few truly popular issues. On the former point, the age factor has been a constantly recurring theme of language acquisition. Moreover, the connection between age and language development is not something which has only recently been commented on. It has cropped up in writings about language over many centuries. Two examples must stand for many. St Augustine, in his *Confessions*, uses language development as virtually a defining criterion of maturation:

> Passing hence from infancy I came to boyhood, or rather it came to me, displacing infancy. For I was no longer a speechless infant but a speaking boy. (*Confessions*: 1.13)

Somewhat closer to our own times Montaigne, writing of the learning of classical languages, tells of 'a method by which they may be acquired more cheaply than they usually are and which was tried on myself' (*Essays*, 1.26). The method in question consisted in exposing him during the first few years of his life to no language other than Latin. The results, according to Montaigne, were excellent as far as his command of Latin went. The results of attempts to teach him Greek formally at a subsequent stage, on the other hand, are depicted as considerably less successful.

With regard to popular interest, everyday conversations about child language continually refer to implicit age norms. How often does one hear remarks like 'Talks very well for her age doesn't she?' or 'Nearly three and he can hardly put two words together!'? Folk wisdom also abounds when it comes to the role of age in second language (henceforth L2)[2] acquisition, as is evidenced by observations of the type: 'I could never learn German at my age' or 'Beginning French at secondary school is no good; kids need to get started when they're young and fresh'. As far as beliefs about the emergence of the first language (henceforth L1) are concerned, these are obviously based on the pooled experience of child-rearing. As for the age

1

factor in L2 learning, to the casual observer the differences between younger and older L2 learners appear perfectly clear:

> ... young children in suitable environments pick up a second language with little trouble, whereas adults seem to struggle ineffectively with a new language and to impose the phonology of their mother tongue on the new language. (Macnamara, 1973a: 63)

Scholarly attention to the part age plays in language acquisition has mainly focused on precisely the assumptions which underlie comments such as those cited above, namely (a) the idea that there are age ranges within which certain things should happen in normal L1 development, and (b) the idea that one's age is a major factor in how efficient one is as a language learner, and in particular as an L2 learner. Approaches to these assumptions have varied from sceptical scrutiny to more or less uncritical acceptance. In the first case the assumptions in question have been the subject of rigorous observation and experimentation; in the second case they have been treated as self-evidently accurate accounts of phenomena to be explained.

Scientific interest in this area has, as one would expect, both a theoretical and a practical dimension. Each of these is explored more fully in the chapters that follow. However, briefly, on the one hand, arguments relating to the age factor have been tied in to arguments for or against particular models of language acquisition and hence for or against particular conceptions of language. On the other hand, they have been deployed in the debate about language in education.

Probably the best known example of the theoretical use of age-related arguments is the linkage of the notion of such arguments to the 'innateness hypothesis', the idea that language acquisition is only possible because of an inborn 'language faculty'. The connection between the age question and this hypothesis is fairly straightforward. If there is an innate language faculty and language develops in a way similar to, say, a physical organ or bipedal locomotion (cf. e.g. Chomsky, 1978, 1988), one can expect to be able to identify age-related stages in such development and periods of particular readiness for such development. To the extent that such age-related phases are discoverable, they can be represented as supportive of the innateness hypothesis.

Nor does the matter rest there. The innateness hypothesis has further ramifications. If there is a faculty concerned specifically with language which is inborn, this not only sets language apart from behaviours which are acquired purely from the nurturing environment, but also suggests that language is an essential, perhaps defining, part of the human make-up, and renders very plausible the notion that language is peculiar to our species.

On a slightly different tack, if there is an innate language faculty, it must be constituted in such a way as to be able to cope with any human language to which it is exposed, and, conversely, all human languages must be amenable to its operations. This implies that human languages have or draw on a common core of properties – universals – which are at bottom biologically determined. Accordingly, evidence of an age factor in language acquisition can be seen as appertaining not only to the innateness hypothesis but also to the idea that the language faculty is unique, both within the range of human capacities and across species, and to the universalist conception of language (cf. e.g. Harris, 1980: 179; Smith & Wilson, 1979: 33).

To turn now to the more applied dimension of scholarly interest in the age question – the relating of the age question to language educational issues – the obvious example of this is the debate about L2s in the elementary curriculum. It is not so long since the wide supposition was that this debate was over, having been lost by the advocates of early L2 instruction some time in the 1970s. Stern (1983: 105) reports, for example, that American interest in foreign languages in the elementary school (FLES) had begun to wane by this time, while in Britain the evaluation of a large-scale primary school French project by Burstall et al. (1974) was widely construed as refuting the notion that an early start in a L2 conferred an advantage. However, the idea that the case was closed was premature. There were always researchers who did not accept the way in which Burstall et al.'s findings had been interpreted (see e.g. Buckby, 1976; Potter et al., 1977), and the question continued to receive attention. For example, in 1978, Ekstrand was reporting on a revival of the discussion about English at grade 1 or 2 in Sweden, and ongoing controversy in Finland and Sweden about when to begin teaching the language of the host country to immigrants (Ekstrand, 1978; reprint: 136f; see also Ekstrand, 1985); in the 1980s the Italian government set in motion a national experiment in the early teaching of foreign languages (see e.g. Titone, 1985a, 1986a, 1986b); during the 1990s early L2 programmes were put in place and evaluated in France, Ireland and Scotland (see e.g. Audin et al., 1998; Favard, 1993; Harris & Conway, 2003; Johnstone, 1996); and in Germany a decision was recently taken that from September 2003 a foreign language would henceforth be taught to all primary-school pupils from grade 3 at the latest, and that, on the basis of local determination, such foreign language teaching might commence in grade 1 and/or take the form of content teaching via the L2 (Niemeier, 2003).

One reason why early L2 instruction has remained such a live issue arises from the notion of a 'critical period' for language development – the notion that language acquisition is only fully possible if begun in the childhood years. This idea, which is quite widespread in the community at large, undoubtedly underlies the pressure to introduce early L2 instruction which has been exerted on politicians – in Europe at least – by that portion of the population with children. Among linguists the idea of a critical period for language acquisition was in the past accepted for the most part without question. Thus Lenneberg's (1967) discussion of the critical period is much more an attempt to provide an explanation for its existence than actually to *demonstrate* its existence. Likewise, Corder's (1973) treatment of the topic (113ff.) is in the main focused on implications of the critical period rather than on the evidence relating to it (to which he devotes just one sentence). Although it is still true that for many linguists the critical period idea remains axiomatic, others conclude that the case for the existence of a critical period is not proven (see e.g. Clark & Clark, 1977: 520; Elliot, 1981: 27; Klein, 1986: 10; Marinova-Todd *et al.*, 2000: 27; Van Els *et al.*, 1984: 109); that, as far as L2 learning is concerned, older beginners in fact do better (see e.g. Burstall, 1975a; reprint: 17; Cook, 1978; reprint: 12); or that younger L2 beginners outperform adult beginners only in respect of oral skills (see e.g. Faerch *et al.*, 1984: 211; Scovel, 1988) or in the long run (see e.g. Krashen, 1982a: 43; Long, 1990).

The other major facet of the age question in receipt of scholarly attention, namely the notion of maturational 'milestones' in the emergence of speech in young children, is less controversial insofar as no one seriously disputes the proposition that in the normal development of vocal activity and early speech there is both a predictable sequence of events and, within certain limits, a predictable chronology. Nevertheless, even in this area there have long been divergences of view, notably with regard to the relationship between the very earliest vocalisations – 'cooing' and 'babbling' – and later speech. Thus Clark and Clark (1977: 389f.) refer to the division of opinion between the *continuity approach,* represented by, for example, Mowrer (1960), and the *discontinuity approach,* represented by, for example, Jakobson (1968). According to the former the development from early vocalisations to later speech is gradual and continuous, whereas according to the latter later speech is unrelated to early vocalisations. In fact, this debate leads us back to the Critical Period Hypothesis, or at least to that version of it which postulates a lower limit as well as an upper limit to language readiness. It is therefore in the context of a discussion of the evidence relating to the onset of the critical period that we shall return to the continuity-discontinuity question.

Given the amount of debate and uncertainty relating to the question of the age factor in language acquisition, there certainly seems to be room for a survey of the relevant research and arguments which goes beyond the article- or chapter-length treatment they usually receive. Just such a survey is attempted in the present work, which sets out to explore impartially the pertinent data, proposals and speculations in all their diversity. Clearly, there are limits to the extent to which even a book-length review can be exhaustive. However, all the points touched on in the foregoing are addressed in subsequent chapters. Chapter 2 examines the evidence relating to speech milestones; Chapter 3 reviews L1-related evidence appertaining to the Critical Period Hypothesis; Chapter 4 looks at L2 evidence of an optimum age for language learning; Chapter 5 outlines and appraises the various explanations that have been offered for the evidence of an age-related factor in language acquisition; and Chapter 6 explores two major language educational issues that are linked to the age question: the question of L2 instruction at elementary level and that of L2s for older adult learners. The concluding remarks in Chapter 7 briefly recapitulate the points emerging from Chapters 2–6, and indicate where, in particular, further research is needed.

Notes

1. *Language acquisition* is not here distinguished from *language learning* (cf. Krashen, 1981a, 1981b, 1982a, 1982b, 1985), both expressions being used throughout the book, unless context indicates otherwise, in a comprehensive sense.
2. *Second language* (L2) refers here and throughout to any language being learned other than the first language.

Chapter 2
Evidence of Speech Milestones

Introductory

The investigation of the development of language in infants and children has a long history. Leopold (1948) states (reprint, pp. 2f.) that the 'exact study of child language began in Germany in the middle of the nineteenth century under the impetus of the philosophy of Herbart', but also mentions 'forerunners' working earlier in that century and indeed at the end of the 18th century (Tiedemann, 1787). Accordingly, we have in this area a database of diary studies which extends back some 200 years (cf. Ingram, 1989), although there is, it has to be said, some variation in the quality of the early data collected up to about the middle of the 20th century (see e.g. Leopold's comments, 1948; reprint: 1f.).

Research conducted during the early part of the twentieth century tended to focus on small groups of individual children in an attempt to establish developmental norms for acquisition, and tended not to be undertaken by professional linguists. The data emerging from such studies will be examined in the sections that follow. From the late 1950s onwards language acquisition became a very active research topic in linguistics because of the influence of the writings of Noam Chomsky (e.g. 1959, 1965) and the excitement aroused by his claims regarding universal aspects of language acquisition and his postulation of an innate mechanism for language development (commonly referred to as the Language Acquisition Device or LAD) as one dimension of a self-contained language faculty or module.

Within psychology too, language acquisition had by the second half of the 20th century become a much-researched topic. The initial emphasis in this case was on the centrality of cognition in the acquisition process, an approach inspired by the work of Jean Piaget (1926), who claimed that language acquisition could be accounted for in terms of general cognitive developmental processes. Within a few years, social explanations for language acquisition gained prominence, with researchers such as Bruner (1975) and Snow (1979) suggesting that the foundations of all aspects of

6

language lay in the social interaction between infants and their caregivers. According to this 'social-interactionist' perspective, all aspects of language, including syntactic categories and rules, are discovered in the formats of parent–child interaction and/or are derived from the specialised linguistic input provided by the caregiver. Productive as the cognitive and social-interactionist accounts of language development were in respect of research generation, they were seen by researchers such as Cromer (1988) and Shatz (1982) as having rather limited explanatory power as far as both the detail and the overall phenomenon of language acquisition was concerned.

Partly owing to the criticisms levelled at the aforementioned cognitive and social-interactionist approaches, the Chomskyan position that language is encapsulated in a discrete innate module gained further credence as a topic for empirical investigation. Advances in linguistic theory, particularly the Government and Binding Framework and Principles and Parameters Theory (Chomsky, 1981), triggered a considerable amount of research based on linguistic approaches to acquisition (see, e.g. Goodluck, 1991; Pinker, 1989; Radford, 1990). Linguists and psycholinguists embarked on a search for the universals which were assumed to characterise the language acquisition process for all children and all languages.

Most textbook accounts of language acquisition describe a general course of L1 development, characterised by a stable and readily identifiable sequence of stages. This course of development is portrayed as proceeding from first words near the first birthday to brief phrases about six months later and then on to more elaborated sentences in the third year. (cf. Ingram, 1989). Health professionals have been eager to make use of such notions of common sequences and stages because disorders of higher cognitive functions in toddlers and preschoolers often initially manifest themselves as language delays/disorders (Tuchman *et al.*, 1991). However, not all research has been keen to associate age norms with these stages, and researchers have frequently taken refuge in statements like: 'the rate of progression will vary radically among children' (Brown, 1973: 408). Crystal *et al.* (1976) treat such caution somewhat briskly, arguing that age norms are an indispensable tool for those involved in the assessment of child language delays/disorders, and that, in any case, to reject the notion of chronological norms would be absurd.

All of us have clear intuitions about norms of fluency and expressiveness in young children. We are aware that some children are 'very advanced for their age' and that others are not very talkative. In the light of this, it is likely that the emphasis on rate variability in the literature is at least partly due to analysis so far having been restricted to intensive studies of a very few children; differences between individuals become more marked under the microscope, and as a larger range of children come to be studied, we predict that striking similarities in rate of acquisition of structures will emerge. When one compares the empirical findings of language acquisition studies, in fact, it is surprising how similar dates of predominant development of the various syntactic structures turn out to be. Onset time may indeed vary, but means display a remarkable correspondence. (Crystal *et al.*, 1976: 31)

As it turns out, Crystal *et al.*'s prediction that future research with larger samples would reveal greater regularity in the course of acquisition has proved to be unfounded. With the advent of computer technology, there has been a substantial increase in sample sizes and a much greater degree of sharing of child language data. However, while studies have documented some measure of regularity in the development of phonology, morphology, syntax and semantics, considerable diversity has also been noted. This will be discussed in greater detail in the following sections.

The first section of the chapter will look at evidence for speech milestones in the first year of life; the subsequent section investigates speech milestones during the second year of life; the third section looks at evidence beyond the second year; and the final section reviews the evidence for milestones in the development of speech processing skills.

The Very Early Stages: First Year Vocalisations

Crystal *et al.*'s (1976) contention that age norms are impossible to ignore clearly holds up for the very early stages. Although stage models referring to the first year of life may not apply uniformly, they do capture genuine regularity and provide an ordered and broadly valid account of the events that mark vocalisations in the first year of life. While different researchers' proposals diverge in some respects, five main stages are generally recognised in the child language acquisition literature (see Kent & Miolo, 1995):

(1) Birth–1 month: Crying and reflexive vocalisations, for example grunts, belches and coughs.
(2) 1–2 months: Vocal play, cooing or phonation. The child starts producing vocalisations with a vowel-like quality.[1]
(3) 2–6 months: Vocal play with an increasing degree of supralaryngeal articulatory behaviour.
(4) 6 months +: Emergence of multisyllabic babbling known as repetitive, reduplicated or canonical babbling. The child starts combining vowel-like and consonant-like sounds

(5) ~9–12 months: More complex babbling or jargon babbling. These utterances can be highly complex in their phonetic and acoustic structure.

Thal and Bates (1990) cite Jakobson's (1942) proposals relating to universals in phonological development, which were based on the concept of 'markedness'. According to Jakobson, all children begin to babble at approximately the same age and start by babbling a set of unmarked phonetic contrasts that are present in every language; every successive stage of phonological development follows a universal markedness hierarchy, with the most complex sounds coming last.

Table 2.1 sets out the relevant pronouncements of a selection of summaries of some early studies of language development during the first year of life and includes the age ranges specified for each individual stage.

Table 2.2 compares a number of the relevant claims regarding very early language development arising from a selection of more recent summaries of child language acquisition research. It includes several stage descriptions of infant phonetic development during the first year of life. The approximate duration of the individual stages reported is shown for each system.

It may be noted that the categories of the studies tabulated are not always unambiguously identifiable with the stages currently under discussion and that the terms used to describe the various types of output differs from study to study. However, with a little reflection, appropriate connections can be made. For example in Table 2.1 'vocalisations' almost certainly refers to utterances other than crying, and in the absence of further qualification can probably be assumed to denote what we have labelled as 'cooing'. Likewise, the expressions 'many syllables', 'several well-defined syllables', etc. very probably include perceived *consonant + vowel* syllables and can therefore be taken as signalling the onset of babbling. There are also two more specific terminological divergences. Gesell *et al.* (1938) clearly do not use 'coos' simply in the above-defined sense of producing vowel-like sounds, since they differentiate it from 'vocalises *ah, uh, eh*'. Cattell, for his part, appears to employ 'babbles' in a rather loose sense, assimilating it to 'coos'. We have dealt with these divergences by (a) giving Gesell *et al.*'s findings in relation both to the vocalising of *ah, uh, and eh* and to 'cooing', and (b) interpreting Cattell's 'babbles or coos' as referring to cooing in our sense. In Table 2.2, various terms are used to describe the various types of output. For example, the stage of development reached after that of the production of basic biological sounds such as crying is referred to by Stark (1986) as 'cooing and laughter', and by Oller (1978) as 'GOOing', while Holmgren *et al.* (1996) use the term 'interrupted phonation with no articulation',

Table 2.1 Age in months at which two early stages of language development are reported in eight major quantitative studies

		Bayley (1933)	Shirley (1933)	Bühler (1930)	Bühler & Hetzer (1935)	Gesell et al. (1938)	Gesell & Thompson (1934)	Gesell (1925)	Cattell (1940)
Cooing stage	'Vocalisation'	1.5							
	'Several (different) vocalisations'						2	4	
	'One syllable'		2						
	'Vocalises ah, uh, eh'					1.3			
	'Cooing'/'Coos'			2	3	3		4	
	'Babbles or coos'								2
Babbling stage	'Articulates many syllables'							6	
	'Vocalises several well-defined syllables'						6		
	'Says several syllables'	6.3							
	'Vocalises ma or mu'					6.5			
	'Vocalises da'					7			
	'Two syllables – 2nd repetition of 1st'					7			
	'Imitating sounds re-re-re'			6					

Adapted from McCarthy. 1946, Table 1, pp. 482ff.

Table 2.2 Ages associated with early speech milestones

Age (months)	0	1	2	3	4	5	6	7	8	9	10	11	12
Stark (1986)	Reflexive crying and vegetative sounds		Cooing and laughter			Vocal play	Reduplicated babble			Non-reduplicated babble and expressive jargon			
Oller (1978)	Phonation		GOOing	Expansion			Canonical babble			Variegated babble			
Holmgren et al. (1996)	Contin-uous. phonation with no articulation		Inter-rupted phon-ation with no articu-lation.	Continuous or interrupted phonation with no articulation			Phonatory variants with or without articulation		Continuous or interrupted phonation with reduplicated babbling				
Elbers (1982)	Vocalising								Repetiti ve	Concatenating		Mixing	
Kent (1990)	Early phonation		Late phon-ation	Simple articulation with phonatory variants			Multisyllabic babbling (Reduplicated and variegated babbling developing in parallel)						
Nakazima (1980)	Reflexive crying		Development of phonatory-articulatory-auditory mechanisms of babbling				Repetitive babbling			Reorganisation of phonatory-articulatory-auditory mechanisms			

After Kent and Miolo, 1995: 324

Elbers (1982) refers to all development prior to babbling at eight months as 'vocalising', Kent (1990) talks about 'late phonation', and Nakazima (1980) terms this phase 'development of phonatory-articulatory-auditory mechanisms of babbling'. However, there is a broad consensus evident among the various studies cited in Tables 2,1 and 2.2 concerning speech progress in the first year of life, and three distinct stages, or milestones, of development in the first year of life are identified. The order of the stages is as follows: vocalisation/phonation, phonation with intonation, babbling. There are also broad age-ranges that appear to correlate with these three basic stages; vocalisation/phonation occurs up to around the first two months, phonation with intonation can continue up until six months and babbling occurs post the six-month range in the normally developing child. The phonological features included in babbling become more varied as the child approaches 12 months of age.

On the other hand, as can be seen from the tables, there can be substantial amounts of variation in the timing of children's cooing and babbling. Normally developing children can begin to produce canonical babbling – i.e. meaningless consonant-vowel strings – anywhere between six and ten months. The content and course of babbling also vary considerably (Kent & Miolo, 1995; Locke, 1988; Vihman _et al._, 1986). As Thal and Bates (1990) observe, some children have a very small repertoire of phonetic contrasts for many weeks, while others have a much larger phonetic repertoire from the outset. Some consonant phonemes are more likely to be present in early output – e.g. bilabial and alveolar stops and nasals. However, some children's early output includes phonemes that are further down Jakobson's markedness hierarchy – e.g. fricative-vowel combinations. While it is clear that individual differences are considerable, there are also obvious convergences. It is difficult to ignore in this connection the possibility that phonetic tendencies in first year vocalisations are biologically determined. In particular, one notes that during the first few years of life, when children are learning to use their vocal apparatus, the apparatus in question is subject to considerable modification (see Kent & Miolo, 1995), a gradual remodelling in a striking evolutionary progression.

Not all phonemes appear in babbling with the same frequency of occurrence. Certain sounds such as plosives and nasals are more likely to occur than others and it is these sounds that crop up more frequently in early lexicons. On the other hand, environmental influences have also been shown to exert considerable influence. While strong cross-language commonalities have been observed in the types of phonemes that children use in the first year of life, there is also evidence that children younger than one begin to adjust their sound patterns to reflect characteristics of their parent language. In order to tune into the parent language, the infant has to ascertain which sounds are contrastive in the language in question (although there is some research that suggests that the new-born is already biased to a certain degree to a particular linguistic system – Kent & Miolo, 1995). Tomasello and Bates (2001: 18) see this process as explaining effects sometimes attributed to maturational constraints: 'the infant's open mind about languages she can learn is closed not by some mysterious maturational process depending on an invariant and inflexible "critical period" but by the very act of learning her own native language'.

In sum, while there is some evidence of variation, in general the very early stages of acquisition point to a stable sequence of speech milestones (crying and reflexive vocalisations → cooing → babbling) occurring within fairly well-defined age-ranges.

First Words

Discussion of language milestones in L1 development tends to focus mainly on production milestones. Comprehension milestones are more difficult to quantify, and distinguishing contextual comprehension from linguistic comprehension in infants can prove difficult. Jusczyk (2001) reviews a number of studies which demonstrate that lexical comprehension begins to develop relatively early in the second half of the first year of life. Thal and Bates (1990), for their part, argue that, while there is very little systematic evidence for word comprehension under nine months of age, there is considerable variability in rate beyond this age. With regard to production, the consensus is that in normally developing children one-word utterances begin to appear between 12 and 18 months and that the onset of two-word utterances follows between 18 and 24 months[2].

Until 20 years ago, the main method for studying early lexical development was the parental diary. Long-term studies that document early vocabulary growth, a selection of which are cited below, reveal that young children often exhibit a sudden upturn in the rate of acquisition of new words during the second year of life (see, e.g. Benedict, 1979; Dromi, 1987; Halliday, 1975). The first words are acquired at a slow rate, with only one, two or three new words being acquired each week. However, around the time when the child's vocabulary has grown to between 20 and 40 words, there is often a vocabulary spurt in which the rate of vocabulary acquisition begins to increase rapidly, and within a few weeks the child may be acquiring eight or more new words a week (Barrett, 1995). Some relevant results from a number of other frequently cited studies are summarised below. The last three studies summarised below – Wells (1985), Bates *et al.* (1988), and Fenson *et al.* (1994) – are examples of larger-scale studies and more variability is demonstrated in these findings.

Bateman (1914) found that 75% of his 35 subjects produced their first word before the end of their first year.

Smith's (1926) subjects had an average productive vocabulary of one word at 10 months ($N = 17$), three words at 12 months ($N = 52$), 19 words at 15 months ($N = 19$), and 22 words at 18 months ($N = 14$). At 24 months their average length of response was 1.7 words ($N = 25$).

Stern and Stern (1928) found that for their 26 subjects the average age of onset of the one word stage was 11½ months, and that in 69% of cases it occurred before the end of the first year.

McCarthy's (1930) study of 140 children ranging in age from 18 to 54 months yielded the following mean lengths of response:

18 months – 1.2 words
24 months – 1.8 words
30 months – 3.1 words

Castner (1940), having surveyed a sample of 40 18-month-olds, discovered vocabulary sizes distributed as follows:

1–5 words – 22%
6–10 words – 30%
11–15 words – 27%
16–20 words – 10%
21–25 words – 0%
26–30 words – 3%
'Innumerable' – 8%

Morley (1957) found that of his 114 subjects 73% were using words with meaning by their first birthday and that 89% were using meaningful combinations by their second birthday.

Nelson (1973) found that a vocabulary size of 50 words was attained by all her 18 subjects between the ages of 1.3 and 2 years.

Benedict's (1979) study of eight children yielded an average vocabulary size of 45 words at 18 months.

Wells (1985) reports that at the commencement of his study, when his younger cohort of 60 subjects were aged 15 months, 75% of them were already at the one word stage. By age 24 months 50% of them were at the two-word stage and by age 27 months 90% had reached this stage.

Bates *et al.*'s (1988) parental report study found that parents of middle-class infants reported a mean of 5.7 words at 10 months. The 12-month-old children were reported to have produced an average of 13.1 words (range 0–83 words). The mean age for the production of novel word combinations was 20 months (range 14–24 months).

Fenson *et al.* (1994), who used a checklist measure of lexical comprehension, found that at 13 months of age children could produce an average of 10 words and comprehend 110 words. At 16 months, on average, children could produce 45 words but could comprehend over 180 words.

One notes discrepancies between the vocabulary sizes reported at various ages, and a comparatively late onset of the two-word stage among a large proportion of Wells's (1985) subjects. However, by and large, there do seem to be some definite broad parallels in lexical development. A selection of case studies – going back more than 200 years – is presented in Table 2.3. Even at first glance, one can immediately see some general points of consensus between the findings of the studies referred to in this table and the above-cited findings. The divergences in study outcomes in relation both to early vocalisations and to the first words stage that are discernible are subject to at least three qualifications. First, in the case of at least some of the quantitative studies cited, some caution is necessary in assigning an interpretation to individual researchers' terminology and in relating particular recorded events to the four stages with which we are concerned. Second, it must be borne in mind that the observation of subjects reflected in these studies varies in terms of regularity and consistency. Finally, it should be noted that the ages mentioned with reference to the Bloom (1970) study and the Brown (1973) study are those of the subjects at the start of observation; that is to say, no data had been obtained from any of these subjects prior to the ages in question.

However, it must be added that variability in early language development has become an active topic of research in recent years and that considerable individual variation in the pattern and progression of early acquisition has been documented. Goldfield and Reznick (1990) demonstrated that not all children exhibit a vocabulary spurt. Five out of the 18 children observed in this investigation acquired words at a much steadier rate throughout the second year of life, and the rate of acquisition only occasionally demonstrated modest upward movements. As we have seen, Crystal (1976) predicted that, as population sizes increased and greater ranges of children were included in child language acquisition studies, striking similarities in the rate of acquisition would emerge. In fact, however, large-scale studies with more diverse populations have actually highlighted variability in the acquisition process.

One of the more widely cited and reproduced studies of qualitative dif-

Table 2.3 Reference to age in respect of four early stages of language development culled from seventeen case studies

	Tiedemann 1787 (boy)	Taine 1877 (girl)	Darwin 1877 (boy)	Preyer 1889	Stern and Stern 1928, Stern 1930		Lewis 1936 (boy)
					Hilde	Gunther	
Cooing stage		At 3½ months vowels only	At 46 days 'little noises [. . .] to please himself				From 1 month, 14 days, various sounds in various states of comfort
Babbling stage	At 6 months, 19 days attempted to initiate 'ma'	After 'several months' consonants added	At 5½ months articulated 'da' without meaning	At 1 month, 15 days [amma] (among other sounds)	At 2 months, 14 days beginning of repetitive chains	At 3 months trains of 'Lallen'(babbling) begin to appear	At 3 months, 21 days 'chains of babbling'
One word stage	At 15 months, 4 days, used *papa* and *mama* with meaning.	By 14 months, 3 weeks, 5 or 6 words used with meaning	At 1 year, used *mum* to mean food	At 11 months, [atta] and variants with reference to disappearance; [mama] with reference to mother	At 10 months, 14 days [didda] with reference to clock	At 11 months14 days [papa] with reference to father	At 1 year, I month, 8 days, plays 'peep-bo' accompanying hiding movement with [ăbo]; [mama] with reference to mother
Two word stage	At 21 months, 13 days, combined with noun and verb				At 1 year, 5 months, first sentence of more than one word.		At 2 years, 16 days, [pu daedi] ('pull Daddy'); [baenkets ɔf] ('blankets off')

Table 2.3 Reference to age in respect of four early stages of language development culled from seventeen case studies

Bowley 1957 (boy)	Scott 1967		Britton 1970	Bloom 1970			Brown 1973		
	Don	Judy	(girl)	Gia	Eri e	Kathryn	Adam	Eve	Sarah
At 4 months, 'made monosyllabic sounds'		At 4 months, 'squeals, gurgles, bubbles, coos'							
At 6 months, 'ki-ki, 'da-da' r-sounds made'	At 8 months 'combines consonants with vowels'	At 8 months, 'says da-da, ma-ma'							
At 10 months, 'said ga-ga (dog), bi-wi (bus)' (first meaningful words)	At 9 months, 'says 'bye-bye''; at 1 year, 3 months vocabulary of 9 or 10 words		At 12 months, 'ung' (for the little brush she likes to hold)						
At 1 year, 5 months, first sentence: 'look-moon-sky'	At 2 years, 1 month, 'asks involved questions'	At 1 year 6 months, 'vocabulary of more than 20 words; uses 3 and 4 word sentences'	At 18 months, combin-ations such as black bow-wow, push pram, wow wow, sit there, more bun, mummy have a cup of tea	At 19 months, 1 week, mean length of utterance = 1.12 morphemes	At 19 months, 1 week, mean length of utterance = 1.10 morphemes	At 21 months, mean length of utterance = 1.32 morphemes	At 27 months, mean length of utterance = 2.06 morphemes	At 18 months, mean length of utterance = 1.68 morphemes	At 27 months mean length of utterance = 1.73 morphemes

ferences in the language acquisition process is Nelson's (1973) study of the first 50 words of 18 children (7 boys and 11 girls), which drew on maternal reports using a diary methodology. On the basis of the number of general nominals used by these children, Nelson divided them into two groups; referential and expressive. Referential children were those whose productive lexicon consisted mostly (70%+) of general nominals. Expressive children were those whose productive lexicon was more heterogeneous, containing fewer object labels, more pronouns, quantifiers and other nonnominals (e.g. more, all gone). Expressive children also produced some fixed phrases which served a social-personal function rather than a labelling function (e.g. I want that, don't do that). Recent normative data from large-scale studies such as the MacArthur Communicative Development Inventory (MCDI) (Fenson *et al.*, 1993) and recent studies using data from the CHILDES (Child Language Data Exchange System)[3] data have confirmed Nelson's conclusion regarding variability among children in this connection and have demonstrated that the variability in question is very wide indeed (MacWhinney & Snow, 1985, 1990).

In recent years, there has been a growing reliance on the MCDI for the study of vocabulary development in English. A growing body of research has indicated that the MCDI is a well-normed, reliable and valid tool. Concurrent and predictive correlates have been reported between MCDI scores and observational data, standardised language measures and Mean Length of Utterance (MLU) at 28 months of age (Fenson *et al.*, 1994; Reznick & Goldfield, 1992). With a sample size of 1803 children on the MCDI, Fenson *et al.* (1994) found far more variability in the onset and development of language ability than had been previously expected from the literature. Excluding children with a known medical condition, prematurity or Down syndrome from the study, they found that at 16 months children in the top 10% had reported productive vocabularies of nearly 180 words, whereas children in the lowest 10% were producing fewer than 10 words, some producing no words at all. The data did not yield strong evidence for the prevalence of the vocabulary spurt that is often reported for individual cases. On an individual level, some slow talkers, who did not present with language delay at a later stage, displayed a slow rise that is best described in terms of a linear function. Other children's vocabulary appeared to develop in a series of small bursts resulting in a step function. Thus, there appears to be significant variability among individual children and the typical pattern described by Barrett (1995) of first words being acquired at a slow rate, followed by a vocabulary spurt and rapid acceleration is far from universal.

Grammatical development in toddlers showed a similar level of variability. At 16 months of age, children scoring in the top 10% showed significant growth, while those in the lowest 10%–25% began to expand some grammatical skills by 30 months but did not demonstrate any growth in other grammatical features. For example, at 16 months the use of morphemes marking regular plural (-s), possessive (-s), progressive (-ing) and past tense (-ed) was relatively uncommon among Fenson *et al.*'s (1994) sample. However, by 22 months, the majority of children were reported to be using plurals, possessives and the progressive. Over 90% of the children were reported to be using these forms by 30 months. The past tense (-ed) emerged more slowly. This is similar to the findings of Brown (1973) and Bates *et al.* (1988). Data concerning the emergence of irregular forms were collected by asking parents about their child's use of the five common irregular plural nouns and the 20 common irregular past tense verbs. When the data were plotted on a graph, the children scoring at the 75th and 90th percentiles demonstrated a relatively steep ascending curve, beginning at 16–17 months and continuing through to 30 months, while those scoring at the median had a more gradual growth curve which began later, at 22 months. Children at the 10th and 25th percentiles were not credited with using any of these irregular forms until 20–22 months. Over-generalisations, which are often viewed as a sign of linguistic progress in the extraction of linguistic rules and regularities, were only prominent in children in the upper 25% of the distribution and then only after 23–24 months. By 30 months, more than half the sample was reported to be producing less than five of the 45 items on the checklist. Sentence length and complexity also varied considerably across the sample, parental report of MLU and observed MLU being highly correlated between the ages of 16 and 30 months. As Lieven *et al.* (1992: 287) note, the phenomenon of variation among L1 acquirers is now taken as a given: 'the fact that variation exists in children's early speech production is no longer an issue for the child development literature'.

The fact that the findings from older studies demonstrate considerably more uniformity and a more readily identifiable set of sequences or stages of lexical and grammatical development may perhaps be attributable to their focus on individual case studies and small population numbers consisting of children from specific closed classes such as researchers' own children or children from university crèches. The earlier studies used more homogeneous groupings and there is a growing literature on the external factors that have been shown to affect language acquisition in children. These can be separated into social factors and individual factors. The social factors include socio-economic status (Hoff-Ginsberg, 1998) and birth-order (Coates & Messer, 1996). It has also been suggested that gender may affect language acquisition. There seems to be a tendency for girls to acquire vocabulary at a slightly faster rate than boys. Although the magnitude of this variation is extremely limited (see Shore, 1995) in comparison to the range of variation that is exhibited within each gender, it may nevertheless account in some measure for the greater overall ranges found in the more recent large-scale studies cited (e.g. Fenson *et al.*, 1994). Individual external factors include education level of caregivers (Hoff-Ginsberg, 1991), language level of caregivers (Barnes *et al.*, 1983) and caregiver-child interaction (Hampson & Nelson, 1993). Internal factors that have been shown to contribute to variability in acquisition include cognitive level, imitative capacity, mastery, motivation, temperament and genetic factors (cf. Shore, 1995).

To conclude, while the research does confirm some definite broad parallels among children during the stage when first words start to appear and the earlier research especially provides strong evidence for a sequence of milestones in this period, more recent large-scale studies involving more diverse populations and larger numbers of data sets used have demonstrated more variability in both the rate and the pattern of acquisition.

Later Stages

As far as the later stages of the emergence of language are concerned, there is fairly good evidence of a stable sequence of syntactic stages, with each of which it is apparently possible to associate a normative age-range. Some interesting evidence concerning further syntactic milestones to which age norms are assignable has been provided by the Wells (1985) study that was referred to briefly in the previous section. Wells worked with two samples of children, one composed (finally) of 60 subjects aged 15 months at the beginning of the study, and the other of 65 subjects aged 39 months when they began to be observed. The younger group was observed over 27 months (i.e. from 15 to 42 months) and the older group over 21 months (i.e. from 39 to 60 months). Accordingly, for the age-range 39 to 42 months data were gathered from both samples. The rationale underlying this overlapping design was that it would enable a sizeable age-range to be covered (15 to 60 months) without involving any set of subjects for more than two and a quarter years, thus minimising the 'wastage' factor. Observations of subjects were made at three-monthly intervals, the major part of each observation consisting in a recording of a sample of spontaneous speech. A programme of language tests was also built into the observations, the original aim being to arrive at an integrated analysis of naturalistic and experimental data. However, because of labour-intensive nature of the project the two approaches were not integrated, as initially intended, with the result that the great bulk of the data used was therefore naturalistic (Wells, 1985: 128). Analysis of these data pointed to a sequence of ten developmental stages, each stage representing a composite of newly emergent items selected for inclusion according to three criteria:

(a) saliency: items should be easy to identify in a sample of spontaneous speech;

(b) order: items chosen within any system should be strongly ordered with respect to each other and selected in such a way as to represent the full range of the sequence of emergence within that system;

(c) frequency: as far as possible, items selected should occur frequently once they had emerged. (Wells, 1985: 205)

The various characteristics of the 10 stages derived by Wells from his data are set out in Table 2.4, and the age norms arrived at for each stage are presented in Table 2.5. It is not possible here to enter into a detailed exposition of each of these ten stages (see Wells, 1985, Chapter 5), nor of the statistical procedures employed in their induction (see Wells, 1985: Chapter 4). The most that can be attempted is an illustration of the kinds of findings that underlie the positing of the age norms (for a full account see Wells, 1985: Chapter 6). Examples at the pragmatic level would be the cases of the functions 'wanting' and 'formulation'. 'Wanting' (Stage I; average age of onset posited < 1.3) had emerged in at least 75% of subjects' speech by 21 months and in 100% of subjects' speech by age 24 months, whereas 'formulation' (Stage VIII; average age of onset posited = 4.0) did not reach the 50% level of emergence until age 42 months and at age 60 months was present in the speech of still only 72% of subjects (Wells, 1985: 230). To take two instances at the semantic level, 'Simple past' time (Stage III; average age of onset posited = 2.0) was being expressed by at least 90% of subjects by age 30 months and by 100% of subjects by age 57 months, while 'frequency' (Stage IX; average age of onset posited = 4.9) had not emerged in the speech of more than 51% of subjects by the time the study ended. As for syntax, convenient exemplifications can be found in the data on the development of noun phrase structure. Singular nouns (Stage I; average age of onset posited << 1. 3) were present in the speech of at least 75% of subjects by age 18 months, at least 90% of subjects by age 21 months and 100% of subjects by 27 months. The structure Determiner + Modifier + Head + Qualifier, in contrast (Stage IX; average age of onset posited = 4.9) had emerged in the speech of only 48% of subjects by age 60 months.

It is interesting to compare these results of Wells's empirical study with the seven syntactic stages hypothesised by Crystal and his collaborators (Crystal, 1976; Crystal & Fletcher, 1979; Crystal *et al.*, 1976), which are presented as 'a descriptive synthesis of what has been discovered about the order and rate of syntactic development' (Crystal *et al.*, 1976: 60) and 'a workable scheme for assessment and remediation' (Crystal *et al.*, 1976: 61).

Table 2.4 Stages of language development in the preschool years

Level	Sentence/Clause Syntax	NP Syntax	NP Semantics
X	Aux + neg + S + V + X wh- + aux + S + aux + V+X		Head: Neg. Adverb Head: 'any'
IX	S + cop + ( ) Aux + S + aux + V +X Polar Interrog. + Sub. Clause S + aux + neg + aux + V + (X)	Prep. + Det. + Head + Qual Det. + Mod. + Head + Qual.	Mod: Ordinal Qual: Adjective Head: Reflex. Pron. Head: 'where' (rel.)
VIII	'Why' Interrogative Three-Clause Declarative Any Relative Clause S + V + i0 + 0 Aux + S + V + ( ) Wh- + aux + S + V + X	Interrog. Adj.+ Head Det. + Head + Def. Clause	Head: 'nothing' Head: 'what'/'that' (relative) Head: 'something'/ 'anything'
VII	Aux + S + V + X + X main Clause + Sub./Main Clause S + aux + aux + V + (X) S + V + (finite) Any Passive Main Clause + Tag Cop + S + X wh- + aux + S + V	Det. + Head + Def. Phrase Head + Def. Clause Prep + Det. + Mod. + Head Dem. Adj. + Mod. + Head/Def. Art + Mod. + Head	Qual: Quantitative Head: 'him'
VI	S + aux + cop + X S + aux + neg + V + (X) S + cop + A A + aux + V + 0 A Aux + S + V + 0/A	Head + Def. Phrase Def. Art. + Npl.	Head: 'we'
V	S + cop + IC S + V + (non-finite) S + aux + V + (O/A) S + V + 0 + A wh- + cop + S	Indef. Art + Mod + Head Dem. Adj. + Nsing.	Head: 'he'
IV	S + cop + C S + V + (0)	Prep. + Det. + Head Def. Art. + Nsing.	Mod: Phys. Attrib.
III	Two constituents	Prep. + Head Indef. Art. +Nsing.	Head: Interrog.Pron Mod: Possessive Head: 'I' Head: 'it'
II			Head: Pronoun Head: Adverb
	One constituent		Head: Noun

Table 2.4 Stages of language development in the preschool years

Modality	Time and Aspect	Conjunction	Sentence Meaning Relation	Function
Inference		'so'/'so that'	(Agent) Change Classif. / Equivalence Purposive	Condition
	Asp: Inceptive Time: Frequency	'that' (comple-mentiser)	Possess/Benefact. + Embed. Cl. (Agent) Change Affect. Exper. Agent Cause Direct. Movement	
	Time: Extent Asp: Habitual	'when' 'if' 'but'	Temporal State/Change	Formulation
Possible		'because'	Benefactive Relation	Query State/Attitude
Obligation/ Necessity			Agent Cause + Embedded Clause	Request Explanation Justification
			(Agent) Change Phys. Exper. Agent Change Existence Cogn. Exper + Embed.Cl.	Suggestion
Permission / Ability	Time: Future		Affective Experience Agent Act on Target Agent Function on Patient Cognitive Experience	Explanation/ Justification
				Request Permission
	Asp: Perfect		Want Exper. + Embed. Cl. Evaluation Attribut. Agent Change Phys. Attrib. (Agent) Change Possession Agentive Cognitive Exper.	Intend
	Asp: Contin.	'and'		Yes/No Question
			Want Experience Classification Agent Change Location	Content Question Express State/ Attitude
	Time: Past		Static Location	Statement Direct Request
			Operator + Nominal	Wanting Ostension Call

Reproduced from Wells, 1985: 206f.

Table 2.5 Age norms arrived at by Wells for the various levels on his scale of language development (age in years and months)

Level	Advanced	Average	Delayed
I	< 1.3	< 1.3	1.9
II	< 1.3	1.9	2.0
III	1.3	2.0	2.6
IV	1.6	2.3	3.0
V	1.9	2.6	3.6
VI	2.0	3.0	4.3
VII	2.3	3.6	4.9
VIII	2.9	4.0	> 5.0
IX	3.3	4.9	> 5.0
X	3.9	> 5.0	> 5.0

Reproduced from Wells (1985: 280).

A summary of these stages is set out in Table 2.6. The last two of Crystal *et al.*'s stages, even as described in fuller form, contain no obvious points of contact with the higher end of Wells's scale. However, Stages I–V in Crystal *et al.*'s scheme are readily comparable with Wells's Stages I–VII, and, as Table 2.7 shows, the relevant postulated age-norms are quite close.

The syntactic stages proposed by Crystal *et al.* (1976) and Wells (1985) are also comparable to Brown's (1973) index of grammatical development in English in terms of mean length of utterance, which is the set of grammatical norms most widely cited in academic research and most widely used in clinical practice. Brown's conception of mean length of utterance (MLU) is based on a count of morphemes – i.e. including inflections (e.g. plural -s and past tense -ed) and function words (e.g. the, of) alongside content-word stems (e.g. cat, house). Brown's (1973) classic longitudinal study of the early grammar of three children (Adam, Eve and Sarah), which is referred to above in Table 2.3, is elaborated upon further below. Brown used the MLU measure to break early language development down into five distinct stages and age ranges. Table 2.8 is adapted from Ingram (1989):

The evidence for a stable sequence of acquisitional stages associated with fairly well defined age-ranges is quite strong, therefore, in respect of the early emergence of syntactic structures. However, the evidence is less clear in other areas of language acquisition. For example, while there is a general trend towards the identification of a sequence in early acquisition from single-word to multi-word speech via vocabulary explosion, this

Table 2.6 Crystal *et al.*'s synthesis of the descriptive findings of the language acquisition literature in seven age-related syntactic stages

Stage	Average age in years and months	Major characteristics
Stage I	0.9–1.6	Single-element sentences, for example, N (daddy), V (gone).
Stage II	1.6–2.0	Two-element clauses, for example, SV (daddy gone), VO (kick ball), Prep N (in box), Det N (that ball).
Stage III	2.0–2.6	Three-element sentences, for example, SVO (daddy kick ball).
Stage IV	2.6–3.0	Four- (or more) element clauses, for example, SVOA (daddy kick ball hard)
Stage V	3.0–3.6	Clause sequence and connectivity, for example, co-ordination (daddy gone in the garden and him hurt his knee).
Stage VI	3.6–4.6	Completions of grammatical 'systems': elimination local child forms, for example, in the pronoun system (he for him above), and the addition of further members of a system, for example predeterminers in the NP (all, both, etc.)
Stage VII	4.6–?	Other structures, for example, sentence connectivity, using adverbials (actually, frankly), emphatic word order variation (it was X that Y etc.)

Adapted from Crystal and Fletcher (1979); reprint: 44f.)

Table 2.7 Comparison of Crystal *et al.*'s first five syntactic stages with Wells's first seven stages

	Crystal et al.		Wells	
Stage No.	Postulated average age	Common features of characterisation	Stage No.	Postulated average age
I	0.9–1.6	1-element sentences	I	< 1.3
			II	1.9
II	1.6–2.0	2-element sentences	III	2.0
III	2.0–2.6	3-element sentences	IV	2.3
IV	2.6–3.0	4(+)-element sentences	V	26
			VI	3.0
V	3.0–3.6	complex sentence structure	VII	3.6

Table 2.8 Brown's index of early grammatical development

Stage I: (0.9–1.6)	Early MLU range:	1.05–1.5	The period of single words to first word combinations
	Late MLU range:	1.50–2.0	The very first inflections appear
Stage II: (1.6–2.0)	MLU range:	2.0–2.49	Productive control over grammar appears
Stage III: (2.0–2.6)	MLU range:	2.50–2.99	Modalities of the simple sentence
Stage IV: (2.6–3.0)	MLU range:	3.00–3.99	Embedding of one sentence within another
Stage V: (3.0–3.6)	MLU range:	4.00 upwards	Co-ordination of simple sentences and propositional activities.

sequence is not universal (Goldfield & Reznick, 1990). It has been demonstrated that there is a significant level of variability in this pattern (see above, and see Shore, 1995 for an in-depth review of the literature). The issues that variability presents for theories of normal language development are discussed at length by Fenson *et al.* (1994). The majority of the research on child language acquisition focuses on developments prior to the third year of life. Indeed, some researchers maintain that language development per se is essentially over at that point (Thal & Bates, 1990) and that later language development is merely a process of continuing lexical acquisition and increasing grammatical fluency. However, a small body of newer evidence has accumulated on language development past the five-year age-range. During this later period, semantic and syntactic knowledge is reorganised in the service of complex discourse function, and it appears that individual differences may be significant in this connection (cf. Nippold, 1998). For most school-age children and adolescents, an individual's written language ability can play an increasingly important role in overall language development. Somewhere between eight and ten years of age, many children begin to use their reading skills to increase their lexicons, access more complex syntactic structures and develop figurative language such as metaphors, proverbs and idioms. The ability to read fluently allows children to acquire a great deal of linguistic knowledge independently. The development of linguistic individualism is promoted as children progress through school, as they can select a greater number of subjects, extracurricular activities and social interactions by choice.

In sum, it seems that the greatest evidence for predictable age-related speech milestones is in the earliest stages of acquisition, that in lexical development even at this stage inter-subject variation is considerable, and that as age level and proficiency increase, individual differences become more and more prominent.

Language Processing Milestones

A further area of interest among language acquisition researchers is the question of whether there are age-related milestones in the manner in which language is processed. It is interesting to note, for instance, that two-year-old children with age-appropriate language skills rarely make word-order errors and generally place the agent before the verb and the patient after the verb (Bloom, 1991; Tomasello, 1992). Also, children as young as two years have been shown to correctly interpret a command such as 'Make the dog bite the cat' (Roberts, 1983, cited by Conti-Ramsden & Windfuhr, 2002). Menyuk (1977), reviewing research on developmental aspects of speech processing, refers to a number of studies which indicate that there may indeed be age-related factors in language-processing attainments.

Bever (1970), for example, proposes that the first mechanisms used by the child are those of reference, followed by predication (actor-action, action-object). According to Bever, at around age three the child starts using 'superficial perceptual strategies', that is to say, strategies that drive semantic function from surface word order. Thus, a child at this stage, says Bever, will interpret any noun – verb – noun sequence as actor + action + object. This is why, the claim continues, children between three and five years old misinterpret 'reversible passives' like The boy was kissed by the girl (interpreted as 'The boy kissed the girl') and cleft sentences like It's the horse that the cow kisses (interpreted as 'The horse kisses the cow'). Interestingly, by the earlier predication strategy this latter sentence receives a correct but incomplete interpretation ('The cow kisses'). Bever contends that by about age five, children can interpret reversible passives and cleft sentences correctly, which suggests that by this age adult-like strategies may be available.

Sinclair and Bronckart (1971) also found marked differences in the decoding strategies exhibited by children of different ages. Their subjects were asked to act out with toys three-word utterances containing only various combinations of nouns and verbs. Menyuk summarises their results as follows:

> At the earliest ages, in acting out the utterance, children either use themselves as actors or provided only a two-part solution (action-object or agent-action). Children aged four to five interpreted the

N[oun] nearest the V[erb] as agent, but provided a three-part solution (agent-action-object). At age five to six they interpreted the N nearest the V as object, and at age five to seven they interpreted the first N as agent and the second as object. (Menyuk, 1977: 138)

There is a rough correspondence between these findings and Bever's, although the former indicate that the strategy which analyses noun – verb – noun as agent + action + object has a slower and more complex genesis and a longer life than Bever suggests. More recent research had suggested that children with age appropriate language skills are sensitive to word order from as young as 16 months (Hirsch-Pasek & Golinkoff 1996). However, as Conti-Ramsden and Windfuhr (2002) argue, having a sensitivity to word order and having a deeper understanding of word order as a syntactic cue in a sentence interpretation may actually imply different levels of knowledge. The use of known verbs in experiments has been criticised, as it may be that children's supposed early sensitivity to word order may reflect their lexical knowledge of verbs as specific lexical items rather than any deeper syntactic knowledge. It is plausible to suppose that young children place the 'doer' of the action and 'the one it is being done to' in the appropriate positions because they have learned to place items in relation to their knowledge of the individual verb. Tomasello and his colleagues (Akhtar, 1999; Akhtar & Tomasello, 1997; Olguin & Tomasello, 1993) demonstrated using novel verbs that children at this stage of development were unable to correctly mark the role of agent and patient when given a novel verb (see Tomasello 2000 for a review). Conti-Ramsden and Windfuhr (2002) cite Skipp *et al.*'s (2001) finding that children with age-appropriate language skills between 2.5 and 3.0 have no general verb knowledge, that they are generally conservative with position, and that they primarily follow the surface structure of the linguistic input provided by the experimenter. Children demonstrate that they have developed, or are in the process of developing, a general category of verb by using verb + inflection structures that they have not heard used by adults – for example, by over-generalising regular past tense morphology in forms such as *wented* and *goed*. Conti-Ramsden and Windfuhr (2002) argue that if one considers children's use of novel verb + inflection structures as evidence of verb knowledge, there is a fairly well-defined sequence and age-range for the acquisition of a verb category in children with normal language development.

A sidelight on the question of maturational factors in language processing is cast by the case of children who present with SLI (Specific Language Impairment), who have particular difficulties with language processing. SLI is the term currently used to describe children with a range of different linguistic profiles, all of which exhibit marked language deficits in the context of normal cognitive ability, where no identifiable cause is present (Bishop, 1997). Therefore, children with autism, general learning disability or physical or neurological damage are excluded from this diagnosis. Children with SLI present with difficulties marking specific items of grammatical morphology such as past tense (-ed), third person singular (-s), and copular and auxiliary be (Ellis *et al.*, 1999). These forms are more consistently poor in the SLI population and are more resistant to remediation than other morphological markers such as plural markers, possessive markers and the present progressive (-ing). It has been suggested that the former group are phonologically weak forms and impose a greater processing load (Eadie *et al.*, 2002). Leonard's (1998) 'Surface Hypothesis' of SLI offers a process-based account of SLI. He argues that the underlying deficit in SLI is reduced language processing ability (see Leonard, 1998 for a review). Several recent studies have attributed poor phonological memory to children with SLI. For example, children with SLI also perform significantly worse on non-word repetition tasks than MLU-matched controls (Bishop *et al.*, 1999), and ability to repeat sentences on sentence imitation tasks has been demonstrated to differentiate between adults with and without SLI (Tomblin *et al.*, 1992). Processing explanations for SLI have gained credence recently as they link limited processing capacity or phonological memory constraints to the reduced capacity of children with SLI to focus on important grammatical detail such as morphology. Conti-Ramsden and Windfuhr (2002) argue that children with SLI have processing deficits that make them less sensitive to phonologically based features in production such as grammatical markers and that, accordingly, they require a greater number of exemplars of this type in the input than children with normal language development before they can reach an 'SLI critical mass' and can abstract and generalise their lexically specific knowledge of individual verbs to a more general category knowledge of verbs.The evidence on normal developing children appears to lend support to the suggestion that there are age-related milestones in processing. However, the evidence from atypical populations such as children with specific language impairment suggests that exposure factors rather than maturation may be key. However, in interpreting all of these findings we need to bear in mind what Ellis and Beattie (1986: 228f.) have to say about the questionable relationship between the processing of language in highly contrived experimental tasks and language processing in natural, everyday communication.

Summary and Conclusions

(1) As far as the very early stages of normal L1 acquisition are concerned,

the evidence points strongly to a stable sequence of speech-related milestones within the first year of life.

(2) Research relating to the second year of life (single word / multi-word stage) confirms some broad parallels between children in terms of sequences of development in relation to age-ranges. However, more recent large-scale studies have increasingly highlighted variation in both the pattern and the rate of language acquisition at this stage.

(3) As regards acquisition up to the age of four years, there is considerable evidence for a stable sequence of syntactic milestones associated with reasonably well-defined age norms but considerably less evidence of such sequential milestones in the lexical, semantic and pragmatic domains.

(4) Beyond the age of four, individual differences play a very significant role in the acquisition process. The later stages of acquisition are discussed in further detail in the following chapter.

(5) With regard to language processing, there is some evidence which points to age-related phases in this area. However, recent evidence from the SLI population calls into question maturationally based explanations of processing development.

Notes

1. In fact according to Stark (1986: 187), these sounds do contain 'brief consonantal sounds also . . . all produced at the back of the mouth, where the tongue and palate are most likely to resume contact with each other during vocalic sounds'. What are later perceived as the first combinations of consonant-like and vowel-like sounds ('babbling') are characterised phonetically by 'prolonged vowel- or consonant-like steady states' and consonantal elements which are 'produced more anteriorly' (Stark, 1986: 158).
2. Cf. Crystal *et al.* (1976: 31): 'every reference we have ever seen to the emergence of two-element sentences cites the age-range between 18 months and 2 years'.
3. The CHILDES website (www.psy.cmu.edu / ~childes) is constantly updated with new data, details of current and previous research projects and literature.

Chapter 3
The Critical Period Hypothesis: L1-related Evidence

Introductory

The popularly held view that there is a 'critical period' for language development is not generally subjected to more than rather superficial scrutiny. Most adults simply take it for granted, for example, that children are of their nature equipped to learn a foreign language with much less effort and in a generally more competent manner than they themselves are able to manage. Introductory psychology texts often treat the matter in a similarly axiomatic fashion but endow the assumptions they make with scientific credentials by introducing concepts and terminology from such domains as neuropsychology and nativist linguistics. This is not to say that the Critical Period Hypothesis is without its critics. Indeed, the question of whether there is a critical period for language development has generated fierce debate among researchers and continues to do so. As was indicated in Chapter 1, the discussion has both a theoretical and a practical dimension and is of interest to L1 acquisition researchers and L2 acquisition researchers alike. For some theoreticians the Critical Period Hypothesis is important because the notion of maturational constraints on language acquisition is seen as related to the idea that language development is underpinned by special bioprogramming. In the more practical sphere of language education, the Critical Period Hypothesis has ramifications with respect to decision-making about the starting point for the introduction of L2 instruction in schools. The L2 issues will be discussed in detail in Chapters 4 and 6. In this chapter we shall be concerned with examining the L1 evidence in respect of the Critical Period Hypothesis.

Defining the Critical Period

Before we proceed further in our discussion of the Critical Period Hypothesis (henceforth CPH), it may be worth pausing to consider how the concept of the critical period is understood in the biological sciences.

Critical period is the term used in biology to refer to a limited phase in the development of an organism during which a particular activity or competency must be acquired if it is to be incorporated into the behaviour of that organism. The example which is usually cited in this connection is that of imprinting in goslings and ducklings. Lorenz (1958) notes that newborn goslings became irreversibly attached to the first moving object they perceive after hatching. Usually, the first moving object in question is the gosling's mother. However, any other moving object will trigger the relevant reaction if it comes into the gosling's line of vision in the post-hatching period. The period during which the attachment of the above kind may be effected is limited in duration, and beyond that period the gosling will no longer fix its following behaviour in the way described. Similarly, De Villiers and De Villiers (1978) refer to the following behaviour of Mallard ducklings, commenting:

> This following behavior only occurs within a certain time period after hatching, after which point the ducklings develop a fear of strange objects and retreat instead of following. Within these time limits is the *critical period* for the following behavior. (De Villiers & De Villiers, 1978: 210)

On the basis of the above, critical periods in biology can, be characterised as follows.

(1) They relate to very specific activities or behaviours.
(2) Their duration is limited within well-defined and predictable termini.
(3) Beyond the confines of the period in question the relevant behaviour is not acquired.

If we are to use the term *critical period* in relation to language acquisition, we have presumably to demonstrate that the language acquisition maturational constraints we are positing are in line with the above criteria. If language acquisition in human beings is rigidly constrained by the limits of a critical period of the above kind, the implication is that L1 development begins only at the onset of this period and that unless it gets under way during the period in question it will not happen at all. A further implication may be that even if L1 development begins within the critical period it does not *continue* beyond the end of that period. Investigations of critical periods in non-humans often adopt an experimental type of methodology, which essentially involves depriving the organism of access to relevant stimuli during the putative critical period. For obvious reasons, this kind of approach cannot be taken in the case of language acquisition in humans. Accordingly, other ways have had to be found to explore the question of whether there is a critical period for language acquisition.

Lenneberg (1967), who is generally acknowledged as the 'father' of the CPH in relation to language acquisition, sees the critical period as beginning at age two and ending around puberty, this period coinciding with the lateralisation process – the specialisation of the dominant hemisphere of the brain for language functions. He adduces a wide range of evidence of changes in the brain occurring during the period in question. However, his claim that lateralisation ends at puberty has been significantly undermined by later studies which reinterpret the relevant data as indicating that the process is already complete in early childhood (see e.g. Kinsbourne & Hiscock, 1977; Krashen, 1973). These studies will be discussed further in Chapter 5. As noted earlier, one can distinguish between a weaker and a stronger version of the CPH. The weaker version claims that, in order to proceed successfully, language acquisition must begin within the critical period, and that the sooner language acquisition begins after the onset of the critical period the more efficient it will be. The stronger version holds that even if language acquisition begins within the critical period it does not *continue* beyond the end of that period. L1-related evidence relevant to the foregoing will be presented in what follows – beginning with an exploration of evidence concerning Lenneberg's suggestion that the critical period begins at age two and going on then to examine evidence in respect of the offset or end of the critical period.

The Onset of the Critical Period

Regarding the beginning of the critical period, Lenneberg (1967) cites some evidence based partly on his own observations of deaf children. He claims that whereas 'children deafened before completion of the second year do not have any facilitation [in respect of oral skills] in comparison with the congenitally deaf, those who lose their hearing after having been exposed – even for a short time – to the experience of [oral] language subsequent to this point 'can be trained much more easily in all the [oral] language arts' (p. 155). He interprets this as indicating that the beginning of the critical period can be located around the age of two years:

> Language cannot begin to develop until a certain level of physical maturation and growth has been attained. Between the ages of two and three years language emerges by an interaction of maturation and self-programmed learning. (Lenneberg, 1967: 158)

Lenneberg's (1967) interpretation of the data from the deaf – to which we shall return in the next section – is very far from universally accepted. Moreover, there is a whole range of other evidence, which runs counter to the notion that the language acquisition process is, as it were, 'switched on' around the age of two years. Actually Lenneberg's own synthesis of the language acquisition timetable in the same chapter of the same work undermines such an interpretation. Thus, although he associates the period 21–36 months with 'acquisition of language', his summary of development between four and 20 months is 'from babbling to words' (1967: 180), which clearly implies that the production of what most people would regard as elements of 'true' language, i.e. words, has normally already begun well before the second birthday; and what has been produced must necessarily have been on its way to being acquired at a prior stage. In fact, current evidence seems to suggest that there is no stage in the infant's development when language is *not* in the process of being acquired.

Some rather dramatic phonological evidence in support of this notion comes from experimental studies (Eimas *et al.*, 1971; Streiter, 1976). The classic study by Eimas *et al.* (1971) provided evidence that infants as young as one month can discriminate between phonologically relevant categories in the same way that adults do. The study focused on infants' sensitivity to voice onset time (VOT) differences. VOT refers to the point in time at which the vocal chords begin to vibrate in relation to the release of a closure:

> In a fully voiced plosive, for example, the vocal chords vibrate throughout; in a voiceless unaspirated plosive, there is a delay . . . before voicing starts; in a voiceless aspirated plosive, the delay is much longer, depending on the amount of aspiration. (Crystal, 1997: 413)

In the experiments in question, sensitivity was tested using a sucking habituation technique. When the same sound was repeatedly played to an infant sucking on a 'blind nipple' his/her rate of sucking gradually decreased. If then a change in the sound stimulus occasioned a renewed increase in sucking rate, this was interpreted as an indication that the difference had been perceived and the habituation effect thus disrupted. Eimas *et al.* (1971) found that American infants of only one month of age discriminated between the synthetically produced speech sounds [b] and [p], but failed to distinguish between sounds which diverged by the same VOT difference as [b] and [p] but which belonged to the same phoneme, i.e. functioned as the 'same sound', in English. Streiter (1976) investigated a group of infants whose average age was 63 days and who were being reared in a home where the only language being spoken was Kikuyu which, unlike English, has a phonetic distinction between prevoiced and voiced stops. Streiter's subjects showed particular sensitivity to the prevoicing-simultaneous voicing transition, a sensitivity that was not reliably shown by Eimas *et al.*'s subjects.

It is now quite clear that the ability to perceive phonic contrasts is present very early, which may imply that it is an innate property of the human auditory system (Tomasello & Bates, 2001). Infants very rapidly sort out the sounds which are functional in the language of their environment, though, interestingly, they fail to distinguish the contrasts in question when the relevant sounds are played backwards – a finding which has been interpreted as suggesting that the perceptual ability in question constitutes something more than a capacity to discriminate between random sound sequences and that it specifically concerns the patterns of human speech. In fact, very recent research has suggested that infants develop a bias towards the sounds of the language of their environment while still *in utero* (cf. Ramus *et al.*, 1999). It should perhaps be noted that, if innate perceptual abilities exist, they are not unique to speech or indeed unique to humans. Categorical perception also occurs with pure tones and sequences of lights. There is, moreover, a growing literature indicating that categorical perceptions occur in non-human species – e.g. chinchillas, quail and tamarin monkeys. Ramus *et al.* (2001), for example, have shown that tamarin monkeys can discriminate the same phonologically relevant contrasts as human infants and, like human infants, cannot distinguish these contrasts when the relevant sounds are played backwards.

Stark's (1986) review of research on pre-speech segmental phonology leads her to conclude that there are definable levels or stages in the infant's vocal development during the first 12 post-natal months, these stages being: reflexive crying and vegetative sounds, cooing, vocal play, reduplicated babbling and non-reduplicated babbling. Particularly pertinent in the present context are her comments on these stages, which suggest that even the earliest vocalising makes a contribution towards later phonological development and that while the various stages can be seen as representing 'landmarks' there is no question of any sharp break in the developmental progression:

> It has been suggested that the earliest productions provide a matrix of primitive metaphonological features from which babbling, jargon and speech ultimately derive (Oller, 1976). Most, if not all, of the articulatory features of speech are present in the earliest sounds of infants in a remarkably well-organised form. For example, the feature stop, produced at the glottis, initiates many cry segments and the feature bilabial place of articulation is present in the brief clicks of sucking. (Stark, 1986: 171)

The term 'landmark' may suggest a discontinuity in vocal development; indeed the major landmarks of vocal development may reflect marked changes in vocal tract configuration resulting from downward and forward facial growth or from the descent of the larynx into the neck. They may also reflect discontinuities of neural development within the speech motor system.

Vocal behaviours that are characteristic of one stage, however, may persist into succeeding stages and new landmark behaviours may have their antecedents in preceding stages. Thus discontinuities of vocal behaviour, although the most salient aspect of vocal development, do not describe that development completely. (Stark, 1986: 171f.)

Crystal's (1986) summary of research into the beginnings of prosody tends in a similar direction. He also isolates (1986: 178–92) a succession of stages: a stage of 'biologically determined vocalisations', a stage of first 'awareness of prosodic contrasts', a stage of primitive 'prosodic patterns' in the infant's vocalisations, a stage where these patterns take on 'an increasingly determinate and systematic character' and finally a stage where 'tonic contrastivity' or 'contrastive stress' appears. Three points relevant to the present discussion emerge from Crystal's exposition: (1) the acquisition of prosody begins very early; (2) the various stages are largely continuous with each other; (3) there is an early interaction between the acquisition of prosody and other aspects of language development.

Crystal sees his second stage as the 'first sign of anything linguistic emerging' (1986: 179). He refers to reports in Lewis (1951) suggesting that this stage can begin around two or three months, but goes on to refer to a number of infant speech perception studies indicating that infants respond to both prosodic and segmental features earlier (1986: 179). His third stage emerges, he says, 'from as early as six months, according to most scholars' (1986: 179). One interesting study cited in this connection is that of de Boysson-Bardies *et al.* (1984), who 'found that adults were able to distinguish French, Arabic and Chinese children of eight months on the basis of their intonation patterns' (Crystal, 1986: 180). His reading of the research (including Lenneberg's) leads him to situate his fourth stage, more vaguely, 'during the second half of the first year' (1986: 181). As for his final stage, his inference from the literature is that its onset coincides 'with the appearance of two-word utterances at around 1.6' (1986: 188). Thus it appears that the acquisition of prosody normally begins well before the end of the child's first six months and that all the basic elements of prosody are already in place in advance of the age at which Lenneberg situates the onset of language acquisition.

Regarding the continuity of Crystal's stages, this emerges clearly from his discussion of research findings. To take just one example, the following is what he has to say concerning the establishment of tonic contrastivity:

> The general developmental process seems clear. Lexical items which have appeared independently as single-element utterances, marked thus by pitch and pauses are brought into relationship . . . At first, the

lexical items retain their prosodic autonomy, with the pause between them becoming reduced . . . Often long sequences of these items appear, especially repetitively . . . The next step is the integration of sequences of items, usually two, into a single tone-unit. How general a process this is, is unclear, but in several English combinations studied it was the case that one item became more prominent than the other; it was louder and had an identifiable pitch movement. There was a rhythmic relationship between the items . . . and intervening pauses became less likely in repeated versions of lexical sequences. (Crystal, 1986: 188f.)

Crystal himself explicitly highlights the gradualness of the progression at the end of this section on stress: 'One general conclusion from these studies must be to emphasise the very gradual nature of the acquisition of stress and associated contrasts' (1986: 192).

Crystal cites a good deal of evidence indicative of an early interplay between prosodic development and other aspects of language acquisition. The examples in the following quotations exemplify on the one hand the role of prosody in providing the child with a stable framework for perfecting the pronunciation of his/her first words and sentences, and on the other the interaction between the acquisition of prosody and the learning of discourse structuring techniques:

In one child studied at Reading, aged 1.2, the phrase *all-gone*, regularly said by the parent after each meal, was actually rehearsed by using the prosodic component only: the child hummed the intonation of the phrase first . . . only then attempting the whole, producing an accurate intonation but only approximate segments The phrase could be easily elicited after any meal, but it was not until a month had gone by that the child's segmental output became as stable as his prosodic. (Crystal, 1986: 181)

The development of 'turn-taking', either between the parent and child (Snow, 1977) or between children (Keenan, 1974) also involves prosodic delimitation and interdependence. One Keenan twin, for example, would regularly take the prosodic character of the other's utterance and 'play' with it. Another child, studied at Reading, marked the end of a jargon sequence with a distinctive two-syllable pitch movement . . . which was openly described by his parents as 'their cue to speak'. (Crystal, 1986: 182)

To shift the focus now to non-phonological aspects of language development, comprehension of at least one linguistically mediated communicative function, namely attention getting, appears to be established early in the second half of the child's first year. Griffiths (1986: 284) cites Leopold's (1939, 1949) observations of his daughter Hildegard, which show her turning her head in response to her name during her seventh month, and Griffiths (1986: 282) refers to Valentine's (1942) study, which reveals subject B evincing 'faint signs of recognition' of 'Baba' at five and a half months and producing a smile every time he heard the word one month later. More recent experimental research has found that children respond to their names (in isolation) at 4.5 months and as early as six months in connected speech (with priming) (see e.g. Mandel *et al.*, 1995).

However, interactionists like Halliday and Bruner would claim that the process of learning how and what language means begins long before the acquisition of such knowledge becomes manifest in linguistic contexts. Thus, Halliday sees meaningful language as the last link in 'some chain of dependence such as: social order – transmission of the social order to the child – role of language in the transmission process – functions of language in relation to this role – meanings derived from these functions' (Halliday, 1975: 5). Similarly, Bruner claims that meanings which eventually come to be mediated linguistically are first mastered as knowledge of the social situations constituted by caregiver–child exchanges, so that:

> ... the child comes to recognise the grammatical rules for forming and comprehending sentences by virtue of their correspondence to the conceptual framework that is constructed for the regulation of joint action and joint attention. (Bruner, 1975:18)

There is a fair amount of evidence around which appears to lend at least general support to such views. The context of the interaction has been shown to affect the linguistic forms utilised. For example, Bateson (1975) examined longitudinal data collected from five children and their mothers. She reports that 'social interactions similar to conversation were recorded for all of the pairs before three months' (p. 102) and comments on the fact that 'in the development of praxis we can see the progressive construction of contexts of communication', which she takes to be contexts of learning' (p. 111). Harris *et al.*'s (1983) longitudinal study, which involved the video-taping of mothers and infants aged between seven and 10 months playing together, found that almost all of the mothers' utterances related to the child's immediate environment, that 70% referred to an object to which the child was at that time attending, and that 67% of changes of topic were responses to changes in the child's activity. Schaffer *et al.* (1983) likewise found that mothers tended to time their directives in such a way that the child was focusing on the relevant object before being asked to do something with it. Tomasello and Todd (1983) for their part found that where mothers and children maintained sustained bouts of joint attention, the children in question had larger productive lexicons. They conclude that the manner in which the mother and child interact and regulate one another's attention is an important factor in early language development. Barrett (1995) also argues that the presence of socio-interactional formats in mother–child interaction is highly significant for early language development; studies of these routines have demonstrated that they are highly structured, are regular, have standardised formats and have clearly assigned roles for both the caregiver and the child. Furthermore, the caregiver produces certain linguistic forms at predictable points in the action sequence (cf. Bruner, 1983).

Whatever the precise degree of explanatory power the interactionist perspective is in the long run shown to have with regard to the specifics of language acquisition, the general notion that caregiver–child shared activity prepares the ground for and is continuous with the development of linguistic interaction seems incontrovertible. Incontrovertible also is the fact that such shared activity typically commences literally as soon as the child emerges from the womb. In any case, there are sufficient indicators from the development of segmental and prosodic phonology to justify deep scepticism concerning Lenneberg's contention that language acquisition does not properly begin until around age two. In fact, the briefest perusal of the child language acquisition literature will lead one to conclude that the first year of life and perhaps even the latter stages of *in utero* development are highly important for language acquisition and the organisation of perception and related production systems. As for Lenneberg's evidence on the development of deaf children, it has to be said that this evidence is somewhat vague and anecdotal in nature. Furthermore, the phenomenon it purports to document is not necessarily to be interpreted as signalling the sudden onset of a critical period for language at the age of about two years. After all, children who have had access to aural input beyond the age of two years have necessarily received such input over a longer period than children who have been deafened before that age. It is surely conceivable that longer duration of exposure to normal aural input could of itself explain the better linguistic performance of those who receive it. In short, there seem no good grounds for believing that there is a particular 'level of physical maturation' in early child development where language suddenly 'emerges' and a critical period for its acquisition begins.

The End of the Critical Period

We turn now to the question of the upper limit of a putative critical period for language acquisition. To put the problem in its simplest and starkest terms, is it the case that human beings who have not acquired language before a certain age cannot acquire it thereafter? The age most frequently posited as the upper limit of the critical period is the early teens, that is to say, the stage at which childhood, as commonly understood, is ending and adolescence, with the onset of puberty, beginning – although, as Snow (1987: 188) notes, 'in reviewing the literature relevant to the CPH, it is important to remember that the end-point of the critical period is as much a matter at empirical issue as is the very existence of a critical period'. In what follows we shall review a number of different categories of evidence which have been discussed in connection with the notion of a cut-off point or end of a critical period for L1 acquisition. Specifically, we shall explore (a) neurological evidence, (b) evidence from language acquisition in the deaf, (c) evidence from feral children and (d) evidence from language acquisition in Down syndrome subjects.

(a) Neurological evidence

There has been considerable interest in evidence from neurology and its implications for the existence or otherwise of a critical period for language acquisition. The notion that children's brains are different from adults' brains is, of course, uncontroversial. It is generally accepted that the immature brain exhibits markedly more plasticity than the mature brain. However, it has not been demonstrated that the diminishing plasticity of the brain is linked to processes specifically and exclusively relating to developments in respect of the specialisation of cerebral structures for language acquisition.

A category of evidence which is frequently referred to in discussions of the notion of an absolute upper age limit on the commencement of L1 acquisition is evidence on the recovery of speech after brain damage or brain surgery. Such evidence is, naturally, cited in support of the neurological perspective on age effects, to which we shall be returning in Chapter 5. Basically, what is in question is the ability of the human organism at different maturational stages to transfer language functions from a damaged or surgically removed area to a still subsistent and healthy area. It has been taken for granted for more than a century that in adults the two hemispheres into which the brain is divided are not equally involved in serving language functions, but that one, usually the left, is clearly dominant in this connection. More recently it has been claimed that injury to or removal of this dominant hemisphere has different long-term effects on the language of the person concerned, depending on the age at which the lesion or operation takes place.

Thus, Penfield and Roberts (1959: 240) report that children are normally able to re-learn language when injury or disease damages speech areas in the dominant hemisphere, whereas speech recovery in adults is much more problematic, and that whereas in young children the speech mechanism is frequently transferred with complete success from the injured dominant hemisphere to the healthy minor hemisphere, such transfers do not seem to occur in the case of adults. On this basis they feel justified in asserting that 'for the purposes of learning languages, the human brain becomes progressively stiff and rigid after the age of nine' (Penfield & Roberts, 1959: 236).

Lenneberg (1967) takes a similar kind of line, but comes up with a different age-limit, namely puberty. He cites (1967: 152f.) Basser's (1962) survey of the relevant clinical literature in support of a claim that where hemispherectomy (i.e. the removal of a cerebral hemisphere) affects the dominant hemisphere, children who have undergone the operation can transfer language functions completely to the non-dominant hemisphere whereas adults cannot. He goes on to link time limitations for language acquisition to 'the far-reaching plasticity of the human brain (or lack of cortical specialisation) with respect to language during the early years of life' (Lenneberg, 1967: 154).

Lenneberg's use of Basser's data was subsequently called into question. Krashen (1973: 65) reanalysed the data cited by Lenneberg from Basser, and discovered that:

> Actual data on transfer of the language function indicates that perfect transfer is definitely possible before five … Lenneberg (1967: 152) notes that Basser's cases were injured 'before teens' and uses this data as evidence that transfer is possible just up to puberty … in all cases, the lesion was incurred before five. For lesions incurred during adulthood, complete transfer has not yet been reported … (Krashen, 1973: 67)

Krashen concludes that the relevant neurological development must be completed by around age five. Analyses based on radiological techniques for assessing hemispheric specialisation have led to similar conclusions. For example, Simmonds and Scheibel (1989) looked at 17 brain specimens from individuals between 0.3 and 6.0. They found that dendrites in the right hemisphere developed earlier than those in the same area in the left hemisphere. However, by the fourth to sixth year, the dendrites in the left hemisphere had caught up with and exceeded those in the right hemisphere.

Adams (1997) has a differing perspective; his six-year case study concerns the speech and language development of a boy who was 8.2 at the onset of the study. Subsequently, the boy underwent a left hemispherectomy at 8.6 and had no speech prior to surgery, his language and cognition being at a 3–4-year-old level. Post surgery and following the withdrawal of anti-convulsant medication at 9.3, he suddenly began to acquire speech and language. This was measured periodically between his 9th and 15th year. The most recent scores at 15 years indicated that his receptive and expressive language were at an 8–10-year-old level.

Snow (1987), for her part, cites a number of studies which suggest that children are as impaired as adults following injuries of similar severity and locus (Robinson, 1981). Even children who appear to have fully recovered from head injury manifest persistent word retrieval deficits (Gilbert *et al.*, 1985), and following even very early left hemispherectomy, children have been found to exhibit considerable learning but also permanent linguistic deficits (Dennis, 1980). These findings suggest that right hemisphere potential for language acquisition, even in the very young child, is not equivalent to left hemisphere functioning.

Clearly, the fact that different researchers have specified different ages as marking the onset of a decline in cerebral plasticity specifically in relation to language functions does not inspire confidence in their assertions. Moreover, neurologists have tended to be increasingly sceptical about special factors operating in the recovery of speech, preferring the more general hypothesis of 'the greater plasticity of the less mature organism as it compensates for function loss due to damage' (Kinsbourne & Hiscock, 1977: 174; cf. Springer & Deutsch, 1985: Chapter 8). Such a position is obviously very far from one that interprets the neurological evidence as directly and unequivocally supporting the idea of a critical age limit specifically for language acquisition. One can indeed pose the question whether evidence concerning compensation for damage to normal speech centres tells us *anything* about putative maturational constraints on language acquisition where these centres are entirely unimpaired.

(b) Evidence from language acquisition in the deaf

As noted earlier, Lenneberg (1967) cited evidence, partially based on his own observations, which purported to indicate that children deafened prior to the age of two years had no speech advantage over those deaf since birth. He used such evidence in support of his (now discredited) view that the critical period begins at two years of age. However, an important Deaf-related issue that Lenneberg failed to look at was the question of age effects in the acquisition of sign languages. Children acquiring sign language from infancy go through the same stages of acquisition at the same rate and through the same process as hearing children (see Emmorey *et al.*, 1995; Morford & Mayberry, 2000). However, as Emmorey *et al.* (1995) point out, these children are in the minority; only 3–8% of deaf children have deaf parents. Thus, more than 90% of deaf children are born to hearing parents who do not have sign language competence. It is argued that these children have no access to effective L1 input in their early years and acquire language only at a later stage when exposed to sign language. Accordingly, it has been suggested that the clearest evidence for a critical period in respect of L1 development comes from studies of such cases

However, it must be borne in mind that even profoundly deaf children who are not exposed to sign language and who do not learn a spoken language spontaneously do develop home sign gestures to communicate. While the individual home signs are unique to each individual child, all home signs have been shown to exhibit a systematic linguistic structure that does not vary on an individual basis and is consistent cross-culturally (Emmorey, 2002; Goldin-Meadow & Mylander, 1990; Kegl *et al.*, 1999). Thus, even profoundly deaf children who cannot access an L1 effectively appear to develop a linguistic system for communication, albeit a limited one. This may perhaps call into question the notion that profoundly deaf children deprived of access to sign language are completely without language.

It has been observed that young deaf children appear to have the ability systematically to regularise the input of non-native sign of their parents. The most widely cited example of this phenomenon is that of Simon (J. Singleton, 1989), whose parents' production of the movement morphemes of American Sign Language (ASL) classifier constructions had about a 70% accuracy rate, while Simon's accuracy was 88% – i.e. on a par with deaf children of the same age who receive native language input. In similar vein, Kegl *et al.* (1999) report a study of the emergence of a sign language in Nicaragua, which, they claim, contributes new and direct evidence in support of the CPH. According to this report, young children were able to use their innate capacities to 'make sense of' or fill in the grammatical gaps in the models available to them (ISN) and in this way to surpass their models and acquire a qualitatively different language (PSN), whereas adult learners were not able to do this. This study certainly provides further evidence that children acquiring their L1 are able to regularise the input that they receive to an extent which adults are not, but the question of whether that which underlies this difference is a critical period is not in fact resolved by evidence such as this.

Numerous studies indicate that the later acquisition of sign language as L1 is characterised by deficits of various kinds. Emmorey (2002) reviews the literature and concludes that there are long-term advantages for individuals who began acquiring ASL in childhood over adult beginners. Likewise, the study of 'Chelsea', a deaf adult who began acquiring ASL as an L1 in her early 30s, reveals good lexical and semantic abilities after six years of exposure, but impaired morphology and syntax (Curtiss, 1988), and a large-scale project reported in Newport (1984) and Newport and Supalla (1987), cited in Emmorey (2002), shows that late/adult learners first exposed to ASL after age 12 fell far short of native standards in their signing. Newport (1990) went on to investigate the ASL competence of American deaf adults who had a minimum of 30 years of daily experience with ASL but were at different maturational stages at the time of exposure to ASL. The subjects were assessed on their ability to produce and comprehend a number of syntactic and morphological structures in ASL. Newport found that age of acquisition had no effect on control of basic ASL word order but that subjects exposed to ASL in early childhood consistently outperformed later learners on tests of ASL morphology (cf. Emmorey, 2002; Mayberry, 1993; Mayberry & Eichen, 1991; Meier, 1991; Meier, 2001). Mayberry and her colleagues have found that phonological processing of ASL seems to be particularly vulnerable to the effects of late acquisition (Morford & Mayberry, 2000). Quite significant claims have been made on the basis of such research regarding the notion of a critical period for language acquisition. The following quote from Emmorey (2002: 225) exemplifies this well:

> . . . studies of Deaf children and adults have provided important insights into the nature of the critical period for language acquisition and into the effects of late language acquisition. The results indicate that the window of opportunity for language acquisition slowly closes during childhood and that late acquisition results in incomplete grammatical knowledge and inefficient language processing that do not improve during adulthood, even with years of experience.

However, one notes that the above studies do not demonstrate that language completely fails to develop after a given maturational point, which is what one might expect in the case of a critical period for language. We should not forget that the late learners in Newport's (1990) study displayed considerable control of the morphological system and that Mayberry and Fischer's (1989) late learners did similarly with phonological system. Indeed, all that the above research demonstrates is that earlier acquirers of ASL have some advantages; they have better control of the morphological system and more developed phonological processing skills. It is, moreover, well known that ASL language learners, like learners of other natural languages, are subject to variability explicable in terms of socio-linguistic principles (Snow, 1987).

Moreover, it is surely conceivable that deprivation of language input during the phase in a child's life when cognitive development is at its most intense may have quite general psychological/cognitive effects, and that it may be these general effects that are reflected in later language development rather than effects relating specifically to a critical period for language. Emmorey (2002) argues quite passionately that delayed language exposure has no lasting effects on general cognitive abilities and cites studies by Vernon (1969), who found the same IQ distribution among the deaf and hard of hearing as that of the population at large, and the work of the Gallaudet office of demographic studies (Schildroth, 1976), which yielded similar findings. Emmory (2002) does acknowledge that deafness can affect short-term memory capacity, but she states that this is resolved in adulthood. She argues that while the linguistic effects of late exposure continues into adulthood, the cognitive deficits are overcome.

Theory of mind research is often cited in this context. Theory of mind is the ability to mentalise or the ability to attribute mental states to others. In other words, the child who develops theory of mind learns that people possess minds capable of such mental states as knowing, believing and wanting. Furthermore, such a child develops awareness that people's behaviour can be predicted on the basis of such states, and that another person's state and knowledge may be completely different from the child's own state and knowledge. Deficits in this area have also been described in children with autism, Asperger's Syndrome, Specific Language Impairment (SLI) and deafness. A test often used in this connection is the 'Sally-Ann' or 'False Belief' Test (Baron-Cohen *et al.*, 1985). The test task requires the subject to recognise a character's false belief in a story about two dolls – Sally and Ann. There are slightly different versions, but the central points are as follows: Sally hides a marble in her basket and leaves the room; Ann then moves the marble to another box. The question put to the test-taker is: 'Where will Sally look for the marble?' This question is correctly responded to by normally developing children between five and seven years. A number of studies have demonstrated that Deaf children from hearing families who have delayed exposure to sign language exhibit a marked delay in theory of mind development, but that native signing children exhibit theory of mind at the same age as their hearing peers (see e.g. Peterson & Siegal, 1995; De Villiers & De Villiers, 1999). Emmorey (2002) argues, and cites literature which argues, that deaf children's theory of mind development can be tied directly to exposure to and acquisition of language, and that the deficit is not permanent, as deaf adults exhibit theory of mind ability. However, other researchers have argued that theory of mind deficits may co-exist with other deficits (Hughes & Russel, 1993), that theory of mind deficits can be far-reaching and that they 'may result in profound and extended problems in understanding people, social events, interpersonal relationships, literary competence and vocabulary' (Lundy, 1999: 2).

It has been claimed that studies of the late-acquired sign language of deaf children of hearing parents provide us with an empirical evidence for the existence of a critical period for language acquisition on the basis that such children have not been able to access an L1 early in childhood. However, as we have seen, these children develop 'homesign', a gestural system that they use to communicate with their caregivers and which exhibits a systematic linguistic structure that is consistent cross-culturally. Therefore, they do have access to a communication system, albeit a limited one, from early childhood. There is certainly plenty of evidence that early learners of sign languages have some advantages over later learners. However, late learners nevertheless demonstrate considerable competence. Moreover, such deficits as are manifest in the sign language of late acquirers may be explicable in terms of general cognitive factors such as problems with theory of mind. In the light of all this it can hardly be said that findings relative to the late acquisition of sign language constitute definitive evidence of the existence of a critical period for language acquisition.

(c) Evidence from feral children

Controlled and rigorous L1-based experimentation aimed at investigating the endpoint of the CPH is obviously out of the question. Coldbloodedly to deprive a child of normal linguistic interaction until it reached sexual maturity for experimental purposes would clearly be monstrous. However, there is a body of observational evidence available which at first sight seems directly to address the issue at hand – namely, reports concerning feral children, children, that is to say, who have grown up in isolation from normal human contact and society. Children who are excluded from normal human contact and caretaking in this way naturally fail to learn language. The question is whether these children will learn language later in life if they are later returned to normal social situations and given appropriate intervention. Because of the view of Lenneberg and others that puberty marks the end of the critical period for language, instances of feral children whose rescue and reintegration occurred around or after puberty would seem to be of particular interest in the present connection. Probably the two best-known and best-documented examples of such cases are those of Victor, the 18th-century 'Wild Boy of Aveyron' and Genie, a 20th-century American girl. These two instances will be discussed in detail. Other less well-documented cases include those of Isabelle, Kaspar Hauser, Peter of Hanover and Kamala and Amala (the Indian Wolf Girls) (for overviews see Candland, 1995; Newton, 2002).

A major problem faced by researchers attempting to assess and interpret evidence concerning feral children is that it is often difficult to determine whether the children in question are of normal intelligence and language learning capacity prior to their isolation. Further vital information is also often missing. To quote Lenneberg:

> The degree and duration of neglect, the initial state of health, the care provided for [the children] after discovery, and many other factors are bound to influence the outcome; in the absence of information on these points, virtually no generalizations may be made with regard to human development. (Lenneberg, 1967: 142)

Victor, the 'Wild Boy of Aveyron'

The case of Victor, the 'wild boy of Aveyron' has received a fair amount of scholarly and indeed artistic attention, and illustrates well the problem pointed to by Lenneberg (see e.g. Lane 1976; Shattuck, 1980). This child made his appearance in 1797, when he was seen running naked and searching for roots and acorns in some woods near Lacaune in south central France. In 1798 he was captured and taken to Lacaune, but escaped a little while later. In the following year he was again caught but after eight days again succeeded in escaping, remaining, however, on this occasion on the plateau between Lacaune and Roquecézière in the department of Aveyron, and occasionally approaching farmhouses for food. Then in January 1800 he turned up in the village of Saint-Sernin. The next day, the government commissioner for Saint-Sernin took charge of him and sent him to the orphanage at Saint-Affrique. According to reports on the boy published by two naturalists, Bonnaterre and Virey, in 1800, he was 12 or 13 years old and unremarkable in appearance except for numerous scars on his body, including a long horizontal one across his throat. This last led Bonnaterre to speculate that a deliberate attempt might at some stage have been made on the boy's life. His organs seemed normal and his senses good, but he occasionally underwent spasms, which appeared to indicate that his nervous system had been affected in some way. With specific regard to language, the boy employed some signs – relating to his principal needs – apparently learned since his capture, but his only vocalisations were cries, grunts and other inarticulate sounds.

In August 1800 the boy was conveyed to Paris by order of the Minister of the Interior. There he was delivered into the hands of Sicard, the director of the Institute for Deaf-Mutes, who, however, did not 'take him on', presumably judging him untrainable. If that was indeed Sicard's judgement, it was seconded by that of Pinel, medical director of the Paris asylums for the insane. A report on the boy prepared by Pinel in November 1800 interprets every aspect of the child's behaviour as symptomising 'idiocy':

> We know the other details of his life from the time he entered society – his judgement always limited to the objects of his basic needs, his

attention captured solely by the sight of food, or by means of living independently, a strongly acquired habit, the total absence of subsequent development of his intellectual faculties with regard to every other object. Do these not assert that the child ought to be categorised among the children suffering from idiocy and insanity, and that there is no hope whatever of obtaining some measure of success through systematic and continued instruction? (As cited by Lane, 1976: 69)

One person at least disagreed with this judgement, namely Itard, newly appointed resident medical officer of the Institute for Deaf-Mutes. He had already taken an interest in the boy before assuming his duties at the institute and, once in post, proposed to develop an educational programme for him. He also gave the boy a foster-mother and a name. The former, Madame Guérin, was a woman without special training. As for the name, Victor, Itard chose this because the boy seemed to react to 'the sound o' more than to others.

The two facts emerging from Itard's reports (1801, 1807) on his endeavours which have particular significance in the present context are (a) that Victor reached puberty shortly after Itard's training programme began, and (b) that despite Itard's efforts Victor never acquired more than a few rudiments of language. With regard to language development, there were at the beginning of Victor's training some encouraging signs. He articulated the word *lait* ('milk'), though, according to Itard, only as 'a useless exclamation of joy' (as cited from Itard 1801 by Shattuck, 1980: 95), and apparently derived from this item other word-like sounds:

> The word 'lait' provided Victor with the basis of two other monosyllables, *la* and *li*. They had even less meaning for him. Only recently he has modified the second sound by adding a second *l* and pronouncing it as in the Italian *gli*, approximately *yee*. One often hears him repeating *lli, lli*, in a tone of voice not without sweetness. . . . I am inclined to think that this different feat of articulation is Victor's way of reaching out toward the name *Julie*. Julie is Madame Guérin's twelve-year-old daughter, who spends all her Sundays with her mother. On that day one cannot help noticing that the exclamation *lli, lli*, becomes more frequent. (As cited from Itard, 1801 by Shattuck, 1980: 95f.)

He also attempted the exclamation *Oh Dieu!* (Oh God!), which he pronounced 'by eliminating the *u in Dieu* and doubling the *i*, so that one distinctly hears *Oh Diie! Oh Diie!*' (As cited from Itard 1801 by Shattuck, 1980: 95.)

Furthermore, he even learned to spell out the word *lait* in metal letters, and to use the duly arranged letters as a request.

One afternoon when [Victor] was ready to set out for the observatory, we saw him take the four letters in question on his own initiative and put them in his pocket; no sooner did he arrive at Citizen Lemeri's house, where as I previously said he goes every day for some milk, than he took them out and placed them on a table in such a way as to form the word *lait*. (As cited from Itard, 1801 by Lane, 1976: 124)

Progress continued in the written medium. Victor learned to respond to simple written expressions and to communicate his own requirements in writing. Moreover, he could apparently cope with and produce meaningful combinations of words he had not previously encountered, and was even able to find interpretations for strings that were semantically anomalous:

When I found myself one day, after successive changes of the objects of the verbs, with such associations of words as *to tear stone, to cut cup, to eat broom,* he evaded the difficulty very well by changing the two actions indicated by the first two verbs into others less incompatible with the nature of their objects. Thus he took a hammer to break the stone and dropped the cup to break it. Coming to the third verb [*eat*] and not being able to find any other to replace it, he looked for something else to serve as the object of the verb. He took a piece of bread and ate it. (As cited from Itard, 1801 by Lane, 1976: 148)

Oral language, however, proved more problematic. Itard, having come to the conclusion that Victor was incapable of the kinds of aural discrimination that would enable him accurately to imitate speech, tried to teach him the dynamics of speech articulation by visual means, modelling the movements of the articulators in an exaggerated manner. These endeavours were to no avail, and it may well be that Itard's failure in the domain of oral language 'marked a change in the entire relationship' (Shattuck, 1980: 141) and was a major factor in his decision in 1805 to abandon Victor's training. The ministry allocated 150 francs a year to Madame Guérin, and Victor went to live with her in a nearby house, where he died, in his forties, in the year 1828.

Is it permissible to interpret Victor's failure fully to develop language as evidence of a critical period for language acquisition? Itard certainly thought so, concluding that 'the articulation of sounds ... must encounter innumerable obstacles at any age other than early childhood' (as cited from Itard, 1801 by Lane, 1976: 129). However, Itard also recognised the role of another factor, namely isolation and its desensitising consequences, on which he laid great emphasis as a general explanation for Victor's condition. Another possible explanation is to be found in Pinel's contention that Victor had significant learning disabilities. One can also speculate that Victor may have been born normal but may have developed psychiatric symptoms prior to being abandoned. Commentators have talked of autism and other possible psychiatric diagnoses (see e.g. Lane, 1976: 176ff; Shattuck, 1980: 169). With particular regard to productive speech, there is in addition Bonnaterre's and Virey's suggestion that Victor's speech physiology may have been affected, perhaps as a result of his wound. Finally, one can point to possible deficiencies in Itard's training programme (see e.g. Lane, 1976: 169f.; Shattuck, 1980: 165ff.) – its failure to build systematically on what Victor achieved, the narrowness of the environment it provided, the disproportionate importance it attached to oral language, and its negligence of the emotional and sexual dimensions of Victor's reintegration.

Given the variety of possible explanations of Victor's language problems, it would be unwarranted to see these problems as simply maturation-related. Nor, on the other hand, can one take Victor's small successes in acquiring language and using it creatively as evidence *against* the hypothesis that post-pubertal language acquisition *ab initio* is absolutely impossible. We do not know whether Victor learned to speak before being abandoned by his parent(s) or guardian(s) or, if he did, what traces of the experience remained to be re-activated later. In other words, we are unable to say categorically whether or not Victor's language development while under Itard's instruction can truly be described as development *ab initio*. It might be imagined that these uncertainties derived from the fact that the case in question is remote in time. However, if one looks at a very recent case of a 'feral child', that of Genie (see e.g. Curtiss, 1977; Curtiss *et al.*, 1975; Fromkin *et al.*, 1974) one finds essentially the same difficulties of interpretation.

Genie

The general facts about Genie's condition when she was discovered, and what is known and surmised about the appalling circumstances of her upbringing, are contained in the following extract from a report by Fromkin *et al.* (1974).

> Genie was first encountered when she was 13 years, 9 months. At the time of her discovery and hospitalization she was an unsocialized, primitive human being, emotionally disturbed, unlearned and without language. She had been taken into protective custody by the police and, on November 4, 1970, was admitted into the Children's Hospital of Los Angeles for evaluation with a tentative diagnosis of severe malnutrition . . .

When admitted to the hospital, Genie was a painfully thin child with a distended abdomen who appeared to be six or seven years younger than her age. She was 54.5 inches tall and weighed 62.25 pounds. She was unable to stand erect, could not chew solid or even semi-solid foods, had great difficulty in swallowing, was incontinent of feces and urine and was mute.

... There is evidence that from the age of 20 months until shortly before admission to the hospital, Genie had been isolated in a small closed room, tied into a potty chair where she remained most or all hours of the day, sometimes overnight. A cloth harness, constructed to keep her from handling her feces was her only apparel of wear. When not strapped into the chair she was kept in a covered infant crib, also confined from the waist down. The doors of the room were kept closed and the windows were curtained. She was hurriedly fed (only cereal and baby food) and minimally cared for by her mother, who was almost blind during most of the years of Genie's isolation. There was no radio or TV in the house and the father's intolerance of noise of any kind kept any acoustic stimuli which she received behind the closed door to a minimum ... Genie was physically punished by the father if she made any sounds. According to the mother, the father and older brother never spoke to Genie although they barked at her like dogs. The mother was forbidden to spend more than a few minutes with Genie during feeding. (Fromkin *et al.*, 1974: 84f.)

Medical examinations revealed 'no discernible evidence of physical or mental disease that would ... account for her retarded behaviour' (Fromkin *et al.*, 1974: 86). Nor was she autistic or pathologically disturbed. Within four weeks of her admission to hospital she was no longer apathetic and withdrawn, but showing signs of 'a lively curiosity' and 'emotional responsivity' (Fromkin *et al.*, 1974: 86).

It is not known whether Genie had ever spoken before her isolation. On admission to hospital, the only sounds she made were noises associated with spitting and 'a kind of throaty whimper' (Fromkin *et al.*, 1974: 86). Tests of linguistic competence produced evidence that Genie understood 'individual words which she did not utter herself, but, except for such words, she had little if any comprehension of grammatical structures' (Fromkin *et al.*, 1974: 87). Over the subsequent two years she developed comprehension of such structures as singular-plural contrasts of nouns, negative-affirmative sentence distinctions, possessive constructions, modifications, prepositional usage, conjunction with *and*, and comparative and superlative forms of adjectives.

Progress in speech production was slower, presumably because Genie had not learned the necessary neuro-muscular controls over her vocal organs. She apparently had difficulties regulating air flow and volume. Her sound productions were acoustically weak and strange in voice quality. Nevertheless, her phonological development approximated to that of normal children. As far as syntax is concerned, Genie learned to combine words in three- and four-word strings and to produce negative sentences, strings with locative nouns, noun phrases, possessives and plurals. Broadly, her progress in the acquisition of language, though slower than is usual, paralleled that of normal English-speaking children. Moreover, relative to her overall stage of linguistic development, she exhibited particular difficulties with written language, in her acquisition of colour words and numbers, in vocabulary-building generally, and in understanding the full range of wh-questions. However, she also demonstrated some peculiar inconsistencies in word order, interpreting simple NVN sentences incorrectly, despite the correctness of her own sentences and her successful performance in tests imposing apparently identical requirements (Curtiss *et al.*, 1975).

Clearly, Genie's language development went further than Victor's ever did. In a very much richer sense than in Victor's case, Genie's language is 'rule-governed behaviour', that is to say, 'from a finite set of arbitrary linguistic elements she can and does create novel utterances that theoretically know no upper bound' (Curtiss, 1977: 204). What is more, she can actually understand and produce speech, whereas Victor's communication through language was all but confined to the written medium. It is therefore difficult to disagree with Curtiss's verdict that 'in the most fundamental and critical respects, Genie has language' (1977: 204). On the other hand, one cannot ignore Genie's difficulties with vocal production nor her syntactic-semantic idiosyncrasies.

Genie's language development has been interpreted as evidence both for and against the CPH. Curtiss suggests that the abnormal aspects of Genie's speech may indicate 'specific constraints and limitations on the nature of language acquisition outside of . . . the critical maturational period' (Curtiss, 1977: 234). Against this, De Villiers and De Villiers read Genie's achievements as running counter to the notion that puberty represents a critical upper limit for language acquisition:

> Genie represents a case of first-language acquisition after the critical age of puberty. To be sure, her development is laborious and incomplete, but the similarities between it and normal acquisition outweigh the differences. (De Villiers & De Villiers, 1978: 219)

In fact, our state of knowledge about Genie's childhood and its psychological repercussions does not justify either interpretation. It would surely be as plausible to attribute Genie's linguistic problems to trauma resulting from her isolation and confinement, and/or to the general effects of not having been reared in the normal sense, as to ascribe them to the fact that her experience of language began after puberty. Contrariwise, it is possible, on the evidence, to argue that Genie may actually have received just enough exposure to language before being rescued – for example, during her mother's brief visits – to provide a basis on which further linguistic development could build.

In sum, the evidence from the oft-cited feral children such as Victor and Genie is incomplete in crucial respects both regarding language exposure and in relation to experiences which would have had significant effects on their overall development and psychiatric well-being. We probably have to concur with Lenneberg's comment that the only safe conclusion to be drawn from cases like Genie's and Victor's 'is that life in dark closets, wolves' dens, forests or sadistic parents' backyards is not conducive to good health and normal development' (Lenneberg, 1967: 142).

(d) Evidence from Down syndrome subjects

Such evidence as there is against language development begun in childhood continuing into adulthood comes from studies of people with learning disabilities, especially those with Down syndrome. Down syndrome is a genetic disorder with a prevalence of approximately 1:600 to 1:700 births. It is strongly associated with mental retardation and is usually identified at birth and confirmed by the identification of a karotype (i.e. cell nucleus profile) showing trisomy (i.e. three copies) of chromosome 21 (Spiker & Hopmann, 1997). Down syndrome children have substantial delays in phonological acquisition. Rosin *et al.* (1988) found that this pattern continues into adolescence; the adolescents in their study had significant poorer intelligibility than a control group of children with developmental delay due to other causes and matched for mental age. Crucially for the present discussion, the diagnosis of Down syndrome is specifically associated with a characteristic pattern of language deficit, even once cognitive status, hearing and chronological age are taken into account. Language comprehension is superior to expression and there are differential rates of development in the lexical and syntactic/morphological domains (Chapman, 1995). Children with Down syndrome also do more poorly on auditory memory tasks than typically developing mental-age or vocabulary-comprehension matched controls. The most widely referred to findings of a cessation of progress in the language development in Down syndrome subjects are those of Lenneberg, Nichols & Rosenberger (1964), who in a three-year observational study of 54 individuals with Down syndrome were able to record progress in language development only in children younger than 14 years. This was taken by Lenneberg (1967: 155) as indicating that 'progress in language learning comes to a standstill after maturity'.

Spiker (1990) cites numerous studies which illustrate the variability in general developmental functioning, caregiver–child interaction styles and responsiveness to intervention in children with Down syndrome. All of the aforementioned factors appear to be highly influential in relation to the development of language in such children. Spiker (1990) stresses the importance of early intervention in Down syndrome in respect of the development of speech and language functioning. Attention has also been given to changes in the brain associated with Down syndrome from early in life; by middle age there is evidence of Alzheimer-like 'plaques and tangles' in the cortex (Holland, 1997) which are not found in subjects who have learning disabilities not associated with Down syndrome. Fowler (1990) found that most individuals with Down syndrome fail to acquire linguistic structures beyond a preschool developmental level – with deficits in syntax, morphology, comprehension and production. A crucial word in the foregoing statement is 'most'; there are a number of documented exceptions.

Although the fundamental language problems of children with Down syndrome are claimed to be not modality-specific (cf. Woll & Grove, 1996), the Down syndrome literature includes reference to numerous instances where alternative systems of linguistic expression have been explored with success in late childhood, the teenage years and beyond. For example, Seagoe (1964) documented the case of Paul Scott, an individual with Down syndrome who learned to write at six and kept a diary until near his death at age 47. According to Buckley (1985) several studies have demonstrated that Down syndrome children manifest reading skills similar to or more advanced than those of normally developing children of the same chronological age. She suggests that mastering a written language may be in some ways easier than acquiring a spoken language for Down syndrome subjects, owing to the phonological and short term memory deficits that are characteristic of the syndrome. Crossley has had considerable success using facilitated communication systems, such as computers, as communication modalities for teenage children with Down syndrome (cf. Crossley, 1994, 1997). The total communication approach (sign, speech, technology, as appropriate) has added considerably to the expressive abilities of Down syndrome children and teenagers (Gibbs & Carswell, 1988; Iacono & Duncan, 1995).

What then are we to say about Lenneberg's (1967) findings? Perhaps what Lenneberg *et al.* observed were not absolute terminations of language development but temporary plateaux. Such plateaux are certainly recognised as a feature of the Down syndrome developmental pattern (see e.g. Cunningham, 1982: 157). Another (not incompatible) possibility is that the halt in language development was a function of deficiencies in the input the children were given rather than of an inherent, maturationally related cut-off point. The research demonstrates that language development can occur into adolescence if targeted using appropriate input strategies. One very strong current in the literature on developmental delay suggests that 'mentally handicapped adults can continue to acquire educational, social and occupational skills *providing they are exposed to skilled and systematic teaching*' (Cunningham & Mittler, 1981: 301; our emphasis). Admittedly these studies do not focus specifically on language development, but it may nevertheless be significant that Lenneberg *et al.*'s subjects were all raised at home and were presumably therefore not exposed to systematic teaching.

First Language Development after Puberty

Given then, that there is little prospect of obtaining unambiguous evidence on the question of the possibility of *beginning* to acquire an L1 after any age posited as critical, it would appear sensible to look at evidence concerning the *continuation* of L1 acquisition beyond the childhood years. If it were the case that L1 acquisition clearly came to a complete halt at a particular point, this could be taken as evidence in favour of a strong version of the critical period. It turns out, however, that most of the evidence, as well as common sense, points in the other direction, i.e. towards a continuing development of L1 competence well into adulthood. In fact, according to Nippold (1998: 1) 'it is difficult to identify any point in the lifespan when the process of language development is truly complete'.

Nippold cites Kamhi's (1987) finding that as children progress through the school system the increased level of freedom afforded to them in the selection of academic work, extracurricular activities and social contacts also promotes the development of 'linguistic individualism'. This continuing development is most obvious on the pragmatic and semantic levels. A number of semantic and pragmatic abilities have been shown to grow in adolescence. These include the development in the ability to define abstract nouns (McGhee-Bidlack, 1991), idioms and proverbs. While the ability to explain idioms and proverbs begins in early childhood, it gradually improves throughout the school-age years and well beyond into adulthood (Brasseur & Jimenez, 1989; Nippold & Rudzinski, 1993; Nippold *et al.*, 1997)

In this connection, Britton has some very pertinent things to say about the way in which 'social speech' develops in adolescence.

Social tact is a kind of generosity and as such is more easily achieved by people who are sure of themselves and their place in society: development of the appropriate forms of speech, therefore, is likely to come fairly late in adolescence. Politeness is highly conventionalised and its conventions vary from society to society. Even in its simpler forms, the formulas of politeness that may have been in use in childhood will sometimes be dispensed with in adolescence, and its subtler forms . . . are a relatively mature form of speech . . . 'getting to know the people we want to know', needs . . . to be . . . defined to include getting on with the people we know and like, enjoying their company, engaging them in the kind of talk that reaffirms commonly held values and opinions. It is in this area of speech that adolescent 'with-it' language flourishes – conversational speech full of slang expressions that changes rapidly with changing fashions.. . . Such linguistic forms have their function in drawing together members of the group or the set, and keeping outsiders out: hence the necessity – as with a password – for a rapidly changing fashion. Such speech may also be used, outside its context, as an offensive weapon, a means of establishing the individual as no longer to be identified with the family group. (Britton, 1970: 234f.; cf. Brown & Levinson, 1987)

The development and role of slang among teenagers is a standard topic of textbooks on adolescence (see e.g. Grinder, 1973: 238ff.; McCandless & Coop, 1979: 272f.) and the development of slang terms unique to a peer group is an important aspect of later language development, particularly during adolescence. The commonly cited relevant studies are those of Schwartz and Merten (1967), Leona (1978) and Nelson and Rosenbaum (1968, 1972). Slang used by adolescents often occurs in the form of meataphors. For example, Schwartz and Merten (1967) studied middle and lower class adolescents attending a high school with a socially mixed catchment area. They found that their subjects divided their peers into 'socies' ('clean-cut', conforming high-achievers), 'hoody-socies' (hedonistic but not seriously delinquent pace-setters), and 'hoodies' (rebels, slow-learners and intellectuals). Leona's (1978) study of adolescents attending a high school near Boston found that the general student population had names for each of the cliques such as 'jocks' who were involved in sport, 'motorheads' who spent most of their time driving and repairing cars, and 'fleabags' who used illegal substances and did not conform to the main-stream lifestyle. In addition, each clique had its own unique slang. For example, the jocks had particular terms for other athletes such as 'the jumping machine' and 'speedy'. Nelson and Rosenbaum (1968, 1972) for their part asked a total of nearly 2000 adolescents to list the slang words they used when talking about school, the police, popularity, and so on. Boys generated more slang terms than girls for topics of money, cars and motorbikes but girls had a greater number of terms relating to the topics of clothing and appearance, boys and popular and unpopular people. They found that the number of slang words produced in response to a particular topic reflected its social saliency, that more slang words were associated with unpopular than with popular topics, and that general knowledge of slang increased with age.

More generally, most mature adults can recall developments at various stages in their adult lives which have involved the acquisition of new ways of using language and new vocabulary. By way of illustration it is interesting to look at Argyle's (1967: 150) discussion of some 'professional skills . . . which are not necessarily acquired as a result of everyday experience' (p.150). The skills he treats (pp.150–80) are: various kinds of interviewing, selling, public speaking, supervising work-groups, teaching, psychotherapy / counselling, and child-rearing – all of which rely to a very large extent on language. It is universally accepted that adults can be trained to perform these skills; nor is there any received doctrine concerning an upper age-limit beyond which such training loses its effectiveness. Argyle's own assumption throughout his discussion is that training in these skills can result in changed behaviour, and he explicitly evaluates (pp.181–201) different kinds of training techniques on the basis of research into their behaviour-changing efficacy. Obviously, changed behaviour in this context includes, in large measure, changed language behaviour. The above is not, one should add, intended to suggest that new modes of language use are acquirable only through special training; the same kinds of language behaviour-changing processes are likely to occur whenever an individual experiences modifications in his / her patterns of work and / or social life that have implications for language use.

Specifically on the question of vocabulary acquisition, Diller's research suggests that there is no point before death at which lexical development can be predicted to cease:

> Twelve-year olds have a recognition vocabulary of about 135,000 words, Harvard freshmen know about 200,000 words, the typical thirty-year-old Ph.D. knows about 250,000 words. . . Vocabulary development continues in a natural, almost unnoticed fashion as long as one lives and is interested in new things. (Diller, 1971: 29)

Carroll's conclusion, based on his review of a number of vocabulary studies, is a little more tentative but broadly similar; he claims (1971: 124) that vocabulary tends to increase significantly up to at least the age of 40 or 50.

Even at a rather basic level it appears that the semantically rooted competencies of post-pubertal teenagers are on average significantly below those of mature adults. Referring to a study of such competencies by Thurstone, McLaughlin remarks on the relative sluggishness of language development:

> Thurstone's analysis of seven primary abilities indicates that verbal comprehension reaches 80% of adult competence at age 18 and word fluency at age 20. In contrast, number and memory factors reached 80% of adult level at 16, space and reasoning at 19, and perceptual factors at age 12 (Thurstone, 1955). In comparison with other mental capacities, then, language capacity does not seem to develop remarkably quickly. (McLaughlin, 1978: 55f.)

Morphological and syntactic development beyond the childhood years is less obvious, but it certainly has been observed. Braine (1971a) reports an unpublished study carried out by Bar-Adon (1959) on children learning Hebrew as their L1:

> Hebrew lexical roots usually consist of three consonants; vowels intercalated between the consonants belong to the formative morphemes distinct from the lexical root. Because they have more than one phonemic realization, several of these consonants have to be considered as morphophonemes, and their varying phonemic shapes are determined in a complex way by the position of the consonant in the root (i.e. whether first, second or third consonant), the conjugation in which the root appears, and the tense form . . . These . . . morphophonemic alterations are not found regularly in children's speech; instead, one shape of the consonant tends at first to be used in all forms of a particular verb . . . Regularizations of this sort may be found as late as adolescence . . . (Braine, 1971a: 28f.)

Similarly, according to Feofanov (1960), Russian-speaking children have problems with Russian prepositions throughout their school years, that is to say, well into their teens. One can also cite in this connection Smedts's (1988) study of L1 derivational morphology in Dutch between ages 7 and 17; Smedts found that his 7-year-old subjects displayed a mastery of, on average, only 14% of a range of Dutch word-formation rules, that his 13-year-olds knew just 51% of the rules tested, and that even his 17-year-olds demonstrated a command of no more than 66% of these rules.

In English speaking populations, it has been found that as school-age children and adolescents mature, they demonstrate increasingly sophisticated use of spoken and written sentence structure; particularly with complex and compound complex structures (cf. Scott, 1988). With regard to sentence formation, Carroll (1971: 117) cites evidence from a study by Zidonis of American ninth graders' written English:

> When rigorous criteria of well-formedness were applied in the analysis of writing samples, almost half of the sentences written by the ninth graders were judged to be malformed. This finding runs counter to the widespread contention of the structural linguist, who is not concerned with well-formedness as a grammatical goal, that children have acquired virtually full command of the grammar of English at an early age. The more likely contention is that the grammar of English is never fully mastered. (Zidonis, 1965: 408)

Carroll goes on to comment:

> Although there are certain aspects of grammatical competence that seem to be well mastered even at the normal school entry age, there are other aspects in which development is slow, at least for many children. We know little about the actual grammatical competence of adolescents or even adults as manifested in either speech or writing. Many of Zidonis's ninth graders were apparently unable to recognize the malformedness of the sentences they wrote. It cannot be concluded that all adults have acquired the degree of grammatical competence assumed by many linguists. (Carroll, 1971: 121)

With respect to sentence length increases during the school-age and adolescent years, this occurs partly as a result of an increase in the use of lower-frequency syntactic structures. Scott (1988) and Scott and Stokes (1995) found that as students mature noun phrases are expanded through the use of appositives, elaborated subjects and post-modification via prepositional phrases, non-finite verbs and relative clauses, while verb phrases are expanded through the use of structures such as modal auxiliaries, perfect aspect and the passive voice. The tendency to combine low-frequency structures is also more characteristic of more mature language use. Through the use of low-frequency structures, the number of words per clause increases, along with density of information expressed. Sentence length also increases through the use of co-ordinating, subordinating and correlative conjunctions and use of adverbial conjuncts. However, it is worth noting that sentence length can vary greatly in relation to discourse mode and the context of the conversation. For example, Nippold (1998) cites Leadholm and Miller's (1992) study, which found that children's MLUs were greater during story retelling than in conversation.

Even some aspects of the phonological system of one's L1 may not be mastered until one is well into adulthood, as is evident from Carroll's account of a doctoral dissertation dealing with stress placement in English:

> Robinson (1967) studied the development, in grade school children and adults, of competence in pronouncing, with correct stress placement, derived words with the suffixes -ity (as in *polárity < pólar*) and *-tion* (as in *generátion < génerate).* She found that these competences develop very slowly; many adults appear not to have acquired rules for the pronunciation of these derived words . . . (Carroll, 1971: 116)

There is also some interesting evidence that conscious phonological judgement improves with age. Pertz and Bever (1975) tested the ability of 40 monolingual English-speaking children (aged 9–11) and 40 monolingual English-speaking teenagers (aged 16–19) to guess the frequency in terms of occurrence in the world's languages of non-English initial consonant clusters. They found that their older subjects' answers were significantly better than those of the children.

To summarise, there is good evidence of all aspects of normal L1 development continuing into adulthood, and indeed of at least some aspects of such development continuing through to middle age and beyond.

Summary and Conclusions

(1) This chapter began with an introduction to and definition of the CPH in relation to language acquisition. The contribution of Lenneberg (1967) to this theoretical framework was discussed. Lenneberg (1967) claimed that the onset of the critical period as being at two years of age. This claim was discussed and shown to be implausible in the light of evidence that language development is in process from birth onwards.

(2) Lenneberg's further claim (1967) was that puberty constituted the cutoff point or offset for the critical period. A variety of evidence was considered in this connection – from neurological research, from deaf studies, from accounts of feral children and from Down syndrome subjects – none of which was found to point unambiguously to a well-defined cut-off point. While some of the evidence in question indicates linguistic advantages associated with early L1 acquisition, there are no clear grounds for believing that language acquisition absolutely cannot occur beyond puberty.

(3) Finally, post-pubertal L1 development in the normally developing population was explored and it was concluded that such development continues into early adulthood and indeed, at least in the semantic and pragmatic domains, through to middle age and beyond.

(4) All in all, the available evidence does not clearly support the notion of a critical period for L1 acquisition as defined by the criteria used to characterise critical periods in the biological sciences.

Chapter 4

The Critical Period Hypothesis: L2-related Evidence

Introductory

Discussion of the notion of a maturational factor in language acquisition as it relates to L2 acquisition has largely revolved around five propositions which can be summarized as follows.

(1) L2 learners whose exposure to the L2 begins in childhood are globally more efficient and successful than older learners.
(2) L2 learners whose exposure to the L2 begins in adolescence/early adulthood are globally more efficient and successful than younger learners.
(3) L2 learners whose exposure to the L2 begins in childhood are more efficient and successful than older learners only in some respects.
(4) Adolescent/adult L2 learners are initially more efficient, but in the long run the younger a learner is when the L2 acquisition process begins, the more successful the outcome of that process will be.
(5) After a certain maturational point the L2 learning process changes qualitatively.

The five sections of this chapter which follow present the evidence relevant to each of the above positions on age-related differences in L2 learning efficiency.

The 'Younger = Better' Position

The position that success in L2 learning is inversely related to age coincides with popular belief on the question. This belief has been brushed aside by some researchers on the basis that 'folk psychology is not a good basis for doing research in second language learning' (Snow, 1983: 149). However, one should perhaps remember that science has frequently found substance in what was previously stigmatised as unscientific popular wisdom. Moreover, the experience underlying the popular view cannot easily be dismissed, and such experience must constitute evidence of a kind. The following remarks from Tomb (1925) concerning British residents in India at the time of the Raj will strike a chord with most people who have had occasion to observe immigrant families in any country:

> It is a common experience in the district in Bengal in which the writer resides to hear English children 3 or 4 years old who have been born in the country conversing freely at different times with their parents in English, with their *ayahs* (nurses) in Bengali, with the garden-coolies in Santali, and with the house-servants in Hindustani, while their parents have learnt with the aid of a *munshi* (teacher) and much laborious effort just sufficient Hindustani to comprehend what the house-servants are saying (provided they do not speak too quickly) and to issue simple orders to them connected with domestic affairs. (Tomb, 1925: 53)

The popular belief about age effects in L2 learning is, moreover, shared by many language teachers, and is not short of anecdotal support (see e.g. Kirch, 1956).

Support of a less subjective kind appears at first sight to come from the body of results from various American studies of the effects of programmes of foreign languages in the elementary school (FLES).[1] For example, Vollmer's (1962) study (reported in Donoghue, 1965) found that FLES graduates continuing to study the language in question, and who were placed in groups at a level a year ahead of non-FLES groups, attained foreign language grades which were approximately 10% higher than those of non-FLES pupils of similar ability despite the age gap of one year. The problem with such evidence is that it was not only age of initial L2 exposure that differentiated the two groups but also length of exposure, the FLES groups having been learning the foreign language for six years longer than the non-FLES groups. A similar difficulty arises with similar findings reported by Brega and Newell (1965, 1967).

A further set of pertinent findings based on a formal instruction situation, but in this case without the problem of unwanted variables, is that of Yamada *et al.* (1980). The subjects for this study were 30 Japanese elementary school pupils distributed evenly across three age-groups – 7 years, 9 years and 11 years – none of whom had had any previous experience of English. The experiment investigated subjects' success in learning a small selection of English words. From a list of 40 English mono- and disyllabic words, the denotatum of each of which was represented in an associated picture, each subject was given four items to learn, along with the corresponding pictures, in two learning sessions separated by a period of 24 hours. In individual tests it was found that 'mean learning scores decrease with age, i.e. the older the age the lower the score' (Yamada *et al.*, 1980: 245).

We return now to evidence from the experience of immigrants acquiring L2s in a 'naturalistic' manner. A number of studies have indicated a relationship between early age of entry into the host country and successful acquisition of its language. One well-known study, conducted by Asher and García (1969), revealed an interaction between age of entry and length of residence, but showed age of entry to be the better predictor of successful acquisition of pronunciation. The subjects for this study were 71 Cuban immigrants to California ranging in age from 7 to 19 years, most of whom had been in the United States for about five years. A panel of 19 native speakers of American English acted as judges of randomly ordered recordings of the Cubans and of a control group of 30 American-born children uttering the same set of English sentences, scoring them for fidelity of pronunciation on a 4-point scale, the extremes of which were 'native speaker' and 'definite foreign accent'. Not one of the 71 Cuban subjects was judged to have native pronunciation; however, many were deemed to speak with near-native pronunciation, and the highest probability of being so judged was associated with children who had entered the United States between the ages of one and six years and had lived there over a period of between five and six years. Moreover, the younger a child had been when entering the United States, the higher the probability of a native-like accent, this probability being further increased the longer the child had lived in the country.

Another oft-cited immigrant study is that of Ramsey and Wright (1974), who in a large-scale survey of 'New Canadians' collected data about age of arrival in Canada and achievement in English. Their method was to take a random selection of 25% of classrooms at the grade 5, 7 and 9 levels across the City of Toronto and to obtain background information and test measures from the 5,000 students in those classrooms. The language tests administered were a vocabulary test and a language skills test comprising subtests in auditory perception, intonation, lexical knowledge, knowledge of functions and knowledge of idioms. On the basis of their analysis of their results Ramsey and Wright concluded that for students who had immigrated at or after age seven there was 'a clear negative relationship between age on arrival and performance' (Ramsey & Wright, 1974: 121). This conclusion was disputed by Cummins (1981) who re-analysed Ramsey and Wright's data and found that, when length of residence was controlled for, age of arrival 'appears to have relatively little effect on the rapidity with which grade norms are approached' (Cummins, 1981: 146). Cummins further argues that, since grade norms are progressively higher, older learners have to learn much more than younger learners in order to come within the same distance of attaining the appropriate norm, and that, therefore, Ramsey and Wright's results indicate an *advantage* for older learners in terms of rate of L2 acquisition.

An interestingly different approach was adopted in Seliger *et al.*'s (1975) investigation of the English and Hebrew proficiency of immigrants to the United States and Israel respectively. In this case the data on subjects' L2 proficiency were these subjects' own perceptions. The data were obtained by interviewing 394 adults who had migrated at various ages and from various countries. The questions asked concerned country of birth, age, age of arrival in the host country and distinguishability from native speakers of their L2. An analysis of these interviews revealed that a majority of respondents who had migrated at or under the age of nine years reported that most speakers of their target language thought they were native speakers. Most respondents who had migrated at or over the age of 16 years, on the other hand, felt they still had a foreign accent. Of respondents who migrated between the ages of 10 and 15 years the number who reported a foreign accent 'was nearly identical to the number who reported no accent' (Seliger *et al.*, 1975; reprint: 15).

We come now to Oyama's work (1976, 1978) on 60 male Italian immigrants to the United States. Her subjects had entered the United States at ages ranging from six to 20 years and their length of residence in the United States ranged from five to 18 years. Oyama tested her subjects for degree of approximation to a native American English accent and for proficiency in English listening comprehension. In the accent study (1976) subjects were required to read aloud a short paragraph in English and also to recount in English a frightening episode from their personal experience. A 45-second extract from each sample was then judged by two American-born graduate students, using a 5-point scale ranging from 'no foreign accent' to 'heavy foreign accent'. The analysis of results, which treated age at arrival and length of residence as separate, independent variables revealed 'an extremely strong Age at Arrival effect . . . virtually no effect from the Number of Years in the United States factor, and a very small interaction effect' (Oyama 1976; reprint: 25f.). Oyama found that the youngest arrivals performed in the range set by the controls, whereas those arriving after about age 12 did not, substantial accents starting to appear much earlier. In the listening comprehension experiment involving the same subjects, 12 short English sentences (five to seven words long) recorded by a native speaker were played to subjects against a background of masking 'white noise' (at a level which did not cause problems of intelligibility to native speakers), following an instruction to repeat what had been understood. Again the scores obtained reveal a clear age at arrival effect: subjects who had begun learning English before age 11 obtained comprehension scores similar to those of native speakers, while later arrivals did less well, those who had arrived after age 16 performing markedly worse than the natives (Oyama, 1978, reprint: 42). Again, too, it was found that no length of residence effect was discernible.

On a much more restricted scale was Kessler and Idar's (1979) longitudinal and comparative study of the morphological development in English of a Vietnamese woman refugee and her four-year-old daughter living in Texas. Progress was measured for both subjects between two stages. For the mother Stages 1 and 2 comprised respectively the first and last eight weeks of a six-month period during which she was communicating in English at work. For the child Stage 1 covered the last three weeks of a nine-week stay with an American family, her first real experience of an English-speaking environment, and Stage 2 was situated a year after the beginning of her stay, i.e. some 10 months after the end of Stage 1. During this time, subsequent to her leaving the American home, she attended an English-speaking kindergarten. The results of a comparison between mother and child in respect of their progress towards acquiring six grammatical morphemes between the two stages are as follows. In the mother's case none of the six morphemes studied was used more than 17% more accurately in Stage 2 than in Stage 1. In the case of the child, on the other hand, improvements of up to 74% were recorded. Since the period between the two stages was four months or so longer for the daughter than for the mother, the comparison is not as tight as one might wish. Nevertheless, these results do suggest a markedly slower rate of progress for the adult than for the child.

Patkowski's (1980) quantitative investigation of the English grammatical competence of immigrants to the United States also appears to offer support for the 'younger = better' hypothesis. His subjects were 67 highly educated immigrants from various backgrounds, all of whom had resided in their host country for at least five years, and his control subjects were 15 native-born Americans of similar backgrounds. All subjects were interviewed in English and transcripts of five-minute samples of these interviews were then submitted to two trained judges for assessment of syntax on a scale from 0 to 5 (with a possible + value for any level except 5). Patkowski's results show a strong negative relationship between age at arrival and syntactic rating. In addition, the distribution of ratings for the 33 subjects who had entered the United States before age 15 years differed from that for the 34 subjects who had arrived after that age. In the former case there was a bunching of ratings at the upper end of the scale, with 32 of the 33 subjects scoring at the 4+ to 5 level. In the latter case, on the other hand, there was a strikingly 'normal' curve centred on the 3+ level, with only five subjects scoring at the 4+ to 5 level and eight subjects scoring at the 2+ to 3 level. The only other variable to exhibit a significant effect was amount of informal exposure, and this was at such a low level of correlation as to explain less than 5% of the variance. Moreover, this relationship disappeared when the effect of age at arrival was eliminated. Two subsidiary experiments were carried out by Patkowski in association with the research described above: 30-second extracts from each of the taped interviews were submitted to the above-mentioned judges for phonological assessment on a scale from 0 to 5, which resulted in a strong negative relationship being found between age of arrival and accent rating, with no other variable showing a significant effect. Patkowski also gathered further data from his subjects by means of a written multiple-choice test of syntactic competence. In this case the age effect revealed was not so sharp, but subjects who had entered the United States before age 15 still tended to do better.

In a later re-analysis of his 1980 pronunciation data, Patkowski (1990) disagregated his sample into an early subgroup (the 33 subjects who had arrived before age 15) and a late subgroup (the 34 subjects who had arrived after age 15). His interpretation of what emerged when he subjected the ratings of two subgroups' accent to regression analysis was that there were different distributions of accentedness in the two groups, which suggested to him a discontinuity in the capacity to acquire L2 phonology specifically occurring around age 15. There is, however, some dispute about this interpretation. Harley and Wang (1997) and Birdsong (2002) point out that the evidence offered by Patkowski for a sudden sharp decline in accent acquiring capacity at age 15 is rather ambiguous, since there appears to be a continuing age-related decline in the late subgroup.

Further evidence of an age-related age effect in the acquisition of accent in an L2 comes from Piper and Cansin's (1988) study of 29 advanced ESL learners in Canada with ages of arrival ranging from pre-age–6 to 28+ . These subjects each participated in an individual interview in which they (a) answered personal questions, (b) read aloud from a short story, and (c) retold a personal narrative. Native speaker judgements of parts (b) and (c) of the interview – based on a 5-point scale – were gathered, and an analysis of these judgements in terms of group means for six age-of-arrival groups indicated that subjects who had arrived in Canada as children tended to have significantly better English accents than those who had arrived later and that length of residence in Canada was not a significant factor.

Mägiste's (1987) investigation is unusual among immigrant studies for its concentration on lexis. Mägiste tested the capacity of 151 young native speakers of German (77 high school pupils and 74 elementary school pupils) who had been resident in Sweden for various lengths of time to name pictured objects and two-digit numbers in German and Swedish. She found that the point at which the response times for naming objects in the two languages intersected occurred after four years' residence as far as the elementary school group was concerned but only after six years' residence in the high school group – from which an advantage may be inferred for the former. With regard to the naming of two-digit numbers, the two groups' response times for Swedish coincided with their response times for German at about the same point – namely after three to four years. Mägiste's comment on this latter result is that 'it is remarkable that the elementary school students achieved the point of language balance at the same time as the high school pupils, despite the fact that this task was more difficult for the younger students', the implication being that the younger learners' lexis-acquiring advantage compensated for their general cognitive disadvantage.

Of all immigrant studies investigating the age question, probably the most widely referred to is that of Johnson and Newport (1989), which looked at the long-term attainments in English of immigrants to the USA as gauged by grammaticality judgement tests. The subjects of the study were 46 Korean and Chinese acquirers of English who had arrived in the United States at various ages but all of whom had resided in America for at least five years. Johnson and Newport report that, while subjects who arrived before age seven performed within the range set by native-speaker controls, performance levels declined linearly with age of arrival between age seven and 15. Among subjects who arrived at around 17 years of age, the distribution of performance was claimed to be more or less random. The Johnson and Newport results appear at first sight to argue strongly for a specific maturational phase – up to about seven years – which is particularly favourable for language learning and a second maturational phase – from about seven years to about puberty – during which the language learning capacity disimproves gradually but subsequent to which there is a qualitative change in the sense that age of arrival is no longer predictive of ultimate proficiency. However, the study in question has been criticised on methodological grounds, and the data it yielded have been re-analysed and re-interpreted. Concerning methodology, Kellerman (1995) casts doubt on the assumption that a non-native speaker participating in a grammaticality judgement task will focus on the same feature or features as a native speaker; he points out that there may be instances where the variables of formal correctness/deviancy and functional plausibility/ implausibility are fatally confounded; and he criticises the failure on the part of the investigators to take cross-linguistic influence into account in the interpretation of results. With regard to re-analysis of the data from this study, carried out by Bialystok and Hakuta (Bialystok, 1997; Bialystok & Hakuta, 1994), this shows significant correlations of scores with age of arrival if the cut-off point is set at 20 rather than 17 years and thus that 'that the tendency for proficiency to decline with age projects well into adulthood and does not mark some defined change in learning potential at around puberty' (Bialystok, 1997: p.122).

In a further immigrant study focusing on grammar – but also on lexis – Hyltenstam (1992) studied subjects who had migrated to Sweden before (in one case during) puberty and whose period of residence in Sweden exceeded five years (except in one case where the length of residence was three years). Swedish data, both oral and written, were elicited from these subjects, and similar data were obtained from a control group of Swedish native speakers. When subjects' errors were analysed it emerged that the numbers of errors – both grammatical and lexical – produced by subjects who had arrived in Sweden after age seven were consistently in a higher range than the numbers of errors produced by the native speakers, whereas the range of numbers of errors produced by subjects who had arrived in Sweden before age six overlapped with those of the other two groups. Like the Johnson and Newport data, these results suggest that any decline in L2 learning capacity begins very early.

To return to the question of accent, another study appearing to show an advantage for L2 younger beginners in phonological terms is Thompson's investigation of 39 Russian-born migrants who had settled in the United States. They had arrived in America at ages ranging from four years to 44 years. Three different samples of these subjects' spoken English were judged by two native speakers of American English for degree of foreign accent on a 5-point scale. Thompson's finding was that the subjects' age on arrival in an English-speaking environment 'was the best indicator of the accuracy of their pronunciation in English (Thompson, 1991: 195). Interestingly, as in the case of Asher and García's (1969) study (see above), none of Thompson's subjects was rated as being at native-speaker level in terms of accent. However, subjects who had arrived in the United States at age ten or younger were judged to have only slight foreign accents, with the best ratings of all being allocated to the two subjects who had arrived at age four.

A number of immigrant studies by Flege and his colleagues (e.g. Flege *et al.*, 1995; Flege *et al.*, 1999) also show that, on the whole, degree of authenticity of L2 accent correlates with age of arrival, with younger arrivals generally outperforming older arrivals. The Flege *et al.* 1995 study focused on native speakers of Italian who had migrated to Canada. Flege (1999: 102) summarises it as follows:

> Flege *et al.* (1995) recruited participants who had been living in Canada for at least 15 years at the time they were tested.. . . The 240 native Italian participants' productions of five short English sentences . . . along with those of a control group of 24 native English participants

were digitized and then presented randomly to native speakers of English from Ontario.. . . As expected, the native English participants received higher ratings than most native Italian participants, whose ratings decreased systematically as age of arrival increased.

The Flege *et al.* 1999 investigation used broadly the same design as the 1995 study, but involved native speakers of Korean rather than Italian and was based in the United States rather than Canada. Once again 240 immigrants representing a range of ages of arrival participated in the study, and once again there was a control group of 24 native speakers of English. Once again, ratings for authenticity of English accent tended to decline as age of arrival increased.

Straddling the borderline between immigrant studies and studies involving shorter-term L2 learners is the work of Tahta *et al.* (1981a, 1981b). They investigated both an immigrant sample (1981a) and a group with only formal exposure to one of the languages in question and no exposure at all to the other (1981b). Their two sets of results are in broad agreement with each other. The immigrant sample consisted of 54 males and 55 females who, from a variety of countries and at various ages, had migrated to the United Kingdom and had resided there for a minimum of two years. Data were gathered by recording these subjects reading aloud a passage of English prose and responding to questions about their L2 learning history. Each recording was listened to by three independent judges, who assigned a rating for accent of 0 ('no foreign accent'), 1 ('detectable but slight accent') or 2 ('marked accent'). The results (Tahta *et al.*, 1981a: 269f.) suggest age of onset of acquisition of English as the factor of overwhelming importance in phonological proficiency: if L2 learning had commenced by age six, the L2 was invariably judged as accent-free; with a beginning age of 7–9 the chances of an accent-free L2 were still high; with a beginning age of 9–11 the chances had dropped to about 50%, and with a beginning age of 12–13 onwards, the chances of an accent-free L2 were minimal. The only other variable which made a significant contribution was use of English at home.

Tahta *et al.*'s other sample (1981b) consisted of 231 English-speaking children and adolescents ranging from five to 15 years and drawn from four state schools in Surrey. These subjects were asked to imitate words and short phrases in French (a language to which most subjects over eight had had some formal exposure) and Armenian (which was unfamiliar to all subjects), and their efforts were rated on a 0–3 scale. In addition, two slightly longer phrases in each language were repeated and subjects' imitations of the intonation patterns were judged as either correct or incorrect. For subjects aged seven and over, if intonation was not correctly copied in both phrases, the less well imitated one was further repeated up to a maximum of 10 times until its intonation pattern was faithfully replicated. The results of this experiment show a generally negative relationship between age and performance. However, a difference does emerge between pronunciation and intonation. As far as pronunciation is concerned, there is a steady linear decline in mean scores with increasing age. With regard to intonation, on the other hand, there is a marked and rapid drop in performance ratings between eight and 11 years and then a slight superiority in the performance of 10–15-year-olds over that of 11–12-year-olds. These findings are consistent across the two languages used in the experiment.

Let us now return to the suggestion from Bialystok and Hakuta's (1994) re-analysis of the Johnson and Newport (1989) data that that there is no period within fixed maturational termini at the end of which L2 learning capacity *dramatically* declines. In this connection, Bialystok and Hakuta (1999) and Hakuta *et al.* (2003) analysed census data on age of arrival and reported English proficiency for Chinese-speakers and Spanish-speakers who had resided in the United States for at least 10 years. What emerged from this analysis was, on the one hand, a steady linear decline of reported English proficiency as age of arrival increased but, on the other, no indication of a dramatically sharper rate of decline at any particular point. Data on the relationship between L2 accent and age of arrival obtained by Flege and his colleagues (see, e.g. Flege, 1999) show a similarly continuous decline, and Birdsong's (2002, 2003a) wide-ranging survey of L2 research on age effects issues in the conclusion that there is no strong evidence of discontiuities of a kind that one would expect if a critical period were operative. It should be noted in this connection that a question-mark has been raised about the reliability of reported proficiency of the type that Bialystok and Hakuta use – notably by DeKeyser (2003), who also claims that much of the other evidence cited in favour of a gradual decline in language learning is amenable to statistical re-analysis which points in the opposite direction.

Highly relevant to this question of a lifelong decline in L2 learning capacity are the relatively small number of studies which look at the L2 learning attainments of older and younger adults. Seright (1985) notes that the few studies which have focused on age-related differential achievement within the adult category indicate an advantage for younger adult L2 learners. In support of this she cites Thorndike's (1928) experiments on the learning of Esperanto, which show younger subjects making more gains than older subjects. She also cites d'Anglejan *et al.*'s (1981) investigation of Canadian immigrants learning French in an intensive programme, which found age to be an important predictor of success, less success being associated with greater age; Halladay's (1970) study of the aural comprehension gains of adults on an eight-week intensive ESL course, which found smaller gains for students in their 40s as compared with younger students; Klein and Dittmar's (1979) research into the varying success of foreign workers learning German in Germany through the social context, which found a strong inverse relationship between age of arrival in Germany and oral syntactic proficiency, those who had immigrated at age 40 or over showing particularly low ratings; and Brown's (1983) study of adults on an eight-week intensive Spanish course, which found that subjects aged 19–23 performed significantly better than those aged 55+ in terms of of oral skills. By way of qualification it ought to be noted that in Thorndike's results the greater gains of the younger groups of adults are 'to be accounted for entirely in terms of one test – oral directions' (McLeish, 1963: 125), and that, as Seright acknowledges, in Klein and Dittmar's study age appears to co-vary with exposure, so that the two variables are confounded. However, Seright's general inference from the above research – that among adult L2 learners 'differential attainment . . . could well be related to age' (Seright, 1985: 457) – is certainly plausible.

Seright's own study compares the L2 achievement of two groups of adult Quebec Francophones learning English in an intensive programme: 50 of her subjects were in the age-range 17–24 years and 21 were in the age-range 25–41 years. An English listening comprehension test was administered in Week 1 of the programme and again after 12 weeks (300 hours) of teaching. Differences between post-test and pre-test scores were interpreted as representing the extent of gains in aural comprehension. In order to control for possible effects of variation in pre-test score, IQ, years of education and years of ESL instruction, two samples of matched pairs were abstracted from the two age-groups, each being arrived at by a slightly different statistical procedure. In both samples, as well as in the global sample, the mean gain was significantly greater for the younger than for the older subjects.

A study not mentioned by Seright, but apparently offering corroboration of her position is that of Von Elek and Oskarsson (1973). This is primarily a comparison of different language teaching methods using a sample of 125 Swedish students of English as a foreign language ranging in age from under 20 to over 60. However, one by-product of the study is the finding that in the results from the various English language proficiency tests administered 'there is a negative correlation between age and achievement' and that 'this is particularly noticeable on the tests which involve auditory discrimination and oral production' (Von Elek & Oskarsson, 1973: 178). Also interesting in this connection is an earlier study of patterns of language use in Israel. Braine's (1971a) analysis of census data on the spread of Hebrew among immigrants to Israel indicates that both preadolescent and adult immigrants tend to use Hebrew as their everyday language within a few years of arriving, whereas Hebrew tends to be used less by middle-aged immigrants and substantially less by elderly immigrants. Braine comments that, whatever the cause, 'if there is a decline in language learning ability with age, it looks as if it is probably a slow decline associated with middle and old age' (Braine, 1971a: 71).

A more recent study of L2 learning outcomes among adults beginning at various ages is that of Birdsong (1992). Birdsong's subjects were 20 native speakers of English who had begun learning French as adults, arriving in France at ages ranging from 19 to 48 years, and he probed these subjects' French competence via a grammaticality judgement task. He was surprised by two aspects of his results, as his own later summary of the study indicate.

> First, among the 20 native speakers of English who began learning French as adults, 15 fell within the range of native speaker performance on a challenging grammaticality task, and several of these 15 participants deviated very little from native norms. Second, I found that performance on the task was predicted by age of arrival (AOA) in France, even though the participants had moved to France as adults. Why should age effects continue to be found after the end of the presumed critical period? (Birdsong, 1999: 9)

The 'Older = Better' Position

Evidence favouring the hypothesis that older L2 learners are more successful than younger ones mostly comes from studies of learning as an outcome of formal instruction, that is, very short-term experimental research, and studies based on primary school L2 teaching projects and L2 immersion programmes. However, the results of some immigrant studies also seem to point to an advantage for older learners. While most of the relevant studies involve children as at least one element of comparison, there is a small miscellany of studies focused on adolescents and adults of different ages whose results also indicate that older learners fare better.

Of the short-duration experiments involving children and adults, one of the best known is that of Asher and Price (1967). Their experimental subjects were 96 pupils from the 2nd, 4th and 8th grades, and 37 undergraduate students. None of the subjects had had any prior experience of the experimental target language, Russian. In three short training units subjects listened to taped commands in Russian and watched them being responded to by an adult model. Half the subjects simply observed, while the other half imitated the model's actions. Each session was followed by a retention test in which each subject was individually required to obey

Russian commands heard during training, and also 'novel' commands comprising recombinations of elements in the learned commands. The results were that the adults, at every level of linguistic complexity, dramatically outperformed the children and adolescents. With regard to these latter groups, the 14-year-olds (8th graders) consistently did significantly better than the 8-year-olds (2nd graders), and the 10-year-olds (4th graders) significantly surpassed their 8-year-old counterparts. Asher and Price acknowledge the possible selectivity effect in relation to the college students, whose mental ability would have been above average. However, citing Pimsleur (1966), they claim that 'general mental ability is a light-weight factor in L2 learning accounting for less than 20% of the variance' (Asher & Price, 1967; reprint: 83).

Cook (1986a) refers to two studies (Kuusinen & Salin, 1971; Locke, 1969) which show older children coping better than younger children with the pronunciation of newly encountered phonological shapes. Another pho-nologically-oriented study (Politzer & Weiss, 1969) involved subjects from the 1st, 3rd and 5th grades of an elementary school and from the 7th and 9th grades of a junior high school. The L2 involved was French, of which the subjects had no knowledge, and the experimental procedure consisted of an auditory discrimination test, a pronunciation test and a recall test. The results show an improvement of scores with increasing age in all three tests. Since almost all subjects above grade 3 level had had some exposure to Spanish and many of the 7th and 9th graders were receiving regular instruction in that language, there may be some question of a progressive effect for Spanish training. However, Politzer and Weiss claim that such training could have directly influenced performance on only the small subset of test items which involved French non-dipthongal vowels. Comparable results emerged from a study by Stapp (1999) in which 28 monolingual Japanese subjects ranging in age from four to 17 years were asked to repeat a list of simple English words containing /r/ and /l/. In the aggregate the adolescents were found to outperform the children, although the high degree of inter-subject variability suggested to the researcher that mimicry ability is less an age-related phenomenon than a talent available to particular individuals irrespective of age. As in the Politzer and Weiss study, the superiority of the older subjects may be attributable to a training effect, especially since in this instance the 13–15-year-olds had had some initial exposure to English, while the 16–17-year olds had had 2–3 years of English instruction. A very different kind of experiment was that of Smith and Braine (1972) (discussed in Macnamara, 1973a: 63f.), which involved the use of a miniature artificial language. Subjects were exposed to a set of sentences in this language and then tested on their progress in 'acquiring' the language in question. In the tests conducted by Smith and Braine in this context the adult subjects performed better than the children. To return to the realm of natural languages, Olson and Samuels (1973) investigated the capacity of English speakers in three different age-groups to learn to pronounce the sounds of German. The groups consisted of 20 elementary school pupils (ages 9.5–10.5), 20 junior high school pupils (ages 14–15) and 20 college students (ages 18–26). None of the subjects had had any previous foreign language learning experience. Each subject participated in the same programme of 10 15–25 minute taped sessions of German phoneme pronunciation drills. On a post-test of pronunciation the two older groups performed significantly better than the elementary age-group. The difference between the two older groups favoured the college group but was not significant. Intellectual ability was not found to be a significant factor.

We turn now to the results of early investigations of FLES programmes. One such study (reported in Ekstrand, 1959, 1964, 1978a) investigated the teaching of English in the early grades of Swedish primary schools. A thousand or so pupils ranging in age from 8 to 11 years, drawn from elementary school grades 1 to 4 were exposed to 18 weeks of English instruction via audio-visual methodology. The pronunciation of a random sample of 355 of these pupils was then tested by means of a procedure which required them to imitate English words and sentences extracted from the teaching materials. Judgement of the accuracy of their pronunciation focused on entire utterances, individual speech sounds and overall impressions. All three methods yielded results which improved almost linearly with age. A listening comprehension test was also administered. Again the scores increased steadily with age. Similar results were obtained by Grinder et al. (1961) who, in a study of the relationship between age and proficiency in Japanese as an L2 among 2nd, 3rd and 4th graders in Hawaii using the same audio-lingual course, found that the older children consistently outperformed the younger ones. We have already noted Donoghue's (1965) report of Vollmer's (1962) research the findings of which are interpretable as evidence of a faster rate of L2 acquisition among older learners. The same interpretation can be applied to Justman and Nass's (1956) study, which found that high-school pupils who had experienced instruction in the foreign language at elementary school had no long-term advantage over those who had not, and to Dunkel and Pillet's (1962) finding that the mean score of 20 pupils tested in French grammar after completing a five-year FLES programme in an independent American elementary school fell short of the norm for independent secondary school pupils on the same test after only one year's work. More direct evidence emerges from a study conducted by Bland and Keislar (1966), involving six 5th-graders and four kindergarteners and based on a programme of oral French deploying a machine that could play back utterances recorded on strips of audiotape affixed to cards, which also displayed graphic representations of the utterance meanings. A hundred of these cards were used, one utterance and one drawing being associated with each card. It transpired that, on average, the younger learners took more than twice as long as the older learners to reach criterion.

In the 1970s the study which undoubtedly had the most impact in undermining the case for FLES was that carried out by Burstall *et al.* (1974) (see below). However, other studies published in that decade also suggested that older children responded better than younger children to formal L2 instruction. One such study was Bühler's (1972) investigation of more than 1500 Swiss school children learning French as an L2. Of these, some had begun French in 4th grade, others in 5th grade. On two separate testing occasions the earlier beginners performed significantly better than the later beginners on various tests of French language skills. Durette (1972) describes the testing of pupils completing a five-year elementary L2 programme in French in listening, speaking, reading and writing skills. The mean scores achieved by these pupils in all four areas on the standardised test in question fell well short of the means achieved by secondary school pupils after only two years' instruction. A further study (Oller & Nagato, 1974) looked at the long-term effect of FLES instruction in Japanese schools. It involved 233 subjects drawn from the 7th, 9th and 11th grades of a private elementary and secondary school system for girls, and at each grade level included some pupils who had experienced a six-year FLES programme in English and some who had not. Subjects' proficiency in English was measured by means of a 50-item cloze test, a separate test having been constructed for each grade. The results were adjusted for IQ level. What emerged was that at 7th grade level there was a highly significant difference between FLES and non-FLES students, at 9th grade level a reduced but still significant difference, and at 11th grade level no significant difference (Oller & Nagato, 1974: 18). These findings are interpreted as evidence against the notion that FLES imparts long-term benefits, the clear implication being that older beginners can learn as much in five years as younger beginners can in 11 years.

To come now to the work of Burstall and her colleagues (Burstall *et al.* 1974, Burstall, 1975b), this was an evaluation of a scheme which in the 1960s and 1970s provided for instruction in French to all pupils from the age of eight years in selected primary schools in England and Wales. The evaluation covered the period 1964–1974, focusing longitudinally on some 17,000 pupils. The results of a comparison of the proficiency in French of pupils who had experienced primary school French with that of pupils who had not are interpreted by Burstall *et al.* as indicating a progressive diminution of any advantage conferred by early exposure to French. This effect is most apparent from comparisons between the experimental sample and control groups of 11-year-old beginners drawn from the same secondary schools and most frequently from the same French classes as the experimental pupils. When the experimental and control pupils were compared at age 13 the experimental pupils significantly outscored the control pupils on speaking and listening tests, but the control pupils' performance on reading and writing tests equalled or surpassed that of the experimental pupils. When the experimental and the control pupils were compared at age 16, the only test on which the experimental pupils still scored significantly higher than the control pupils was the listening test; the two groups performed similarly in speaking, but the control pupils maintained their superiority in reading and writing (Burstall *et al.*, 1974: 123). Given the three-year start of the experimental pupils this looks like evidence of the superiority of the older learner, and more direct evidence emerged from another comparison in the study. When the experimental group was compared at age 13 with control pupils who had been learning French for an equivalent amount of time, but who were, on average, two years older, the older pupils' performance on all the tests was consistently superior to that of the experimental pupils (Burstall *et al.*, 1974: 122). The Burstall *et al.* report had its critics. Stern (1976) and Buckby (1976), for example, argue that the authors are inconsistent in explaining the results cited in age-related terms while opting for environmental explanations in respect of sex- and social class-related differences revealed by other parts of the study. Stern also points to the possible blurring effects of mixing experimental and control pupils within the same classes, and Buckby criticises the nature of the tests used. Potter *et al.* (1977), for their part, emphasise the possible role of less than adequate resources. On the other hand, Burstall *et al.*'s conclusions concerning the relative rates of formal L2 learning of older and younger pupils clearly concur with the findings of earlier and subsequent FLES assessments.

Among the latter, one can cite Stankowski Gratton's (1980) investigation of the results of a programme of after-school German lessons offered by an Italo-German Cultural Association in Trento. Two classes, each composed of 11 children and both having a similar gender distribution, were involved in the project. One drew its pupils from the 1st grade (average age six years) and the other was made up of 3rd grade pupils (average age eight years). The programme, which was spread over one school year, proceeded at a rhythm of three 45-minute lessons per week, and used a basically audio-lingual methodology. Three tests were administered to both groups, a questionnaire designed to establish the motivational profiles of the two classes, an aptitude test adapted from the Modern Language Aptitude Test (Carroll & Sapon, 1959) and a final test aimed at determining the extent of linguistic gains. A similar motivational distribution emerged across the two groups, but the older group's average score on the aptitude test was higher than the younger group's – a difference attributed by Stankowski Gratton (1980: 130) to the fact that 'certain capacities which facilitate the learning of a language increase and mature as the child grows' (our translation)[2]. With regard to the final linguistic test[3] the very construction of this instrument is revealing, since more items were included in the grade 3 test than in the grade 1 test, to take account of the fact that the older group had covered more ground during the year. When the absolute gains of the two groups were compared, the older group's lead was found to stand at more than 17%.

Also to be noted in this context are two major projects being conducted in Spain – at the University of the Basque Country and the University of Barcelona – on the introduction of a foreign language to schoolchildren at different ages. The project based at the University of the Basque Country involves subjects who are already functionally bilingual in Basque and Spanish and to whom English is taught as a third language. The language was traditionally introduced in the 6th year of primary school (when the pupils are aged 11), but has more recently begun to be introduced in the 3rd year (when the pupils are aged eight). The project compares the progress of 11-year-old beginners with that of eight-year-old beginners and also looks at children participating in a scheme which introduces English in the 2nd year of kindergarten (when the pupils are aged four). Essentially what emerges from this project is that – across a whole range of performance categories – oral proficiency, listening comprehension, grammaticality judgement, sound perception and pronunciation, written comprehension, written production – when the number of hours of instruction are held constant, the older beginners significantly outperform the younger beginners (see e.g. Cenoz, 2003a, 2003b; García Lecumberri & Gallardo, 2003; García Mayo, 2003; Langabaster & Doiz, 2003). Essentially the same message emerges from the Barcelona Age Factor Project (see e.g. Muñoz 2003a, 2003b) which involves Catalan-Spanish learners, to whom English was introduced as a third language between two and six years of age, at age eight, age 11, age 14 or beyond age 18. Comparisons so far effected between the eight-year-old and the 11-year-old beginners reveal that under conditions of equal exposure time the older beginners significantly outperform the younger beginners not only in written tests but also in oral story-telling and oral interaction. The one set of results which constitutes an exception to this trend is that relating to a listening comprehension test composed of 25 items which required subjects to select a picture (out of three) that corresponded to the oral stimulus (word or sentence) they heard. In this case too the older beginners' scores were higher, but not significantly so.

Turning now to the evidence from L2 immersion programmes, Harley (1986) investigated the effects of different varieties of immersion programme available in Canada, placing her study in the context of two further pertinent Canadian studies based on the immersion situation (Genesee, 1979/Adiv, 1980; Tremaine, 1975). In a study of the comprehension of syntactic contrasts in French and English by early total immersion students and other young learners of French as an L2 in Ottawa, Tremaine (1975) found that the more cognitively mature a child was the better his/ her L2 comprehension. With regard to the Genesee (1979)/Adiv (1980) study, this established that English-speaking pupils who had been exposed to an early French immersion programme starting in kindergarten did not do better in French than those whose immersion programme had not begun until grade 7 – which suggests more rapid L2 learning among the latter. Harley's own study involved 12 Anglophone pupils who had experienced approximately 1000 hours of a French total immersion programme starting in kindergarten, 12 who had experienced equivalent exposure to French via a total immersion programme beginning grade 8, and 12 of the same age level as the latter group, who had been exposed to a (partial) French immersion programme from grade 1 onwards. Two control groups of native French-speaking pupils were included in the investigation, one of 12 1st graders and the other of 12 10th graders. The focus of the study was the French verb system, and the testing instruments used were a prescripted task (for the older groups only), an interview, a story repetition and a translation task. Of the two total immersion groups the late immersion group on the whole performed better; and of the two older groups, while that with experience of early partial immersion and thus much greater exposure to French outperformed the late immersion group in general terms, its lead was limited and not consistent. Both results concur with those of the other immersion studies cited in suggesting a faster acquisition rate among older learners in an L2 immersion situation. One can also cite in this connection Swain's (1981a) finding that English-speaking pupils in a late French immersion programme surpassed early immersion students in French reading comprehension test and as well as the early immersion pupils on a French cloze test, although the early immersion pupils did better in French listening comprehension. Evidence from subsequent Canadian studies is broadly consistent with the foregoing. Turnbull *et al.* (1998: 33) cite many such studies and in their own study found that, at the end of secondary schooling, despite vastly more exposure to the L2, early immersion students did not outperform middle immersion or late immersion students on a multiple choice-based listening comprehension test nor on any test involving literacy skills, although they did do better on another measure of listening and on speaking tests.

Some immigrant studies also suggest that L2 learning improves with age. Ervin-Tripp (1974), for example, investigated 31 English-speaking children ranging in age from four to nine years who had been exposed to French in Switzerland for up to nine months. On tests of comprehension of syntax and morphology, imitation and English-French translation, and taking into account diary records and taped natural conversation, the older children outperformed the younger ones across the board. Similar results were obtained by Ekstrand (1976a) in his investigation of the proficiency in Swedish of 2189 immigrant children of school age in Sweden. Tests for pronunciation, transcription from dictation, listening comprehension, reading comprehension, free oral production and free written production were administered, and all test results, with the exception of those for free oral production, were found to correlate positively and significantly with age, but not with length of residence, suggesting to Ekstrand that L2 learning ability 'improves with age' (Ekstrand 1976a; reprint: 130). Skutnabb-Kangas and Toukomaa (1976 – reported by Harley, 1986: 28) also showed that children of Finnish migrants who had been born in Sweden or who had entered Sweden before age 9–11 years were not only less proficient than those who had migrated later, but also below the normal level of monoglot Finnish- and Swedish-speakers of similar non-verbal IQ. North American immigrant studies provide further evidence tending in the same direction. Walberg *et al.* (1978) investigated the English proficiency of Japanese children and young adults living in the United States: 352 such subjects ranging in age-level from kindergarten to 12th grade were asked to rate the relative difficulty of English and Japanese in respect of reading, writing, speaking and listening. In addition, the American teachers of an overlapping sample of 360 Japanese pupils from grades 1 to 9 were asked to rate the pupils on a 4-point scale with respect to reading, writing, vocabulary, and the expression of facts, concepts and feelings. No evidence emerges from these two sets of ratings of an advantage for younger learners. On the contrary, since the older children reached American peer-norms in the same amount of time as the younger children took to reach the lower norms of their American age-peers, it can be inferred that 'older children learn faster' (Walberg *et al.*, 1978: 436, note 1). As we have seen, using similar reasoning, Cummins shows that Ramsey and Wright's (1974) findings (see above) also indicate an advantage for older L2 learners. A further study, by Ferris and Politzer (1981), involved 60 13–14-year-old Hispanophone subjects resident in the United States, 30 of whom had been born in the United States and schooled entirely through English, the remainder having been born in Mexico and having received at least three years of education through Spanish. Ferris and Politzer found that the partly Mexican-schooled group performed as well as the entirely American-schooled group in English written composition except in respect of verb structure.

Let us now return to evidence from studies of adult L2 learners of different ages. Thorndike's (1928) research (see above) found that younger adults made greater gains than older ones in learning Esperanto as far as 'oral directions' were concerned. However, if one takes these oral gains together with gains in vocabulary, handling printed directions and reading paragraphs, 'the difference between age 22 and age 40 in the ability to learn a logical systematic language is small' (Thorndike, 1928: 46). Moreover, a group comprised partly of very young adults (age-range 9–18 years) 'having over twice as much class study as the group 35 years old and over (and more than twice as much home study . . .) gained little more than half as much' (Thorndike, 1928: 46). Other parts of Thorndike's research focused on the learning of natural L2s. Cheydleur reports (1932: 259f.) that in one of Thorndike's experiments, dealing with gains made on standardised tests in French by students in two evening high schools, it was estimated that compared with students from 20 to 24 those from 14 to 16 made gains of 59%, that those from 17 to 19 gained 86%, that those from 25 to 29 gained 89%, and that those who were 30 or over gained 86%. In other words, the adults made better gains than the two youngest groups, although the oldest group did less well than those from 20 to 24. Similar results were obtained in respect of German, Latin and Spanish. Cheydleur himself (1932) compared the achievements in French of a group of 39 adults (average age 33 years) attending evening classes in that language at the Madison Vocational School, Wisconsin, with those of a group of 54 first semester students following a similar course at the University of Wisconsin. The same instructor (the researcher himself) taught both groups and the comparison was based on scores attained on the same standardised test (the American Council Alpha French Test). However, whereas this test was administered to the younger adults (i.e. the university students) after 64 hours of instruction, it was given to the older adults after only 42 hours of instruction. The results favour the older group. On the one hand, whereas only 28% of the university students gained A or B grades, 38% of the evening class students attained this level. On the other, both groups had a mean score of around 56%, and since the instruction time for the older group was about a third less than for the younger group, this implies a markedly faster rate of acquisition on the part of the former.

A rather different kind of study is that of Horwitz (1983), the purpose of which was to ascertain whether there was any relationship between conceptual level and competence in an L2. Conceptual level is seen by Horwitz in the perspective of Hunt's model of conceptual development (Hunt, 1971;

Hunt *et al.*, 1978), which represents conceptual level as indexing both cognitive complexity and interpersonal maturity and which envisages four stages of development from uncompromising self-centredness to flexibility and social awareness. Horwitz's subjects were 61 English-speaking female pupils drawn from four schools in the United States. Their ages ranged from 14 to 18 years, the mean being 15.9, and all were at approximately the same stage in learning French, having reached roughly the same point in their common textbook. Tests were administered to determine subjects' conceptual level, their foreign language aptitude, their linguistic competence in French and their communicative competence in French. Horwitz (1983: 72) found conceptual level and foreign language aptitude to be related to both communicative and linguistic competence. However, foreign language aptitude was not found to be related to linguistic competence when conceptual level was statistically controlled, whereas conceptual level was found to be related to communicative competence when foreign language aptitude was statistically controlled. Horwitz's conclusion is that conceptual level appears to be an important individual variable in second language learning. While she herself does not explicitly connect these findings with the age issue, a connection is not hard to discern.

The results of the above studies are not necessarily in serious conflict with those cited earlier (previous section). Two of the three studies showing an advantage for older adults start from a rather younger baseline, whereas those studies indicating an advantage for younger adult learners tend to compare learners approaching or in their 20s with learners over the age of 30. However, the notion that the L2 learning capacity peaks before and declines after puberty does seem to be undermined by the adult studies cited in this section, which, on the face of it, appear to suggest a continuing improvement in L2 learning capacity at least through the teens. With regard to counter-evidence to the general hypothesis that older L2 learners are globally better than younger ones, the reader is referred not only to the previous section but also to the two that follow.

By way of a coda to this section it may be worth referring to a number of non-comparative studies which show child learners performing rather poorly in their L2 and adult learners performing extremely well. In relation to the former, one can cite the disappointing message emerging from evaluations of L2 programmes in primary schools around Europe. For example a report of the Scottish Education Department in 1969, based on the observation of the learning of French in 106 primary schools in eight areas, found pupils' ability to understand spoken French 'reasonably satisfactory' (p.15), their degree of fluency 'very varied' (p.16), their stock of acquired vocabulary 'poor' (p.16), and their ability to redeploy what they had learnt in new situations 'disappointing' (p.16), a majority of classes visited yielding no evidence at all of skill transfer (p.17). Also relevant is Harris's (1984) series of large-scale surveys of primary school learners of Irish in the Republic of Ireland, where Irish is part of the curriculum from the infant grades onwards. Although precise estimates of numbers vary considerably (see Baker, 1997; Hindley, 1990; Mac Mathúna, 1988; Markey 2003; Ó Murchú, 1984; Salminen, 1993–1999), no one disputes that only a tiny proportion of the population of the Republic are native speakers of Irish and / or use it on a regular basis. Thus, the overwhelming majority of the pupils involved in Harris's research were learning Irish as an L2. Harris found that only about a third of the pupils surveyed had mastered the points tested (all of which were based on syllabus objectives). A further third were judged to have made some minimal progress in relation to these points, but the remaining third had apparently failed to achieve even this much. More dispiriting still are the conclusions of Audin *et al.*'s (1999) report on the outcome of a study which involved the observation of 30 foreign language classes (the languages in question being English, German, Italian and Spanish) in the French primary schools at CM2 level – i.e. in the 4th year of the primary cycle:

> . . . actual language gains are minimal and very fragmentary. The pupils know isolated words and can recognize and use chunked utterances in an extremely limited number of situations. These few gains are not re-deployed when a new situation appears (Audin *et al.*, 1999: 41; our translation[4])

Concerning the L2 performance of adults, it is worth quoting the studies cited by Hill (1970) of L2 learning customs in other cultures. Sorenson (1967), for example, notes that among the Vaupes River Indians of Colombia and Brazil successful adult acquisition of L2s is commonplace and that individuals continue to perfect their knowledge of all the languages at their disposal until very late in life. Salisbury (1962) reports a similar cultivation of adult multilingualism among the Siane of Australian New Guinea. Some very striking evidence of how well adults can perform as L2 learners comes from Neufeld's (1977) study of a group of students at the University of Ottawa who had submitted themselves to 18-hour individualised courses in Japanese and Chinese. When imitated utterances in the language in question were recorded from the experimental sample and evaluated by native speaker judges (three for each language) on a 5-point scale, ranging from unmistakably native' to 'heavily accented', nine of the 20 subjects tested convinced the judges that they might be native speakers of Japanese, and only five performed at lower than point 3 of the scale. The results for Chinese were similar, eight subjects scoring at native-speaker level and only four receiving scores of less than 3. In a later study Neufeld

(1979) found that of seven Anglophone subjects who had acquired French as adults and who had recorded the same short corpus of French (150 words), five were judged by at least 75% of the 55 French Canadians who listened to the recordings to be native speakers of French.

Since the early 1990s there has been a positive proliferation of studies which have focused on older beginners who attain very high levels of L2 proficiency. For instance, Birdsong (1992) found that 15 out of his 20 Anglophone adult subjects who began acquiring French as adults in France fell within the range of native speaker performance on a grammaticality judgement task; Ioup *et al.*'s (1994) study of two subjects who learned Arabic as adults in an Arabic-speaking environment established that both were attaining levels of performance close to native norms across a range of areas (see also Ioup, 1995); White and Genesee (1996) found that there were no significant differences between English grammaticality judgement scores attained by native-like Francophones who had begun learning English after age 12 and those attained by native-speaker controls; Bongaerts *et al.* (1995) demonstrated that Dutch learners of English who began learning English in a formal instructional setting after age 12 were able to attain English pronunciation ratings within the same range as those attained by native-speaker controls. More recently Bongaerts and his colleagues have expanded upon their earlier study (see, e.g., Bongaerts, 1999, 2003). A further investigation has been conducted in respect of the learning of English as an L2 by Dutch subjects (Bongaerts *et al.*, 1997), and there have also been studies of the learning of French as an L2 by Dutch subjects (Palmen, Bongaerts & Schils, 1997) and the late learning of Dutch as an L2 (Bongaerts *et al.*, 2000). These studies essentially replicate the findings of Bongaerts *et al.*'s 1995 study in showing that some learners whose experience of an L2 begins after age 12 can nevertheless acquire an L2 accent which is perceived as native by native speakers. A recent study by Van Boxtel *et al.* (2003) focuses on the grammatical proficiency of very advanced German and French late learners (age of arrival >/= 12) of Dutch as compared with that of 44 (highly educated) native speakers of Dutch. The grammatical measure deployed consisted of an elicited imitation task and a grammaticality judgement task in which participants were tested on their knowledge of dummy subject constructions – notoriously difficult for learners of Dutch as an L2 to acquire. The results show that three German and four French participants were able to attain to the native speaker range on the grammaticality judgement task and that, of these, all three German speakers and one French speaker also performed within the native range on all items in the imitation task.

Two additional studies worth mentioning in this connection are Moyer's (1999) investigation of the L2 phonetic/phonological attainment

of 24 Anglophone graduates in German and Birdsong's (2003) investigation of the L2 phonological attainment of 22 Anglophone learners of
French. With regard to Moyer's subjects, none of these had had any
exposure to German before age 11. In general, the ratings for their German
accents did not overlap with those obtained by native speaker controls.
However, one of the subjects *was* mistaken by the raters for a native
speaker. This individual had begun learning German at age 22 and was
largely self-taught. What distinguished him from his peers was a particularly deep fascination with the German language and culture and a
particularly strong desire to sound German. Birdsong's subjects were
resident in France and had begun acquiring French no earlier than age 18,
their mean age of onset of acquisition being 24.5 years. Two of these
subjects exhibited native levels of phonetic/phonological attainment both
in terms of native-speaker ratings and in terms of the results of an acoustic
analysis of specific segments. Both the subjects in question had high levels
of motivation in regard to learning French and both had experienced some
measure of training/correction in respect of their French pronunciation.

The 'Younger = Better in Some Respects' Position

Faced with a collection of evidence which offers two directly contradictory hypotheses both comfort and discomfiture, some researchers have
inclined towards more differentiated positions, suggesting that younger
L2 learners may be better than older learners in some very specific respects.
The particular areas of discussion that we shall examine here are: (1) the
question of whether the degree of efficiency of phonology acquisition is
age-related; (2) the notion that younger learners are more efficient at
acquiring basic communicative skills while older learners outperform
younger learners in the more academic domain; (3) the idea that the
acquirability of aspects of language which are claimed to be bio-
programmed may remain constant through life, while the acquirability of
aspects which do not fall within the sphere of bioprogramming may
diminish with increasing age.

One very common contention is that younger learners are specifically
more efficient at acquiring a native-like accent in the target language, the
strong version of this position being that unless exposure to the L2 begins in
the childhood years an authentic accent will not normally be acquired.
Thus, Scovel (1988: 101) affirms that pronunciation is the one area of
language which shows age effects because it has a 'neuromuscular basis';
he suggests that acquiring vocabulary and morphosyntax is fundamentally different from learning pronunciation because the former, unlike the
latter, does not have a 'physical reality'. He goes on to claim that those who

begin to be exposed to an L2 after age 12 cannot ever 'pass themselves off as native speakers phonologically' (Scovel, 1988: 185) (a position which he has more recently qualified – Scovel, 2000). A differentiation between accent acquisition and the acquisition of other competencies in the age context can be seen as compatible with some tendencies discernible within the research literature. Many of the studies which point to greater success on the part of younger learners have focused specifically on phonetic/phonological performance – studies such as those of Kirch (1956); Asher and García (1969); Seliger *et al.* (1975); Oyama (1976) and Tahta *et al.* (1981a, 1981b); Piper and Cansin (1988); Thompson (1991); Flege *et al.* (1995); Flege *et al.* (1999). Moreover, a consistent finding of studies confined to different age-categories of adult L2 learners is that in tests which specifically focus on oral-aural skills learners over 30 do worse than their juniors. On the other hand, a number of those studies reviewed in the previous section which suggest an advantage for the older L2 learner have focused on competencies other than accent: for example, Cheydleur, 1932; Smith and Braine (1972); Oller and Nagato (1974); Stankowski Gratton (1980); Ferris and Politzer (1981).

More direct evidence of a difference between phonetic/phonological skills and other skills in terms of age-related acquirability comes from an early study by Dunkel and Pillet (1957) and from two studies conducted by Fathman (Fathman, 1975a; Fathman and Precup, 1983). Dunkel and Pillet (1957) compared the proficiency in French of pupils taking a FLES programme in that language and groups of beginning students of French at university level. In various comprehension tests, both written and aural, the university students outperformed the elementary pupils. However, the researchers' impression of the younger learners' pronunciation was that it was 'generally much superior to that achieved by older beginners' (p. 148), and in a survey based on tape-recordings of 20 sample pupils 85% were graded 'good' or 'fair' at French pronunciation and only 15% 'poor'. In their conclusions the authors designate pronunciation as 'the most rewarding aspect of the [elementary school] program' (p.151). In her 1975 study Fathman (1975a) tested the English of 140 immigrants to the United States of diverse language backgrounds and with ages ranging from six to 15 years. An oral production test was used, based on a series of pairs of pictures. In addition, each student was asked to give a general description of a composite picture. The scores for the more structured part of the test were related solely to morphological and syntactic accuracy, whereas the discursive descriptions were rated on a 5-point scale for pronunciation and fluency as well as grammar. As far as pronunciation was concerned the younger children, aged six to 10 years, were assigned significantly higher ratings than the older group, aged 11 to 15 years, despite the fact that all the children had been exposed to English for a similar period of time. On the other hand, the older children performed significantly better on the morphology and syntax subtests (Fathman, 1975a: 249). In a subsequent study Fathman and Precup (1983) gathered speech samples and measures of oral proficiency in English from (1) a group of 20 adults and 20 children learning English in the United States in primarily informal settings, and (2) a group of 20 adults and 20 children learning English as a foreign language in Mexico primarily in formal settings. The study found that in both settings the children scored better than the adults in English pronunciation, while the adults scored better than the children in English syntax.

Also worth quoting in this context is a study by Snow and Hoefnagel-Höhle (1979) which seems to show that phonetic/phonological skills are a relatively self-contained dimension of L2 proficiency: 51 English speakers learning Dutch naturalistically in The Netherlands were tested at three points during their first year in the L2 environment. The tests probed pronunciation, auditory discrimination, morphology, syntax, vocabulary, comprehension of continuous speech, fluency and metalinguistic judgement. When the results were subjected to factor analysis it became clear that by the end of the year two major factors had emerged – (1) grammar plus vocabulary and (2) phonological ability. This structure is distinct and interpretable in the results from the third testing occasion, less distinct but discernible in the results from the second testing occasion, and indistinct and unidentifiable in the results from the first testing occasion. Snow and Hoefnagel-Höhle take these results as suggesting that there are separate components of L2 ability: control of grammatical skills and control of phonological skills (Snow & Hoefnagel-Höhle, 1979: 157). Such a finding clearly renders more plausible the suggestion that phonology and grammar/lexis relate differently to maturational influences.

A very different tack on accent is taken by Hill (1970), who argues that the notion of authenticity of accent is culture-bound:

> South India is an example of an area where many adults speak several local languages and also English, using rather similar phonetic systems throughout the multilingual repertoire. In this situation, would it be as easy for a native speaker of, say, Kannada, to recognize a Tamil accent when a native speaker of Tamil speaks Kannada as an adult-acquired second language as it is for an American English speaker to recognise a French speaker who learned English as an adult? ... Another area that displays extreme multilingualism of a type that might lead to the disappearance of the concept of 'foreign accent' is the Philippines. A discussion of Philippine multilingualism by Hunt (1966) suggests that not all the Filipino multilinguals whom he observed had the same kind

of consciousness of whether or not they were speaking second languages well . . .

I suspect that the concept 'foreign accent' may not have been operative in the American Indian language which I studied at the time when it was a viable speech community. In working with Cupeno, a remnant Uto-Aztecan language of Southern California, 1 often had the experience of reading back phonetically transcribed text in what must have been rather imperfect pronunciation and having people claim that 1 was indistinguishable from the natives. Many linguists who have worked with exotic languages have reported similar experiences; often the native speakers on hearing this sort of performance will simply assume that the linguist speaks the language and proceed accordingly . . . (Hill, 1970: 243f.)

Hill's arguments suggest that there may be a language- or culture-specific dimension to the definition of phonetic/phonological skills. Moreover, a study by Munro and Derwing (1995) suggests that a strong foreign accent does not necessarily entail a reduction of comprehensibility; and Cook (1995), for his part, claims that accent may be the least important aspect of L2 proficiency, and that older learners who fail to acquire a native-like accent lose little. On the other hand, common experience indicates that phonological deviancy on the part of an L2 user can from time to time occasion breakdowns in communication, and that even in less extreme cases a poor accent can induce interlocutors to 'switch off' during conversations and/or to avoid further interactions with the L2 user in question.

To return to the issue of age and accent acquisition, an interesting sidelight is thrown on this question by a consideration of regional/national variations of accent among speakers of the same language. Labov (1966, 1970) claims that people rarely acquire the accent of a particular region if they move into that region after puberty. Christophersen (1973: 48), on the other hand, asserts that at least some adults do change their accent. Support was lent to Christophersen's view in a review of BBC coverage of the 1980 Winter Olympics and in particular some interviews with the British skater Robin Cousins, who in the latter stages of his career had trained in America. Clive James noted in *The Observer* (24.2.80: 20) that Cousins spoke 'with a noticeable American accent – an indication that his gift has been brought to flower somewhere else than here'.

With regard to L2 acquisition, even in studies which seem to indicate that younger learners acquire a native-like accent more efficiently than older learners, the evidence is for a trend rather than for an inexorable law. For example, in Asher and García's (1969) experiment, in which the best assessment obtained by any of the experimental subjects was that their speech 'indicated a near native speaker', 7% of those who had entered the United States after the age of 13 were judged to have attained this level. Similarly, in the surveys conducted by Seliger *et al.* (1975), 7.6% of those who had learnt English/Hebrew as adults claimed no foreign accent. In addition there are studies which paint a very rosy picture indeed of adult L2 learners' capacity to acquire an authentic accent. The studies cited in the previous section conducted by Neufeld (1977, 1979) and more recently by Bongaerts and his colleagues (Bongaerts, 1999, 2003; Bongaerts *et al.*, 2000; Bongaerts *et al.*, 1995; Bongaerts *et al.*, 1997; Palmen *et al.*, 1997) suggest that substantial proportions of adult L2 learners could pass as native speakers of the L2s in question. Some studies (e.g. Ervin-Tripp, 1974; Kuusinen & Salin, 1971; Locke, 1969; Olson & Samuels, 1973; Stapp, 1999 – also cited in the previous section) show older L2 learners outperforming younger ones in pronunciation. There are also studies which challenge the notion that children are particularly adept at accent acquisition. Lengyel's (1995) investigation, for example, involving nine-year-old Hungarian children without L2 experience repeating recorded Russian words, shows that young children's capacity to repeat foreign words accurately is distinctly limited. Nor, according to Harley *et al.*'s (1995) findings, do younger L2 learners pay more attention than older learners to phonological cues when interpreting sentences.

Given such counter-evidence, a more fruitful avenue might be a perspective which differentiated language competencies along different lines. While accent has been foregrounded in much discussion of the age factor in L2 acquisition, many of the questions raised in relation to age have had a rather broader scope, concerning oral communication generally rather than pronunciation alone. A much-cited version of such a broader differentiation is Cummins's distinction between 'basic interpersonal communication skills' (BICS) and 'cognitive/academic language proficiency' (CALP):

> CALP is defined as those aspects of language proficiency which are closely related to the development of literacy skills in Ll and L2. Basic interpersonal communicative skills (BICS) and Ll such as accent, oral fluency and sociolinguistic competence may be independent of CALP for a variety of reasons . . . (Cummins, 1980: 177)

This distinction he later relates to the extremes of a continuum of context-embeddedness, his claim being that the more context-embedded communication is, the less cognitively demanding it is:

> . . . in context-embedded communication the participants can actively negotiate meaning (e.g. by providing feedback that the message has

not been understood) and the language is supported by a wide range of meaningful paralinguistic and situational cues: context-reduced communication, on the other hand, relies primarily (or at the extreme end of the continuum, exclusively) on linguistic cues to meaning . . . (Cummins, 1983: 120; see also Cummins, 1984: 136ff.)

Cummins argues that his distinction is relevant to L2 acquisition and performance. He refers to Genesee's (1976) finding that while certain French language skills of Anglophone pupils in French immersion and core French programmes in Montreal, notably reading, grammar and vocabulary, correlated with IQ, most oral skills did not; to Ekstrand's (1977) finding that Swedish data from immigrants in Sweden showed a correlation with IQ in respect of reading comprehension, dictation and free writing but not in respect of listening comprehension, free oral production and pronunciation; and to Skutnabb-Kangas and Toukomaa's (1976) finding that although parents, teachers and the children themselves considered Finnish immigrant children's Swedish to be fluent, tests of the children's Swedish necessitating cognitive operations yielded disappointing results (see previous section). The particular advantage offered by Cummins's model is that the distinction it draws does not precisely coincide with any distinction between linguistic levels or means of production. It thus seems to suggest a way forward in reconciling contradictions in the evidence about age-related differences among L2 learners. Cummins's proposals in relation to the age question are:

> . . . that older learners, whose CALP is better developed, would acquire cognitive/academic L2 skills more rapidly than younger learners; however, this would not necessarily be the case for those aspects of L2 proficiency unrelated to CALP (i.e. L2 BICS). (Cummins, 1979: 199ff.)

He cites not only many of the studies quoted above in support of the notion that younger L2 learners are advantaged in respect of accent acquisition, but also, for example, Oyama's (1978) study (see section before last) showing a L2 listening comprehension advantage for subjects who had begun learning the language before age 11. He also refers to studies which show older learners outperforming younger learners except in some aspect of oral communication – such as Ekstrand's (1976a) investigation of immigrants' proficiency in Swedish, which found older immigrants' Swedish to be better than that of younger immigrants in all respects except free oral production, and Snow and Hoefnagel-Höhle (1978a) study of L2 learners of Dutch in The Netherlands, which found that adolescent and adult learners outperformed the younger learners in the short term except as far as pronunciation and auditory discrimination were concerned.

Burstall *et al.*'s (1974) findings are also susceptible to a Cumminsian interpretation. The skills in which the pupils involved in this study who had experienced French in the primary school showed a lead over control pupils were, at age 13, speaking and listening comprehension and, at age 16, listening comprehension only. Moreover, this study is criticised by Buckby (1976) precisely because the tests administered at age 16 included no tests of pronunciation or free conversational ability. Buckby's very telling comment (1976: 344) is that, accordingly, 'what were generally recognised, at least in the pilot schools, as being two of the most important objectives, for learners and teachers alike, were not assessed', but there is the further point that, if Cummins is right, these are areas in which learners with earlier exposure might in any case be expected to excel. Other studies which have seemed to show an advantage for older learners have also failed to test skills that obviously relate to BICS; one thinks, for example, of the studies by Smith and Braine (1972), Oller and Nagato (1974), Stankowski Gratton (1980) and Ferris and Politzer (1981), discussed above. Other findings which have a bearing on Cummins's thesis are those emerging from studies by Swain (1981a) and Cummins *et al.* (1984). Swain (1981a) found that English-speaking pupils in a late French immersion programme (with about 1400 hours of French to their credit) performed better than early immersion students (with over 4000 hours of French) in a French reading comprehension test and as well as the early immersion pupils in a French cloze test, but that 'the performance of the early immersion students was superior to that of the late immersion students on a test of French listening comprehension' (pp. 3f.) (cf. similar results from other immersion studies – e.g. Turnbull *et al.*, 1998). Cummins *et al.* (1984), investigating the English proficiency of Japanese and Vietnamese immigrant students, found that on more academic proficiency measures those who had entered Canada at older ages did better, but that length of residence was a more important factor than age of arrival in predicting per-formance in oral conversation. Harley's (1986) results also seem relevant; she found that the one area in which her early total immersion subjects did as well as the late total immersion subjects was the expression of simple time distinctions, which presumably constitute a component of basic communication.

Alas for Cummins's hypothesis, the results from a large number of other studies are not supportive of the notion that younger L2 learners acquire basic interpersonal communicative skills more readily than older learners. The findings of Olson and Samuels (1973), Ervin-Tripp (1974), Neufeld (1977, 1979) and Bongaerts (Bongaerts, 1999; Bongaerts *et al.*, 2000; Bongaerts *et al.*, 1995; Bongaerts *et al.*, 1997; Palmen *et al.*, 1997) have already been noted in connection with accent acquisition. Also worth recalling are results from various studies cited in the last section:

Ekstrand (1959, 1964, 1978a) found that the English pronunciation and listening comprehension of a sample of FLES pupils improved linearly with age.

Bland and Keislar (1966) found that kindergarteners took longer than 5th-graders to learn to 'speak correctly' the French utterances used in an individualised foreign language programme.

Asher and Price (1967) found that their adult and adolescent subjects consistently performed better than their younger subjects in responding to oral directions in Russian after a brief programme of instruction in that language.

Politzer and Weiss (1969) found that in a sample of 1st, 3rd, 5th, 7th and 9th grade subjects with no previous knowledge of French there was a general improvement of scores with age on French pronunciation and auditory discrimination tests.

Locke (1969) and Kuusinen amd Salin (1971) found older children to surpass younger children in coping with the pronunciation of newly encountered phonological shapes.

Durette (1972) found that mean scores of graduates from a five-year FLES programme on listening and speaking tests fell well short of means achieved by secondary school pupils on the same tests after only two years of foreign language instruction.

Tremaine (1975) found that French aural comprehension among early total immersion pupils correlated with cognitive maturity.

Ekstrand (1976a) found immigrants' pronunciation of Swedish to correlate positively with age.

Horwitz (1983) found that in a sample of adolescents and young adult L2 communicative competence correlated with socio-cognitive maturity as reflected in conceptual level.

Stapp (1999) found Japanese adolescents to outperform Japanese children in the pronunciation of English words containing sounds which were particularly difficult for L1 speakers of Japanese to distinguish – /l/ and /r/.

To come back to the point made earlier about the CALP/BICS distinction not necessarily coinciding with that between literate and oral-aural skills, it could be argued that the measures on which some of the above findings are based are too context-reduced genuinely to reflect basic interpersonal communicative skills. It is true that many of the studies in which older learners outperformed younger learners in the oral-aural domain involved imitation and other rather highly structured tasks bearing little resemblance to normal interactive communication. However, not all of them are vulnerable to this charge. Ervin-Tripp (1974), for example, took into account records of spontaneous natural speech, and Horwitz's communicative competence text was specifically designed to elicit skills used in real communicative contexts. Moreover, some of the studies showing an advantage for younger learners in oral-aural performance are not immune to the charge of remoteness from ordinary communication; Asher and Garcia's (1969) experiment and Tahta et al.'s (1981a; 1981b) work are cases in point. With regard to the other part of Cummins's claim, namely that older L2 learners acquire cognitively demanding skills more efficiently than younger learners, counter-evidence seems to emerge from the studies by Kessler and Idar (1979), Patkowski (1980), Johnson and Newport (1989) and Hyltenstam (1992), all of which focus on grammar and all of which suggest an advantage for younger beginners. It is true that some of the data in question are based primarily on recordings of conversations and might therefore be deemed to reflect BICS rather than CALP. This is not true of all the relevant data, however. Patkowski's subsidiary experiments elicited data by means of a written multiple choice syntax test, Johnson and Newport's data are from a grammaticality judgement task, and Hyltenstam's data are written as well as oral. Interpretation of such findings is not helped by the vagueness of Cummins's exposition of his distinction, which, as Harley (1986: 31) points out, fails to clarify exactly what aspects of L2 competence, other than phonology, are supposed to be more readily acquirable by younger learners.

A further perspective on the 'younger = better in some respects' position is that arising from the notion that innate mechanisms and capacities guide certain aspects of language acquisition. Martohardjono and Flynn (1995) make a distinction between those aspects of L2 proficiency which can be seen as facilitated by 'biological endowment' and those aspects which may be considered to lie outside of the ambit of the posited innate mechanisms and capacities and thus to be subject to various developmental vicissitudes. Martohardjono and Flynn take the line that access to biologically endowed supports for language acquisition continues into adulthood and so they are able to apply the above-outlined distinction to questions about age-related effects in syntax acquisition and phonology acquisition beyond the end of the so-called critical period. They argue that, whereas non-innate aspects of L2 proficiency may be susceptible to age-related degradation, innate aspects are likely to be immune to such degradation. We shall return to the issue of post-pubertal access to Universal Grammar (UG) in the final section of this chapter and in the next chapter. However, it is probably useful immediately to review some of the evidence referred to by Martohardjono and Flynn.

One study they describe is Martohardjono's (1993) investigation of reactions to ungrammatical sentences in English by two groups of subjects who had begun to be exposed to English after age 15 and who were native speakers of Chinese and Indonesian, two languages which do not exhibit syntactic movement in questions and which therefore do not instantiate movement constraints. The ungrammatical sentences in the instrument included illicit extractions from relative clauses, sentential subjects and adjunct clauses. Martohardjono found that both groups tended to reject the ungrammatical sentences in question, from which she concluded that they had solid knowledge of the relevant movement constraints, and that since these constraints were taken to be UG-derived, UG principles which are not instantiated in the L1 remain available to adult L2 learners. Concerning aspects of phonological acquisition which are claimed to be supported by innate capacities, Martohardjono and Flynn cite evidence that new phonemic categories which exist in the L2 but not in the L1 are quite easily perceived by non-native speakers across a range of ages. They refer to Best *et al.*'s (1988) report that a sound such as the Kikuyu click, which is completely novel to native speakers of English, is perceived equally well by infant and adult L1 English speakers. They also cite Werker and Tees's (1983) study, which found that contrasts (such as /th/-/dh/) which are phonemic in Hindi but not in English, were detectable by both children and adults whose L1 was English – although the adults required some training to bring them up to criterion. They interpret such evidence as suggesting that basic sensory abilities to perceive novel contrasts are not eroded by increasing age.

According to this perspective, then, the only elements of language which *do* become difficult or impossible to acquire with increasing age are those which are not supported by biological endowment. The problem is that, given the variations and rapid changes in linguistic models which make claims about innate capacities, it is extremely difficult to determine in advance in a detailed manner which elements are supposed to be in some sense biologically given and which are supposed to be otherwise developed. Identification of these latter can only be made *ex definitione* once the age-related effects have been noted, which is, of course a circular way of proceeding. Moreover, since there is as yet no consensus as to the exact nature or degree of consistency of the effects in question, even this *post hoc* approach is very far from being a precision instrument. More fundamentally, the question of whether and in what measure language acquisition is supported by innate mechanisms remains highly controversial, and it should be noted that even those who accept the innateness hypothesis differ on the issue of whether and to what extent innate language acquisition capacities remain available beyond the end of childhood. As we shall see later, some nativists in fact explain age-related effects in terms of such capacities becoming *unavailable* around puberty.

The 'Younger = Better in the Long Run' Position

Problems of definition also arise in relation to the other major attempt to make sense of the contradictions in the evidence, namely that of Krashen *et al.* (1979). The main distinction drawn by Krashen *et al.* is between short-term and long-term attainment in L2 acquisition. However, other, subsidiary distinctions are also embedded in their hypothesis, the precise terms of which are as follows:

(1) Adults proceed through early stages of syntactic and morphological development faster than children (where time and exposure are held constant).
(2) Older children acquire faster than younger children (again, in early stages of syntactic and morphological development where time and exposure are held constant).
(3) Acquirers who begin natural exposure to second languages during childhood generally achieve higher second language proficiency than those beginning as adults. (Krashen *et al.*, 1979; reprint: 161)

In limiting their claim about the short-term attainment of adults and older children to syntax and morphology, Krashen *et al.* are incorporating into their hypothesis a distinction similar to those discussed in the last section; and in limiting their claim about the long-term attainment of children they are further distinguishing between formal and informal learning contexts.

Support for part (3) of the hypothesis comes from a number of the immigrant studies discussed earlier – e.g. Oyama (1978), Patkowski (1980), Johnson and Newport (1989), Hyltenstam (1992). In Oyama's, Patkowski's and Johnson and Newport's studies all subjects had been in the United States for at least this length of time. Hyltenstam's subjects' period of residence in Sweden also exceeded five years (except in one case where the length of residence was three years). In all of these cases, as we have seen, subjects whose experience of the target language had begun early in life were shown on the whole to have reached higher levels of proficiency in that language than those whose experience had begun around and beyond puberty. With regard to parts 1 and 2 of the hypothesis, evidence is cited from many of the studies discussed earlier in this chapter in relation to the 'older = better' hypothesis. The claim that older learners proceed through the early stages of L2 grammatical development more rapidly than younger learners clearly finds support in a study such as that of Ervin-Tripp (1974), where older children demonstrated superiority over younger children on tests of L2 syntax and morphology reception after an exposure to the language not exceeding nine months, and that of Ekstrand (1976a) in which older children outperformed younger children in a range of L2 tests after a length of exposure the median of which was 10.5 months and which in more than 90% of cases did not exceed two years. Less obviously tied, perhaps, to the very early stages of grammatical development in an L2 is Fathman's (1975a) study, which shows older children with up to three years' natural exposure to the L2 doing better in terms of syntax and morphology production than younger children with similar amounts of exposure to the language. Here we are faced with the problem, to which we shall return, of different possible interpretations of terms like 'early', 'eventual', 'short-term', 'long-term', etc.

Probably the best evidence in favour of a short-term / long-term distinction in regard to the age factor in L2 acquisition comes from two studies conducted by Snow and Hoefnagel-Höhle (1978a; 1978b). In the former a total of 69 English-speaking subjects living in The Netherlands were given tests in Dutch pronunciation, auditory discrimination, morphology, vocabulary, sentence repetition and translation. The 27 subjects who had been resident in The Netherlands for at least a year were classed as 'advanced' and were tested once only, whereas the remaining 42, who had arrived in the country within three months of the commencement of testing were classed as 'beginners' and were tested three times at 4½-month intervals. The results of these tests reveal little or no age differential in relation to phonetic/phonological skills. As far as other areas of competence are concerned, adult and adolescent 'beginners' evinced a distinct initial advantage over younger learners, the adolescents achieving the highest scores. However, this advantage was shown to be progressively eroded with longer residence in the L2 environment. Thus, in the results for the 'beginners', age differences decreased in size by the second testing session, and in the results for the 'advanced' group no significant advantage for older learners was discernible in respect of any test except the vocabulary test. Snow and Hoefnagel-Höhle adopted much the same procedure in the latter study (1978b), which involved 81 English speakers resident in Holland – 51 'beginners' who had arrived in The Netherlands within six months of the start of the testing programme and 30 'advanced' learners who had spent at least 18 months in the country. The former group was tested three times at 4- to 5-month intervals, while the latter was tested only once. The tests were in Dutch pronunciation, auditory discrimination, morphology, sentence repetition, sentence translation, sentence judgement, vocabulary, story comprehension and story telling. The results resemble those outlined above. On the first testing occasion significant age differences were noticed among the 'beginners' on all tests except the imitation condition of the pronunciation test. In all cases the adolescent and adult subjects outperformed the younger subjects, the highest scores being attained by the adolescents except in the case of spontaneous pronunciation, where the scores improved linearly with age. However, by the second and third testing occasions the younger learners had begun to catch up with and, in some cases, overtake the older learners.

There seems to be no direct counter-evidence to the notion that in a natural acquisition situation children learning an L2 generally do better than adult learners in the long run. The proposition that older learners initially outstrip younger learners in terms of grammatical development, however, is somewhat called into question by Kessler and Idar's (1979) finding that a Vietnamese mother made slower progress in acquiring the morphology of English than her four-year-old daughter during their first months in an English-speaking environment. Admittedly the periods of exposure involved were not identical, but the daughter's attainments were so markedly superior to the mother's that the conclusion that the former was progressing more rapidly in terms of morpheme acquisition would be very difficult to rebut. On the other hand, this was a very limited study of a situation in which special factors may have been operative.[5] A further study (Slavoff & Johnson, 1995) finds no differences between the rate of L2 acquisition of younger and older learners – children of migrants to the United States – over the first three years of exposure, as gauged by performance on a grammaticality judgement task. However, since the two groups were prepubertal at the time when exposure commenced (ages 7–9 years and 10–12 years respectively), these results fall outside the strict terms of the Krashen _et al._ (1979) hypothesis. Slavoff and Johnson relate their results to the fact that their subjects were all L1 speakers of languages which were typologically distant from the L2, English; they suggest that the initial advantage that emerges for older children in Snow and Hoefnagel-Höhle's (1978b) study may somehow be a consequence of the high degree of similarity between the L1 (English) and the L2 (Dutch) in question.

Beyond the strict terms of Krashen _et al._'s hypothesis the evidence concerning short-term versus long-term L2 attainment is more confused. With regard to the early stages of phonetic/phonological development, we have already seen in earlier sections that while some studies of a short/short-to-medium-term character show an advantage for younger learners (e.g. Dunkel & Pillet, 1957; Fathman, 1975a; Fathman & Precup, 1983; Tahta *et al.*, 1981b) others show quite the opposite (e.g. Ekstrand, 1959, 1964, 1976a, 1978a; Politzer & Weiss, 1969; Ervin-Tripp, 1974; Olson & Samuels, 1973; Stapp, 1999). An especially interesting piece of research in this connection is another of Snow and Hoefnagel-Höhle's studies. In this case Snow & Hoefnagel-Höhle (1977) conducted both a laboratory study and a naturalistic study. In the laboratory study 136 English-speakers ranging from five to 31 years in age were tested on multiple imitations of five different Dutch words recorded on a stimulus tape. When their efforts were assessed by a Dutch native speaker on a 5-point scale it was found that scores increased linearly with age. In the naturalistic study 47 English speakers ranging in age from three to 60 years, all in their first year of residence in The Netherlands, were tested for Dutch pronunciation at intervals of four to five months, the first testing occasion occurring within six weeks of their starting to speak Dutch. The test consisted of 80 words and had both an imitation and a spontaneous production condition. The subjects' pronunciation of the difficult sounds in the words was scored by a native speaker on the same scale as in the laboratory study. The results in this instance showed an initial advantage for older subjects but a rapid catching up by the younger learners so that 'the younger subjects had become better at pronouncing some of the sounds after a period of 10 to 11 months' learning' (Snow & Hoefnagel-Höhle, 1977; reprint: 90). In a follow-up test (after 18 months' exposure) involving a subgroup of the original sample 'the adults showed somewhat lower scores than the children' (Snow & Hoefnagel-Höhle, 1977; reprint: 90). These results, which are broadly in line with those of Snow & Hoefnagel-Höhle's 1978a and 1978b studies, can be taken as suggesting that, whether or not older learners have an initial advantage in respect of L2 phonetics/phonology, any such advantage is short-lived, at least in a natural exposure situation (cf. Krashen *et al.*, 1979; reprint, note 6: 170).

    With regard to L2 vocabulary learning (cf. Singleton, 1998) the findings are on the whole in keeping with those which relate to morphosyntax. That is to say, short-term 'naturalistic' studies, almost all short-term formal instructional studies and all long-term formal instructional studies show adult and adolescent beginners progressing more rapidly than children in acquiring vocabulary, and older children progressing more rapidly than younger children; on the other hand, long-term 'naturalistic' studies suggest that the younger one starts the better the proficiency one is likely to

attain eventually in lexis as in other areas. The obvious short-term naturalistic research to cite in this connection is that of Snow and Hoefnagel-Höhle
(1978a, 1978b), which has already been mentioned. This shows adult and
adolescent naturalistic acquirers of Dutch outscoring younger beginners in
the short term on a version of the Peabody Picture Vocabulary Test – but
starting to be overtaken by their juniors after about a year. As far as short-
duration formal instruction-based experiments are concerned, a typical
school-based investigation is that of Stankowski Gratton (1980), also
mentioned earlier, which involved a younger and an older group of Italian
primary school pupils (mean age six and eight, respectively) following a
beginners' course in German over a school year. The end-of-year test, half
of which was focused on lexis, revealed the older group to be substantially
ahead of the younger group. There is, however, one piece of short-duration
instruction-based research that fails to conform to the trend illustrated by
the Stankowski Gratton study – namely, the already-noted study by
Yamada *et al.* (1980), which appears to show an *immediate* vocabulary-
leaming advantage for younger L2 beginners. The inconsistency of these
results with those of other research involving instructed leamers might
perhaps be connected with the artificial, decontextualised and very limited
nature of the learning task in question. In any case, however, the clear trend
of findings from other instruction-based studies is for younger beginners to
perform less well at L2 lexical learning in the short term. Turning now to
somewhat longer-term investigations of L2 lexical acquisition, as an
example of an instruction-based study, one can cite again Oller and
Nagato's (1974) research, which used a cloze test as its instrument and
which therefore had a strong lexical dimension. The implication of this
study, it will be recalled, was that in a formal intructional setting older
beginners could assimilate as much in five years as younger beginners
could in 11. As for evidence from long-term naturalistic research with a
lexical focus, this is typified by Hyltenstam's (1992) study, from which it
emerged that the numbers of L2 errors – including lexical errors – produced
by subjects who had arrived in the L2 environment after age seven were in a
higher range than those produced by native speakers, whereas the range of
numbers of errors produced by subjects who had arrived in the L2 environment before age six overlapped with those of the native speakers.

Finally in this section we come back to the question of the eventual L2
attainment of different age-groups of learners in formal educational
settings. Most of the FLES studies cited above seem to indicate, in Harley's
words, 'that older learners eventually catch up to those who started
learning the L2 at a younger age' (Harley, 1986: 36). To illustrate her point
Harley cites the study by Burstall *et al.* (1974), which seemed to show that
by age 16 non-FLES learners were performing as well as their FLES peers in

virtually every area, that by Dunkel and Pillet (1962), which indicated that after five years of FLES learners were not doing as well as pupils of the same age with only one year of L2 instruction, and Oller and Nagato's (1974) study, in which pupils exposed to a FLES programme from grade 1 to grade 6 were found not to do better on a cloze test than pupils of the same age whose L2 experience had begun in grade 7. Harley also refers to the research on L2 immersion pupils carried out by Genesee (1979) and Adiv (1980), which showed late immersion pupils performing as well as early immersion pupils by the end of grade 8. A large number of the other studies cited in the section before last, including, of course, Harley's own, point in the same direction.

Before rushing to the conclusion that formal instructional conditions lead to different age-related results from natural exposure conditions in terms of eventual L2 attainment, we should perhaps pause to consider the sense to be attached to 'eventual'. Clearly, a period of, say, five years of natural exposure to a L2 would in most circumstances involve much more exposure than five years of formal L2 instruction, where the language was being treated as one school subject among many. Even in comparison to five years' immersion, five years' natural exposure would typically involve a great deal more experience of the L2. Thus, if the length-of-exposure variable is held constant, 'eventual' attainment in a formal instructional setting needs to be associated with much longer real-time periods than 'eventual' attainment in a natural exposure situation. Unfortunately, such studies of 'eventual' L2 attainment in formal settings as have been conducted to date have not extended over sufficient periods of time for exposure to be considered comparable with that involved in 'long-term' naturalistic studies. Hence, there are no real grounds for saying that the eventual attainment of older learners is better than that of younger learners in a formal learning situation if 'eventual' is to have the same content as in relation to naturalistic learning situations. There is, moreover, a small amount of evidence that, in fact, the same phenomenon of progressive reduction of older L2 learners' lead over younger learners as emerges from Snow and Hoefnagel-Höhle's findings in respect of natural exposure situations also occurs in formal instructional settings. Research on the effects of the introduction of English as a foreign language into grades 4, 5 and 6 of Danish elementary schools (Florander & Jensen, 1969; Mylov, 1972; reported in Ekstrand, 1976a) revealed that, after 80 hours of English, of the 300–400 pupils investigated those in grade 6 performed best on grammar, vocabulary and listening comprehension tests, their lead being a signifi-cant one. After 320 hours, however, this lead, though still significant, had diminished considerably. Also, as we have seen, some studies of L2 immersion programmes indicate that early programmes yield better long-term results than late programmes – at least in some domains (cf. Holobow *et al.*, 1991: 180).

There is thus a fair amount of evidence suggestive of a general long-term advantage for learners whose experience of the target language begins in their childhood years. There is no counter-evidence to this proposition from natural exposure studies, and what looks like counter-evidence from research into formal language learning cannot be accepted at face value because of the length of exposure factor, which calls into question the applicability of 'eventual' to the attainments investigated. With regard to short-term attainment, the picture is more confused. However, the balance of evidence does seem to indicate an initial advantage for older learners at least as far as grammatical development is concerned. One should note that the corollary of observations made above concerning the term 'eventual' is that where target language exposure is limited, as in a school setting, to a set number of hours per week, 'initial' is to be interpreted liberally – in terms of many years rather than months.

The Qualitative Change Position

Some researchers take the view that at a particular maturational point a qualitative change occurs in the nature of language acquisition. Three (not incompatible) commonly advanced views are the following: (1) after a certain maturational point successful L2 learning requires markedly more effort than before this point; (2) after a certain maturational point L2 learning is no longer subserved by the same mechanisms that subserve child language acquisition; (3) after a certain maturational point the L2 learner is no longer capable of attaining native-like levels of proficiency. These three perspectives clearly begin to encroach on the territory of the next chapter, where we shall return to them. In the present context we shall principally be concerned with taking a first look at the kinds of evidence that has been used in relation to the claims in question. We shall also look at some evidence relating to (4) the progress of L2 learning which would appear to bear on the notion of a qualtitative change.

(1) Evidence relating to the claim that later L2 learning is more effortful

Lenneberg's (1967) view is that post-pubertal L2 learning is no longer automatic, that 'automatic acquisition from mere exposure to a given language seems to disappear [after puberty], and foreign languages have to be taught and learned through a conscious and labored effort' (Lenneberg, 1967: 176). A particular version of the above position is that different age groups of L2 learners respond differently to different language learning environments. Thus, it has often been speculated that younger learners require only informal exposure to their target language whereas adults need in addition some kind of formal instruction. This issue is one to which Krashen (e.g. 1976, 1981a, 1982a, 1985) has devoted considerable attention. The evidence reviewed below is that to which he refers.

A number of studies suggest that younger learners do not actually benefit from instruction. Hale and Budar (1970), investigating immigrant adolescents in Hawaiian junior high schools noted that the immigrants fell into two categories: (1) speakers of less common languages who were isolated from other speakers of those languages and who were not provided with instruction in English as an L2, and (2) subjects who were able to associate with other speakers of their L1 and who did have TESOL[6] classes. What Hale and Budar found was that the former group made better progress in English than the latter. Fathman (1975b) examined the results of the oral testing of 120 Korean and Spanish immigrants to the Washington DC area who ranged in age from six to 14 years and were distributed between two different types of learning environment – a programme where the children had many teachers during the day, including one who provided special English instruction, and a programme where the children were with one teacher for the entire day and received no special English instruction. No significant differences emerged between the group mean scores on the various subtests. On the other hand, there is at least one study which shows instruction to be helpful to child L2 learners – Brière's (1978) investigation of the acquisition of Spanish as an L2 among 920 Mexican children who spoke a local Indian language as their mother tongue. From this study instruction in Spanish emerged as a better predictor of Spanish test scores than mere exposure to Spanish.

Regarding the putative instruction-dependence of adults, Krashen cites three studies of adult L2 learners of English in the United States in which he himself was involved: Krashen *et al.* (1974); Krashen and Seliger (1976); Krashen *et al.* (1978) (cf. Krashen, 1981a: 44). In the first study, in only six cases out of 14 pairs of students matched for years of formal study of English did the student with more exposure show a higher ranking than his partner with less. Similarly, in the second study, more exposure was associated with a higher score in only 10 out of 21 cases. When students were matched for exposure scores, however, it transpired that more instruction correlated with more proficiency. In the first study, this was true of seven out of nine cases, and in the second it was true of eight out of 11 cases, which in both studies was statistically significant. The third study looked at the placement test scores of 115 students of English as an L2 in an American extension programme, comparing these scores with the students' reports of their period of formal study of English and the amount of time spent in

English-speaking environments. The results resemble those of the earlier studies, with years of formal instruction emerging as a better predictor of English proficiency than time spent in an English-speaking environment. One further study referred to by Krashen (Chihara & Oller, 1978) examined adult learners of English as a foreign language in Japan and found a positive correlation between a range of test scores and amount of instruction in English, but no significant relationship between test scores and amount of exposure to English.

Such results indicate only that the instruction helps adults L2 learners, not that instruction is necessary or sufficient for adult L2 learning (Schumann, 1978a: 103). Moreover, there is some counter-evidence. Upshur (1968) found that of three groups of 10 adult non-native speakers of English enrolled in a summer session for law students, the group which scored highest on the English entrance tests was that which had been provided with no classes in English. The group which had had two hours of English classes daily scored lowest, and that which had had one hour of English daily attained a mean score intermediate between those of the other groups. Mason (1971) examined the progress of foreign students at the University of Hawaii who were excused from the classes in English which their level of English would normally have rendered compulsory. These students' scores in end-of-semester tests were not significantly different from those of students who had taken the English classes. Carroll (1967), investigating the L2 proficiency of American college seniors majoring in foreign languages, found a strong positive relationship between time spent in the target language community and test performance. Also, students whose parents used the L2 in the home were found to outperform those whose parents did not or could not speak the target language. Both findings point to the importance of naturalistic exposure to the target language for adult learners.

The picture is further confused if one looks more closely at the variables involved in the above studies. As Krashen says (e.g. 1981a: 45ff.), the variable 'exposure', which tends to be treated as a monolithic phenomenon, in fact subsumes a whole spectrum of language-using experiences, from virtually constant communicative use of the target language to only sporadic participation in target language exchanges. The same can be said of 'instruction'. Krashen (e.g. 1982a: 33ff.) draws attention to the fact that for some learners the language class may be the main or only source of target language input, whereas for others it may be just one minor source alongside other more important sources. One could add that 'instruction' covers a multitude of styles and practices, and is more accurately regarded as a complex of variables than as a single variable. Another point, illustrated by Long's (1983: 363ff.) discussion of Hale and Budar's study, is that the comparisons involved in such studies may not take account of the confounding effects of other variables. Long shows that the groups compared by Hale and Budar differed not only in respect of amount of formal instruction received, but also in terms of social class and contact with other speakers of their L1, the higher scoring group being drawn from more advantaged social milieux and having fewer opportunities to associate with members of their L1 community. Given the contradictory nature of the evidence and the difficulties of interpretation, firm conclusions about age-related differences in the relative contributions of exposure and instruction to the L2 learning process are not possible. Krashen's contention that only adult learners can benefit from the latter must, on the evidence, be regarded as speculative.

More recently, Bongaerts (e.g. 1999: 154–5) has suggested that the near-native performance that he and his colleagues have observed in some late L2 beginners may be partly explicable in terms of the very intensive training received by his subjects – thus appearing to give credence to the proposition that post-pubertal L2 learning is not an automatic affair.

As Bongaerts would be the first to acknowledge, however, the evidence which underlies his suggestion is no more than anecdotal in nature. It is not at all clear that 'input enhancement' of the kind described by Bongaerts is a prerequisite for successful late L2 learning. One can refer in this context to the work of Ioup, one of whose highly successful adult learners of Arabic was untutored. It is true that there was a certain amount of self-generated input enhancement in her experience, since she consciously worked on certain areas of linguistic form, but her performance was native-like even in relation to structural regularities pertaining to the subtle aspects of syntax and morphophonology of which she was unaware and on which she certainly had not, therefore, consciously focused (Ioup, 1995: 118).

To conclude, it is worth saying that even if it is the case that post-pubertal L2 learning *is* more consciously effortful than pre-pubertal L2 learning, this is not a clinching argument in favour of a qualitative change specifically relating to language learning. Krashen (1975) mentions in this connection the possible role of the onset of a particular stage posited by Piaget in general cognitive development – that of 'formal operations'. However, one does not have to be a Piagetian to recognise that the conscious, deliberate dimension of learning in *all* domains increases as cognitive development advances.

(2) Evidence relating to the claim that later L2 learning is subserved by fundamentally different mechanisms

With regard to the idea that children and adults may have fundamentally different mechanisms at their disposal, this has been espoused by some (though by no means all – see above) adherents of the Universal Grammar (UG) school of thought, who claim that post-pubertal L2 language learning has no access to UG principles and parameters. Cook and Newson summarise the kinds of arguments that have been put by such researchers in the following terms.

> General arguments in favour of no access are: the knowledge of the L2 is not complete (Schachter, 1988; Bley-Vroman, 1989); some L2s are more difficult to learn than others (Schachter, 1988); the L2 gets fossilized (Schachter, 1988); and L2 learners vary in ways that L1 learners do not. The proponents of no access have therefore sought to find explanations for how it is possible to learn an L2 without UG; the typical solution is seen as general problem solving combined with the knowledge of the L1 (Bley-Vroman, 1989). (Cook & Newson, 1996: 295)

On the other hand, much research indicates that post-pubertal L2 learners deal in the same way as L1 acquirers with features purportedly having a UG basis. An early study in this domain was conducted by Ritchie (1978b) on a group of adult Japanese learners of English, with reference to the presence in their internalised English grammar of the 'right roof constraint', postulated to account for the non-occurrence of sentences in which an element is 'moved to the right' out of the embedded sentence in which it 'originated', e.g.:

> *[That a gun went off] surprised no one which I had cleaned.*
> *(cf. [That a gun went off which I had cleaned] surprised no one.)*

Ritchie argues that this constraint is not acquired by children on the basis of linguistic input, but is innate. Japanese is a language which does not contain 'right movement' of any kind, so that the acquisition of Japanese does not call for the operation of the right roof constraint. Accordingly, if the constraint were manifest in the English of a group of Japanese adult learners, this could plausibly be regarded as evidence of the survival into adulthood of an innate universal principle. Ritchie's test – a grammaticality judgement task – appeared to establish the presence of the right roof constraint in the English of his Japanese subjects, which, in his view, lent 'support to the assumption . . . that linguistic universals are intact in the adult' (p. 43). Martohardjono's (1993) study, summarised earlier, and other evidence discussed by Martohardjono and Flynn (1995) and Flynn (1987) yield similar conclusions, as do later studies such as those of Dekydtspotter *et al.* (1998) and Bruhn de Garavito (1999). In other words, the empirical basis for the Bley-Vroman/Schachter perspective is highly dubious (cf. Hawkins, 2001: 353–59). Braidi (1999: 67) points out that recent changes in

Chomskyan theory now render evaluation of earlier studies extremely difficult, but she also notes that 'L2 learners do not seem to exhibit grammars that are not sanctioned by UG'.

With regard to non-UG-oriented research bearing on the notion of age-related qualitative change in L2 learning, a study conducted by Liu *et al.* (1992) examines how age of first encounter with the L2 affects the processing of L2 sentences (in terms of the use of word order and animacy as cues to interpretation) by Chinese learners of English. Their results suggest that, whereas those who began to acquire English after age 20 transferred Chinese processing strategies into English, those who began before age 13 deployed the same strategies as monolingual English speakers. This is an interesting result, but it can be explained without recourse to the notion that at a particular maturational point language acquisition mechanisms undergo a qualitative shift – namely, in terms of the increasing extent to which the L1 influences L2 processing as a function of years of experience of the L1 and the degree to which it is entrenched. We shall return to this question in Chapter 5.

Another strand of non-UG-focused research relating to what underlies L2 learning at different ages is that which looks at the question of whether older learners draw to a greater extent than younger learners on general IQ and verbal analytical skills. Genesee (1976) investigated Anglophone pupils from grades 4, 7 and 11 of a French immersion programme in Montreal and of the regular French programme in the same schools. The students in question were classified as average, above average or below average according to their most recent score on the Canadian Lorge-Thorndike Test of Intelligence. This classification was subsequently compared with pupils' performance on a French listening comprehension test, a French reading test, le Test de Rendement en Français (focusing on spelling, vocabulary, grammar, usage and reading comprehension in French), le Test de Rendement en Mathématiques (focusing on mathematical skills exercised in the French medium), and a test of interpersonal communicative skills in French, this last being administered to only a subsample of subjects. Students' performance on the three tests of academic language skills proved to be positively correlated with IQ level, but no consistent association was found between IQ level and performance on the measures of interpersonal communication skills (Genesee, 1976: 278). No effect was found for age. However, in a later study (Genesee, 1978/9) an age effect was detected. In the latter instance it was found that the French literacy skills of Anglophone pupils in grades 1–6 of a Montreal French immersion programme co-varied with IQ level, but that their French listening comprehension and oral production skills did not, which confirms the finding of the earlier investigation. On the other hand, among pupils enrolled in a *late* immersion programme (commencing at grade 7), evidence concerning IQ level and French competence was 'less clearcut' and is interpretable as suggesting that among older learners 1Q has a more important role in the acquisition of interpersonal communication (Genesee, 1978/9: 25). Harley (1986: 48) comments that these findings 'raise the possibility that in young children the acquisition of oral L2 skills is relatively independent of the kind of skills measured in a written 1Q test, while for adolescents, such skills may be more intimately involved'.

Further evidence tending in the same direction comes from Harley's own (1986) comparison of the L2 performance of early and late immersion students with approximately the same amount of exposure to their target language (French). Her first calculation of Spearman rank-order correlation coefficients between IQ and within-group ranks for early total, early partial and late immersion groups revealed no statistically significant relationship, although coefficients ranging from 0.41 to 0.45 for the late immersion students suggested a possible relationship for the older beginners (Harley, 1986: 111). This last-mentioned relationship was confirmed when school class and exposure to French outside school were controlled for. As Harley says, these findings can be interpreted as indicating 'that for the late immersion students, the cognitive skills measured by their IQ tests have been more intimately involved in L2 acquisition than for the early total and partial immersion students who began acquiring French at an earlier age' (Harley, 1986: 112).

The evidence, then, on age and the contribution of IQ to L2 learning can be interpreted as suggesting that this contribution is greater in respect of older beginners than of younger ones. However, one has to bear in mind the danger of reductionism in dealing with the IQ measure. As Calvin (1997) puts it: 'IQ is certainly one fascinating aspect of intelligence, but it doesn't subsume the others; we shouldn't make the mistake of trying to reduce the subject of intelligence to a simple number on a rating scale' (Calvin, 1997: 10–11). One also needs to take into consideration the doubts that have been raised about intelligence testing (see e.g. McDonough, 1981: 126ff.), particularly in relation to minority groupings (see e.g. Cummins, 1984: 18lff.). Also, the comment offered earlier in respect of putatively higher levels of consciousness in later language learning can be repeated *mutatis mutandis* in the present context. It is surely *only to be expected* that general intelligence resources will be increasingly drawn upon with advancing cognitive development – not only in relation to language learning but in all learning contexts.

With regard to verbal analytical skills, Harley and Hart (1997) investigated the role of language aptitude in two groups of Anglophone secondary school students who had entered French immersion programmes in grade 1 and grade 7 respectively. It emerged that the early beginners' L2 outcomes 'were much more likely to be associated with a memory measure than with a measure of language ability' (p. 395), whereas the reverse was true of the later beginners. Moderate further support for this view came from a later study by Harley and Hart (2002) involving students on a three-month exchange programme who had begun intensive exposure to the L2 at different ages. DeKeyser's (2000) study yields not dissimilar results: the adult beginners in his study who scored within the range of the child beginners had higher levels of verbal analytical ability, an ability which, according to him, played no role in the performance of the child beginners. On the basis of his results DeKeyser suggests that maturational constraints apply only to implicit language learning mechanisms. Bialystok (2002a) has criticised DeKeyser's study on a variety of grounds – including the choice, the truncation and the translation of the language aptitude test used (the MLAT – Carroll and Sapon, 1959) – and by Bongaerts (personal communication) on the ground that the language aptitude scores, which are low even for the late beginners, have been over-interpreted. Commenting on their findings, Harley and Hart (1997) point to the possible influence of different instructional styles associated with primary versus secondary-level education. A further possibility (which DeKeyser (2003) himself seems to favour) is that the above results are relatable to general cognitive changes which impact on language learning but not *only* on language learning.

(3) Evidence relating to the claim that later L2 learners cannot attain native levels of proficiency

A number of researchers in recent years have affirmed that there is a maturational limit beyond which it is simply impossible to acquire an L2 (or certain aspects thereof) to native levels. As we have seen, for example, Scovel (1988) claims that those who begin to be exposed to an L2 after age 12 cannot ever acquire a native accent, a position which Long (1990: 274) endorses, also claiming that the *sine qua non* for the acquisition of L2 morphology and syntax to native levels is exposure to the L2 before age 15. The evidence cited in favour of this position is typically based on the observation that older L2 beginners do not usually end up being taken for native speakers: 'adult learners fail, often miserably, to become indistinguishable from members of the ambient speech community' (Eubank & Gregg, 1999: 77). Much of the evidence cited in earlier sections bears out this observation, but a particular study which is often cited in this connection is that of Coppetiers (1987) who used a written questionnaire to investigate semantic and grammaticality judgement in a group of 21 very advanced users of French as L2, all of whom had learned the language in adulthood.

Coppetiers also taped lengthy interviews with each of his subjects during which they were prompted to offer comments on the judgements they had provided. What he found was not only that the non-native speakers exhibited significantly more variation in their judgements in quantitative terms, but that comments elicited during the interviews indicated an even greater divergence at the qualitative level: 'the extent of the gap between NSs [native speakers] and NNSs [non-native speakers], particularly in the interpretation of basic grammatical contrasts, points to qualitative, not simply quantitative, differences between the two groups' (p. 565).

On the other hand, one has to take account of the great wealth of studies (already referred to) focused on older beginners attaining very high levels of L2 proficiency: Birdsong's (1992) finding that a majority of his adult beginner subjects performed in a native-like way on a grammaticality judgement task; Ioup *et al.*'s (1994) documentation of native-like performance across a range of areas of two subjects who learned Arabic as adults; studies conducted by Bongaerts and his colleagues (Bongaerts, 1999; Bongaerts *et al.*, 2000; Bongaerts *et al.*, 1995; Bongaerts *et al.*, 1997; Palmen *et al.*, 1997) demonstrating that among L2 learners whose experience of their L2 began after age 12, some were able to attain pronunciation ratings within the same range as those attained by native-speaker controls; Moyer's (1999) investigation of the L2 phonological attainment of 24 Anglophone graduates in German, which revealed that the one subject who was mistaken for a native speaker had begun learning German at age 22; and Van Boxtel *et al.*'s (2003) finding that some late learners of Dutch from French-speaking and German-speaking backgrounds were able to attain native levels of accuracy in a grammaticality judgement task and an elicited imitation task. It is true, as Hyltenstam and Abrahamsson (2000: 155) claim, that there is no case on record of a post-pubertal L2 beginner who has been demonstrated to behave in every linguistic detail like a native speaker. However, it is also true, as Hyltestam and Abrahamson recognise, that the more closely we study very early L2 beginners the more we realise that, at the level of subtle detail, they too differ from monoglot native speakers. On this latter point recent studies (e.g. Ekberg, 1998, cited Hyltenstam & Abrahamsson, 2000: 161; Hyltenstam & Abrahammson, 2003) have shown that even very young L2 beginners diverge at the level of fine lexico-grammatical detail from native speakers. Much the same seems to be true at the phonological level; Flege (e.g. 1999, 2002) cites a number of studies in which he was involved which show that subjects who begin to be exposed to an L2 in an L2 environment as young children are nevertheless quite likely to end up speaking the L2 with a non-native accent (e.g. Flege *et al.*, 1997; Guion *et al.*, 2000; Piske *et al.*, 2001) and to be less good than monglot native speakers at vowel and consonant perception in their target language (Flege *et al.*, 1999; MacKay *et al.*, 2001).

It may well be, therefore, that the maturational issue is less important in this connection than the very fact of the possession of knowledge of another language (cf. e.g. Cook, 1995; Grosjean, 1992). It seems also to be the case that the degree of distance between the L1 and the L2 plays a role. McDonald (2000) found that learners of English from a Spanish-speaking background who had begun to be exposed to the language before age five were able to perform to native levels on an English grammaticality judgement test, whereas Vietnamese speakers with pre-age five experience of English were not. We shall return to a discussion of cross-linguistic perspectives in Chapter 5. An immediate conclusion from the foregoing, however, is that the appropriate comparison in the investigation of age-related effects in L2 acquisition is not between post-pubertal L2 beginners and monoglot native speakers but between post-pubertal L2 beginners and those who begin to acquire an L2 in childhood. Cook's recent criticism of both sides of the ultimate attainment debate is very much to the point:

> Both sides of the debate judge the L2 user against the native speaker; ultimate attainment is a monolingual standard rather than an L2 standard. Differences from native speakers represent failure; 'Very few L2 learners appear to be fully successful in the way that native spearkers are' (Towell & Hawkins, 1994: 14).
>
> While the question of what ultimate attainment means in a second language is not yet resolved, there is no intrinsic reason why it should be the same as that of a monolingual native speaker. (Cook, 2002: 6)

A further obvious point that emerges from the above – one made some years ago by, among others, Kellerman (1995) – is that comparisons between older and younger learners' attainments always need to take account of L1 background.

(4) Evidence from the progress of L2 learning

A major contribution to research into the way in which L2 learning progresses were the L2 'morpheme studies'[7] inaugurated by the work carried out by Dulay and Burt in the 1970s (Dulay & Burt, 1973, 1974a,b,c) under the inspiration of L1 morpheme studies (notably Brown, 1973; De Villiers & De Villiers, 1973). Dulay and Burt's research design was cross-sectional. From their results they derived an accuracy order for the morphemes under scrutiny and assumed that this accuracy order reflected the acquisition order for the morphemes. The results of L2 morpheme studies can be seen to bear on the age issue in two ways. First, the accuracy order derived from such studies can be compared with accuracy / acquisition orders derived from L1 morpheme studies, and, second, accuracy orders of L2 learners of different ages can be compared. Concerning the first possibility, since the fact that a language is labelled as an L2 implies that the experience of that language began at a later stage and age than experience of some other language, the age issue is implicit (alongside other issues) in any comparison of L1 and L2 performance. This has a special pertinence to evidence from morpheme studies, since such evidence was used by Dulay and Burt in the elaboration and testing of their hypothesis that L2 acquisition (at least in childhood) could be *equated* with L1 acquisition (Dulay & Burt, 1974a: 107f.) with respect to the kinds of errors made and to the morpheme accuracy/acquisition order. It transpired, however, that, while many of the errors produced by L2 learners do resemble the developmental errors of L1 learners of the same language, many do not, and also the morpheme accuracy/acquisition orders which emerge from L2 studies differ somewhat from those established by L1 studies. Dulay and Burt were obliged by such findings to withdraw from their 'L2 acquisition = Ll acquisition' position, their explanation for the differences being in terms of the fact that 'children learning an L2 are usually older than Ll learners; they are further along in their cognitive development, and they have experienced a language once before' (Dulay & Burt, 1974d: 225) – i.e. interestingly, not simply in terms of age *per se*. With regard to comparisons of results from L2 learners of different ages, these tend to show similar orders for adults and children (Bailey *et al.*, 1974; Krashen *et al.*, 1976; Krashen *et al.*, 1978), and for older and younger children (Fathman, 1975a,b). A further adult study (Larsen-Freeman, 1975) yielded orders which varied according to the elicitation instrument used, but the orders obtained on two tests do correlate with Dulay and Burt's findings for child learners.

Cross-sectional morpheme studies are not without their critics:

> . . . it has been argued that there is not a sufficient theoretical base for assuming that the accuracy with which learners use morphemes corresponds to the order in which they are acquired. The case studies have shown that learners may begin by using a grammatical form correctly, only to regress at a later stage, which makes a mockery of attempts to equate accuracy and acquisition. Other doubts . . . include the suspicion that the orders obtained are an artefact of the Bilingual Syntax Measure[8]; and criticism concerning the choice of morphemes for investigation and the methods used to 'score' each morpheme. Also Rosansky (1976) has argued that the rank correlation statistics used to compare the orders achieved in different studies disguise much of the variability in the data. (Ellis, 1985: 69)

There is also some evidence (see Larsen-Freeman, 1976) that morpheme accuracy orders may reflect frequency of occurrence rather than an 'internal syllabus'. Against such criticisms one can quote, for example, Fathman's (1979) finding of a significant correlation between the morpheme accuracy orders obtained from a sample of 60 children on two testing occasions separated by time periods in the order of 6, 9 or 12 months. Krashen (1981) concludes from his survey of morpheme studies, including longitudinal as well as cross-sectional studies of learners of various ages, that where account is taken only of morphemes for which there were at least 10 obligatory occasions of use, there is 'an amazing amount of uniformity . . . in all studies where language was used for communication' (Krashen, 1981a: 57).[9] Larsen-Freeman and Long (1991), for their part, note that the early morpheme studies have been followed by dozens of later studies, including some dealing with non-Indo-European languages, and argue that that 'despite . . . limitations in some areas, the morpheme studies provide strong evidence that ILs [interlanguages] exhibit common accuracy/acquisition orders' (Larsen-Freeman & Long, 1991: 92). Even if it cannot be definitively inferred that younger and older learners exhibit a similar 'internal syllabus' in respect of L2 grammatical morphemes, one can at least say that the morpheme studies do not yield any striking counter-evidence to this hypothesis, or any findings which point to qualitative age-related differences in the L2 learning process.

We turn now to some studies which compare L2 with L1 patterns in areas other than morphological development. Cook (1973) looked at L2 and L1 patterns in respect of the imitation and comprehension of relative clauses and the comprehension of sentences with the same surface structures but different deep structures. In the first case Cook found that children learning English as their L1 and adults learning English as an L2 'seemed to have tackled the tasks of imitation and comprehension of relative clauses in much the same manner' (Cook, 1973: 20). He discovered eight similarities and only three differences between the results from the two groups. The differences were:that the children but not the adults: (1) sometimes substituted *what* for the relative pronouns in the stimulus sentences; (2) shifted the subject of the relative clause to the main clause; (3) sometimes imitated only the last few words of the stimulus sentences.

Difference (1) is explicable in terms of dialectal differences in the input to which the two groups were exposed. Difference (2) is more difficult to account for; Cook's somewhat puzzling observation is that 'it may be the by-product of the audio-visual teaching method' (p. 1). His explanation of difference (3) in terms of age-related differences in short-term memory capacity does, however, have the ring of plausibility. Cook's second experiment repeated an experiment conducted by Cromer (1970) testing English-speaking children's comprehension of pairs of sentences like 'The duck is happy to bite' and 'The duck is hard to bite'. Cook's version used the same sentences, but with a group of adult non-native speakers of English. He found that he could divide his subjects up in the same way that Cromer had been able to: into 'primitive rule users' (those who consistently interpreted the surface structure subject as the subject of both verbs); intermediates' (those whose interpretations were on a hit-or-miss basis); and 'passers' (those whose interpretations were consistently correct). These categories represented for both Cromer and Cook developmental phases in the acquisition of English sentence structure. On the whole, then, Cook's experiments both suggest broad similarities between the ways in which L1 and L2 learning proceed and thus between language learning processes at earlier and later maturational stages.

Other studies customarily quoted in discussions of similarities and differences between L1 and L2 acquisition are those which have focused on developmental stages passed through by learners in the acquisition of syntactic structures such as interrogatives and negatives (for a discussion of a range of relevant research see Braidi, 1999: Chapter 2). Prominent among the L2 studies most frequently referred to in this connection are those of Ravem (1968, 1970, 1978); Wode (1976); Adams (1978); and Cancino *et al.* (1978), the L1 points of comparison being, notably, the studies by Brown and his collaborators (e.g. Brown, 1968, 1973; Brown *et al.*, 1971; Bellugi, 1965; Klima & Bellugi, 1966).

Basically, the whole trend of results from L2 syntax studies has been to show 'striking similarities' (Ravem, 1970; reprint 140) between the developmental phases evidenced by L2 and L1 learners. As Larsen-Freeman and Long note (1991: 95), the results of such studies 'are consistent with the notion that IL [interlanguage] development is a process of gradual "complexification" or *recreation* of the L2 in much the same way that children "recreate their mother tongue in first language acquisition"'. For example, all learners of English, whether as an L1 or an L2, appear to pass through a stage in the acquisition of wh-questions where declarative order is maintained, as in e.g. *What she (is) doing?*, before arriving at the stage where an inversion rule is incorporated. Similarly, both L1 and L2 learners of English seem to go through a stage of marking *yes/no* questions by intonation alone, as in e.g. *John come too?*, and of forming negatives by simply preposing a negative element in front of the main verb, as in e.g. *He no like it.* Instances of L2 learners' developmental syntactic stages diverging from those of L1 learners do occur, but find a ready explanation in terms of L1 influence. For instance, Ravem (1968), when analysing his (Norwegian) six-year-old son's acquisition of English in Britain, noted sentences such as:

> *Drive you car to-yesterday? Like you food?*
> *Like you me not, Reidun?*

Learners of English as an L1 do not normally produce such structures, even transitionally. However, such structures can be related to Norwegian *yes/ no* questions which do have this form, e.g.:

> *Gjorde du det?* (Lit. 'Did you it?')
> *Likker du ikke iskrem?* (Lit. 'Like you not ice-cream?')

Likewise, Wode (1976) recorded English negatives produced by German learners which were of the type:

> *John go not to the school*

Such structures do not resemble L1 transitional negatives, but can be linked to the German negative structure:

> *John geht nicht . . .* (Lit. 'John goes not . . . ')

One further piece of research that needs to be mentioned in this context is Ervin-Tripp's (1974) study, which has already been referred to and which, it will be recalled, investigated the L2 progress of 31 Anglophone children aged between four and nine years learning French in Switzerland. On the basis of her data from testing as well as taped natural conversation and diary records Ervin-Tripp inferred the following similarities between L2 and L1 acquisition:

(1) 'Learning . . . occurs first for the material which is predictable and for which the meaning is apparent' (p.115).
(2) 'Meaning recurrences provide basic categorization devices for mapping of forms' (p.116), so that the basic preference of the learner is 'for a principle of one meaning – one form' (p.117),
(3) 'The first features of sentences to be used in comprehension rules are those which survive in short-term memory best' (p.117) and 'the relation of order to meaning' is relatively early acquired (p. 17).

In sum, then, Cook's work, the research bearing on developmental syntactic stages and Ervin-Tripp's study concur in suggesting that the L1 and L2 acquisition processes are broadly similar. Such divergences as do emerge can be ascribed to factors such as cognitive development, memory development and influence from an earlier learned language; they certainly do not necessitate the postulation of a qualitative age-related change in the manner in which language acquisition proceeds.

With regard to findings from studies other than morpheme studies comparing the progress of L2 learners of different ages, again the picture that emerges is one of an acquisition process which largely transcends age. An interesting set of experiments with a bearing on this issue was conducted by Braine (1971b). These experiments focused on pattern-learning mechanisms that could plausibly be considered relevant to language learning. The experimental task was to internalise the grammar of an artificial L2 on the basis of a number of strings generated by that grammar or those strings plus an admixture of 'ungrammatical' strings. The experiments involved both young adults and nine-year-old children, and one of the findings of the research was that there were no major differences between these two groups in terms of how they went about the task – which led Braine to the conclusion that 'the pattern-learning mechanisms of these two types of subjects seem to be rather similar for the kind of procedure and learning material used' (Braine, 1971b: 162 note 3). Ervin-Tripp (1974) reaches a similar conclusion in respect of older and younger children: across the whole age-range of her subjects (four to nine years) the indications were that L2 learning proceeded in broadly the same way. Also of relevance is Selinker *et al.*'s (1975) conclusion, based on their analysis of errors made by English-speaking children in grade 1 of a French immersion programme, that essentially the same processes of language transfer, over-generalisation and simplification are at work in child interlanguage as in adult interlanguage. A similar conclusion was reached by Snow (1981) in a study which, over about a year, examined, by means of a translation test, the acquisition of Dutch syntax by 51 English-speaking children, adolescents and adults living in The Netherlands. The major difference found was that the older learners generally learned faster than the younger ones over the period in question. On the other hand, the younger learners tended to distinguish earlier than the older ones between one particular pair of temporal conjunctions (*toen* and *wanneer*). Otherwise, all groups approached the learning task in similar ways: 'the majority of hypotheses adopted and errors made were found for subjects in all age groups' (Snow, 1981: 248). For example, all age groups went through approximately the same stages in the acquisition of temporal conjunctions, and similar kinds of transfer errors were recorded from all groups.

Harley's (1986) comparison of the L2 performance of early and late immersion students with approximately the same amount of exposure to their target language (French) (see above) also yields broad similarities between the groups with respect to the patterning of errors:

> . . . both immersion age groups tend to make more accurate use of relatively unmarked French verb forms *vis-à-vis* more marked forms, particularly within the confines of a particular semantic domain. The two age-groups also tend to make generally similar types of formal

errors in realising functions for which they currently lack the appropriate French verb forms . . . To the extent that Ll transfer appears as a factor in the errors made, it is at least as prevalent among the younger early immersion students as among the older late immersion students. (Harley, 1986: 110)

Such differences as were found between the groups could in large part be ascribed to differences in input (1986: 114).

All in all, it is difficult to disagree with McLaughlin's conclusion of 25 years ago: results of research into various dimensions of the way in which L2 learning proceeds suggest that age differences between adults and children are of little significance as far as the L2 acquisition process is concerned and 'that the adult uses basically the same strategies as the child, in spite of a great deal more experience with language' (McLaughlin, 1978: 70).

Summary and Conclusions

(1) The available evidence does not consistently support the hypothesis that younger L2 learners are globally more efficient and successful than older learners.
(2) Nor is it possible to conclude from the evidence that older L2 learners are globally more efficient and successful than younger learners.
(3) With regard to the notion that different age-groups excel in different aspects of L2 learning, the evidence does not consistently support the hypothesis that younger learners are inevitably more efficient than older learners in the phonetic/phonological domain. On the question of a differentiation in terms of basic communicative versus cognitive-academic skills, it is impossible to make a definitive evaluation until the relevant concepts are more tightly defined. With respect to the proposal that biologically endowed aspects of L2-acquiring capacity are immune to maturation-related degradation whereas other aspects may not be, this is a far from universally accepted view among nativists and, on the present evidence, must be seen as speculative.
(4) Concerning the hypothesis that those who begin learning an L2 in childhood in the longrun generally achieve higher levels of proficiency than those who begin later in life, one can say that there is some good supportive evidence and that there is no strong counter-evidence. The data from school-based investigations which seem to contradict this hypothesis do not in fact bear on it, if one takes naturalistic situations as the basis for one's definition of 'long run', 'eventual', etc., since L2 exposure-time involved in studies focusing on formal learning situations never approaches that involved in long-term naturalistic studies.

(5)   The idea that there is an age-related qualitative change in language learning at a particular developmental point is not unambiguously supported by the available evidence. It has not been demonstrated that post-pubertal L2 learning is necessarily more consciously effortful that pre-pubertal learning, and even were this to be the case it could be explained in general cognitive terms. It has not been shown either that there is a fundamental difference between child and adult language learning mechanisms. Such differences as there are in the learning approach of younger and older learners can again be explained in general cognitive terms and/or in terms of increasing L1 influence. With regard to the notion that post-pubertal L2 learners cannot attain to native levels of proficiency, this is undermined by some recent studies, but in any case failure to attain to such levels can be explained in terms of cross-linguistic interaction, especially given the fact that early L2 learners also fail to behave like monoglot native speakers. Finally, concerning the idea of age-related differences in the way in which L2 learning proceeds, L2 learners have been shown to follow a learning route which, despite some divergences of detail, broadly resembles that followed by L1 learners. Similarly, younger and older L2 learners exhibit developmental patterns which in the vast majority of respects coincide. Such divergences as do exist are explicable in terms of general cognitive factors and/or cross-linguistic influence.

Notes

1.   For convenience, the *FLES* acronym is used throughout the book to denote second/foreign language instructional programmes at elementary/primary level.
2.   ' . . . certe abilità che facilitano l'apprendimento di una lingua aumentano e maturano col crescere del bambino.'
3.   The test was in two parts. The first was designed to probe 'la conoscenza delle strutture-base' ('knowledge of basic structures') and the second 'le conoscenze "staccate" imparate durante l'anno, come p.e. gli oggetti, i colori, le particelle, ecc.' ('"separate" items of knowledge acquired during the year, such as e.g. objects, colours, particles, etc.').
4.   '. . . les acquis proprement langagiers restent minimes, très atomisés. Les élèves connaissent des mots isolés, savent reconnaître et utiliser des énoncés dans un nombre de situations extrêmement limité. Ces quelques acquis ne sont pas réutilisés lorsqu'une situation nouvelle se présente.'
5.   Kessler and Idar's subjects were refugees rather than ordinary immigrants. The authors themselves stress 'the role of affective variables and the retarding effect of negative attitudes arising from difficult adjustments to a new culture' (p. 78).
6.   This acronym stands for 'the teaching of English to speakers of other languages'.
7.   The morpheme is defined as 'the smallest functioning unit in the composition of words' (Crystal, 1997: 248), and thus includes 'content words' as well as 'func-

tors'. The 'morpheme studies' discussed here concentrate on the latter, i.e. *grammatical* morphemes such inflections, articles, auxiliaries and copulas.

8. The Bilingual Syntax Measure (Burt *et al.*, 1973) was the elicitation instrument used in the Dulay and Burt studies and in some other morpheme studies cited.

9. With regard to variations in the orders elicited by Larsen-Freeman (1975), these can be interpreted as resulting from different degrees of 'form-focusedness' induced by the tests employed (see e.g. Krashen, 198la: 52). Since these variations occurred within an entirely adult sample, and since at least some of the findings correlate with those from child studies, they hardly constitute evidence of age-related learning differences.

Chapter 5

Theoretical Perspectives

Introductory

Many professionals and researchers involved in one way or another with language simply assume that there is a critical period for language acquisition. Thus, we find an article in an Irish medical journal (Breathnach, 1993) largely echoing Lenneberg's views – speaking of a 'transitory sensitive period' for language (p. 43) and claiming that 'the infant learns to pronounce and use the language he hears around him with ease and perfection', while adult L2 learning 'demands a systematic and determined effort' (p. 44). Likewise, in a very widely used handbook of psycholinguistics we find the notion of a critical period treated as unquestioned fact:

> . . . just as with the development of stereovision in primates or the acquisition of songs by birds . . . , there is a critical period for language development in humans. If exposed to language prior to the age of seven, children are capable of becoming totally fluent, but after this age the prognosis becomes gradually worse. (Bloom, 1994: 744)

In the light of the content of previous chapters, one would have to say that statements such as the above go beyond what is strictly licensed by the evidence. However, there are undoubtedly effects in language development which can be related to age, and this chapter is concerned with various of the theoretical explanations that have been offered for such effects. The explanations in question can be grouped under the following headings:

- explanations which focus on sensory acuity;
- explanations in terms of competition between languages;
- neurolinguistic explanations;
- explanations which seek to link age-related differences to cognitive growth;
- explanations of an affective-motivational kind;

- explanations which point to differential factors in the quality of input received by younger and older learners;
- an explanation which posits the 'decoupling' of the internalised grammar from the processes of speech perception and production at a particular stage;
- nativist explanations;

The Ageing of the Senses

We begin by examining the point of view that accepts the reality of a maturationally determined decline in language learning capacity, and attributes this to a decreasing sharpness of the senses. For obvious reasons, the particular sense focused on in this connection is that of hearing. Hatch (1983a), reviewing the L2 evidence, suggests that pronunciation and inflectional morphology are 'areas where we may continue to find differences with age' and declares an inclination to 'buy' physiological explanations for this phenomenon. She poses the question:

> . . if adults are less proficient in pronunciation than children, is it because the adult learner is unable to intake – hear – the incoming material accurately (e.g. are the cochlear hairs worn down)? (Hatch, 1983a: 197)

Similarly, Joiner (1981) makes a passing reference to the critical period question in the context of a discussion of auditory impairment, claiming, on the basis of work by Kowalski and Cangemi (1978), that auditory acuity peaks between ages 10 and 14, and noting that this period marks the putative endpoint of the 'so-called critical age for language learning'.

If it is the case that there is a decline in hearing acuity beginning in the mid-teens, this must be taken seriously as a possible factor in subsequent language learning success. The question is whether the alleged end-of-childhood deterioration in auditory acuity is of a magnitude that can be plausibly expected to impede language learning. Some evidence against this proposition can be seen in the findings of Streiter (1976; see above, Chapter 3) and of Eilers *et al.* (1979). It will be recalled that Streiter's study suggests that infants raised in a Kikuyu-speaking environment were at two months already able to distinguish the pre-voicing from the simultaneous voicing of stops, this distinction being one which is functional in Kikuyu. What has not so far been mentioned, however, is that this study also appears to reveal that these infants were in addition able to distinguish between voiced and voiceless stops – a distinction not made by Kikuyu – that 'adult Kikuyus showed the same discrimination pattern as the infants' (Streiter, 1976: 40). Eilers *et al.* (1979) similarly found that their adult subjects could distinguish VOT differences which had no role in the system of their own language. In other words, despite the fact that a phonetic distinction is not functional in the ambient language system, adults can be shown to be sensitive to it in much the same way that infants are. This suggests that post-pubertal hearing is not inferior to child hearing to any extent which is likely to be relevant to the perception of speech sounds.

Further evidence against a linguistically significant decline in hearing acuity as childhood ends is to be found in those L2 studies cited in Chapter 4 which indicate that, in fact, adults can perform to a very high degree of accuracy on pronunciation tests, to the extent sometimes of surpassing younger subjects in this domain and indeed being taken for native speakers. Presumably, if adults can produce L2 sounds accurately they must be able to hear them accurately. Nor, as we have seen, is the excellence of adults' L2 performance confined to the phonetic/phonological area. On the contrary, age comparisons of L2 syntactic and semantic proficiency show virtually without exception that at least in the initial stages adults do better. All of this argues against the notion that there is a linguistically relevant auditory deterioration around puberty.

There is, though, another dimension to the issue of the interaction between age effects on sensory acuity and language learning capacity. While deterioration in hearing between childhood and adulthood seems to be normally slight, a much greater decline is discernible in middle age and senescence. According to Schaie and Geiwitz (1982), 19% of 55 year-olds and 75% of 79 year-olds suffer from some form of hearing loss. Following Hand (1973), Joiner cites a United States National Health Survey which showed that 'while 85% of children between the ages of five and 14 have normal hearing, only 12% of those over 65 can make that claim' (Joiner, 1981: 12). According to Joiner, 'the rate of hearing impairment increases gradually until the 50s, when there is an abrupt increase followed by an even sharper climb beginning at around age 70' (Joiner, 1981: 12). Such losses in threshold audibility are most readily attributable to changes in the sensori-neural receptive machinery in the inner ear and/or to degenerative changes in the receptor apparatus that widen sensory filters and thus diminish frequency discrimination. A third factor seems to be the loss of temporal acuity – i.e. the ability of the auditory system to respond to rapid changes in the envelope of a sound over time, resulting in a diminution in the extent to which the internal representation of the sound faithfully represents the temporal changes present in the physical stimulus (see e.g. Frisina *et al.*, 2000). This is analogous to the reception of blurry, out-of-focus images in the visual domain and implies that elderly listeners require greater voice-onset contrasts in order to categorise the two sounds as being different from each other.

Such hearing decrements in later life (cf. Cross, 1981: 156; Schleppegrell, 1987) may go some way towards explaining the available data in language learning differences between different age-categories of adults. These differences (see Chapter 4) do not point consistently in the direction of a global superiority for younger adults. However, there is at least one consistent finding, which is that among mature adults older subjects tend to perform less well than younger subjects in the oral-aural domain – a finding which, moreover, accords with anecdotal evidence from educators:

> Older learners usually no longer have the great capacity for auditory imitation and memorizing, and this often results in trial-and-error fumbling. Their oral response is decidedly slower . . . (Brändle, 1986: 19)

Hence Joiner's (1981: 12f.) and Brändle's (1986: 18ff.) recommendation that those involved in teaching L2s to learners of advanced years should develop techniques and materials to compensate as far as possible for such learners' less acute hearing.

As well as a decline in auditory acuity, older adult learners also face increasing problems in the visual sphere. Citing reviews by Hand (1973) and Weinstock (1978), Joiner relates vision to age as follows:

> Visual acuity, which peaks at about age 18, declines gradually but steadily until age 45. There is a decrease in the rate of decline beyond 55 . . . ; by age 65, however, half the population has 20/70 vision or less, and many elderly people perceive even bright colors as faded. (Joiner, 1981: 12)

It is true, as both Joiner (1981: 12) and Brändle (1986: 19) note, that visual difficulties can be corrected more satisfactorily than auditory difficulties. Spectacles and contact lenses are, by and large, a good deal more effective than hearing aids. Nevertheless, corrective lenses do not totally resolve visual problems, and it is fairly obvious that, at least in the classroom situation, quality of eyesight could well be a very important factor; formal instruction of virtually any kind tends to rely heavily on written materials, and courses for the elderly may actually involve an increase in such materials in order to compensate for older learners' aural difficulties (cf. above). Certainly, Joiner (1981: 12) advises that teachers of L2s to the elderly take their students' poorer eyesight into consideration (cf. also Draves, 1984: 9). Quoting Knox (1978), Joiner recommends 'longer exposure time, combined audio and visual presentation, simplified sequences of information, and increased time for adaptation between lighted and darkened surroundings' (Knox, 1978: 314).

Age and Competition Between Languages

Since competition between languages clearly implies the presence of more than one language, explanations which rely on the positing of such competition are obviously not applicable to monoglot L1 acquisition. Such explanations have been proposed to account for differences between younger and older L2 learners, and have played a part in discussions about the benefits/disadvantages conferred by bilingualism and bilingual education.

An early explanation in this category is that based on the behaviourist model of language. This model represents L1 acquisition as the establishment of habitual verbal responses to given stimuli through a process of 'conditioning', that is through imitation by the acquirer of the responses in question, reinforcement of those responses by addressees through rewards of one kind or another (food, attention, approval, etc.) and repetition by the acquirer of the same responses in similar situations in the expectation of further rewards. As far as L2 acquisition is concerned, this is represented as the formation of another set of habits but with the complication of influence from the first set of habits. On this view the younger learner is more efficient at acquiring an L2 because '[h]e does not have the sets of reflexes and habits which the adult has acquired and practiced' (Dunkel, 1948: 68) and which 'continually interfere' (1948: 70) with L2 production. According to some versions of this position the difficulties of the older learner have to do with the limitedness of stimulus-response (S-R) connection-forming capacity. Bever retails the argument thus:

> . . . the more [S-R] connections are accumulated in one's first language use, the fewer are available for a second language. Thus by age fifteen, the child has spent twelve years talking in his first language and, in effect, has used up the mechanisms that underlie the formation of new S-R links in language. (Bever, 1981: 181)

There are a number of problems with any explanation based on behaviourist learning theory. The first, and most obvious, is that, according to a very wide consensus, 'learning theory cannot in principle account for the acquisition of linguistic knowledge in the L1, and therefore cannot be resorted to for an explanation of a critical period in an L2' (Bever, 1981: 181). In his review of Skinner's (1957) book, Chomsky (1959) pointed out the difficulties posed by the attempt to extrapolate from the training of laboratory animals to perform relatively simple tasks to the complexity and unboundedness of human language behaviour. Another difficulty with the behaviourist account is that 'such a view would predict that learning a third language would be more difficult (and less possible with age) and learning a fourth language more difficult still' (Bever, 1981: 181), whereas, in fact, learning a fourth language before age 15 appears to be no harder than learning the second. A third problem with this account has to do with the negative and undifferentiated view of language transfer that it implies. Behaviourist theory recognises 'positive' as well as 'negative' transfer, but in applications of the theory to L2 acquisition it is almost always the 'interfering' role of the L1 that is emphasised. It is surely plausible to suppose that the experience of having already learned one language will actually help the L2 learner in many ways. Precisely how much of the experience will be helpful will depend, in part at least, on how closely the languages in question resemble each other and on the learner's perceptions of such resemblances (cf. e.g. Kellerman, 1977, 1979; Ringbom, 1987; Singleton, 1987a, 1987b).

Another approach which relates the age factor to language transfer is that of Flege (1981). This adopts a cognitivist rather than a behaviourist perspective and does not assume that younger learners are superior in an absolute sense – only that very young learners have a better chance of acquiring a native accent than older learners. Flege's explanation for this is that very young children acquiring two languages learn the sounds of these languages independently, whereas older learners 'translate' the sounds of one language in terms of the phonological categories of the other. After reviewing some of the studies on L2 accent acquisition and noting the contradictoriness of the evidence, Flege concludes that 'there does not appear to be evidence of a fundamental difference between children and adults in their ability to learn to pronounce an L2' (p. 447). However, he goes on to point to evidence from Leopold (1947) and Major (1977) suggesting that young children who acquire two languages simultaneously before about age three produce both with an authentic accent. Flege's tentative inference is that '[p]erhaps such children learn the sounds occurring in the phonetic surface of their two languages independently, much as if each sound were a separate phoneme in an enriched, pan-language system' (Flege, 1981: 448).

The next stage in Flege's argument is the citation of evidence that, whereas before about age three bilingual children do not seem to be aware that they are speaking two different languages (McLaughlin, 1978; Redlinger & Park, 1980), somewhat older bilinguals do distinguish between their languages and seem to be aware of the similarity of the sounds these contain (Tervoort, 1979).

> For example, a young American boy speaking French used English words spoken with a French accent when he didn't know the French equivalent (Valette, 1964). English-speaking children have been

observed trying to 'speak' Spanish by producing English words with a Spanish accent (Hernandez-Chavez, cited in Ervin-Tripp, 1974). American children exposed to French for only a month showed in an informal experiment that they were able to produce English words with French sounds (Ervin-Tripp, 1974). This kind of linguistic behavior suggests that even children are capable of *phonological translation* (Catford, 1965) between the sounds of two languages, a factor that may potentially influence their production of sounds in both languages. (Flege, 1981: 449)

Flege illustrates the principle of phonological translation from data on voice onset time (VOT)[1] differences for stops produced by monolingual speakers of English, monolingual speakers of French and French/English bilinguals. In monolingual speech French and English stops are realised differently in terms of VOT. However, studies by Caramazza *et al.* (1973) and Caramazza and Yeni-Komshian (1974) reveal that the VOT of English stops produced by bilingual French Canadians is intermediate between monolingual English and French values. To Flege this suggests that 'the French Canadians based their production of English words on a composite of corresponding sounds ... occurring in both languages' and that the compromise arrived at 'may reflect a restructuring of the phonetic space so that it encompasses two languages' (Flege, 1981: 451). Convergence of this kind will, according to Flege's hypothesis, occur whenever L2 learning commences after the learner has reached an age where he/she is aware that the L2 in question is different from that already at his/her disposal. The hypothesis predicts that even where learners beginning L2 learning after this stage appear to acquire a native accent, fine-grained acoustic analysis will reveal compromise features of the kind discussed.

Much of the more recent work by Flege and his colleagues has demonstrated the importance of environmental factors for L2 pronunciation, with time spent in a country where the target language is in use (Riney & Flege, 1998) and time spent in the company of native speakers (Flege *et al.*, 1997) emerging as major determinants of quality of L2 accent (see also, e.g. Guion *et al.*, 2000; Piske *et al.*, 2001). Flege continues to see a trade-off between L2 and L1 proficiency and in his Speech Learning Model (Flege, 1995) continues to take an 'interactionist' line according to which 'the phonic elements of the L1 subsystem necessarily influence influence phonic elements in the L2 system, and vice versa' (Flege, 1999: 106). According to this view, as L1 phonology continues to be refined, its influence on L2 phonology acquisition continuously increases accordingly: 'L1 vowel and consonant categories become more powerful attractors of the vowels and consonants encountered in an L2 as they develop through childhood and into adolescence' (Flege, 2002: 238). This implies that in older L2 beginners, the pattern will tend to be for the L2 accent to be more highly influenced by L1 phonology and therefore less authentic than in the case of younger L2 beginners, whereas these latter, on the other hand, may acquire a good L2 accent at the expense of their L1 accent.

Environmental and language competition factors are also central to Jia and Aaronson's (1999) approach. They point out that older arrivals in an L2 environment tend to make choices which bring them into frequent contact with fellow native speakers of their L1 and which limit their contact with the L2; such choices may have to do with the avoidance of isolation in the new environment and/or the desire to maintain a particular linguistic and cultural identity. Fewer choices may be available to younger arrivals – because of compulsory schooling. In any case, their linguistico-cultural identity is unlikely to be as fully formed as that of their elders, and so the desire to maintain it may be much weaker. According to Jia and Aaronson (1999) what results from these contrasting circumstances is that, whereas immigrants arriving at ages older than 10 tend to maintain their L1, immigrants arriving before age 10 seem to switch their dominant language from the home language to the language of the host country.

It seems then that acquiring an L2 in childhood may impinge significantly on L1 development. This notion is in line with current views on the interaction between L2 and L1 in general (see e.g. Cook, 1992, 1995, 2003; Herdina & Jessner, 2002; Kecskes & Papp, 2000) and has a fairly long history. Jakobovits (1970) talks about the 'balance effect', and claims that Macnamara's (1966) review of 77 studies of situations where an L2 figured in the primary school curriculum 'confirmed the balance effect indicating that on the whole children who were required to learn, use, or be educated in two languages had a weaker grasp of either language than monolingual children' (Jakobovits, 1970: 57). Macnamara's own investigation of the effects of Irish language instruction in Irish primary schools appears to indicate that English-speaking Irish pupils 'do not achieve the same standard in written English as British children who have not learned a second language' and that they do not achieve either 'the same standard in written Irish as native-speakers of Irish' (Macnamara, 1966: 35). Macnamara's interpretation of his results is controversial (see e.g. Cummins, 1977), and other studies paint a more positive picture of early bilingualism. Jakobovits refers to Peal and Lambert's (1962) study, which 'shows that French-Canadian children in one bilingual setting in Montreal who have developed a good grasp of English are superior in both verbal and non-verbal intelligence to their French-speaking monolingual peers' (Jakobovits, 1970: 58). Also, Swain and Lapkin's (1982) review of research based on French immersion schemes for Canadian Anglophones (cf. also Lapkin & Swain,

1990) yields no evidence of long-term negative effects on L1 development but rather evidence of improved language development generally, especially in respect of metalinguistic awareness (Swain & Lapkin, 1982: 36f.). Moreover, as Hamers and Blanc (2000: 89) point out, advantages for bilinguals have been found in relation to abilities such as the reconstruction of perceptual situations, verbal originality, sensitivity to semantic relations, performance in rule-discovery tasks, divergent thinking, verbal transformation, symbol substitution, grammatical judgement and analogical reasoning (cf. Bialystok, 2001, 2002b).

How is one to reconcile the seemingly diametrically opposed results regarding the effects of early bilingualism? Cummins (1984: 101) draws attention to the prejudice against bilingualism which existed in the first half of the 20th century, when many of the studies with negative results were carried out and also (1984: 103) notes that the '[f]ailure to control for factors such as SES [socioeconomic status], urban-rural differences and language of testing render [*sic*] most of the findings uninterpretable'. In addition, he refers to Lambert's (1975) observation that the early studies mostly focused on immigrant or minority children whose L1 was being replaced by the language of the majority population. Likewise, almost all of the more recent studies showing negative effects for early bilingualism 'have been conducted in Western cultures with children of minority groups schooled in the majority language' (Hamers & Blanc, 2000: 93). This kind of bilingualism Lambert calls 'subtractive' in contrast to the 'additive' bilingualism of children whose L1 is dominant, prestigious and not threatened with replacement by their L2. Cummins comments (1984: 107) that most studies showing advantages associated with bilingualism have been carried out in 'additive' situations. The distinction between additive and subtractive situations is illustrated by differences between French immersion programmes in Canada and what are called 'immersion' but are in fact 'submersion' programmes in the United States:

> The Canadian French immersion programs include instruction in, and about, the first language. Once mother tongue instruction is introduced, it is provided on a continuing basis throughout schooling. Few minority language students [in the United States] enjoy this privilege in public school systems. Yet, given the overwhelming use of the majority language in school and the wider environment, speakers of a minority language constantly face the possibility of the second (i.e. majority) language replacing the first . . .
>
> Furthermore, in the French immersion programs, all children who enter the program at the primary level do so with the same level of target language skills – none. This is in contrast to the situation – which

in the United States is often referred to as 'immersion' – where children who are to learn the target language are mixed together with other children who are native speakers of the target language . . . Additionally, their teachers may not understand the children's first language, which, it has been suggested, may lead to the teaching of a prescribed curriculum which relates little to the existing interests or knowledge of the children . . . (Swain, 1981b: 18f.)

'Subtractive' situations, which are posited as leading to the impoverishment, ultimately the suppression of the L1, seem not to be particularly effective at promoting L2 proficiency either. It has been suggested that they result in a kind of 'double semilingualism' (see e.g. Skutnabb-Kangas, 1984: 248–63). Examples of reports of 'double semilingualism' cited by Skutnabb-Kangas are:

Bloomfield's (1927) description of an Indian called White-Thunder, who spoke less English than Menomini, and whose Menomini was 'atrocious';

Hymes's observation on the Oucchua Indians who 'so to speak gave up their Quechua before they had learnt Spanish' (Hymes, 1974: 72);

Claims by researchers such as Toukomaa (1972) and Heyman (1973) that the language proficiency of Finnish immigrants in Sweden in both Finnish and Swedish is deficient.

According to Cummins (e.g. 1984, 1991), language proficiency in its cognitive-academic dimensions is not to be conceived of as language-specific but as a common base underlying performance in any of the learner's languages. On this view L2 cognitive-academic proficiency is a function of L1 cognitive-academic proficiency – at least in the initial stages of L2 acquisition; in addition, L1 cognitive-academic proficiency must be established to a certain threshold point if cognitive deficits are to be avoided, and an L2 proficiency threshold must also be attained if cognitive advantages are to accrue. Evidence for this perspective comes from the earlier-quoted study by Cummins *et al.* (1984) of Japanese and Vietnamese immigrant students in Toronto, whose scores on academic measures of English correlated positively with their scores on academic measures of, respectively, Japanese and Vietnamese. Similarly Skutnabb-Kangas and Toukomaa, in their 1976 study (also referred to earlier) found that the level of proficiency of Finnish immigrants on arrival in Sweden was important not only for the maintenance and continued development of L1 skills, but also for the development of cognitive academic skills in Swedish. Other relevant findings include those of Rosier and Farella (1976) in respect of Navajo students at Rock Point in the United States who had previously been schooled through English alone, and whose performance in English was below normal grade level. When these students were subsequently provided with a bilingual programme which introduced literacy through Navajo, their levels of English performance improved markedly, and, as they proceeded through the grades, moved progressively closer to national norms (see also, e.g. Duncan & De Avila, 1979; Hakuta & Diaz, 1984; Lemmon & Goggin, 1989).[2]

Cummins frames his interdependence hypothesis in terms of L2 dependence on L1. However, there is also evidence of L2 proficiency having an impact on L1 proficiency. Hamers and Blanc cite a report which gives an account of Swedish children learning English as an L2 and which notes that 'elementary-school children who already had a high competence in their mother tongue and who started to learn a foreign language at an early age would improve their competence in their mother tongue more than peers who did not have exposure to a foreign language' (Hamers & Blanc, 2000: 98). One can also find evidence of bidirectionality in Swain and Lapkin's above mentioned (1982) finding that where immersion students differ from non-immersion students in terms of general language development they typically outperform the latter 'in such areas as punctuation, spelling, vocabulary and usage' (p. 37). The point is that in the case of Canadian-type immersion programmes, while literacy skills are not necessarily established in the L1 prior to the introduction of the L2, they are gradually introduced, and in any case the L1 has been established to a very high level so that 'most immersion children come to school with the prerequisites to literacy that Wells's (1979) study has indicated to be important' (Swain, 1981b: 27).

There are undoubtedly difficulties with the interdependence perspective. As noted in Chapter 4, it is not clear precisely what is to be included under cognitive-academic proficiency. Another problem is that the hypothesis addresses only cases where languages are acquired sequentially and is silent on the question of the simultaneous acquisition of two or more languages. A third is that it leaves largely out of account influences which are not language-related on cognitive-academic development and indeed on language development itself. On the other hand, the interdependence hypothesis does seem to provide the beginnings of a plausible explanation for the differing outcomes of immersion and submersion. It also offers a different angle on the discussion of the topic of developmental competition between languages by suggesting that knowledge of one language can actually support and improve knowledge of another language. This more positive approach is at odds with the emphasis in behaviourist accounts on 'interference'. It also might be interpreted as running counter to Flege's and Jia and Aaronson's idea that the longer experience (and the continued heavy use) of the L1 in older L2 beginners supplies an explanation for the fact that such learners generally do not ultimately attain the same levels of L2 proficiency as younger learners. However, such an interpretation would be ill conceived.

It should be remembered that the interdependence hypothesis relates only to certain aspects of language proficiency – roughly those which involve decontextualised and cognitively demanding uses of language. However unsatisfactory the definition of cognitive-academic proficiency may be, it can presumably be taken to exclude such dimensions as phonetics/phonology, everyday lexis, and the morphosyntax of routine oral communication. The interdependence hypothesis states that in these kinds of areas young L2 learners are not dependent on the establishment of a common base via the L1, which is why they may do better than older learners in these domains. However, the corollary of this position is that in such areas, even if a common base is established, it is not operative in a supportive role in respect of the L2. In respect of such areas, therefore, the hypothesis has nothing to say about the proposition there is developmental competition between languages. It is clear from the work of Flege and his colleagues that in the phonetic/phonological sphere there is indeed competition between L1 and L2 phonetics/phonology – which results in various kinds of outcomes which are not found in the phonetics/phonology of the monoglot native speaker. One can assume similar processes in respect of everyday vocabulary and morphosyntax. Certainly, research into the operations of the bilingual and multilingual mental lexicon (see e.g. Cenoz *et al.*, 2003; Singleton, 1999: Chapter 4) clearly demonstrates L1-L2-Ln interaction in the lexical sphere; and syntactic research has yielded much the same conclusions in respect of grammar (see e.g. Braidi, 1999: chapter 2). It is also worth recalling that, as we saw in Chapter 4, at the level of fine linguistic detail even very young L2 beginners differ from native speakers (see e.g. Ekberg, 1998; Flege, 1999; Hyltenstam & Abrahamsson, 2000, 2003), which suggests that L1-L2 interaction/competition is present at all ages and at all stages.

A further point to bear in mind is that, as far as L2 acquisition by immigrants is concerned, it is likely that the vast majority of child migrants do not receive the kind of support for their L1 that Cummins posits as necessary for the common base to be put in place. This implies that in most cases their L2 acquisition is 'subtractive' and replacive. For example, English-only programmes for Spanish-speaking minorities in the United States, which are labelled as 'immersion education' in fact lead to a situation where the children in question become essentially Anglophone in the academic context, while the prevalence of English, their L2, in the media and in most public domains means that opportunities for the fostering of cognitive-academic skills in the L1 outside the classroom are also severely limited (cf. e.g. Johnson & Swain, 1997: 12). The implication of this, according to Cummins's hypothesis, is that the interaction between the L1 and the L2 is not positive and mutully supportive. The common base is not established and there is no bulwark against competitivity between languages – with the result that – according to Cummins's hypothesis – most immigrant children will end up with their L2 dominant and their L1 weakened in precisely the way Jia and Aaronson suggest (cf. Bialystok, 1997: 123).

Neurolinguistics and the Critical Period

We turn now to the best known category of explanation of the putative age factor in language acquisition, namely that which invokes the maturation of the brain. In order to contextualise these arguments it may be worth borrowing a few sentences from Obler and Gjerlow's (1999) introduction to the topic:

> . . . the largest portion, and by far the most important for issues in speech and language is the cerebrum . . . The cerebrum . . . is divided into two hemispheres, right and left. The cerebral hemispheres are not entirely separate: they are connected by fiber bundles, the most important of which is the corpus callosum. The surface of the cerebral hemispheres is the cortex[3] which is distinguished by its convolutions: the hills and valleys known as gyri and sulci respectively. (Obler & Gjerlow, 1999: 17f.)

The way in which the cerebrum relates to the functioning of the organism is primarily contralateral in nature (Obler & Gjerlow, 1999: 23f.). That is to say, the left hemisphere is largely responsible for what happens on the right side of the body, and the right hemisphere is largely responsible for what happens on the left side. For example, if one stimulates a cortical area in the left hemisphere, this occasions movement in muscles on the right side of the body. However, there is some representation in each of the two hemispheres for ipsilateral or same-side muscles. This pattern is also found in respect of the control of perception. Thus, most of the auditory and visual pathways are contralateral, but ipsilateral pathways also exist.

Since the 1860s neurologists have noted a connection between lesions of the left hemisphere and speech disturbance – with lesions in left cerebral hemisphere in adults leading to irreversible forms of language breakdown or 'aphasia'- and have concluded that language functions in the brain are generally lateralised to the left. On the basis of certain exceptions to this tendency involving left-handers, for whom, given the contralateral relationship between cerebrum and functions, the right hemisphere is in general dominant, it was also for a while hypothesised that in the case of the left-handed it was the right hemisphere that was dominant for language too. However, further research showed that, in fact, most left-handers (98%) also had their language functions principally subserved by the left hemisphere (see e.g. Penfield & Roberts, 1959: 102). The issue of which hemisphere does what is a recurring theme in neurological discussions of the critical period. Such discussions have indeed principally concentrated on cerebral plasticity and hemispheric specialisation. Accordingly, much of the present section is devoted to debate in this area. However, it is worth noting that one neurological approach discussed here, the so-called 'thalamus theory' shifts the focus from the cerebrum to the area surrounding the brain stem.

Cerebral plasticity in children and the 'ganglionic record'

Penfield and Roberts (1959) adduce evidence (see above, Chapter 3) that, when disease or injury damages speech areas in the brain, transference of speech functions from the affected dominant hemisphere to the healthy minor hemisphere is less problematic for children than for adults. Evidence continues to accrue of a remarkable degree of neural plasticity available to the immature brain (Eisele & Aram, 1995). Generally, young children with injuries to the language centres of the brain resulting in acquired childhood aphasia (ACA) make a remarkable recovery, in many cases recovering language functioning to age-appropriate levels. The onset of ACA typically follows a period of normal language development but it can be observed in children with lesions acquired within the first months of life.

Damage to the brain in childhood can arise from a variety of causes including:

- cerebral trauma (head injury e.g. road traffic accident, gunshot wound, fall);
- cerebral vascular accident (stroke – i.e. arterial blockage or bleeding);
- asphyxia (serious depletion of oxygen supply to the brain);
- brain tumour;
- infections (e.g. measles, whooping-cough);
- poisons;
- ionising radiation;
- seizure (convulsive) disorder.

According to Lees (1993), effects range from a localised, focal lesion (e.g. a gunshot wound) to damage to the whole brain (e.g. in the case of cranial irradiation associated with the treatment of a brain tumour), but ACA is most likely to result from focal brain damage. Research suggests that the majority of children with significant lesions to the language areas of the left hemisphere attain age-appropriate levels of language ability (Aram, 1998; Kolb & Whishaw, 1996; Lees, 1993), although a growing number of longitudinal studies are documenting language delay in this population and subtle linguistic deficits in older children with brain lesions (see below).

From evidence of language recovery in brain-damaged children Penfield and Roberts argue that after age nine language learning of all kinds becomes increasingly hampered by stiffness and rigidity in the brain, so that 'when languages are taken up for the first time in the second decade of life, it is difficult . . . to achieve a good result . . . because it is unphysiological' (Penfield & Roberts, 1959: 255). A similar point of view is championed by Lamendella, who claims that 'mature neural systems are less adaptable than immature systems, and this puts the adult SL [second language] learner at a disadvantage' (Lamendella, 1977: 191).

Penfield also notes that electrical stimulation of the brain during an operation will sometimes 'cause the patient to re-experience the past', from which he infers the existence of 'a ganglionic record of past experience which preserves the individual's current perceptions in astonishing detail' and for which he assumes 'some subsequent purpose' (Penfield, 1958: 34f.). The relevance of the 'ganglionic record' to language learning is, he claims, that early experience of an L2 will never be wasted. He cites the cases of his own children who were exposed only to German in the nursery from the ages of six months and 18 months and who subsequently, at ages three and four, entered a French nursery school, where they spent two years. When, years later in an English-medium school, they were introduced to French and German as ordinary curriculum subjects, they found the work easy and had good accents, from which Penfield infers that '[h]idden away in the brain of each were the speech units of all three languages waiting to be employed in the expansion of a vocabulary which normally takes place in later school-years' (Penfield & Roberts, 1959: 254f.).

Considerable scepticism has been expressed about Penfield's perspective. Dechert (1995) argues that Penfield's views in relation to L2 learning owe more to the above-described experience of immersing his own children in foreign languages at an early age than to his work as a scientist. With regard to the notion of a 'ganglionic record' Christophersen (1973: 49) observes that Penfield's patients needed prodding with an electric wire, that the return of the memories was entirely random, that the subjects in question were suffering from epilepsy, and that there was no evidence regarding the veracity of the alleged early memories. Concerning the claim that adults find language learning difficult because beyond the first decade of life it is 'unphysiological', Newmark and Reibel (1968: 154f.) pose the question: if it is 'unphysiological' for an adult brain to learn a new language, how is it possible at all? They note that many adult learners learn new languages very well, which seems to cast doubt on the idea that adults are qualitatively different kinds of L2 learners. Penfield himself admits that it is 'not impossible' for adults to learn an L2 (Penfield & Roberts, 1959: 225), citing Joseph Conrad as an example of an adult L2 beginner who became a 'master' of his target language (English). He also undermines his own case in his claim that adults exposed to the Berlitz Method 'do quite well' (Penfield & Roberts, 1959: 24).

More recent accounts of age effects in L2 learning have continued to posit a decline in cerebral plasticity as the underlying cause of such effects. One such account is that of Pulvermüller and Schumann (1994). Pulvermüller and Schumann note that, as the different areas of the brain mature, the axons[4] of neurons[5] in those areas are progressively wrapped by glial cells, whose purpose is to supply the neurons with nutrition so that they can conduct electrical signals more efficiently. This process is often labelled myelination – after the substance myelin which is contained in the glial cells. Pulvermüller and Schumann acknowledge that there are no clearly established causal links between myelination and loss of plasticity, and they accept the possibility that myelination may be 'an epiphenomenon of an unknown process which also affects plasticity' (Pulvermüller & Schumann, 1994: 710f.). However, they go on to discuss several mechanisms associated with myelination that might have a role – the restriction of space for neuronal growth and the forging of new contacts, the reduction of plasticity of the synapses or connections between neurons, and the production by glial cells of 'neurite growth inhibitors', which reduce axonal growth. Their claim is that in most people plasticity declines in the language areas of the brain until around puberty and then remains low, and that this is what explains age effects in language acquisition. On the other hand, they recognise that this does not account for the fact that some early learners of two languages do not consistently attain native levels in both, nor that some older L2 beginners attain native-like levels in their target language. The former effect they account for in terms of varying levels of motivation, and the latter in terms of a speculation that 'the level of ultimate myelination and plasticity of the language cortex may vary among individuals, allowing some late learners to achieve native speech norms' and also that very high motivation may cause levels of activity in the midbrain that compensate for loss of plasticity in the cortex (cf. section below on motivation).

Lateralisation

Alongside Penfield, the other major figure in early manifestations of the neurological school of thought on the age factor in language acquisition is Lenneberg. Like Penfield, Lenneberg pointed to the remarkable recovery of children presenting with ACA. The early reports (pre-1970) of acquired aphasia in childhood were clinical observations made by neurologists and clinicians such as, besides Lenneberg himself (1967), Freud (1897) and Guttmann (1942). Such reports revealed that persistent language disorders appeared to be rare in children presenting with right hemiplegia – i.e. paralysis of the right side of the body. Prior to the advent of modern brain imaging procedures hemiplegia was taken to be an indicator of unilateral brain damage. Traditionally, ACA was conceived of as a homogeneous disorder characterised by the following features:

- a period of mutism or markedly reduced expressive output;
- non-fluent telegraphic language;
- word-finding deficits;
- lack of jargon, paraphasias (incorrect word-use) or neologisms;
- relatively preserved auditory comprehension.

ACA was seen often to be linked to right hemisphere lesions. Early accounts of ACA tend to be characterised by a favourable prognosis, complete and rapid recovery often being reported, but prognosis has always been recognised to be related to age at onset, a more favourable prognosis being associated with early onset ACA. Lenneberg (1967) observed that children up to 10 years of age presenting with ACA due to unilateral lesions made a full and rapid recovery while children over 10 years had persistent linguistic deficits. He argued that there are differences between the functional organisation of language in the developing brain and the adult brain – on the basis of: (1) the qualitatively different pattern of language impairment in children as compared with adults following focal brain damage, (2) the greater incidence of linguistic deficit resulting from right hemisphere lesions in children as compared with adults, and (3) the relationship between age at onset and recovery,

According to Lenneberg, left hemisphere dominance for language comes about through the ontogenetic specialisation of the two hemispheres, which is contingent on the maturation of the two hemispheres and exposure to the linguistic environment. On this view, initially both hemispheres have equal potential (equipotentiality) with respect to specialisation for language functions, but there subsequently ensues a gradual establishment of left hemisphere language specialisation and a decrease in the involvement of the right hemisphere in language functioning. According to this perspective, if a young child suffers a brain injury, it is possible for the right hemisphere to become specialised for language and thus for full language recovery to be achieved. This potential of the right hemisphere to assume control of language is seen as being closed down at the onset of puberty.

Lenneberg's views on the critical period are of a piece with his general biological optique on language. He claims that there are good reasons for suspecting the presence of 'biological endowments in man that make the human form of communication uniquely possible for our species' (Lenneberg, 1964; reprint: 32). These reasons fall under five general headings:

(a) *Anatomic and physiologic correlates*
There is increasing evidence that verbal behaviour is related to a great number of morphological and functional specializations . . . and . . . sensory and cognitive specializations prerequisite for language.
(b) *Developmental schedule*
The onset of speech is an extremely regular phenomenon appearing at a certain time in the child's physical development and following a fixed sequence of events . . .
(c) *Difficulty in suppressing language*
The ability to learn language is so deeply rooted in man that children learn it even in the face of dramatic handicaps.
(d) *Language cannot be taught*
There is no evidence that any non-human form has the capacity to acquire even the most primitive stages of language development.
(e) *Language universals*
Although language families are so different, one from the other, that we cannot find any historical connexion between them, every language, without exception, is based on the same *universal principles* of semantics, syntax and phonology. (Lenneberg, 1964; reprint: 32f.)

Lenneberg contends 'that the appearance of language is primarily dependent upon the maturational development of states of readiness within the child' (Lenneberg, 1967: 242). The claim is not that environmental contingencies play no role, but that the way in which environmental stimulation is utilised during a particular phase of development is determined by internal biological factors. He also suggests that 'the primary acquisition of language is predicated upon a certain developmental stage which is quickly outgrown at the age of puberty (1967: 142). For Lenneberg the crucial aspect as far as the critical period for language acquisition is concerned is what he sees as the progressive specialisation of the cerebral hemispheres. He interprets the evidence as indicating that, from childhood on, one of the cerebral hemispheres, usually the left, is dominant for language functions. He recognises that the minor hemisphere plays some role in subserving linguistic communication, but claims that this role diminishes with age, as the hemispheres become more and more specialised and language functions become increasingly lateralised. He posits that the lateralisation process is complete by puberty, and that at this point the developmental phase of language readiness is over. He cites in this connection (cf. Chapter 3) Basser's (1962) survey of the clinical literature on unilateral brain damage and evidence relating to hemispherectomy. The former, he claims, indicates that injuries to the right hemisphere cause more language disturbance in children than in adults, while the latter (cf. above) suggests that children are able completely to transfer the speech function to the minor hemisphere, whereas adults are not.

As we saw in Chapter 3, Lenneberg links his notion of critical period acquisition to his observation of the language development of deaf children and of Down syndrome children. He also makes the connection between lateralisation and L2 acquisition:

> Most individuals of average intelligence are able to learn a second language after the beginning of their second decade, although the incidence of 'language-learning-blocks' rapidly increases after puberty. Also automatic acquisition from mere exposure to a given language seems to disappear after this age, and foreign languages have to be taught and learned through a conscious and labored effort. Foreign accents cannot be overcome easily after puberty. (Lenneberg, 1967: 176)

This point of view, which was immediately popularised in L2 research circles by, for example, Scovel (1969), is reminiscent of Penfield's suggestion that language learning in the second decade of life is 'unphysiological'. Newmark and Reibel's critique of that suggestion (see above) applies here too. Lenneberg attempts to dodge such criticism by claiming that L1 acquisition provides a basis for a degree of L2 learning in adulthood thanks to language universals:

> . . . a person can learn to communicate in a foreign language at the age of forty. This does not trouble our basic hypothesis on age limitations because we may assume that the cerebral organization for language learning as such has taken place during childhood, and since natural languages tend to resemble one another in many fundamental aspects . . . , the matrix for language skills is present. (Lenneberg, 1967: 176)

However, a command of these 'fundamental aspects' would fall far short of enabling one to 'communicate in a foreign language'.[6] One notes that those who share Lenneberg's position concerning a biological endowment for language now take the view, as Cook (1995: 63) points out, that what is universal in language is merely a broad set of syntactic principles, that languages diverge in their lexicons (interpreted broadly) and that 'language acquisition is in essence a matter of determining lexical idiosyncrasies' (Chomsky, 1989: 44). Clearly, if language acquisition is mostly a matter of learning language-particular specifics, the notion of a universal matrix triggered by L1 acquisition is of very limited value as an explanation of successful L2 acquisition.

To return to the lateralisation question, a modicum of empirical evidence interpretable as supporting the hypothesis of maturation-related progression in lateralisation comes from Woods's (1980) results from a study which tested the Performance and Verbal IQ of 50 patients who had sustained unilateral non-progressive lesions during infancy or childhood.

> . . . perinatal lesions of the right hemisphere lower Verbal IQ ratings, whereas childhood lesions of the right hemisphere do not affect the verbal ratings. This more limited effect of 'later' right-hemisphere lesions is found even with damage incurred early in the first decade. (Woods, 1980: 69)

On the other hand, the validity of such tests as indicators of linguistic impairment is questionable, since, as Dennis and Whitaker point out (1977: 99), they do not directly measure knowledge of linguistic structure.

There is much more evidence challenging Lenneberg's position on lateralisation. In his re-analysis of Basser's (1962) data Krashen (1973 – cf. above, Chapter 3) notes that 'in all cases of injury to the right hemisphere resulting in speech disturbance, the lesion was incurred before five' (Krashen, 1973: 65), and that: '[s]tudies that include descriptions of children injured after five indicate that the effect of right lesions in older children is the same as in adults' (1973: 65). He concludes from the above 'that lateralization is established around age five' (1973: 65). His review of the evidence concerning the ability of the minor hemisphere to take over when the dominant hemisphere is disabled leads to the same conclusion, since again in all cases where transfer was successfully effected the lesion had occurred before age five (1973: 67f.). In the same paper and others (e.g. Krashen & Harshman, 1972), Krashen reviews evidence from dichotic listening tests[7] carried out on children ranging in age from four to nine years. In such reviews he finds '[n]o significant change in degree of lateralization or right ear advantage . . . from four to nine' (Krashen, 1973: 66) and a degree of lateralisation in the children which is 'the same as that shown by adults tested under similar conditions' (1973) – all of which again points to lateralisation being completed pre-age-five.

Kinsboume (see e.g. Kinsboume, 1975; Kinsbourne & Hiscock, 1977) is sceptical about the whole notion of progressive lateralisation, claiming (Kinsbourne, 1975: 245) that such an idea has no model whatever in the neurophysiological literature for any species. With respect to the data used by Lenneberg to justify his claim that for children damage to either side of the brain is likely to cause aphasia, he calls into question the trustworthiness and the representativeness of the case material, the reliability of the evidence cited for lateralised lesion and aphasia, and the logic of the inferences drawn. For example, he notes (Kinsbourne, 1975: 245f.) that whereas a properly conducted investigation of effects of right hemisphere damage would need to show (1) selective damage in the right hemisphere and (2) language effects of such damage, it is (1) difficult to establish lateralisation of brain damage in the absence of autopsy and (2) difficult to interpret the evidence presented of language interruption, which typically relates only to output and usually consists merely in a report that the child did not speak to the clinician. His view is that at best Lenneberg's data accord only with the weaker claim that the younger brain is more adaptable, better able to transfer particular functions from one hemisphere to the other (Kinsbourne & Hiscock, 1977: 174). As Kinsbourne and Hiscock illustrate, much evidence suggests that laterality of language functions is established earlier than even Krashen suggests. Many dichotic experiments (e.g. Bever, 1971; Gilbert & Climan, 1974; Ingram, 1975) yield a right ear advantage for verbal material in children as young as two and three. The results of studies by Kinsbourne and his associates point in the same direction: '[a]symmetries are seen in children as young as three years, and the asymmetries remain constant until age 13' (Kinsbourne & Hiscock, 1977: 186).

Other evidence indicates that asymmetry of function can be traced back to an even earlier point. Segalowitz (1983b) reviews a range of studies which suggest that such asymmetry of function is actually present in early infancy – including the following:

> Barnet *et al.*'s (1974) discovery of a significant interaction between stimuli – speech (name of child being tested) versus a click – and the event-related potential (ERP) amplitude over the left and right hemispheres, the name producing a greater left-sided ERP, the clicks a greater right-sided ERP.

> Molfese's (1977) report that in an experiment testing the auditory evoked potential – the gross response of a large population of neurons to a stimulus – in the left and right temporal area of infants (mean age 5–8 months), children (mean age 6.0 years) and adults (mean age 24 years), the general pattern for all subjects was that for non-speech

stimuli there was a greater right hemisphere response and for speech stimuli a greater left hemisphere response;

Entus's (1977) study, which involved the administration of a dichotic test 48 infants between the ages of 22 and 140 days, using music and speech as stimuli and measuring reaction in terms of the infant's increase in rate of sucking on a nipple when the stimulus was changed, and which found that in the speech experiment 71% of the infants showed a right-ear superiority; and in the music experiment 79% showed a left-ear superiority;

Glanville *et al.*'s (1977) finding that heart-rate dishabituation was greater when speech was played to the right ear of infants, and conversely dishabituation was greater when musical tones were played to the left ear;

Hammer's (1977) finding of a greater incidence in eye movements to the right when listening to speech (through both ears) and more left movements when listening to white noise[9];

Gardiner and Walter's (1977) study, which measured reaction by electroencephalogram (EEG)[8] and which also found assymetric responses to running speech versus music in very young infants;

Segalowitz and Chapman's (1980) research which looked at responses in infants to speech and music in terms of limb tremor movements and which too established asymmetric response patterns.

Despite some reported failures in replicating the above findings (see e.g. Vargha-Khadem & Corballis, 1979), such evidence in favour of early asymmetry of function is clearly impressive.

The notions of initial equipotentiality, early diffuse representation of language and later hemispheric specialisation are further challenged by more recent discussion of ACA. For example, Woods and Teuber (1978) suggest that the higher incidence of right hemisphere involvement in ACA in earlier studies may be due to undetected bi-lateral involvement stemming from pre-antibiotic infections and a shift in aetiology from diffuse systemic bacterial infections to more discrete focal lesions. In addition, in this connection, one can note that Lenneberg's conclusions were based on clinical observations of clients presenting with hemiplegia and pre-dated the advent of modern brain imaging; accordingly, in some of the cases in question brain damage may have been less or more diffuse than was apparent from clinical observation. Cranberg *et al.*'s (1987) and Van Dongen *et al.*'s (1985) findings are also relevant; they demonstrate that ACA occurs with greater frequency in children with left hemisphere damage, that left hemisphere-related ACA occurs in children as young as age four, and that it may persist up to two years post initial onset. Other studies report specific subtypes of ACA analogous to those seen in adults following left hemisphere brain damage. Woods and Teuber (1978) describe a five-year-old child with damage to the left hemisphere who developed a severe receptive aphasia and expressive jargon-like output, while Van Hout *et al.* (1985) also report cases of children with ACA presenting with receptive dysphasia and neologistic jargon as expressive output. These children had fluent production and concomitant word retrieval deficits that resulted in paraphasias.

Current thinking among ACA researchers is, accordingly, that the left hemisphere becomes specialised in the very early development and localisation of language functioning (Paquier & Van Dongen, 1993). For example, the consensus now seems to be that ACA in left hemisphere damaged children is not especially rare and that it such damage results in approximately equal risk in children as it does in adults. Likewise, the incidence of ACA arising from right hemisphere damage is similar in adults and children (Satz & Bullard-Bates, 1981). There is no evidence for a systematic relationship between age at onset and the long-term linguistic outcome (see e.g. Pitchford 2000; Van Hout *et al.*, 1985); Woods & Teuber, 1978).

Table 5.1 summarises differences which emerge between early and more recent studies of ACA. How can we account for such differences? With respect to linguistic features, the differences centre on fluency of linguistic expression. These differences may be explicable in terms of the duration of the time-lapse between the onset of brain injury and the timing of the initial speech and language assessment. If recovery is timely and assessment delayed, fluent features may be missed. Also. early studies did not have access to brain-imaging technology and relied on impairment of muscular strength or paralysis affecting one side of the body as the clinical indicators of ACA, and it transpires that such symptoms are more often associated with non-fluent types of aphasia. In addition, paraphasias are often revealed by the use of confrontational naming tasks of the kind included in formal speech and language therapy assessment tools, and these have been employed only in the more recent studies. Finally, medical developments have led to a reduction in the rate of childhood mortality and have thus allowed access to information on long-term outcomes and prognosis for children presenting with ACA. With regard to differences in prognoses, later studies report more mixed outcomes and these differences may be

Table 5.1 A summary of the differences between early and recent studies of Acquired Childhood Aphasia

	Early reports (pre-1970)	*Recent studies (post-1970)*
Linguistic features	Homogeneous features	Heterogeneous features similar to adult subtypes
Incidence	Rare but often occurred following right hemisphere lesions	Equal to adults presenting with similar neurological damage
Prognosis	Favourably related to age at onset	No direct relationship to age at onset
Theoretical framework	Progressive lateralisation of language functioning	Early hemispheric specialisation for language functioning

accounted for by the criterion of 'recovery'. Earlier reports often referred to clinical recovery while more recent studies have adopted a more stringent criterion for recovery: recovery to pre-morbid age-appropriate linguistic status as measured by standardised speech and language assessment. Furthermore, more recent studies have tended to group children according to site of lesion damaged as opposed to broad physical consequences of brain damage (e.g. hemiplegia). Some researchers argue (see Eisele & Aram, 1995; Satz *et al.*, 1990) that children's recovery from ACA may be accounted for by a latent activation of alternative non-dominant brain regions following injury rather than initial bilateral representation of speech and language functions.

Anatomical studies, re-analyses of hemispherectomy data and studies of congenitally brain-damaged children also call into question the notion of intial equipotentiality. Anatomical studies of the brains of foetuses and infants (Chi *et al.*, 1977; Wada *et al.*, 1975) cited by Springer and Deutsch (1985: 193; cf. also Obler & Gjerlow, 1999: 70) have found that the temporal plane – or planum temporale – of the left hemisphere tends to be larger than that of the right hemisphere. These findings may have a bearing on the early differential functioning of the hemispheres in respect of language (cf. Witelson, 1983: 128). With regard to hemispherectomy evidence, Dennis and Whitaker (1977) conclude in the light of a review of such evidence and of a study of their own that from the perinatal (newborn) stage onwards the cerebral hemispheres already differ as to the ranges of functions they can most proficiently perform. As far as research into the effects of congenital brain damage is concerned, Stiles *et al.*'s (2002) study of the language acquisition of 10 children with congenital left and right hemisphere damage over a 10-year period found delayed babbling and first words in both groups of children. During the period of early lexical development, the children with right hemisphere damage presented with comprehension delays and the children with left hemisphere lesions presented with production delays. All the children exhibited syntactic delays but the children with lesions in the left temporal cortex were most affected. However, the study found little evidence of the direct lesion site-symptom associations observed in some adult aphasics. Overall, Stiles *et al.*'s findings support the notion of early left hemispheric specialisation

It is possible to argue that, even if the left-hemisphere is specialised from birth onwards, 'this does not necessarily mean that it remains unchanged from infancy to senescence' (Witelson, 1977: 269), nor that it extends to all language functions. With regard to the possibility of further development, one of Molfese's experiments yielded results indicating developmental differences in hemispheric functioning. In this study (1977: 29–33) he measured the auditory evoked potential of adults and eight neonates in response to a speech syllable into which, after 15 repetitions, a voicing change was introduced which crossed the phoneme boundary. In five of the six adults the response to this change came from the left hemisphere, whereas is the six infants in whom a response was registered both hemispheres responded in the same manner. This is taken by Molfese to suggest a developmental dimension to hemispheric asymmetry. Moscovitch (1977: 206f.) suggests that the timetable for any such further development may be different for different functions. His view is that, whereas the lateralisation of certain 'low-level' functions of phonetic and/or phonological character may be 'complete by the first year of life', the sensorimotor cognitive structures underlying the child's early use of syntax and semantics may be 'represented in both hemispheres', in which case 'his meaningful linguistic utterances will be mediated by both hemispheres, although perhaps not to the same degree'. He suggests that 'language becomes more strongly lateralised to the left hemisphere' as the child's linguistic and cognitive skills develop. This approach predicts a multiplicity of critical periods, with the phonetic/phonological one being posited as complete very early on (cf. Seliger's, Walsh and Diller's and Walz's proposals below).

On the other hand, Obler and Gjerlow (1999: 67ff.) cite a study by Aram (1988) which challenges the notion that there are differences between the effects of brain injury at the time around birth as compared with the effects of such injury later in early childhood. In this study an analysis was conducted of the speech of left- and right-hemisphere-damaged children and that of normal controls matched for such factors as age, gender, socioeconomic status and non-neurological health factors. What Aram found was that the language performance of right-hemisphere-damaged children was very similar to that of the controls. The left-hemisphere-damaged children, on the other hand had difficulties with both syntax and the naming of objects. Particularly interesting in the present context is the fact that Aram found absolutely no effect for the age at which the brain injury occurred. This result clearly runs against both the idea that the two hemispheres are equipotential for language at birth and the idea that asymmetry of function in this domain develops with maturation.

In sum, the evidence on lateralisation does not seem to support the notion of a starting point of absolute hemispheric equipotentiality in respect of language functions. Nor does the available evidence clearly favour a developmental position which would postulate a continuing lateralisation process of relatively long duration. We are far from understanding the biological constraints that charcterise linguistic development following early hemispheric damage. However, the evidence does seem to suggest that complete acquisition of all aspects of linguistic functioning requires the normal operation of both hemispheres from the earliest point in development.

Ultimate degree of laterality of functions

A further aspect of the lateralisation issue which merits examination is the question of the ultimate degree of laterality of language functions. Jackson (1865 – see Taylor, 1958) first drew attention to the contribution of the right hemisphere to linguistic performance, suggesting that it might mediate the less propositional, more automatic aspects of language such as emotional utterances. The current view is that the right hemisphere plays a role in language-based communication in those of its aspects that extend beyond the literal or surface aspects of words and sentences (see e.g. Fabbro, 1999: 46f.; Moscovitch, 1983a; Myers, 1994; Obler & Gjerlow, 1999: 78–90; Perecman, 1983). There is also a specifically L2-related dimension to this question; that is to say, some researchers have suggested that the right hemisphere has a more prominent role in respect of L2 processing than in L1 processing, while others have claimed that this is true only where the L2 has been acquired after a certain age.

Much-cited in discussion of right hemisphere participation in language processing is evidence from 'split-brain' patients; that is, patients suffering from severe epileptic conditions who have undergone an operation, known as commissurotomy, which involves the severing of the fibres of the nerve tract linking the two hemispheres of the brain (cerebral commissures), with a view to preventing the spread of epileptic discharges from one hemisphere to the other. This brings about a situation in which the two cerebral hemispheres have to function in isolation from each other. Early research on split-brain subjects (e.g. Gazzaniga, 1970; Levy *et al.*, 1971; Sperry & Gazzaniga, 1967; Sperry *et al.*, 1969) was interpreted as indicating that certain basic linguistic abilities were reflected in both hemispheres (see e.g. Foss & Hakes, 1978: 363; McLaughlin, 1978: 51), Split-brain patients were asked to pick up unseen objects or carry out commands with the left hand; since this is controlled by the contra-lateral hemisphere, such tests were seen as providing information about minor (right) hemispheric functioning. Similarly, words were presented 'to the minor hemisphere (i.e. the left field of vision) and subjects had to indicate with the left hand when the written word matched a spoken word. Whereas split-brain patients were not generally able to name pictures or say printed words shown only to the right hemisphere, if the word they were shown was the name of an object, they were able to select that object from among several others using the left hand. They could also draw pictures of such objects with the left hand, but not with the right hand. Work on split-brain patients was taken further by Zaidel, using an instrument called the Z-lens, which allows the subject to move his/her eyes without restriction during the experiment, while ensuring that only one hemisphere receives visual information from experimental stimuli (see e.g. Zaidel, 1983; Springer & Deutsch, 1985: 38ff.). From Zaidel's auditory vocabulary tests, in which the patient heard a single word and then had to select the corresponding picture from a display viewed through the Z-lens, it emerged that the tested disconnected right hemispheres had 'a surprisingly rich auditory vocabulary' (Zaidel, 1983: 107). Other experiments revealed a (more restricted) reading vocabulary in the disconnected right hemispheres tested, as well as a capacity to distinguish words from non-words.

These results have been taken by some to suggest that the neurological substrates of language functions are not exclusively located in the major hemisphere. This interpretation has, however, been called into question by a researchers such as Gazzaniga (1983), Geschwind (1983) and Millar and Whitaker (1983), who point out that the right hemisphere results obtained in split-brain studies may simply reflect a pre-commissurotomy shift of language functions to the right hemisphere induced by early lesions in the left hemisphere and may be totally unrelated to normal right hemisphere functioning. Also to be noted is work by Sidtis and his collaborators (Holtzmann *et al.*, 1981; Sidtis & Gazzaniga, 1983) suggesting that even after commissurotomy some information may still be shared by both hemispheres. Obler and Gjerlow (1999: 88f.) comment that results from split-brain patients do not undermine the notion that the dominant hemisphere is 'more talkative' – i.e. language-involved – than the minor hemisphere.

Some evidence from normal subjects has also been construed as suggesting a language processing role for the right hemisphere. For example, Moscovitch's reaction-time studies (see e.g. Moscovitch, 1973, 1979, 1983b) show a consistent advantage for the left hemisphere in the identification of tachistoscopically presented words,[10] but also appear to indicate an adequate performance of the right hemisphere on such tasks. Likewise, Zaidel (1983) reports that when a word-identification test with a semantic priming element was used with normal subjects its results suggested that both hemispheres were competent to distinguish words from non-words and that in both cases the decision was facilitated by the prior presentation of a semantically related 'prime'. In the phonological sphere, citing Blumstein and Cooper (1974), Obler and Gerlow (1999: 81) report that dichotic listening test-based studies involving normal subjects which actually appear to show a left ear advantage and therefore right-hemisphere dominance for the processing of both linguistic intonation (e.g. distinguishing questions from statements) and emotion-related intonation. However, the reliability of all of the above evidence is open to doubt, given the speed of brain processes and the collaborative functioning of the two hemispheres in normal subjects (see e.g. Millar & Whitaker, 1983: 88; Obler & Gjerlow, 1999: 30f.).

Neurolinguists consider the best evidence on the question of the role of the right hemisphere to be that which comes from studies of brain-damaged subjects. Damage confined to the right hemisphere results in a variety of cognitive and perceptual problems including deficits in attention, affect, visual perception and also communication deficits at the prosodic, linguistic and discourse levels (Myers, 1999). One oft-cited example of a study involving right hemisphere damaged subjects is that of Hier and Kaplan (1980), which looked at 34 such subjects and found mild verbal comprehension deficits – specifically, difficulties in grasping spatial and passive relationships and problems in interpreting proverbs. In the light of Hier and Kaplan's and other similar studies, and of their own experiments involving 10 right-hemisphere-damaged patients, Berndt and Caramazza (1982) conclude that right hemisphere damage results in difficulties in the integration of verbal information entailing some kind of cognitive transformation (e.g. relating *not small to big)*, and therefore that the contribution of the right hemisphere to language comprehension 'is not purely linguistic but involves some other aspect of the cognitive system' (Berndt & Caramazza, 1982: 277). Such a conclusion is, of course, founded on the assumption that semantic processing is not 'purely linguistic', and indeed that the expression 'purely linguistic' actually means something. Leaving such issues aside, more recent findings – those of Joanette and Goulet (1994) – lend weight to the general thrust of Berndt and Caramazza's claim insofar as they suggest that right-hemisphere damage has an impact on the processing of lexical meanings but not of lexical forms.

Myers's (1994) review of the literature indicates that some individuals with right hemisphere damage make errors on simple expressive and comprehension tasks such as naming, word discrimination, following simple verbal commands, word definitions, reading and writing, and fluency. However, there are conflicting results. For example, several studies, including those of Diggs and Basili (1987) and Gainotti *et al.* (1981), found that right-hemisphere-damaged subjects had impaired single-word naming compared to non-brain damaged controls while others, such as Cappa *et al.* (1990) and Rivers and Love (1980), found no difference in performance. However, clinicians and researchers agree that deficits in linguistic form tend to be relatively mild in right-hemisphere-damaged subjects, and that their errors on standardised assessments do not mirror those of individuals presenting with aphasia. Linguistic deficits in right hemisphere lesions are more subtle, and in many cases the individuals concerned are not routinely referred for speech and language evaluation (Shields, 1991). On the other hand, when assessment focuses on the full range of communication ability, rather than linguistic form alone, communication problems are readily identifiable. Extralinguistic or pragmatic deficits represent the heart of the impairment for individuals with right hemisphere damage. *Extralinguistic* is applied here to factors that affect communication but are not conventionally linguistic in nature. Extralinguistic aspects of communication relate to the context in which communication takes place and allow one to understand and convey intentions and emotional tone (Myers, 1994). Studies of individuals presenting with right hemisphere damage report deficits in the following areas:

- difficulty using contextual cues to understand the meaning of complex narratives;
- difficulty understanding humour or the subtleties of irony;
- difficulty expressing personal intended meaning;
- difficulty in using extralinguistic cues that convey emotion through gesture and prosody.

Right hemisphere deficits thus impair the individual's ability to grasp the essence of events and to experience a sense of connectedness with the outside world.

This conclusion can also be seen as being supported in some measure by evidence that right hemisphere damage is associated with difficulties in coping with affective aspects of communication. For example, Ross (1981), having systematically examined patients with focal damage to the right hemisphere for disorders of prosody, concludes that the prosodic elements of language are a dominant feature of the right hemisphere and that the functional anatomic organisation of prosody in the right hemisphere mirrors the organisation of 'propositional language' in the left hemisphere. In his discussion of right-hemisphere involvement in control of affective prosody, Fabbro (1999: 47) reports the case of a right-hemisphere-damaged primary-school teacher whose pupils could not cope with his intonational impairment, and who consequently had to give up teaching. Earlier studies (Heilman *et al.*, 1975; Tucker *et al.*, 1977) had indicated impairments in identifying the affective but not the propositional components of language among right hemisphere damaged patients. A study by Blonder *et al.* (1991) yielded some interestingly mixed results. It revealed that (1) right-hemisphere damaged subjects were able to infer the affective content of sentences referring to emotionally charged situations (such as the anniversary of a child's death), whether or not the emotiveness of the situation was explicitly indicated; (2) such subjects did, however, have difficulty interpreting emotional states signalled by facial expressions; and (3) they in addition had problems accessing the affective messages conveyed by descriptions of facial expressions and of emotional manners of speech.

However, not all of the evidence from right-hemisphere damaged subjects points to a restriction of right-hemisphere involvement to the more cognitive and/or affective aspects of language processing. Obler and Gjerlow note – referring to a study by Schneidermann and Saddy (1988) – that right-hemisphere damaged subjects also seem to have less flexibility than normal subjects in assigning structural properties to sentences:

> For example, in order to appreciate the ambiguity of a sentence such as The boy hit the man with the cane, it is necessary to see both the possibilities: 'with the cane' can be an adjective phrase describing the man or an instrumental phrase modifying the way in which the boy hit the man. The patients tested by Schneiderman and Saddy could not identify both possibilities. (Obler & Gjerlow, 1999: 82)

Myers (1994) has suggested that 'inference' may summarise the right hemisphere's communicative function, inference being defined in terms of the *interpretation* of sensory data depending on at least four operations: (1) attention to individual cues; (2) selection of relevant cues; (3) integration of relevant cues with one another; and (4) association of cues with prior experience. Viewing right-hemisphere damage as an 'inference deficit' provides a framework for exploration into and addressing of the apparently disparate communication deficits which result from such damage. Problems in producing informative content, integrating narrative information, generating alternative meanings, comprehending and expressing emotion, and comprehending and expressing prosody can all be seen as flowing from deficits in respect of the generation of inferences in the above sense.

There is a specifically L2 dimension to the debate about right-hemisphere involvement in language processing. One may perhaps presume (see e.g. Seliger, 1982) that if the right hemisphere has a role in language processing, this role extends to L2 processing and acquisition. What is more interesting, however, is the possibility that the presence of an L2 may influence the magnitude of such a role. Brain damage data indicate strongly that all of an individual's languages are subserved by essentially the same brain base (see e.g. Kinsbourne, 1981), while data from electrical stimulation of the bilingual brains[11] reveal localisation for the different languages which is at least overlapping (see e.g. Whitaker *et al.*, 1981). On the other hand, it may well be that the right hemisphere has a particular function in relation to L2 learning. One possibility is that the right hemisphere may have a particular role in the early stages of L2 learning. This hypothesis, which has been labelled the 'stage hypothesis' is associated with the name of Obler (see e.g. Obler, 1981), who, in a review of 14 experimental studies focusing on normal subjects with a knowledge of two languages, found that 'twelve yielded data consistent with the notion of differential dominance' in respect of the languages in question, and also discovered that one of the studies scrutinised suggested more right hemisphere involvement in beginning stages of L2 learning than in subsequent stages. A modified version of the stage hypothesis was elaborated by Galloway and Krashen (1980), who suggested that greater right hemisphere involvement might be a feature only of the initial stages of 'acquiring' (in Krashen's sense – i.e. unconsciously 'picking-up') an L2. However, subsequent experimentation furnished no evidence in support of this suggestion (see e.g. Galloway, 1981; Fabbro, 2002).

The evidence of Carroll's (1980) series of dichotic listening studies involving L2 learners tends in a rather different direction. The suggestion in this case is that a greater right-hemisphere participation in L2 than in L1 processing is associated with subjects with exposure to the L2 before age six and with subjects who learn the L2 in immersion situations. Genesee's (1982) review of the relevant clinical and experimental literature (including Carroll's work) leads him to reject the first of the above hypotheses and to conclude that the bulk of research 'supports the hypothesis that there is greater RH [right hemisphere] involvement in SL [second language] processing the later the SL is acquired relative to the first' (Genesee, 1982: 317). On the question of the manner of acquisition Genesee's reading of the literature is more congenial to Carroll's proposal, to the extent that it finds some support for the notion that informal learning situations promote greater right hemisphere involvement than formal ones. As far as the stage hypothesis is concerned, Genesee's survey uncovers very little empirical support for this.

With regard to the suggestion that the crucial factor in determining the extent of right-hemisphere involvement in L2 processing is the age at which the L2 is acquired, Obler and Gjerlow (1999: 138) cite a review of the bilingual laterality literature by Vaid (1983), which concludes that late L2 acquirers are more likely to show increased right-hemisphere participation in language processing. Obler and Gjerlow (1999: 138f.) also summarise a study by Wuillemin and Richardson (1994), which employed a tachistoscopic presentation whereby Papua New Guinean university students had words presented to their left or right visual fields in their L2 – which for some subjects was English and for others Tok Pisin. In respect of both languages, the results suggested clear left-hemisphere dominance for individuals who had learned their L2 before age four, but rather more right-hemisphere involvement for subjects who had learned it after age nine. If this is the case, the obvious question that arises is whether differences between the patterns of organisation of L2 functions in the brain of early and late beginners might constitute an explanation for age effects in L2 learning. One should treat such an interpretation with caution. Given the recognition by the neurosciences that the direction of causation may be the reverse of the one usually assumed – that is, that brain differences are as likely to reflect different kinds of learning experience as to determine these experiences (see e.g. Bialystok & Hakuta, 1999; Gazzaniga, 1992; Robertson, 1999) –, one has to accept that differences of L2 organisation in the brain may be the consequence rather than the cause of lower proficiency among later beginners (cf. Marinova-Todd *et al.*, 2000: 17–18; cf. also discussion in the next section).

Clearly, the debate about the right hemisphere's contribution to language processing is set to continue for some time. Since, as we have seen, there is not yet agreement on what constitutes good evidence in this matter, the inference must be that resolution of the substantive issues is still some way off. However, even researchers as sceptical about much of the evidence as Millar and Whitaker are prepared to admit that 'enough data have accumulated to challenge the simple view that the LH [left hemisphere] is the language hemisphere and the RH [right hemisphere] does something else' (Millar & Whitaker, 1983: 110). In other words, there is enough evidence around to call into question Lenneberg's strictly dichotomous representation of mature laterality of functions, and to cast doubt on any absolute interpretation of the 'completion' of lateralisation.

Proposals regarding multiple critical periods

Finally on the question of lateralisation and cerebral plasticity, mention should be made of Seliger's 'multiple critical periods hypothesis' (Seliger, 1978) and Walsh and Diller's proposals concerning the differential maturation of different nerve cell types (Walsh & Diller, 1981). Like Molfese, Moscovitch and Witelson, Seliger accepts the evidence of very early laterality, but, again like them, posits a continuing process of specialisation. For Seliger, though, this process is one of *localisation* as well as *lateralisation*. He quotes evidence which seems to indicate that similar cerebral lesions cause different (Alajouanine & L'hermitte,1965), and more specific (Brown & Jaffe, 1975) aphasias in adults as compared with children – except in the case of anomalous dextrals (right-handers who are mixed dominant or not clearly left-lateralised) and some left-handers, who show similar aphasia profiles to those of aphasic children (Brown & Hécaen, 1976). From these findings Seliger argues that, just as each type of aphasia is determined by the state of the localisation process at the moment of brain damage, so the acquirability of a particular aspect of language at a particular time may depend on the state of that same process – i.e. that there may be a different timetable for the acquisition of different aspects of language. This would explain, says Seliger, why an authentic accent in an L2 is not usually acquirable beyond puberty, whereas syntactic skills are acquirable much later in life. Evidence that the localisation process is arrested in anomalous dextrals and some left-handers is taken by Seliger to indicate that these populations maintain the state of plasticity necessary for certain kinds of acquisition and to explain why certain adult learners succeed in acquiring such subsystems as the phonology and phonetics of an L2, while the majority do not.

Seliger's whole approach runs into the problem that the evidence on age effects in relation to accent acquisition (see Chapter 4) is not as straightforward as he assumes. Much the same can be said of Walsh and Diller's (1981) claim that phonetic/phonological skills are subserved by a different variety of cell from that which subserves grammatical skills. Diller notes that of the two major types of neurons, pyramidal and stellate, the pyramidal cells develop early – by age six or eight – and that is these neurons that make long-distance connections with their long axons and which are crucial in establishing links between the language centres in the brain and other centres of neural control. Diller (Diller, 1981a: 76) argues that only at a very young age, while the pyramidal neurons are still developing, can new language centres be formed in the right hemisphere to compensate for left-hemisphere injury. He notes further that pyramidal cells have a crucial role in neuromuscular control, and that changes in the plasticity of these cell systems might be reflected in the emergence of pronunciation difficulties. With regard to stellate cells, or local-circuit neurons, Diller observes that these short-axon cells are linked with higher order cortical functions, with cognition and learning in particular, and that they are characterized by relatively slow differentiation in the brain, and by continued maturation over at least two to three decades. He suggests that the continued neuroplasticity of the local-circuit neurons explains why it is not 'unphysiological' to continue to learn new things – including new languages – after age six or eight, and why the cognitive aspects of new languages are learned better by relatively mature people even though the neuromuscular control of pronunciation might present certain difficulties. Unfortunately for these proposals, the evidence on age and accent acquisition is, as we have seen, contradictory. Moreover, even studies which indicate an advantage in this area for younger learners often show also a substantial minority of counter-examples. A further problem is that correlating a precise linguistic level with a particular kind of neuron can at our present state of knowledge only be speculative. This point is well illustrated by the fact that other researchers have made somewhat different correlations. Wallace and Macaskie (1984: 197ff.), for example, associate the shorter maturational timetable of the pyramidal cells with the rather general insecurities experienced by older L2 learners as well as their difficulties in acquiring authentic accents.

Arguments concerning localisation which have emerged from brain-imaging-based research

To return to the question of localisation of language functions, a research approach to investigating this issue which has become available in recent times is that of brain-imaging. Two major technologies are used to image the brain in the study of language processing: Positron Emission Tomography (PET) and Functional Magnetic Resonance Imaging (fMRI). Both technologies image the brain in a dynamic way, thereby making it possible to detect changes over time. Almost all right-handed and most left-handed subjects are shown by brain-imaging to exhibit language-related activation that is strongly lateralised to the left hemisphere (Matthews *et al.*, 2003). However, interpreting the images generated by these technologies is fraught with difficulty, as experimental tasks typically activate many different areas of the brain simultaneously. Moreover, different modes of language use – e.g. speaking versus reading – seem to involve the activation of different areas of the language centres (Scott *et al.*, 2000). Posner and Pavese (1998) explain that brain-imaging cannot provide us with a definitive answer as to how language works or identify very specific locations for very specific functions. Complex neural networks are activated by tasks involving even single words; when words are combined into phrases and sentences the networks become still more complex, owing to the activation of many pragmatic and affective as well as linguistic areas. These difficulties are replicated in almost all studies using fMRI and PET to investigate human cognitive tasks (Posner & Pavese, 1998).

Some brain-imaging research has addressed the question of whether early L2 acquisition results in different spatial representations in the brain from late acquisition. For instance, Kim *et al.* (1997) used magnetic resonance imaging[12] to investigate the spatial representation of L1 and L2 in the cerebral cortex of early and late bilinguals during a sentence-generation task. The results revealed little or no age-related separation of activity in Wernicke's area, the area traditionally associated with comprehension and semantic processing, but differences did emerge in respect of activity in Broca's area, the area traditionally associated with output and syntactic processing. Among the late bilinguals two distinct but adjacent centres of activation were revealed for L1 and L2, whereas in the early bilinguals a single area of activation for both languages emerged. This looks like evidence of different kinds of brain organisation in early and late bilinguals.

Wattendorf *et al.* (2001) attempted to replicate Kim *et al.*'s research for multilinguals some of whom (early bilinguals) had been exposed to two languages before age three and to a third after age 10, and others (late multilinguals) who had experienced only one language up to age 10 and had then been exposed to two further languages. Basically, the results of this study show that in the early bilinguals the neural substrate in Broca's area activated by the use of the first two languages in a narration task overlapped, whereas in the late multilinguals the pattern of activation was more diffuse. Evidence from the above two studies has been interpreted as indicating different kinds of brain organization in early and late bilinguals in relation to syntax but not in relation to the lexicon.

However, there are reasons to treat such evidence with caution. For one thing, as indicated above, and as Fabbro (2002) notes, there are important limitations to the methodology of neuroimaging:

(a) the time needed to study the cerebral representation of a function is expressed in seconds, whereas language processes are expressed in milliseconds;
(b) subtractive comparisons between the two tasks [general cognitive and linguistic] are often difficult to interpret;
(c) often results of neuroimaging studies do not correspond to clinical neuropsychological findings;
(d) neuroimaging techniques do not allow one to determine whether acti-

vation of a structure depends either on an increase in activation processes or in neurophysiological inhibition processes; and, lastly,

(e) brain activation was studied with tasks that . . . generally simultaneously activate many linguistic, pragmatic and affective structures, thus making it difficult to interpret data. (Fabbro, 2002: 209f.)

There is also at least a dubium over the relationship between traditionally identified language areas in the brain and the functions which they have been assumed to subserve (see e.g. Obler & Gjerlow, 1999: 9–11 and *passim*). Finally, Marinova-Todd *et al.* (2000) note that in Kim *et al.*'s study there is no control of the proficiency level of the later beginners. Accordingly there is the possibility 'that the adult learners assessed . . . were poorly selected and do not represent highly proficient adult bilinguals' (Marinova-Todd *et al.*, 2000: 17–18). If this were so, then the neurological differences observed might simply reflect different proficiency levels (see discussion above). Likewise, proficiency rather than age may have been the critical factor in relation to the late trilinguals in the Wattendorf *et al.* study; they are reported to have all used their three languages in their daily lives, but this hardly constitutes a detailed evaluation of their proficiency levels. Other studies have indeed suggested that proficiency is a 'critical factor in shaping the functional brain organization of languages' (Abutalebi *et al.*, 2001: 187). Contributions to a recent roundtable on cognitive neuroscience came to similar conclusions, identifying proficiency level rather than age of onset as the crucial factor (Friederici, 2003; Ullman, 2003; Green, 2003).

In sum, brain-imaging research has had an important role in corroborating other evidence with respect to the determination of brain areas normally involved in language processing and with respect to the notion of hemispheric dominance. However, the complexity of the neural networks activated during language tasks has made it extremely difficult for brain imaging to provide specific information about the exact location of specific linguistic skills and processing activities, and methodological problems attaching to brain-imaging studies focused on age effects call into question the conclusions of such studies.

Thalamus theory

We come now to the so-called 'thalamus theory', propounded by Walz (1976). This resembles other proposals (see above) in postulating different rates of development for areas or elements of the brain subserving different language functions but diverges from them in positing the location functions ('grammar' and 'accent') not in the cerebral cortex, but in the limbic system (i.e. the area surrounding the brain stem), specifically in the *thalamus*. The thalamus, like the cerebrum, is divided into two portions, left and right, which appear as asymmetric egg-shaped nuclear masses lying obliquely across the cranial end of the brain stem' (Mateer & Ojemann, 1983: 173). The notion that this part of the brain might have a role in language processing is by no means new; Penfield and Roberts (1959) hypothesised that it had a linking function in relation to different language areas of the cerebral cortex. Walz, however, makes some very specific claims. His argument runs as follows (1976: 101): 'damage to the cerebral cortex produces linguistic impairment with the exception of grammar and accent'; since grammar and accent are mastered 'at an early age', and 'once mastery is attained, the two remain virtually unimpaired', these functions are likely to be seated in an organ which is itself 'ready to function fully at a very early age' and remains 'relatively inviolate'; an organ which meets both these criteria is the limbic system. Other linguistic functions (writing, spelling, comprehending, etc.) which are more vulnerable to impairment are assumed by Walz to be located elsewhere – namely in the cortex:

The most obvious objection to this suggestion from a neurolinguistic point of view is that, as Ekstrand (1980) points out, the great bulk of findings in this field indicate strongly that language functions above the most primitive levels are predominantly subserved by the cortical areas of the brain. Evidence from language disorders (see e.g. Fabbro, 1999: 82f.; Mateer & Ojemann, 1983) suggests that the thalamic contribution lies rather in the lexical than in the grammatical or phonetic/phonological sphere, and is somewhat indirect. Specifically, data from studies of thalamic lesions show an association between such lesions and naming and retrieval errors as well as mild comprehension deficits. Data from electrical stimulation studies also reveal an interaction between the thalamus and verbal expression: 'during electrical stimulation of the most anterior left thalamic nuclei subjects exhibit a strong compulsion to speak, accompanied by the production of words, sentences, or speech irrelevant to the contextual situation' (Fabbro, 1999: 83). To Mateer and Ojemann these data suggest that the role of the thalamus is to provide 'attentional mechanisms' for 'alerting' the cortex (with which it is bidirectionally connected). Fabbro, for his part, notes that the left thalamus contains a substance (noradrenaline) which enhances the impulse to speak and enhances verbal fluency. A further perspective on this issue comes from Pulvermüller and Schumann (1994), who suggest that the thalamus contributes to regulating activity and is relevant for 'selectively attending to incoming stimuli' (Pulvermüller & Schumann, 1994: 703). All of the above conclusions are remote from Walz's suggestion that 'grammar' and 'accent' are located in the thalamus. Another point that Mateer and Ojemann's survey makes clear is that serious disruption of language following damage to the thalamus is usually quite short-lived – which clearly runs counter to the notion that the thalamus subserves deep-seated, very basic language functions. Walz's proposal is not well supported either by data from language acquisition studies. It predicts that the critical period for the acquisition of accent and grammar will end before the age of five, since 'the Limbic System is almost fully developed at the age of about four' (Walz, 1976: 101). This prediction is not borne out by the facts: neither in the case of accent nor in the case of grammar can a case be sustained for the notion that acquisitional capacity disappears before age five.

In this section, we have looked at elements of the neurolinguistics literature which bear on the Critical Period Hypothesis. The support provided by this literature for the hypothesis is less than persuasive. We have seen that the cause–effect relationship between brain and language may be bidirectional. New learning – in adulthood as well as childhood – can induce striking new changes in the brain region related to the learning of the new task (Kleim *et al.*, 1997). Clancy and Finlay (2001) describe brain development in terms of an overlapping and interconnected series of multi-modal additive and regressive neural events, noting that these neural events may drive or alternatively reflect developmental behaviours such as motor development, social and emotional development, intellectual development and language development. Moreover, there is no evidence to support a direct mapping of sequences of speech and language acquisition to discrete neurological events. The complexity of the interactions between developmental neurological events and developmental experiences of the child remains to be researched.

Cognitive Developmental Views

Studies of populations with atypical language development have sharpened our awareness of the connections between language and cognition. For example, in her book on such populations Tager-Flusberg (1994) argues that, while some evidence for the autonomy of syntax and morphology emerges from individual case studies, cognitive and social factors clearly play a role in acquiring language, most especially semantics and pragmatics. In addition, as we saw in Chapter 2, some recent studies relate the reduced capacity of children with Specific Language Impairment to focus on grammatical detail to limited processing capacity or phonological memory constraints (cf. Conti-Ramsden & Windfuhr, 2002). Clinical data indicate that there may not be a simple cause and effect relationship between cognition and language development but an intertwining and interdependence of the two during development. We have also encountered the notion that age-related differences in L2 learning capacity may be associated with cognitive differences between children and adults. We have in addition examined suggestions that post-pubertal L2 learners no longer have access to the purportedly innate cognitive subsystem claimed to be dedicated to language acquisition/processing (Bley-Vroman, 1989; Schachter, 1988), and that IQ (Genesee, 1976, 1978/9) or verbal analytical skills (Harley & Hart, 1997; DeKeyser, 2000) may play a greater role in later than in earlier L2 acquisition.

The dominant paradigm of language emergence as a function of cognitive development is provided by Piaget, according to whom the child comes into the world equipped with elementary intelligence which consists in the capacity to *assimilate new* experience to his/her internal organisation of the world and to modify or *accommodate* the latter to take new experience into account. On this view it is through the interaction between these basic intellectual functions and experience of the environment, that the child becomes progressively less circumscribed by immediate experience and more aware of the wider world and his/her place in it, 'and finally conscious of and capable of reflecting upon his own intellectual processes' (Gruber & Vonèche, 1982: xxviif.). The concept of a progressive expansion of consciousness or *decentration* is vital to the Piagetian understanding of the emergence of language. According to Piaget, as the child's experience grows, he/she begins to imitate what he/she perceives, then to imitate objects and events subsequent to their disappearance or cessation, and in the end to develop mental images of objects and events which can be evoked at any time. For Piaget this gradual escape through intellectual growth from the 'here and now' provides the foundation for language development.

The phase during which language emerges is labelled by Piaget the '*pre-operational*' stage, which is posited as following the 'sensori-motor stage during which action-schemes' are constructed 'with the sole support of perceptions and movements and thus by means of a sensori-motor co-ordination of actions, without the intervention of representation or thought' (Piaget & Inhelder, 1969: 4). When language begins to develop, it does so, according to Piaget, as just one aspect of the 'semiotic or symbolic function' – 'the ability to represent something . . . by means of a "signifier"' (Piaget & Inhelder, 1969: 51). This representative capacity is manifested first in deferred imitation and subsequently in symbolic play, verbal behaviour and drawing. It is important to note, however, that this is presented not as an abrupt development but as one which is continuous with sensori-motor behaviour, the child's first words being described 'intermediary between symbolic or imitative signifiers and true signs' (Piaget, 1962: 218). Piaget's answer, then, to the question of why language emerges when it does in the maturation of the child is merely a particular application of the general Piagetian principle that each cognitive stage is 'an essential epistemological preparation for those that will follow' (Boden, 1979: 31). For Piaget, the onset of language occurs when the child's intellect has accumulated the requisite experience and elaborated the requisite schemas for this to be possible.

A major problem with the Piagetian approach to child development is that it tends to relate rather loosely to empirical data, which has prompted the criticism that the theory is 'so vague as to be virtually unfalsifiable' (Boden, 1979: 153). Such vagueness is certainly a problem when it comes to the Piagetian account of language acquisition. Chomsky is scathing on this point:

> As for Piaget's . . . claim that the facts of language acquisition . . . can . . . be explained as the 'necessary' results of constructions of sensorimotor intelligence I will only say the obvious: The literature contains no evidence or argument to support this remarkable factual claim, nor even any explanation of what sense it might have. (Chomsky, 1976a: 17)

Inhelder observes (1979: 201) that Chomsky is mistaken in suggesting that Piaget supposes sensori-motor intelligence to be the sole basis for all language acquisition – a suggestion which fails to do justice to the Piagetian conception of cognitive growth as a dynamic compound, constantly enriched and complexified by new experience. However, the fact remains that a detailed Piagetian account of the interaction between cognitive and linguistic development has yet to be written.

Various researchers subscribing to the Critical Period Hypothesis – notably, Krashen, Rosansky and Felix – have drawn on Piaget's work as a source of explanations of the critical period. As we have seen, Krashen (1973) made a major contribution to the amassing of evidence against Lenneberg's proposals regarding lateralisation. However, he continued to read the evidence as supporting the existence of the critical period (Krashen, 1975: 219). His (1975) explanation for the phenomenon referred to the Piagetian 'formal operations' stage, the relevant aspect of which for him was the development of an interest in general 'systems' and 'theories' rather than *ad hoc* solutions (Inhelder & Piaget, 1958: 339). In his 1975 paper Krashen suggests that this 'general tendency of adolescents to construct theories' (Inhelder & Piaget, 1958: 336) might inhibit the 'natural' and complete acquisition of an L2. He argues that the person who has reached the stage of formal operations may have the need to construct a conscious theory (a grammar) of the language he is learning; that this might cause the adult to adopt a rule-by-rule approach to language learning; and that, since it is difficult to express all of a natural language in terms of isolated rules, such an approach might limit the adult's access to competence in the target language.

Rosansky also found persuasive the evidence against the hypothesis that lateralisation continued until puberty, but placed her trust in the 'solemn belief in a critical period for language acquisition' and in the anecdotal evidence and personal experience of ESL teachers and researchers which 'tell us that children learn second languages with greater facility and with better accents than do adults' (Rosansky, 1975: 94). Rosansky examines the relationship between the Piagetian notion of decentration and language acquisition. According to Piaget, while initial language acquisition is associated with a self-centred, very limited perspective, at later stages of development 'the child begins to search for both the similarities and the differences between two problems' (Inhelder & Sinclair-de-Zwart, 1969: 20). It is this aspect of decentration that is postulated by Rosansky as being deleterious to language acquisition and, like Krashen, though for different reasons, she sees the formal operations stage as critical:

> . . . if awareness of contradictions acts as an incentive to decentration, then perhaps what acts as a 'block' to language learning, is precisely the *awareness* of differences. This new consciousness of differences seems to supplant the child's previous limitation of being able to only focus on the underlying similarities. (Rosansky, 1975: 98)

Felix (1981) also focuses on the significance of the formal operations stage. As reported by Harley (1986), Felix attempts to reconcile this Piagetian concept with the Chomskyan notion of an innate faculty specifically and uniquely for language acquisition:

Felix (1981) hypothesises that there are highly developed 'language specific cognitive structures' (LSC) of a formal, abstract nature that are activated in Ll acquisition and in childhood L2 acquisition. With the development of formal operations at age 10–12, the individual also has access to separate 'problem-solving cognitive structures' (PSC), which intervene in the acquisition of an L2. Adults, Felix maintains, are typically incapable of suppressing PSC structures in the L2 learning process, even though such structures are inferior for the purposes of language acquisition (Harley, 1986: 12). According to Felix, it is the competition between these language-acquiring structures and problem-solving structures that explains the relative inferiority of adults in the matter of L2 learning.

All three of the above explanations, then, seek to account for the critical period in Piagetian terms, all three basing themselves on the premise that a major cognitive shift – the onset of formal operations occurs during adolescence. For Krashen the crucial factor is the theorising tendency of adolescents; for Rosansky it is their new awareness of contradictions; while for Felix it is the competition in the learners' mind between two different varieties of cognitive structure. The three proposals are not incompatible, but the variation of emphasis does expose the fact that the modalities of the relationship between cognitive development and language acquisition have, as has already been indicated, still to be worked out by Piagetians (cf. Hakuta, 1975; Schumann, 1978a: 105). It is worth emphasising also that the Piagetian explanations of the critical period outlined above do not really constitute an *alternative* to a neurophysiological approach, since Piaget himself certainly regards the onset of formal operations as being 'linked to maturation of cerebral structures' (Inhelder & Piaget, 1958: 337). Thus, a Piagetian perspective on the critical period does not provide an escape-route from neurological questions.

There are at least three further possible objections to the proposals discussed above. The first – aired by Krashen himself (1975: 220) – is this: if, as Lenneberg claims (see above, Chapter 3), the linguistic development of some mentally retarded children ceases at puberty and if, as the above-discussed proposals suggest, the close of the critical period is caused by the onset of formal operations, then the implication is that mentally retarded children reach the highest stage of cognitive development at puberty, i.e. at the same time as unretarded children (although, in fact, as we have seen, the value and relevance of Lenneberg's data in this context is highly questionable). The second objection is that, since these proposals claim that success at language learning depends on one's stage of cognitive development, they imply that people at the same developmental stage should be more or less equally successful language learners. Empirical findings do not, however, bear this out. Schumann's (1978a) study, for example, shows that, of three subjects at the same developmental stage in Piagetian terms, one was a considerably less successful language learner than the other two (Schumann, 1978a: 105). The third objection is that these proposals imply a universal sharp decline in overall language learning ability at puberty, a proposition to which there is a great deal of counter-evidence.

In addition to its strictly cognitive aspects, Piaget's theory of human development also has an affective dimension, and Krashen, Rosansky and Felix all take account of this. The particular manner in which they do so is dealt with in the next section along with other proposals of an affective-motivational nature.

Moving on now to cognitive developmental approaches which do not posit a global decline in language learning capacity at puberty but which, on the contrary, see some language learning advantages in greater maturity, we find an early example of such an approach in Ausubel's (1964) comments. Ausubel takes the view that children may have some superiority in respect of accent acquisition and that, because their intellects have not yet been firmly shaped along particular lines, they tend to be 'more venturesome and less rigid in undertaking new learning tasks' (Ausubel, 1964: 421). He goes on to argue, however, that adults are better equipped for further language learning in two major ways. On the one hand, adults' concept development is far ahead of children's so that, when adults are faced with the task of learning the vocabulary of a new language, progress in that task, Ausubel claims, depends rather on appropriate attachment of labels to already existing concepts than, as in the case of children, on actual concept construction. On the other hand, adults, says Ausubel, are much assisted by their ability to reason consciously about grammatical generalisations and to apply their deductions appropriately, and children, who have to rely on 'less efficient' inductive processes, are distinctly disadvantaged in this regard.

Taylor (1974) cites Ausubel with approval. He is sceptical about the notion of a physiologically based critical period, quoting Krashen's (1973) re-analysis of the evidence on lateralisation (see above, previous section). On the question of cognitive maturity he has this to say:

> There is no cognitive reason to assume that adults will be less efficient than children in language learning. In fact, as already suggested, it seems logical to assume that the adult's more advanced cognitive maturity would allow him to deal with the abstract nature of language even better than children. (Taylor, 1974: 33)

He explains such evidence as there is in favour of children being better language learners than adults in terms of affective factors deriving from cultural attitudes which are neither inevitable nor universal (see next section).

We have already encountered Cummins's views. As we saw in Chapter 4 Cummins (e.g. 1979, 1980) distinguishes between basic interpersonal communicative skills (later deconstructed – e.g. 1983, 1984, – as skills deployed in communicative situations which are context-embedded and relatively undemanding cognitively) and cognitive-academic skills (later related to context-reduced, cognitively demanding communication). What he claims is that cognitive maturity interacting with the accumulation of experience in the more sophisticated, literate uses of the L1 greatly facilitates the acquisition of L2 cognitive-academic skills; and that this is why older L2 learners often excel in terms of grammatical accuracy. However, Cummins also takes into consideration evidence which suggests that younger learners are more successful acquirers of at least some aspects of L2 proficiency. Such evidence he accounts for by the postulation of the principle that tasks making similar contextual/cognitive demands are likely to be performed with similar degrees of success across languages: 'significant relationships would be predicted between communicative activities in different languages which make similar contextual cognitive demands on the individual' (Cummins & Swain, 1986: 155). From this principle it follows that, since the cognitive-linguistic level of even very young learners enables them to engage fluently in face-to-face interactions in their L1, they will find such interactions manageable in their L2 also. This is how Cummins explains the fact that 'oral fluency and accent are the areas where older learners most often do not show an advantage over younger learners' (Cummins, 1979: 201).

We return now to Krashen's work. Whereas, as we have seen, in the mid-1970s Krashen was the partisan of a fairly straightforward version of the Critical Period Hypothesis, in his later writings he adopted a different interpretation of the evidence on the matter and made a different use of cognitive-developmental arguments. For the later Krashen (see e.g. Krashen, 1981a, 1981b, 1982a, 1985) there is a basic distinction to be drawn between the unconscious assimilation or 'picking up' of a language, which he labels '*acquisition*' and the conscious mastering of its rules, which he calls '*learning*'. '*Acquisition*', says Krashen, is what the child engages in when developing his/her L1 but also when confronted with other languages. Adults retain this 'acquiring' capacity, according to Krashen, but are able to supplement it with conscious 'learning'. The relevance of the foregoing to the age question is that, in Krashen's view, 'significant Monitor use is only possible after the acquirer has undergone formal operations' (Krashen, 1982a: 44). However, whereas formerly Krashen linked the onset of formal operations at puberty to a decline in L2 success, he later suggested that it *advantages* the adult, at least in the short run. This putative advantage is related to Krashen's conception of L1 influence on L2 performance in terms of Newmark and Reibel's (1968) 'ignorance hypothesis', which posits that 'transfer' is merely the result of a falling back on L1 resources when L2 competence is insufficient to meet communicative needs. According to Krashen, conscious monitoring enables performers simply to 'utilise the surface structure of their first language, and then employ the conscious grammar as a Monitor to make alterations to bring the L1 surface structure into conformity with their idea of the surface structure of the second language' (Krashen, 1982b: 210). He suggests that this 'L1 plus Monitor' mode helps to account for the rapidity of adult progress in L2s evidenced in many studies (1982b: 210).

Apart from bringing these direct benefits, the 'L1 plus Monitor' mode is seen by Krashen (1982b: 210) as yielding indirect benefits in terms of getting the learner into interaction with native speakers of their target language, and thus promoting access to meaningful, comprehensible input

-for Krashen the sole necessary condition for 'acquisition' in his sense (Krashen, 1985: 2). Thus, according to Krashen, the 'Ll plus Monitor' mode constitutes a mechanism for turning 'learned' knowledge to account in the furtherance of 'acquisition'. The input obtained in this way is, says Krashen, all the more likely to be comprehensible because of the adult's greater cognitive maturity and, indeed, for this same reason a higher proportion of L2 input in general is likely to be of more use to adults than to children (Krashen, 1985: 12). Furthermore, cognitive maturity is seen by Krashen as also having a role in conversational management, in the sense that adults 'work harder in encouraging more language from their conversational partner, indicate more when they have not understood, and are better at keeping conversations going' (1985: 13 – cf. below). According to Krashen's later position, then, the onset of formal operations yields a short-term advantage for older language learners, as does their general accumulation of cognitive experience. It will be recalled, however, that Krashen *et al.* (1979) interpret the L2 evidence on age as suggesting that younger learners do better than adults in the long run (see Chapter 4). Krashen accounts for this eventual superiority ascribed to younger learners in terms of affective factors – to which we shall return in the next section.

The proposition that cognitive maturity yields language learning advantages has some intuitive appeal. However, when it comes to specifics, problems begin to arise. Ausubel distinguishes between accent acquisition, which he sees as not having cognitive implications and, accordingly, as being more efficiently performed by younger learners, and other aspects of language acquisition, which he perceives as being facilitated by cognitive maturity. Unfortunately, the empirical evidence does not unambiguously support this dichotomy (see Chapter 4); nor is there universal agreement about the cognitive demands of acquiring phonetic/phonological skills (see e.g. Cummins & Swain, 1986: 154f.). Taylor is too vague on the question of what precise advantages are bestowed by cognitive maturity for his proposals to be evaluated in detail, and Cummins's position runs into similar delineation difficulties, which have already been discussed. As for Krashen, although his assumptions about age-effects are broadly in line with the L2 evidence, his explanation of some of these effects in terms of Monitor Theory has to be seen against the barrage of criticism that has been levelled at that theory (see e.g. – among many others – Long, 1983; Brumfit, 1984a; Skehan, 1984; Wallace & Macaskie, 1984). On the other hand, what Krashen has to say about the general benefits of cognitive maturity in regard to rendering input comprehensible and facilitating conversation management is unlikely to be widely disputed.

Finally in this section, mention should be made of two very recent perspectives on the role of general cognitive factors in relation to the age question. As we saw in Chapter 4, Bialystok and Hakuta's re-analysis of earlier age-focused L2 research (Bialystok, 1997; Bialystok & Hakuta, 1994) and their own analysis of census data (Bialystok & Hakuta, 1999) point to a general gradual decline with age projecting well into adulthood, rather than a defined change in learning potential at puberty. They suggest that an explanation for this gradual decline may be found in the deterioration over the lifespan in such areas as capacity to perform tasks under time-pressure, risk-taking, establishing long-term memory codes, and ability to recall details. They comment (p. 172): 'if age-related changes in ultimate language proficiency are to be attributable to these cognitive changes . . . then the decline in ultimate proficiency . . . should . . . be gradual and constant'. According to the evidence they and others (e.g. Birdsong, 2002, 2003a; Harley & Wang, 1997) adduce, this is precisely how it is. However, as was indicated in Chapter 4, doubts have been expressed about the reliability of the census data presented by Bialystok and Hakuta, and there has also been some statisical reinterpretation of other dimensions of the evidence in question (DeKeyser, 2003).

We also saw in Chapter 4 that DeKeyser interprets the fact that the adult beginners in his (2000) study who scored within the range of the child beginners had high levels of verbal analytical ability as suggesting that maturational constraints apply only to implicit language learning mechanisms. His conclusion from this and later studies (e.g. DeKeyser & Montgomery, 2002) as communicated in a recent conference paper (DeKeyser, 2003) is that there is an inescapable decline in language acquiring capacity because of cognitive maturation. Specifically, he suggests that there a diminishing capacity for the implicit learning of complex abstract systems – including language. There are clear connections of a general kind between DeKeyser's proposals and some of the earlier proposals discussed under the heading of cognitive developmental explanations. One problem with his position is that it depends on a hard and fast distinction between implicit and explicit learning, a distinction which is not necessarily easy to operationalise in interpreting results from the kinds of study that yield age-related results. For example, is the learning of L2 phonology in a school context explicit simply because of the setting? Is the learning of L2 syntax through interaction with native speakers implicit simply because no textbook or instruction are involved? A conservative answer to both questions would have to be: not necessarily. Moreover, much of the criticism of Krashen's position regarding the a rigid distinction between conscious and unconscious learning modes could be applied, *mutatis mutandis*, to DeKeyser's perspective.

Affect and Motivation

Apart from the most obvious physiological distinctions between different age-groups, what separates them is probably as much a matter of *feeling* as of *thinking*. The emotional life of adolescents and adults very obviously differs in major respects from that of children. A number of researchers have ascribed a great deal of importance to such differences in their treatment of age-related effects in language acquisition and have evoked them in attempting to explain the putative language learning superiority of children.

For those taking a Piagetian line on language learning affective factors are inextricably bound up with cognitive development. Thus, Rosansky (1975) writes that affective and cognitive factors 'cannot in any meaningful way be divorced one from the other, since it is likely that they interact in determining the receptivity of the language learner' (Rosansky, 1975: 94). For Felix (1981) also environmental and personality factors play a role in determining what the problem-solving cognitive system of the post-formal operations learner receives to operate on. Citing Elkind (1970), Krashen (1975: 220f.) makes the connection between formal operations, the personality changes occurring at puberty and language learning in terms of the adolescent's capacity to conceptualise the thought of other people and his/her resulting self-consciousness and feelings of vulnerability, which he sees as having a negative impact on L2 learning. For all of the above researchers the affective repercussions of the development of formal operations are deleterious to language learning. Krashen in his later work re-expresses this claim in terms of the 'affective filter', a notion introduced by Dulay and Burt (1977) but subsequently incorporated into Krashen's model. What the affective filter is supposed to do is to 'impede or facilitate the delivery of input to the language acquisition device' (Krashen, 1982a: 32) depending on levels of motivation, self-confidence and anxiety. Krashen suggests that the changes brought on by formal operations at puberty 'affect the strength of the affective filter' (Krashen, 1982b, 216):

> While the filter may exist for the child second language acquirer, it is rarely, in natural informal language acquisition situations, high enough to prevent native-like levels of attainment. For the adult it rarely goes low enough to allow native-like attainment. (Krashen, 1985: 13)

Krashen thus explains the evidence that adults' L2 progress is initially more rapid than that of children but in the long run (at least in 'natural' environments) less successful in terms of cognitive advantage (see last section), ultimately outweighed by affective disadvantages.

There is a logical problem involved in tying the inhibition of language learning to the affective dimension of the onset of formal operations. If the claim is that language learning difficulties are occasioned by the self-consciousness and sense of vulnerability to the judgement of others which Piagetians associate with this stage of development, how is it to deal with what Piagetians go on to say about the rapid diminution in the intensity of such feelings? According to Elkind, Krashen's own source, such 'egocentrism', in the above sense, 'tends to diminish by the age of 15 or 16, the age at which formal operations become firmly established' (Elkind, 1970: 70). If, then, this particular type of egocentrism is fastened on as *the* critical affective factor inhibiting language learning, the implication is that the language learner is thus inhibited for only two or three years. The further implication is that the language learner is less inhibited at 16 than at 14 years, and that, accordingly, language learning in one's late teens is likely to be more successful than language learning in one's early teens. This does not seem to be consistent with Krashen's (1975) assumptions about the critical period (nor indeed with Rosansky's or Felix's perspective).

Taylor, whose views on cognitive development and language learning are, as we have seen, not narrowly Piagetian, also takes a broader line on the question of affective influences:

> The affective variables of motivation, empathy, ego-boundaries, and the desire to identify with a cultural group all seem to contribute to the uniform success of children in learning their native language. Whereas child language acquisition seems to be a means toward an end – social-ization – . . . lack of such motivation in adults and the absence of a positive attitude toward language learning and the target language and culture may be responsible for the lack of success in most adult second language learning. (Taylor, 1974: 33)

Taylor's references to ego-boundaries evoke Freud, of course, and, indeed, an extremely interesting account of putative age-related differences among language learners in terms of 'identification', 'superego' development, 'libidinal relations to objects' and 'narcissism' is to be found in an early article by the Freudian psychologist Stengel (1939).

The process of 'identification' was described and illustrated by Freud as follows:

> . . . the assimilation of one ego to another one, as a result of which the first ego behaves like the second in certain respects, imitates it and in a sense takes it up into itself . . . If a boy identifies himself with his father,

he wants to be *like* his father . . . his ego is altered on the model of his father . . . (Freud, 1964; reprint: 94f.)

According to Stengel, identification, the desire to be like others, underlies the phenomenon of 'echolalia', i.e. the quasi-automatic repetition of words by children learning (and aphasics re-learning) language, but plays no role in normal adult language learning (Stengel, 1939: 471f.). In the Freudian scheme the process of identification is the basis for the development of the 'super-ego'. The child's tendency to identify with his parents (and later with other authority-figures) leads to the formation of a set of internal inhibitions – in traditional terms, a conscience (Freud, 1964; reprint 93f.).

Stengel (1939: 472f.) attributes to the super-ego a monitoring role in language use. It is, according to him, the relaxing of the severity of the super-ego that is responsible for the kinds of aphasia which cause individuals to 'produce either wrong words or newly created words' (1939: 472). A strict super-ego is claimed to be damaging in other ways as far as the adult is concerned, underlying 'doubts whether some chosen word really reflects the idea of the object' and thus having 'a retarding effect on the development of speech' (Stengel, 1939: 473). The child, on the other hand, is seen by Stengel as unhampered by such inhibitions: 'it is not afraid of wrong words and does not shrink from forming new expressions on the spur of the moment, if the one generally used is not at hand' (Stengel, 1939: 473).

By 'libidinal relations to objects' is meant the way in which the 'libido', in its later, comprehensive sense of 'life instinct . . . all drives to survival as well as the instinctual sexual drive itself' (Stafford-Clark, 1965: 194)[13] apprehends and assesses aspects of external reality in relation to its own needs and wants. Stengel assumes that 'our libidinal relation to an object denoted by a word in a foreign language is somewhat different from our relation to the same object denoted by a word in the native language' (1939: 474), and suggests that this difference might have a connection with the following phenomenon:

> . . . the word 'slaughter-house', spoken in the native language, may produce the picture of a house, but in the new language the picture of the act of slaughtering an animal. . . . Words in the native language call up a picture of a simple lifeless pattern, while the corresponding words in the foreign language are more primitive and concrete. (Stengel, 1939: 473f.)

More generally, he sees libidinal relations to objects as a factor in the adult's resistance to a new language, and their less developed state in children as a factor in younger learners' greater openness to new languages (Stengel, 1939: 474f.).

In addition to the libido's relations with external reality, the Freudian psychologist also recognises the existence of relations between the libido and the ego. The latter are subsumed under the label '*narcissism*'. For Stengel, narcissism permeates attitudes towards language and is operative in the different perspectives adults and children have in regard to their performance in a new language. Many adults according to Stengel (1939: 475f), harbour the hope of 'converting the strangers to their own language', which they think of as more universal, richer, more advanced, even somehow truer than foreign languages. Narcissism also, for Stengel, underlies the 'sense of shame' many adults feel when they start to use a new language, which, he claims, arises from their being back in an 'infantile situation' where 'their narcissism is deeply hurt by the necessity for exposing a serious deficiency in a function which serves as an important source of narcissistic gratification' (Stengel, 1939: 476). Another factor related to narcissism is that of 'exhibitionism':

> Some persons in the first stage of using a foreign language, have a feeling as though they were wearing a fancy dress. Thus it is very probable that the feeling of shame . . . which often appears after a successful linguistic act, originates in exhibitionism. The child's position with regard to these difficulties is quite different. To give a young child an L2 means to give him a second method of play. The impulse to communicate . . . makes use of the new language with pleasure. There is no fear of talking nonsense, for talking nonsense is a source of pleasure. Nor is there any fear of fancy-dress – the child loves to wear it. The adult will learn the new language the more easily, the more of these infantile characteristics he has preserved. (Stengel, 1939: 477)

Fascinating and intuitively appealing though this account may be, it does have a number of weaknesses. With regard to its treatment of child language, it is even vaguer than the Piagetian account and offers no detailed model of the interplay between affect and linguistic development. It also suffers more generally from a dearth of reference to evidence other than impression and anecdote. Where relevant independent evidence exists – notably in relation to differences between child and adult L2 learning – it does not justify Stengel's simplistic 'younger = better' assumptions (see Chapter 4). On the other hand, this account does not postulate a *rigidly* defined critical period or cut-off point. Nor does it set hard and fast boundaries between what is possible for a child and what is possible for an adult. Rather, it suggests that the degree to which the child's approach to language learning persists into adulthood depends on general psychological development and, indeed, that this approach may be largely reverted to in certain circumstances. Some measure of variability is also predicted by Guiora's proposals, which like Stengel's have a Freudian basis.

Guiora (1972) introduces a new construct –*'language ego'* – which is represented as a sort of specialised linguistic version of the Freudian notion:

> In a manner similar to the concept of the body ego, language ego too is conceived as a maturation concept and refers to a self-representation with physical outlines and firm boundaries . . . The permeability of the language ego boundaries, specifically the flexibility of the pronunciation boundaries, is developmentally and genetically (in the psychoanalytic sense) determined. . . . Thus a child can assimilate native-like speech in any language. Once ego development is concluded, flexibility will be sharply restricted forever. (Guiora *et al.*, 1972a: 112)

> Essentially, to learn a second language is to take on a new identity . . . we propose that the most sensitive index of the ability to take on a new identity, i.e. the degree of permeability of language ego boundaries, is found in the ability to achieve native-like pronunciation in a second language. Considering the empathic capacity is also dependent upon the ability to partially and temporarily give up one's separateness of identity, we propose that individual differences in the ability to pronounce a second language should reflect individual differences in empathic ability. (Guiora *et al.*, 1972b: 422)

Schumann (1975a: 223–4) suggests that Guiora's concept of ego permeability might be seen as having an 'internal' as well as an 'external' phenomenon – a notion later accepted by Guiora (1992). Schumann relates the internal dimension to a perspective expounded by another Freudian theorist, Kris (1952), who proposes the idea that in many types of creative processes the ego relaxes and reverts from 'secondary process', which is essentially verbal and follows the laws of syntax and logic to 'primary process' thinking, which is redolent of the childhood years and is characterised by an absence of negatives, conditionals and other qualifying conjunctions.

> It has no sense of time and does not distinguish among past, present and future. Opposites can appear in place of one another and mutually contradictory ideas can exist in harmony. Also, a part of an idea or an object can represent the whole and several different thoughts can be represented by a single thought or image (Brenner, 1957). It is possible that primary process modalities provide an appropriately unbiased mental set in which the second language can be acquired, and that successful adult second language acquisition is accomplished by the

> learner's access to primary process through an ability to undergo an
> adaptive regression. (Schumann, 1975a: 223–4)

As far as the 'external' dimension of ego permeability is concerned (i.e.
the way it relates to what lies outside the individual organism), the above
quotations from Guiora and his collaborators make it clear that this is
conceived as bound up with 'empathic capacity'. For Guiora, L2 learning
'poses a challenge to the integrity of basic identifications', since it
demands that the learner 'step into a new world' and 'take on a new
identity' (Guiora *et al.*, 1972a: lllf.). He defines 'empathy' as 'a process of
comprehending in which a temporary fusion of self-object boundaries, as
in the earliest pattern of object relation, permits an immediate emotional
apprehension of the affective experience of another, this sensing being
used by the cognitive functions to gain understanding of the other'
(Guiora, 1972: 142). The relevance of this process to language learning is,
according to Guiora and his colleagues, that people who are particularly
sensitive and receptive in their interactions with others could be hypothesised to have 'an enhanced capacity to discern those cues and nuances
which, when incorporated in speaking, produce native-like pronunciation' (Taylor *et al.*, 1969: 463).

Some of the experiments carried out by Guiora and his collaborators to
test this hypothesis (Guiora *et al.*, 1967; Taylor *et al.*, 1969; Guiora *et al.*,
1972a) were inconclusive in their results. However, one of Guiora's experiments did seem to confirm at least his general line of thinking (Guiora *et al.*,
1972b). It involved assessing subjects' pronunciation of an L2 after the
ingestion of alcohol. Guiora viewed the lowering of inhibitions through
alcohol as a means of 'operationally inducing a state of greater permeability of ego boundaries or the ability to partially and temporarily give up
one's separateness of identity' (Guiora *et al.*, 1972b: 427). In fact, Guiora and
his associates found that the consumption of small amounts of alcohol did
improve their subjects' pronunciation of the L2. Replications of this experiment were subsequently carried out using hypnosis and valium. In the first
case – reported in Schumann *et al.* (1978) – it was found that deeply hypnotised subjects performed significantly better than less hypnotised subjects
on an L2 pronunciation test, which may indicate that a willingness to 'let
go' is a good predictor of L2 pronunciation performance, which in turn is
very much in line with Guiora's claims regarding ego-boundary permeability. The valium study – reported in Guiora *et al.* (1980) – produced less
clear-cut results, but did yield further evidence that relaxation, anxiety
reduction and disinhibition, in this instance brought about by the administration of a psychotropic drug, were associated with improved L2
pronunciation.

Such findings cannot be taken as proof of Guiora's hypothesis. His perspective may be intuitively appealing, but it has not been definitively substantiated (cf. Schumann, 1975a: 224). In any case, it has to be said that the precise terms of Guiora's hypothesis are not entirely clear. There seems to be some uncertainty as to whether 'empathic capacity' is seen as related to authentic pronunciation alone or to L2 performance in general. For the most part it portrays pronunciation ability as 'a unique feature of second language learning' claiming that 'individual differences in that skill appear to be directly related to flexibility of psychic processes as contrasted with highly integrated ego functioning which plays a major role in learning and manipulating grammar, syntax and vocabulary' (Guiora *et al.*, 1972a: 427; cf. also Guiora, 1992). There are, however, suggestions that 'empathic capacity is related not only to pronunciation ability, but also, in yet to be determined ways, to the overall capacity to acquire a second language' (Guiora, 1972: 145–6). The former position, taken together with the claim that 'pronunciation permeability will correspond to stages in the development of the ego' (Guiora *et al.*, 1972a: 112) assumes a clear superiority on the part of younger learners in acquiring L2 accents but not other aspects of L2 competence. The latter position, on the other hand, assumes a general L2 learning superiority among younger learners. In either case the explanation seems to be too strong for the available data.

However, Guiora's proposals, like Stengel's, do have the advantage of an inherent flexibility about them, in the sense that the age-related psychological barriers they posit are not envisaged as unshakeable. On the contrary, the possibility of changing adults' receptivity levels lies at the very heart of Guiora's approach. Thus, in fact, Guiora's account implies an explanation for adult success as well as failure in L2 learning.

> . . . it views ego flexibility as inducible. If artificial agents such as alcohol can foster permeability of ego boundaries and reduce inhibitions then it would not be unreasonable to assume that, given the right concatenation of natural psychological factors, permeability of ego boundaries might be possible for everyone. (Schumann, 1975a: 226)

Schumann (e.g. 1975a, 1975b, 1978a) placed Stengel's and Guiora's work in the perspective of other research and discussion concerned with acculturation, attitude and motivation. Collating material from these various lines of investigation, Schumann found 'several indications . . . that language learning difficulties after puberty may be related to the social and psychological changes an individual undergoes at that age' (Schumann, 1975a: 229). Citing Larsen and Smalley (1972) and Nida (1957/8) he noted in particular the stress and shock 'resulting from the disorientation encountered upon entering a new culture' (Schumann, 1975b: 25) – 'problems that can produce negative reactions to the new language and its speakers' (Schumann, 1975a: 210) and which can undoubtedly stand in the way of the learning of the language associated with the culture in question. Various researchers have identified the crucial factor in overcoming 'culture shock', 'culture stress' and indeed 'language shock' as the degree of willingness of the learner to accept for a time the position of child-like dependence on others. Such researchers have assumed that children are more willing to accept this kind of position than adults, and that herein lies an explanation for the supposed superiority of children as L2 learners. Such considerations may be relevant to the generality of L2 learners. According to Curran (1961):

> ... children acquire second languages more easily than adults because they are less threatened by the sounds of the new language and because they are willing to depend on others for support in learning. The adult, on the other hand, has acquired a basic security in his own language and is not ordinarily threatened by rejection when he speaks it. But when he attempts to communicate in the new language his normal linguistic securities are undermined, and he finds himself in a dependent state which he may resist. (Reported by Schumann, 1975a: 230)

The influence of attitude and motivation on L2 learning has long been investigated within the so-called 'social-psychological paradigm' by Gardner, Lambert, Smythe and their collaborators (see e.g. Gardner, 1968, 1979, 1980, 1985, 2001; Gardner & Lambert, 1972; Gardner & Smythe, 1975; Gardner *et al.*, 1985; Gardner *et al.*, 1979; Gardner *et al.*, 1976; Gardner *et al.*, 1974; Lambert, 1975; Lambert & Klineberg, 1967; Lambert *et al.*, 1970; Smythe *et al.*, 1975). From such research emerged the view that intelligence and aptitude on the one hand and attitude and motivation on the other operate as independent variables in L2 learning. As far as attitude and motivation were concerned, two orientations were isolated – instrumental – 'reflecting the practical value and advantages of learning a new language' (Gardner & Lambert, 1972: 132) and integrative – 'reflecting a sincere and personal interest in the people and culture represented by the other group' (1972: 132). The suggestion was 'that an integrative orientation would sustain better the long-term motivation needed for the very demanding task of second-language learning', a suggestion which appeared to be confirmed by some empirical studies, though not all. With regard to the age question, some research has been interpreted as indicating that children of around the age of 10 are less likely to be hostile to cultures other than their own (i.e. more likely to be integratively oriented) than older (or indeed younger) children (Lambert & Klineberg, 1967).

Schumann (1975a: 230) saw the findings from these various areas of research as converging, at least in general terms, and as conspiring to suggest 'that social and psychological maturation may be as important or even more important than neurological maturation in accounting for difficulties in adult and L2 learning' (but cf. Pulvermüller & Schumann, 1994 and discussion below). The implication of this conclusion for Schumann was that cases of successful adult L2 learning might be explained by the fact that 'under the right conditions the affective factors in the adult can be ameliorated to permit successful second language acquisition' (Schumann, 1978a: 107).

Schumann also refers with approval to Macnamara's (1973a, 1973b) contention that child–adult differences in L2 learning success have to do with degree of involvement in 'vital communication' with peers (see also next section). For Macnamara the adult's failure to become as involved as the child in 'vital communication' with his/her peers in caused by affective-motivational factors of one kind and another. One such factor in the case of immigrant L2 learners may be differing levels of peer-group pressure. As Smythe *et al.* (1975) point out, this pressure may be particularly acute in the case of children: '[e]normous pressure is brought to bear on the child to learn the language so that he can fit in and be accepted by his new playmates' (Smythe *et al.*, 1975: 17). For adults this pressure may be of a less compelling order, and/or there may be countervailing pressures. The adult may, as Diller (1971: 31) suggests, perceive some advantages in *not* having perfect mastery of the L2 since such mastery allied with an imperfect knowledge of the relevant culture may give the impression that one is a 'rather stupid and uncultured' native speaker. Another dimension to this question may be the *quality of* the peer group pressure, in the sense of the specific kinds of demands it makes in linguistic terms. Magnan (1983) reports an experiment in which she tested the affective reactions of native French speakers in three age-groups to 15 types of grammatical error made by Americans speaking French. The three age-groups in question were composed, respectively, of adolescents, young adults and mature adults. Magnan's results show an inverse relationship between age and sensitivity to gender errors. Other studies cited by Magnan also indicate age-related differences in sensitivity to particular categories of error. Politzer (1978) found that whereas for most of his native German speaker judges L2 users' vocabulary errors were most irritating, his youngest judge (a 13-year-old) did not follow this trend. Delisle (1982) obtained similar results for errors in written German: 13 to 17-year-old native speakers were most irritated by vocabulary errors whereas 10 to 12-year-olds were most irritated by gender errors.

To return to Schumann, the explanation he proposed in the 1970s in respect of putative age-related differences among L2 learners was merely one aspect of a whole approach to L2 acquisition originally known as the Pidginisation Hypothesis and later as the Acculturation Model (see, in addition to the Schumann references already given, Schumann, 1975c, 1976a, 1976b, 1978b, 1983; Schumann & Stauble, 1983a, 1983b). What this model claims is that success in L2 acquisition depends on the extent and quality of contact between the learner and the target language and culture, which in turn depends on the degree of social and psychological distance between the learner and this language and culture. Social distance in this context refers to learner group and target language group attitudes and expectations, to the relative size and cohesiveness of the two groups, and to the measure of congruence between their respective cultures. Psychological distance refers to learners' degree of case or unease with the target language and culture, as well as their personal motivation and the degree of permeability of their ego. On this view, where social and psychological distance is great, the learner's interlanguage will fossilise at a stage of development which is formally comparable to a pidgin language; where, on the other hand, the social and psychological distance is small, the learner's interlanguage will develop steadily towards target language norms in much the same way as a pidgin complexifies when it begins to be spoken as a native language – i.e. becomes a creole – and then restructures itself under the influence of a prestige variety of the language supplying the majority of its elements – i.e. becomes decreolised.

Evidence for pidginisation comes from Schumann's case study of Alberto, a Costa Rican immigrant to the United States whose interest in and contact with English-speaking Americans was minimal, and whose English had apparently stabilised at a level which was morphologically highly reduced (see especially Schumann, 1978a). With regard to depidginisation and decreolisation, Schumann and Stauble (1983a) note resemblances between the development of negation in the depidginisation of Hawaiian Pidgin English and that evidenced at primitive levels by learners of English as an L2, and similarities between the ways in which the negative structure evolves in the decreolisation of Guyanese Creole and those which emerge when one investigates the interlanguage development of learners of English as an L2 over time. Andersen (1983b) adds to Schumann's model by focusing on internal processes. He distinguishes the assimilation of input to the learner's internal conception of the L2 system ('nativisation') in the beginning stages of learning from the accommodation of internal norms to the specifics of the input ('denativisation') as learning progresses. Valdman (1983), for his part, emphasises parallels between early L2 acquisition and creolisation. General empirical support for Schumann's position comes from a number of studies of immigrants where lack of L2 progress has been found to be attributable to social and / or psychological distance (see e.g. Dittmar, 1982; Klein, 1981; Meisel, 1983; Wong-Fillmore, 1976). Schmidt (1983), studying a Japanese adult immigrant to Hawaii found that, despite the absence of a significant social distance factor, his subject made little progress in English in grammatical terms. However, this subject was an effective L2 performer in communicative terms and, moreover, Schmidt did discover some factors which were relatable to psychological distance.

On the other hand, Ekstrand (1976b) found that teachers' judgements with respect to immigrant pupils' social and emotional adjustment did not correlate with their performance on Swedish L2 language tests. Also noteworthy is Green's (1975) finding that among a group of classroom learners of German in Britain attitudes towards the German language had little bearing on achievement in the subject, and attitudes towards German speakers no bearing at all. Burstall *et al.*'s (1974) findings are more ambiguous. They report that although through both primary and secondary school in Britain attitudes towards learning French are associated with success in the language, early success at French is more often linked to later favourable attitudes than early favourable attitudes are related to later success. There have also been a number of attacks on the Acculturation Model from a theoretical point of view. Eckman and Washabaugh question what they see as its nativist and universalist assumptions – assumptions which Schumann (1983) disavows. Rickford (1983) points to a major difference between decreolisation and L2 acquisition: whereas individuals involved in decreolisation situations retain access to creole structures when they develop more standard-like forms, L2 learners progressively replace and thus lose structures as they move along the interlanguage continuum. Schumann and Stauble (1983b) reply that this latter claim needs to be established empirically, and that earlier interlanguage forms may in fact remain available to the learner as he / she advances. Ellis (1985: 254f.) criticises the lack of specificity of the model in regard to internal processing mechanisms, a point which McLaughlin (1987: 127) takes issue with, while himself (p.132) questioning the measurability of social and psychological distance and therefore the falsifiability of the theory.

To sum up, there is no doubt that the Acculturation Model has a great deal of intuitive appeal and that, at least as far as 'natural' L2 learning situations are concerned, it has a fair amount of empirical support. However, it is impossible to disregard the difficulty of quantifying social and psychological distance. Indeed, as McDonough (1981: 142f.) has pointed out, even to define a concept like motivation with any kind of rigour presents significant problems. Also, the applicability of the Acculturation Model to classroom language learning is somewhat unclear (cf. Ellis, 1985: 255), given not only its naturalistic emphasis, but also the unconvincing attitude-success correlations among classroom learners. With specific regard to the age question, the model is appealing in at least two ways. On the one hand, its suggestion that children normally have less difficulty than adults in adapting themselves to a new culture is in line with everyday experience and with some research findings on the subject of immigrant adjustment (see e.g. Taft & Cahill, 1981). On the other, it does not postulate an inevitable maturationally determined decline in language learning capacity but, on the contrary, allows for the possibility of completely successful L2 learning at pretty well any age, which accords with the fact that some adults do learn L2s to native-like levels.

In more recent times Schumann has increasingly turned his attention to neurolinguistic aspects of L2 acquisition (see e.g. Schumann, 1997, 2001a, 2001b). He now sees age effects in L2 acquisition as principally explicable in terms of a decline in plasticity in the language areas of the brain. On the other hand, he continues to take the line that positive attitudinal/motivational factors in adult beginners may cause levels of activity in the midbrain that compensate for loss of plasticity in the cortex and to this extent continues to posit a certain flexibility in relation to the age factor. He recognises that some older L2 beginners do attain native-like levels in their target language and accounts for this in terms of very high motivation which compensates for the limitations caused by the maturation of the cortex. He relates motivation to stimulus appraisal, which he in turn relates to a three-part system of neural mechanisms consisting of the amygdala, the orbitofrontal cortex and the body proper (1997: 37ff.). The amygdala is located in the temporal lobes and is assumed to be involved in assessing values associated with physical and social well-being. The orbitofrontal cortex is highly connected to the amygdala but is located in the prefrontal area of the brain. It subserves 'preferences and aversions acquired in the lifetime of the organism' and also 'value associated with culture, religion, and education' (Schumann, 1997: 37). As far as the body is concerned, it is seen as becoming involved 'when the amygdala and the orbitofrontal cortex foster bodily states that produce positive or negative feelings about agents, objects, and events in the environment' (1997: 37). Stimulus appraisal results in neurotransmitter systems releasing chemical messengers such as dopamine into various parts of the cortex.

Positive appraisals generate approach tendencies that involve perception, attention and cognitive activity toward the stimuli such that the characteristics of the stimuli may be learned. Negatively appraised stimuli are cognized so that they can be dealt with to the extent necessary, recognized in the future, and avoided if possible. (Schumann, 1997: 53f.)

To return to the age question, the areas of the brain responsible for stimulus appraisal appear to remain plastic until late in life, perhaps throughout life (see e.g. Schumann, 1997: 176ff.). This means that older learners retain the capacity for positive evaluation of situations, with the result, according to Pulvermüller and Schumann (1994), that successful late L2 learning remains a possibility.

> Positive evaluation of learning situations leads to amygdala-midbrain associations of language elements. Such evaluation connects linguistic assemblies to neurons in the amygdala and the midbrain. In turn, activation of these forebrain-midbrain networks enhances midbrain input to . . . forebrain structures and thereby facilitates learning in general and further language acquisition in particular. (Pulvermüller & Schumann, 1994: 721)

Age and Quality of Input

We turn now to perspectives on the age factor in language acquisition which focus on differences in the kinds of input experienced by language learners of different ages. These are of two types: those which assume a language learning superiority for children and explain this in terms of the kinds of interaction in which children typically engage, and those which acknowledge that older learners may have an initial advantage and account for this in terms of the former's greater efficiency at obtaining appropriately 'tuned' input.

One can include under the first heading the behaviourist conception of language acquisition according to which, as we saw earlier, the inchoate vocalisations of the infant are gradually shaped into 'verbal behaviour' by a process of 'selective reinforcement'. This process is envisaged as one whereby the caretakers of the child encourage, by repeated modelling and various kinds of reward, the production of those sounds which approximate to units in their language and ignore utterances which do not fall into this category (see Skinner, 1957). While this model provides an account of how speech emerges in the child, it does not explain why speech milestones normally occur within well-defined age-ranges. With regard to the L2 learner, the teaching methodology based on behaviourism, namely the audio-lingual/audio-visual approach, which developed during and after World War II, assumes that in order to promote maximally efficient L2 learning one needs to provide the same kind of modelling and reinforcing input as is supplied to infants (see e.g. Brooks, 1960; Stern, 1983: 30). Missing from the behaviourist account is any explanation of how 'naturalistic' L2 learners – immigrants, for example – can attain to high levels of proficiency without the benefit of 'selective reinforcement' from either their home (where a language other than the target L2 may be spoken) or their school or workplace (where the target language is simply a general medium of instruction/communication).

A non-behaviourist account of child language acquisition which lays great stress on interaction with caretakers and the resultant input is that of Bruner (see also Chapter 3). For Bruner (e.g. 1975) the structure of early language is a reflection of the child's pre-existing conception of the structure of co-operative action. This in turn, according to Bruner, develops from interactions with caretakers, particularly games such as 'Peek-a-boo', in which gesture, action and elements of language are used together to regulate joint attention and activity. Bruner is not specifically concerned with the age question, even in respect of early speech milestones, but one can point to proposals which seem to draw on the same kind of assumptions as Bruner's model and which do address the age issue. The reference here is to Asher's suggestion (see e.g. Asher & Price, 1967; Asher, 1981) that children acquire comprehension and fluency more efficiently than adults because they learn language initially through play activity which is rooted in physical reality, whereas adults' interactions tend to be physically static and larded with abstractions. Asher's Total Physical Response method of teaching foreign languages to older learners rests precisely on the assumption that teaching needs to be based on interactions which are concrete in orientation and which require of the learner an active, physical response – interactions, in other words, which ape those entered into by the child beginning to learn his/her L1. As Joiner (1981: 30) points out, other language teaching methods such as 'community language learning' and 'suggestology' also 'rely on regression or infantilization to liberate the child, i.e. the good language learner, within each student.' However, in these cases the 'regression' aimed for is less to a particular type of linguistic/pre-linguistic interaction than to a more open, less anxious state of mind (cf. discussion in last section).

Another input-oriented account of L1 acquisition is that which focuses attention on the particular features of speech addressed to children by their caretakers – variously labelled 'baby-talk', 'motherese', 'caretaker-talk', and 'child-directed speech' (see e.g. Jusczyk, 1997; Snow, 1986). One dimension of the distinctiveness of child-directed speech (CDS) lies in the phonetic domain:

. . . the speech tends to be slower, the pitch higher and more pauses inserted than would occur if the same sentences were spoken to mature speakers. Also more words are given stress and emphasis. (Steinberg, 1993: 22)

A further dimension is the grammatical simplicity but well-formedness of utterances in CDS. Every measure used in studies of grammatical complexity or of well/ill-formedess has revealed that speech addressed to children aged 18–36 months is simpler but also more grammatical than speech addressed to adults. One study by Newport (reported Steinberg, 1993: 143) with 15 mothers reports an incidence of only one ungrammatical utterance in 1500! Also, the semantic content of CDS is extremely restricted. Caregivers limit their utterances to the present tense, to concrete nouns, to comments on what the child is doing and what is happening around the child, and the words used tend to be 'basic' – *see* rather than *notice, go and see* rather than *visit, (all) gone* rather than *disappeared*, etc.

As McShane (1991:140) says, it is difficult not to assume that CDS 'makes it easier' for young children to identify the units of which utterances are composed. However, the precise effect of caregivers' input on children's language development is a matter of debate (see e.g. Harris, 1992: esp. Chapters 2–5) especially with respect to the effect of the presence, absence and/or frequency of particular features in adult speech on children's grammatical development. The role of input tuning as likely aids to the child's basic isolation of units is less of an issue, although Cutler (1994: 86f.) argues that the above-described features of CDS cannot be absolutely indispensable to isolating word-units, as there are cultures in which CDS does not exhibit such features. The question of cultural variation in relation to CDS is one which is widely used as an argument against its having a truly important role in language acquisition (Foster-Cohen, 1999: Chapter 5; Pinker, 1994: 39ff.), notwithstanding Snow's (1986: 85ff.) demonstration that a culture which does not make use of Western-style CDS may use other devices to supply the child with comprehensible formulae/chunks which can be progressively used as a basis for the discovery of linguistic regularities. In short, the precise connection between the features of CDS and the emergence of language in the child remains mysterious. Nevertheless, much has been made in some quarters of the divergences between CDS and adult-directed speech and their likely consequences. Thus, Macnamara (1973a, 1973b) claims that older language learners do not benefit from input tuning and that, therefore, to compare child L1 learning success with adult L2 learning failure and to draw from this comparison conclusions about intrinsic abilities is to oversimplify.

The above does not address the instance of the child learning an L2 from sources other than a full-time caregiver – as in the case of the child of immigrants who continue to use the language of their country of origin in the home. Hatch (1978b) suggests, however, that one can discern a distinction here, too, between the kind of input received by child and adult learners respectively. From her examination of data from relevant L2 interactions she infers a tendency for speech directed at children in any language and from any source to be more concretely oriented and context-embedded than speech directed at adults (Hatch, 1978b: 424; Warner-Gough & Hatch, 1975: 306f.). Hatch's work draws its inspiration from that of Scollon (1974, 1979), who shows that in L1 acquisition 'horizontal' structures, i.e. combinations of linguistic elements, develop out of interactions in which such elements are deployed 'vertically' in successive turns. Hatch finds the same kind of 'vertical' structures in data from children acquiring an L2. For example:

Juan:	teacher lookit (holds up a quarter)
NS [native speaker]:	Mmhmm. A quarter
Juan:	quarter
NS:	For what?
Juan:	For Monday (the day milk money is due)
NS:	On Monday? For what?
Juan:	For milk.

(Cited by Hatch, 1978c: 144)

As far as adult L2 learners are concerned, on the other hand, the development from 'vertical' to 'horizontal' construction is 'less strong' (Hatch, 1978b: 431), a fact which Hatch relates to the longstanding establishment of the syntactic expression of semantic relationships in the adult's L1. Whatever the reason, Hatch's findings indicate that children in the beginning stages of language learning receive more support and cues than adult beginners from their interlocutors . It might be added, however, that, whatever about scaffolding, there seems to be a tendency for input addressed by native speakers and teachers to L2 novices (of any age) to be broadly tuned to their needs (see e.g. Arthur *et al.*, 1980; Ferguson, 1975; Henzl, 1973), and that to this extent Macnamara's claim that adult L2 learners do not benefit from input tuning is overstated.

Hatch (e.g. 1980: 181) is very frank about the tentativeness of her proposals and is reluctant to draw any very firm conclusions about input-type and age-differences in language learning. Actually, she seems inclined to relate any such differences as much to age-related 'lack of inter-action opportunities' as to 'quality of the input' (Hatch, 1983c: 75). However, her suggestion that amount of input reduces with age is questionable. It seems more plausible to argue, as Krashen does (see above) that adults' better 'conversational management' skills enable them to obtain *more* input from their interlocutors. Krashen (e.g. 1981: 119–37) also addresses the issue of quality of input. He regards CDS as significant because it seems to be roughly tuned to the child's linguistic level, thus providing intelligible but stretching input, and because the attentiveness it implies suggests optimal affective-motivational conditions. He refers too to the earlier-mentioned evidence that speech addressed to L2 learners also shows signs of being adjusted to the addressees' proficiency level. Subsequently (e.g. Krashen, 1985: 4ff.) he took on board the above-mentioned evidence of cross-cultural differences in CDS suggesting that 'simplification' is not a universal feature of speech addressed by adults to infants. Krashen acknowledges that there may be some variation across cultures with respect to the mode of input presentation, its source and its amount, but goes on to affirm that '[t]here is nothing in the cross-cultural data to suggest that comprehensible input is not the essential ingredient for language acquisition' (Krashen, 1985: 8). Another possible response might be to replace the concept of 'simplification' and 'simple codes' with something which is more widely applicable[14] . The point to be retained, though, is that differences between speech addressed to child language learners and speech addressed to adult language learners may not always and everywhere be as vast as some researchers have supposed. On the one hand, older L2 learners also receive input adjusted to their needs, and, on the other, infants do not in all cultures receive input marked by the stereotypical features of CDS.

So much for input-based explanations of age differences in language learning which assume that the younger a learner is the more efficiently he/she will acquire (at least some aspects of) the target language. Scarcella and Higa (1982: 175), however, wish to account for the 'growing evidence that older learners are able to acquire a second language . . . faster than younger learners, at least in the initial stages of L2 acquisition'. They hypothesise that older learners are more active than younger learners in the 'negotiation work' in face-to-face interactions, and that they are in consequence more successful than younger learners at eliciting input which meets their needs. They further hypothesise that younger learners receive more simplified input but that because such learners are not so actively involved in 'negotiating', the adjustments to which their input is subject are often ill-judged and unhelpful. In an experiment designed to test these hypotheses Scarcella and Higa obtained data from 14 Spanish-speaking learners of English as an L2 – 7 children, aged 8.5 to 9.5 and 7 adolescents aged 15.5 to 16.5. The data were elicited by pairing a group of 7 native speakers of English alternately with each of the experimental groups and requiring each resulting dyad to participate in a block-building task. The analysis of the conversations which occurred during this 10-minute activity shows that with the younger learners the native speakers did a great deal more work in the conversation than with the older learners and that, accordingly, the older learners took much more of a role in shaping the discourse than did the younger learners.

On the basis of these findings Scarcella and Higa conclude (1982: 193f.) that older learners' 'headstart' in L2 acquisition derives from active involvement in conversation, which 'charges' the input and allows it to 'penetrate' deeply, and which enables older learners to obtain clarifications that are precisely relevant to the gaps in their understanding. Younger learners' initial disadvantage is explained in an exactly converse fashion – on the basis that such learners do not employ these strategies to the same extent, and that even the simplified input that they receive may thus contain structures and vocabulary which they do not understand. This account clearly ties in with the point made by Krashen about older learners having superior 'conversational management' skills. It has an agreeably commonsensical ring to it and does not appear to make any unwarranted assumptions about age-effects. However, as Scarcella and Higa readily acknowledge, the evidence it relies on is extremely limited and leaves the question of cause and effect essentially unanswered.

The 'De-coupling' Hypothesis

We come now to the 'de-coupling' account of age effects in language learning proposed by Bever (1981). Bever is not impressed (1981: 179) by the paucity of hard evidence for the critical period, claiming there is 'ample individual evidence' that older L2 learners find it difficult to attain native-like proficiency. The explanation of the age-linked decline in language learning ability which he postulates revolves around the relationship between the 'psychogrammar' (i.e. internalised linguistic knowledge) and the processes of speech perception and production, out of the mediation between which, according to his hypothesis, the psychogrammar develops. His thesis is, essentially, that once the psychogrammar is established it becomes 'decoupled' from language perception and production processes and thus unavailable for further language learning. The analogy Bever uses is that of cell differentiation. Early in their development all membranes of individual cells are permeable to fluid and therefore to bio-chemical information from adjacent cells. This information influences the individual cell's development as a function of its surrounding cells. However, as the cell matures, a critical point is reached when, owing to internal growth processes, an impermeable layer is formed on the cell wall.

From that point on, further differentiation is independent of external influence. The 'moral' of this discovery for Bever is that 'the facts of a critical period are accounted for by the normal processes of growth' (1981: 184), processes which cause partially independent systems to become fully independent.

Bever first attempts to show that speech perception and speech production are independent of each other in the adult. Second, he tries to establish the reality of the existence of the psychogrammar in the adult. Finally, he tries to demonstrate that the psychogrammar's function is to mediate between language perception and production as these develop in childhood. With regard to the first stage of the argument, he claims that *prima facie* evidence for the independence of language perception and production in the mature individual is supplied by:

- the conflicting needs of perception and production (maximum explicitness on the one hand, maximum economy on the other);
- the differing major planning units of the two processes (deep meaning-based sentoids[15] and surface structure clauses respectively);
- the fact that we can understand utterances which we could not ourselves produce, and can produce utterances which we should fail to understand if they were produced by someone else.

In the second stage of his argument, Bever notes that most areas of psychological research postulate a distinction between what we 'know' and what we 'do' – to account, for example, for the results of experiments using optical illusions where subjects *know* that two lines are equal in length and yet continue to *perceive* them as unequal. He goes on to refer to the 'prodigious' achievements of that approach to the study of language which has posited a dichotomy between 'competence' (knowledge about one's language) and 'performance' (actual linguistic behaviour). He also observes that certain linguistic sequences are well-formed but unusable, while others are ill-formed but usable. An example of the former is: 'The dog the cat the cricket chirped at meowed at barked at me'. This sentence is extremely difficult for the behavioural system to cope with, even though it is structurally identical to the unproblematic sentence: 'The reporter everyone I met trusts had predicted Lance's resignation'. As an example of an ill-formed but usable string Bever cites: 'Everyone forgot their coat.' He states that sequences of this kind are very widely used, despite the fact that they are ill-formed in the same way as the unusable string: 'Harry forgot their coat.'

On the question of the role of the psychogrammar in L1 development, Bever first argues (1981: 191) that there must be some 'initial internal language common to the systems of perception and production' since otherwise children 'might never map the same kind of structures for the same kind of idea-utterance pairs'. He also suggests that the psycho-grammar is necessary to organise language behavioural data for storage purposes. Of a piece with these proposals is his claim that the psychogrammar develops in part because the independently developing perception and production systems need to be brought roughly into line with each other. He sees evidence of the necessity for such 'equalibration' in the way in which perceptual and production strategies in L1 develop-ment seem to 'leap-frog' each other, so that a shift in the interpretation of a particular structure-type may not be followed by a change in production patterns until much later. Finally, Bever refers to evidence that children are aware of a distinction between what they say and what they 'ought' to say, citing (1981: 192) the following exchange:

Child: Mommy goed to the store
Father: Mommy goed to the store?
Child: No, Daddy; I say it that way, not *you!*
Father: Mommy wented to the store?
Child: No!
Father: Mommy went to the store
Child: That's right Mommy wen . . . Mommy goed to the store.

He claims that the psychogrammar is the developing repository of such awareness.

In summary, then, Bever argues that the psychogrammar constitutes the interface between what is acquired via speech perception and what is acquired via speech production, and that it translates from one domain to the other, regulating conflicts between the two separate emerging capaci-ties. However, he conceives of this function as extending only to the onset of adulthood, by which time 'the systems of perception and production are in almost complete register' (1981: 192), and the psychogrammar is no longer needed to mediate between them. At this point, according to Bever's model, 'the communication channel falls into disrepair because of disuse' (1981: 193), although by this time the psychogrammar has become so thor-oughly entrenched that it remains as an independent representation of utterance-idea relationships. The consequences of this putative break in the link between psychogrammar and processing systems are envisaged as follows:

> After this age, the problem of language learning is how to map each of the distinct and separate L1 behavioral systems onto the correspond-ing systems in the second language, in partial independence of each

other. This is not only likely to make the job of learning a language more difficult; it will certainly make it more disjointed. (Bever, 1981: 193)

Bever sees several virtues in his interpretation of the critical period for language learning. First, it relates the critical period to the intrinsic properties of language acquisition rather than treating it as something special which is 'tacked on' to other aspects of language acquisition. Second, it accounts for the 'commonly reported fact' that people who continue to learn new languages do not experience a decline in language learning capacity. According to Bever's model, in such cases the normal 'decoupling' of psychogrammar from processing systems simply does not occur. Thirdly, the model's predictions are consistent with a number of experimental findings, detailed below.

One prediction which Bever claims for his model is that age of starting to learn an L2 will correlate with measures of speech performance but not with measures of linguistic consciousness. This follows, says Bever, from the posited disjointedness of L2 learning after 'decoupling', and the consequent imbalance between production and perception in the older language learner. The prediction is borne out by Oyama's (1976) finding that, although the age of arrival of her subjects in the United States correlated with their linguistic performance in English (see Chapter 4), there was no such correlation between age of arrival and ability to detect ambiguity or decode semantic relations – suggesting that the critical period relates to productive skills rather than to higher level linguistic consciousness.

Oyama's findings are again used by Bever to test a further prediction of his model, namely that the critical age will differ for different levels of linguistic skill. Because the phonological system of the mother tongue is mastered earlier than its syntax or semantics the phonological dimension of the communication channel between psychogrammar and processing systems is postulated as falling into disuse earlier than the other dimensions. This implies that the critical age for phonological learning will be younger than for acquiring syntax and semantics. Bever re-analyses Oyama's data with a view to calculating the year-to-year rate of improvement as a function of decreasing age of arrival:

A simple measure is the median age of the year-to-year transitions of greater-than-average improvement on a test. This median age is ten years for phonological accent and thirteen years for the syntactic-semantic measures which Oyama used. That is, the critical age does appear to differ for the different aspects of linguistic structure. (Bever, 1981: 195)

Further evidence cited by Bever in respect of the early acquisition of phonology and of the independence of conscious introspection from actual performance in this domain are the findings of Streiter (1976) and Pertz and Bever (1975) (referred to in Chapter 3). He interprets Streiter's findings as indicating that the infants in her study were less sensitive to those VOT transitions which were not functional in the language of their immediate environment. This suggests that their acquisition of the phonology of the latter was well under way even at this very early stage. Pertz and Bever (1975), on the other hand, found that children's capacity to predict the probability of certain non-English consonant clusters occurring in other languages improved with age. Bever's comment is: '[w]hile the ability to respond to fine phonetic features may decrease with age, the ability to make conscious introspective judgements may increase' (Bever, 1981: 196).

Finally, with regard to the predicted mutual influence of perception and production in the early stages of acquisition and their later independence, Bever cites some research he conducted with N. P. Denton into comprehension strategies. It is well known that young children learning English as an L1 pass through a stage of interpreting all *noun-verb-noun* sequences as representing *subject-verb-object*. Bever suggests that this strategy – which leads to worse comprehension at age four than at age two of sentences like *It's the cow that the horse kisses* – is influenced by productive patterns. Bever and Denton found the same strategy being used by Spanish-speaking children learning English as an L2 (all under eight), as their proficiency in the language increased. However, when Bever and Denton used the same procedures to test Spanish-speaking learners of English in their late teens (all over 16), they found no evidence of this strategy.

One has to say that Bever's treatment of the evidence is somewhat partial. For example, in relation to Oyama's work, he fails to comment on her finding that not only accent but also comprehension correlated negatively with age of arrival (see Oyama, 1978, discussed in Chapter 4). This obviously does not sit well with Bever's claim that later language learning is disjointed and that therefore the critical age will relate only to production. (Actually, the argument that later disjointedness of language learning implies an imbalance in one particular direction is in any case a *non sequitur*). With regard to the putative early decline of the capacity to acquire phonology, Bever neglects to mention that Streiter's subjects also showed a significant sensitivity to the voiced-voiceless transition, which is not functional in the language of their environment, and that even Kikuyu-speaking adults retained this sensitivity. He also draws a veil over all the other evidence that runs against the notion of an early decline in phonology-acquiring capacity (see Chapter 4). As for the non-appearance of the comprehension strategy for *noun-verb-noun* sequences among older L2 learners, Bever fails to take into consideration either differing degrees of cognitive maturity or the fact that by age 16 lessons from long experience of L1 use would probably militate against the adoption of simplistic strategies. Also, of course, no account is taken of the abundant evidence (see Chapter 4) that older learners have at least an initial L2 learning superiority.

A further difficulty with the model is its assumption that, except in those abnormal cases where new languages are continually acquired through childhood and adolescence into adulthood, there is an identifiable stage in the mid-teens where language learning can be said to have ceased. As we have seen in Chapter 3, this assumption is difficult to justify. Most evidence suggests that, on the contrary, the acquisition of pragmatic rules and lexis continues well into adulthood – being bounded perhaps only by death – and that even morphosyntactic and phonological development may persist well beyond puberty. This implies that communication between the processing systems and the psychogrammar has to remain open, so that the whole idea of a 'decoupling' of the former from the latter at the end of childhood is fundamentally implausible.

The Age Factor and Nativism

'Nativism' or, as it is sometimes called, 'innatism', is primarily associated with Chomsky and his followers. Its principal claim is that language acquisition is explicable only if one posits an inborn 'language faculty', including a 'language acquisition device', which is pre-informed as to the nature of what is to be acquired. This claim is linked to the suggestion that all human languages share the same general design characteristics, are subject to the same formal constraints, and draw on a common pool of primitive elements, and that these 'universals' derive from the characteristics of the language faculty. A further claim is that the language faculty is unique and species-specific, that is, distinct from all other human cognitive systems and not possessed by any known species other than *homo sapiens*.

The beginnings of Chomsky's nativism can be seen in his early discussion of the Skinnerian account of language acquisition. In his celebrated (1959) review of Skinner's *Verbal Behavior* (1957), having dismissed, because of lack of evidence, the behaviourist notion that language learning vitally depends on 'selective reinforcement', he points to the possibility of an internal rather than an experiential basis for the way in which language develops, suggesting that the 'suddenness' of the induction of the rules of the language being acquired is essentially a function of the point to which the human brain has evolved. He notes in later writings that, on the basis of what he characterises as 'a small amount of rather degenerate experience'

(Chomsky, 1978: 435), language – 'a system of remarkable complexity' (Chomsky, 1976b: 4) – emerges very early in the maturation of the normal child and that, despite many differences in the specific conditions operating from child to child and from environment to environment, it develops in a consistent manner. A consideration of these facts leaves, he says, 'little hope that much of the structure of the language can be learned by an organism initially uninformed as to its general character' (Chomsky, 1965: 58) and inevitably leads to the idea of 'rigid programming' (Chomsky, 1978: 435) – the idea that 'the child approaches the task of acquiring a language with a rich conceptual framework already in place and also with a rich system of assumptions about sound structure and the structure of more complex utterances' (Chomsky, 1988: 34). He returns again and again to this theme: The basic similarities of human languages are taken by Chomsky as further evidence for an innate language faculty, and the investigation of 'universal grammar' (UG), which seeks 'to formulate the . . . conditions that a system must meet to qualify as a potential human language' (Chomsky, 1972: 27) is seen as 'a study of the nature of human intellectual capacities'.

With regard to the uniqueness of the language faculty, Chomsky construes the evidence about the nature of the human linguistic capacity as suggesting that this is qualitatively different from other cognitive capacities. He argues (e.g. 1972: 90) that the grammar internalised by the language acquirer bears little resemblance to any other cognitive system and that, similarly, the 'schema of universal grammar' which he claims to be a necessary condition of language acquisition is unlike any other system of mental organisation. Moreover, to postulate an innate faculty for a particular kind of behaviour is already, by implication, to endow that behaviour and that faculty with a certain specialness. As Smith and Wilson (1979: 33) argue, 'if linguistic knowledge is different in kind from non-linguistic knowledge, then it is more likely that we need special programming to learn it; and if we have such special programming, then it is more likely that the result of language-learning will be different in kind from other systems not so programmed.

As for species-specificity, again there is *prima facie* evidence that language is a peculiarly human phenomenon. Chomsky (1972: 10) notes that even at pathological levels of intelligence humans achieve a proficiency in language which is unattainable by apes, despite the fact that in respect of problem-solving capacity and other adaptive behaviour apes may be superior. Again there is a mutual reinforcement between the claim that the language faculty is innate and the claim that it is species-specific. To say that language arises out of special programming is equivalent to a claim that the language faculty is 'inherent to what one might call "human nature..."[16] (Nique, 1974: 9), from which it is a short step to proposing that it is a *distinguishing* aspect of human nature. The other side of the coin is that if independent arguments concerning the distinctiveness of human language are accepted, then the 'postulation of an innate language acquisition device could . . . be used to explain why language is specific to *homo sapiens* and does not correlate across species with other forms of apparently "intelligent" behaviour' (Harris, 1980: 179).

As we have seen, part of the nativist argument is age-related, having to do with the early emergence of language in the young child. A further dimension of the link between the age issue and nativism is the early Chomskyan endorsement of Lenneberg's work. As we saw earlier, Lenneberg sets out a number of grounds for believing that the language capacity is uniquely human; proposes that the basis for this capacity may be transmitted genetically; and relates his species-specific, nativist perspective both to the age-related sequence of speech milestones and to his conception of the critical period of language readiness. Chomsky endorses these arguments. He is responsible for an appendix in Lenneberg's (1967) book in which he shows solidarity with Lenneberg's 'innate conception of "human language"' (Chomsky, 1967: 401), and elsewhere he is perfectly explicit in his sympathy with Lenneberg's notion of a critical period for language:

> There is reason to believe that the language-acquisition system may be fully functional only during a 'critical period' of mental development. See Lenneberg (forthcoming[17]) for an important and informative review of data bearing on this question. (Chomsky, 1965: 206f., note 32)

Other theorists working within a nativist framework have taken the critical period as given and have used its existence as an argument in support of a nativist conception of the language faculty. For example, Smith and Wilson include the following in their case for a 'special programming' view of language acquisition:

> If we measure general intellectual development in terms of logical, mathematical and abstract-reasoning powers, these powers are still increasing at puberty, when the ability to acquire native fluency in a language is decreasing rapidly. (Smith & Wilson, 1979: 33)

Similarly, Pinker takes for granted the notion that 'acquisition of a normal language is guaranteed for children up to the age of six, is steadily compromised from then until shortly after puberty, and is rare thereafter' (1994: 293). His basic thesis (p. 45) is that language is a 'specific instinct' with an 'identifiable seat in the brain' and perhaps a 'special set of genes', the neurological circuitry for which is dismantled '[o]nce the details of the local language have been acquired', on the basis that 'any further ability to learn (aside from vocabulary) is superfluous' (p. 294) and that it incurs metabolic costs. One can relate Pinker's perspective to Chomsky's notion of the language faculty as a unique subsystem and also to his comparison of the 'growth' of language to the 'growth' of physical organs (see e.g. Chomsky, 1978: 434).

Against this tendency for the age question to be associated with Chomskyan nativism has to be set the fact that in detailed discussion of his model Chomsky (e.g. 1965: 32) idealises away from developmental issues to a mechanism which is represented as operating in an instantaneous fashion. Obviously, Chomsky does not believe that the device actually functions thus. He accepts (e.g. 1965: 202, note 19) that the elaboration of a detailed account of the actual process of language learning would necessitate facing a whole range of developmental issues, but it is simply not his concern to contribute to such an account. For his purposes an idealisation focusing solely on the moment of 'selection' of the appropriate grammar is adequate.

One might add that Chomsky sometimes appeared to draw back from a firm commitment to a particular view of how the child's learning theory interacts with maturation and, specifically, from a definite stance on the critical period issue (see e.g. Chomsky, 1976b: 122f.). However, he continued to use the metaphor of physical growth – with all that this implies in maturational terms – when discussing language development (see above; see also e.g. Chomsky, 1976b: 10ff.; Chomsky *et al.*, 1979: 121ff.; Chomsky, 1988 *passim*). Noteworthy also is the fact that, in pointing to similarities between the development of language and the development of vision, he refers to critical periods for certain aspects of visual development (Chomsky, 1988: 159). Moreover there are clear indications from his writings that he simply takes it for granted that adult language learning is qualitatively different from child language acquisition (e.g. 1988: 179).

Not only dyed-in-the-wool Chomskyans are attracted to the notion of a 'pre-wired language module'. Skehan (2002: 81ff.), for example, speculates that just such a module uniquely adapted for the learning of syntax might be operative in the childhood years but not subsequently, with the result that later L2 learners have to make use of 'more general learning mechanisms', a view which broadly coincides with that of the advocates of the 'no access hypothesis' (see below). On the other hand, it has to be said that the whole idea of the existence of a self-contained, encapsulated innate language faculty is far from universally accepted. Many linguists and psycholinguists simply do not accept that language is 'walled off from other cognitive functions' (Deacon, 1997: 269). As Crystal notes, the issues of whether a biologically endowed language faculty exists and whether or not linguistic knowledge can be specified independently of other factors are both highly contentious: 'controversy abounds' (1997: 198).

Turning now to the question of the relevance of nativist perspectives for the Critical Period Hypothesis in its application to L2 acquisition, we saw in Chapter 4 that some L2 researchers working within a UG framework (e.g. Bley-Vroman, 1989; Schachter, 1988) have wished to claim that age effects in L2 acquisition are explicable in terms of post-pubertal L2 learners' no longer having access to UG. However, we also saw that this is far from the consensual position of L2 researchers with broadly Chomskyan allegiances. There are, in fact, four different points of view on this issue – summarised by Mitchell and Myles (1998: 61f.) as follows.

(1) *No access hypothesis*: UG is not involved in [late] L2 acquisition; it atrophies with age, and [late] L2 learners have to resort to more general problem-solving skills.

(2) *Full access hypothesis*: UG is accessed directly in [early and late] L2 acquisition, and L1 and L2 acquisition are basically similar processes, the differences observed being due to the difference in cognitive maturity and in the needs of the learner.

(3) *Indirect access hypothesis*: UG is not directly involved in [late] L2 acquisition, but it is indirectly accessed via the L1; therefore, there will be just one instantiation (i.e. one working example) of UG which will be available to the L2 learner, with the parameters already fixed to the settings which apply in the L1.

(4) *Partial access hypothesis*: some aspects of UG are still available and others not; for example, principles might be available, but some parameter settings might not. This approach needs to be differentiated from the indirect access hypothesis, as it takes UG and its various subcomponents as the starting point, rather than the L1, hypothesising that some submodules of UG are more or less accessible to the L2 learner.

The fact that there is such a dramatic absence of consensus on this issue among nativist L2 researchers does not inspire confidence. As was indicated in Chapter 3, the evidence is simply unclear, but it certainly does not point unambiguously in the direction of the proposition that post-pubertal L2 syntactic acquisition proceeds in a qualitatively different manner from L1 or early L2 syntactic acquisition. Accordingly, explanations of age-effects in L2 learning by reference to curtailment or reduction of access to UG have to be treated with a great deal of caution – to say the very least.

It is clear that there is an interaction between the notion of an innate language faculty and that of a critical period for language. We have seen that the speed with which language emerges in the young child, the stability of the sequence of age-related speech milestones and such evidence as there is of a critical period have all been exploited as arguments in favour of an innate language faculty, and that, in turn, 'special programming' has been used to explain age-related effects. With regard to L2 acquisition, some researchers have claimed that late L2 learning is less successful because the post-pubertal language learner no longer has access (or no longer has full access) to UG; this claim is, however, controversial even among nativists. As a footnote, one might add that it is perfectly possible to support the Critical Period Hypothesis without signing up to Chomskyan-style nativism; for example, one of the strongest recent proponents of the Critical Period Hypothesis has been DeKeyser, who (e.g. 2003) simply dismisses the Chomskyan conception of an innate language faculty.

Summary and Conclusions

(1) A number of quite diverse explanations have been offered for the age factor in language acquisition. These focus, respectively, on:
   (a) sensory acuity;
   (b) competition between languages;
   (c) neurolinguistic factors;
   (d) cognitive developmental factors;
   (e) affective-motivational factors;
   (f) quality of input factors;
   (g) the 'decoupling' of the processing systems from the psychogrammar;
   (h) innate 'programming'
(2) With regard to (a):
   (i) The idea that language learning capacity is impaired by a deterioration in hearing acuity beginning in adolescence is undermined by the fact that adults continue to perceive voicing distinctions not functional in their own language and also by evidence of adult learners' superiority in L2 performance – at least in the initial stages of learning.
   (ii) Evidence of significant hearing loss in old age can be invoked to help explain why elderly L2 learners have particular difficulties in the oral-aural domain.
   (iii) Evidence of a considerable decline in visual acuity in senescence can also be seen as a possible factor in classroom language learning undertaken by the elderly.

(3) With regard to (b):
(i) The behaviourist conception of earlier established L1 habits inhibiting the subsequent formation of L2 habits has been shown to be
inadequate on general theoretical grounds; furthermore, as customarily presented, the behaviourist explanation makes incorrect
predictions, overemphasises negative transfer, and takes no
account of evidence that older learners may outperform younger
learners.
(ii) On the other hand, there is a fair amount of support in the literature
for the general notion of a trade-off between L1 and L2 proficiency,
and, to the extent that entrenched L1 proficiency at later ages may
be taken to militate against the acquisition of high levels of L2 proficiency, this may bear on the question of L2 age effects; contrariwise, on this basis, the acquisition of an L2 may be assumed to have
an impact on L1 acquisition and use; however, the suggestion that
the early acquisition of an L2 seriously disrupts L1 acquisition is in
conflict with recent evidence on bilingual education, except that
which relates to so-called 'subtractive' situations.

(4) With regard to (c):
(i) Penfield's claim that because of decreasing cerebral plasticity language learning beyond the end of the first decade of life is
'unphysiological' runs into the problem that there are many examples of highly successful adult L2 learning, which suggests that, if
there is a physiological dimension to age effects, it is not all-
determining.
(ii) Concerning Lenneberg's proposal linking a critical period for language learning, ending at puberty, to the process of lateralisation
of language functions, the available evidence does not support the
notion of a starting point of absolute hemispheric equipotentiality
in respect of language functions; nor does it clearly favour a position which would postulate a continuing lateralisation process of
relatively long duration.
(iii) With regard to ultimate laterality the available evidence challenges the simple view that the left hemisphere is *the* language
hemisphere and that the right hemisphere has no involvement in
language processing, which calls into question Lenneberg's strictly
dichotomous representation of mature laterality of functions, and
casts doubt on absolutist interpretations of the 'completion' of
lateralisation; in relation to L2 acquisition, there appears to be
some evidence of greater right hemisphere involvement in subserving late-acquired L2 competence than in subserving early-
acquired L2 competence, although the evidence is not unambigu-

ous and, moreover, differences of L2 organization in the brain are interpretable as the consequence rather than the cause of lower proficiency among later beginners.

(iv) Proposals that posit a continuing process of localisation or different maturational timetables of different neuron-types, and, on this basis, a series of critical periods relating to different language skills are based on questionable interpretations of the neurological evidence and make assumptions (e.g. in respect of age constraints on accent acquisition) that are not unambiguously supported by language acquisition evidence.

(v) Claims arising from brain-imaging research that L2 age effects are related to different cerebral organisation for early and later L2 beginners are probably insufficiently cautious in their interpretation of the brain-imaging evidence and in any case fail to take account of the possibility that such differences as have been identified may be a function of proficiency-level differences rather than of maturational factors.

(vi) Walz's suggestion that accent and grammar acquisition is subserved by the early-maturing thalamus is inconsistent both with evidence from language acquisition research that accent and grammar are not necessarily unacquirable or less efficiently acquirable beyond the very early years and with neurological evidence associating rather different functions with the thalamus.

(5) With regard to (d):

(i) Piaget's explanation of the emergence of language in the child as resulting from the expansion of consciousness occasioned by the child's learning to co-ordinate sense perceptions and movement, in other words, by the constructions of the 'sensori-motor' phase, is unsatisfactorily unspecific.

(ii) Attempts to relate a putative decline in language learning capacity at puberty to the onset of 'formal operations', the fourth and final Piagetian stage of cognitive development, are rather divergent in the particularities of their argumentation. They also seem to have implausible implications for the cognitive attainments of mental retardates whose language development appears to cease at puberty, seem to make wrong predictions about the relationship between degree of cognitive maturity and language acquiring capacity, and cannot account for evidence against a consistent global superiority for younger language learners.

(iii) Other accounts, which suggest that greater cognitive maturity confers some language learning advantages, at least initially, are intuitively appealing but are troubled by evidential problems when they attempt to specify precisely which language skills are more easily acquired at later stages; Krashen's later version of the role of cognitive development in language learning also has particular theoretical underpinnings which are highly controversial.

(iv) Bialystok and Hakuta's suggestion that age effects in L2 ultimate attainment may relate to the deterioration over the lifespan of various general cognitive capacities is plausible only to the extent that age-related changes in language learning capacity can be shown to be gradual and constant; there is a good deal of evidence pointing in this direction, but some of this is controversial.

(6) With regard to (e):

(i) Explanations which link adults' supposed language learning inferiority to the increased self-consciousness which is said to accompany the onset of 'formal operations' do not appear to take into consideration the fact that Piagetians see the intensity of this self-consciousness as diminishing rapidly.

(ii) Stengel's Freudian account of the emergence of language in children and of an assumed decline in language learning capacity in later years is vague, and its unqualified 'younger = better' assumptions are unjustified by the evidence; on the other hand its perspective on the posited decline in language learning capacity is not rigidly deterministic, and does allow for variability among learners.

(iii) Guiora's discussion of the age-factor in language learning in terms of the increasing impermeability of the 'language ego' is based on somewhat inconclusive evidence, is unclear about the precise aspect(s) of language learning which is/are supposedly affected by language ego impermeability and, like Stengel's account, rests on simplistic 'younger = better' assumptions, although, also like Stengel's account, it does imply that given the right affective conditions adults can be successful language learners.

(iv) Schumann's attempt to integrate various insights from research into affective-motivational aspects of language learning, and to explain L2 learning failure among adults as a function of social and psychological distance receives general support from studies of immigrant learners of L2s and has no difficulty in accommodating cases of successful adult language learning, but the concepts of social and psychological distance are difficult to define rigorously – which leads to verification problems – and Schumann's account offers no explanation of older learners' initial L2 learning *superiority*. His more recent neurologically oriented account of motivation specifically offers an explanation for the successes reported among older L2 beginners as well as for younger beginners' general tendency to do better, but remains hypothetical.

(7) With regard to (f)

    (i) The behaviourist claim that 'verbal behaviour' emerges in the child because of the 'selective reinforcement' of certain of his/her vocalisations by his/her caretakers and that L2 teaching is optimally based on a similar approach provides no explanation of the stable, age-related sequencing of speech milestones nor of language learning from sources other than caretakers and is, in any case, inadequate to account for the facts of ordinary language acquisition and use.

    (ii) Non-behaviourist discussion of input which suggest that language input received by children is superior for language learning purposes to that received by adults are flawed by simplistic younger = better' assumptions, but also tend not to give appropriate weight to the fact that the effect of differing input on actual acquisition has yet to be demonstrated, to the fact that L2 learners of any age may receive 'tuned' input, or to the fact that child-directed speech is not universally characterised by the kinds of specific features that are usually associated with it in Western cultures.

    (iii) Scarcella and Higa's speculation that older L2 learners' 'headstart' results from their greater efficiency at obtaining input which is precisely relevant to their needs, while apparently in line with language acquisition research evidence about age-effects, is as yet based on rather sparse evidence regarding differences between input to younger and older L2 learners and regarding the impact of such differences on learning.

(8) With regard to (g), Bever's suggestion that older language learners are disadvantaged because the channel of communication between their language processing systems and their psychogrammar has broken down is based on a very partial treatment of the language acquisition evidence and makes what seem to be false assumptions not only about age-related differences among language learners but also about the cessation of language learning in normal individuals.

(9) With regard to (h):

    (a) Discussion of the age issue has interacted with discussion of the notion of an innate language faculty. The early emergence of speech, the stability of the sequence of age-related speech milestones and evidence for a critical period for language acquisition have all been referred to in this context. However, the idea of an innate language faculty remains highly controversial.

(b) Some reseachers have attempted to explain age-related effects in L2 acquisition in terms of curtailment or reduction of access to UG at the end of childhood. However, by no means all UG-oriented L2 researchers take this line, and the multiplicity of views on this issue casts doubt on the validity of the proposition, even if one accepts the reality of UG.

Notes

1. Cf. Chapter 3.
2. Titone (1985a) discusses a further study which provides rather novel support for the interdependence hypothesis, namely Ghenghea's (1984) investigation of reading skills in Romanian (as an L1). This study indicates a transfer of such skills not only from Romanian to German but also in the opposite direction.
3. The cortex is generally regarded as the most advanced portion of the brain. Essentially it is the outer surface of the cerebrum and for this reason is sometimes called the 'pallium' or 'cloak' of the brain. It is about one-eighth of an inch thick but has an area (enlarged by fissures, grooves and folds) of about 400 square inches (cf. Smith, 1968; Pelican edition: 405).
4. 'The axons . . . can . . . be called the nervous wiring of the body. Each axon is part of a neuron, a nerve cell, and the axon is one finely stretched extension of that neuron, It is so fine that it is often only a hundredth of a millimeter in diameter, and yet its length may be several feet' (Smith, 1968; Pelican edition: 421).
5. I.e. nerve cells.
6. Under 'language universals' linguists include general design characteristics such as double articulation (i.e. the organisation of meaningless units sounds – into meaningful units – morphemes, words – and of the latter into larger meaningful units – phrases sentences), formal universals such as constraints on the operation of rules, and substantive universals, that is, the primitive elements out of which grammars must be composed (noun phrase, verb phrase, etc.). Clearly, knowledge of fundamental aspects such as these would not go very far in even the most rudimentary communication.
7. 'In dichotic listening, subjects are presented with competing simultaneous auditory stimuli, one to each ear. In right-handed subjects the right ear generally excels for verbal material, reflecting left hemisphere specialisation. The left ear excels for certain non-verbal stimuli indicating right hemisphere dominance' (Krashen, 1973: 66).
8. 'In 1929, an Austrian psychiatrist named Hans Burger discovered that patterns of electrical activity could be recorded from electrodes placed at various points on the scalps of human beings. These patterns were called the *electroencephalogram* (EEG), literally meaning "electrical brain writing". Although the EEG is monitored from the scalp, Burger was able to demonstrate that some of the activity it records originates in the brain itself and is not simply due to scalp musculature' (Springer & Deutsch, 1985: 94).
9. I.e. an electronic hiss.
10. 'The technique called tachistoscopic presentation allows normal subjects to react to a visual stimulus presented to only one visual field. The stimulus is flashed to one or other side of the fixation point so briefly that subjects do not

have time to change their gaze, allowing the image to be part of the other visual field' (Obler & Gjerlow, 1999: 30).

11. This technique, pioneered by Penfield (see earlier discussion), involves directly stimulating exposed areas of brain tissue with an electric current. The patient is conscious during the procedure and, whenever the stimulation of a particular area causes *aphasic arrest*, i.e. temporary speech loss, the area in question is noted as part of the language area of the brain. In the case of the bilingual, differing effects of stimulation according to the language being used results in a different neurological 'map' being drawn for each language.

12. 'Magnetic resonance imaging (MRI) . . . can show brain morphology through the creation of a magnetic field around the head that modifies some characteristics of the hydrogen atoms present in cerebral structures' (Fabbro, 1999: 67).

13. Cf. also J. A. C. Brown's comment: 'Libido is best conceived as drive energy, the principal components of which are sexual . . . but Freud never subscribed to the view that no other instincts existed or that everything is sex' (Brown, 1961: 22).

14. There are good grounds for dispensing with this kind of terminology in relation to speech addressed to L2 learners also. It is certainly not the case that such speech is consistently 'simpler' than other discourse in terms of length of utterance or morphosyntax. Making an utterance comprehensible to a non-native speaker may actually entail linguistic complexification in order, for example, to make presuppositions, implicatures, etc. more explicit. For some examples and further discussion see e.g. Maclaran and Singleton (1984a, 1984b).

15. I.e. sentence-like structures.

16. Our translation: 'inhérente à ce que 1'on pourrait appeler "la nature humaine"'.

17. The reference here is to Lenneberg's (1967) book.

Chapter 6

The L2 Educational Dimension

Introductory

This chapter examines the role of age in language learning from an educational point of view. Clearly, if extended to all aspects of education in its broadest sense and to all varieties of language learning, such an examination could fill several books rather than a single chapter. Discussion is therefore confined here to education in the formal sense of the term and to the learning of languages other than the mother tongue. Even within these bounds, however, possible discussion points are myriad. In fact, just two topics have been selected for consideration: the much debated, but still unsettled, question of the advantages and disadvantages of introducing L2s into the primary school curriculum and the less frequently treated topic of L2 programmes for older adult learners.

L2s in the Early School Years

The case for the introduction of L2s into the initial stages of formal education tended in the past to be based on the premise that young children learned languages, or at least some aspects of languages, more efficiently than their elders. As Stern (1983: 132) notes, the movement advocating foreign languages in the elementary school (FLES) in the 1950s and 1960s was much influenced by the 'younger = better' ideas of Penfield and the neurological evidence he adduced in their support (see above, Chapter 3 and Chapter 5). However, there is little doubt that a powerful factor in the widespread acceptance of 'scientific' arguments like those of Penfield was the anecdotally based folk-wisdom according to which language learning that begins in childhood usually produces better results than later language learning (see above Chapter 4).

We have seen that, in fact, the hard evidence from studies of the age factor in language acquisition effectively puts paid to the strongest and most straightforward versions of the 'younger = better' position. In Chapter 3 it was shown that there was no unambiguous L1 evidence for an abruptly ending critical period of language readiness, and that the capacity to expand L1 knowledge remained operative into adulthood and beyond. As far as L2 evidence is concerned, Chapter 4 demonstrates clearly that, on the basis of this evidence, it is impossible to sustain the claim that the younger L2 learner is in all respects and at all stages more efficient and successful than the older learner. Nor does the evidence on the acquisition of L2 phonetic/phonological or basic communicative skills consistently support the hypothesis that younger learners excel in these particular domains. However, it is true that long-term studies of 'naturalistic' L2 learners show that after a period of about five years learners whose exposure to the L2 began in childhood are in general outperforming learners whose experience of the L2 began in adulthood.

The evidence that is least congenial to the younger = better position arises from studies of experiments in early L2 instruction. As we saw in Chapter 4, what generally emerges from evaluations of early L2 programmes is that the lead they confer on those who benefit from them over those who do is fairly short-lived. In other words, within a few years of FLES and non-FLES pupils coming together in the same L2 classes, the latter have all but caught up with the former in terms of L2 performance. What is at first sight puzzling about such findings is that they seem to be exactly contrary to the findings from the naturalistic L2 studies referred to earlier which show younger learners catching up with older learners and eventually outperforming them. Reference was made in this connection in Chapter 4 to Stern's (1976) claim that in the Burstall *et al.* study there might have been a blurring effect resulting from mixing early beginners and later beginners in the same classes at secondary level. It is perhaps worth expanding on this argument, which applies with equal force to many school-based age studies.

> Any teacher knows that if pupils who already have some experience of a given school subject are mixed with beginners and subjected to instruction which merely takes them over ground they have already covered, the result is boredom and demotivation – hardly ideal conditions for learning. In any case, if learners are not being given new material to work on, how can their knowledge do other than stagnate? Furthermore, pupils who, because of previous tuition, are markedly more proficient in a given domain than their peers quickly learn to hide the fact, in order to silence sarcastic comment; obviously, such pressure to conceal knowledge from others will hardly favour its development or even its retention. (Singleton, 1995: 159)

A further point made in Chapter 4 was that the apparent discrepancy between naturalistic and school-based findings might be related to the vastly greater amount of exposure to the L2 implied by a naturalistic situation as opposed to a classroom situation. It was argued that if 'eventual' attainment in the context of naturalistic learning denoted a state of competence arrived at after about five years, a comparable 'eventual' state of competence for the formal learner in terms of amount of exposure would be reached only after many times five years and that, since none of the FLES studies involved a learning period of this kind of duration, it was impossible to be certain what FLES learners' eventual' attainment might be. We can take this line of reasoning a stage further. The studies of naturalistic L2 learning carried out by Snow and Hoefnagel-Höhle (see above, Chapter 4) which appear to indicate that the initial language learning superiority displayed by older learners gradually diminishes suggest that it takes about a year for this 'headstart' to be eroded. Now, let us assume that a naturalistic learner receives L2 input for an average of 10 hours a day – a conservative estimate, especially in an age of 24-hour broadcasting. On this basis, the older learner's superiority wears away after 3650 hours of input. Assuming that the formal L2 learner receives one hour of L2 instruction per school day for 40 weeks of the year – a generous estimate – i.e. 200 hours per year, in terms of input time the naturalistic year of L2 learning represents more than 18 years of formal learning! In other words, if one accepts the premise of an initial advantage for older learners and an 'eventual' advantage for younger beginners, and if one takes the Snow and Hoefnagel-Höhle studies as providing evidence of the time-scale involved, then the 'eventual' advantage for younger beginners can be expected to manifest itself only at a stage well beyond the end of normal schooling.

One may entertain some doubts about a simple equation between 3650 hours of input over 12 months and the same amount of exposure over nearly two decades. However, what cannot be in doubt is the general importance of constantly bearing in mind the varying relationship between real time and exposure time when comparing different categories of L2 learners. The main point here is that the effect of non-FLES pupils catching up with FLES pupils shown by the above-mentioned studies can be attributed to the same initial language learning superiority associated with greater maturity that is revealed by naturalistic studies, the difference being that under a regime of very sparse exposure this superiority may last for several years. Much the same kind of point can be made about immersion studies (see above, Chapter 4). The fact that, for example, the early and late total immersion students compared in Harley's study performed at roughly similar levels could be ascribed to the fact that each group had received only about 1000 hours of L2 input and that the 'eventual' superiority of the younger beginners had therefore not had sufficient time – in exposure terms – to manifest itself. If 1000 hours of exposure time accounts for a year plus in real time in the context of total immersion – as it

seems to in Harley's estimation – then, on the basis of our earlier calculation, a year's worth of naturalistic L2 learning is equivalent in input terms
to something approaching four years of total immersion in a school
situation.

Exposure time *per se* is widely recognised as a crucial factor in differenti-
ating levels of language proficiency. Some researchers have seen the critical
distinction between L1 and L2 acquisition as residing in the exposure time
difference. Kennedy, for example, writes:

> . . . above all, the importance of the difference between the amount of
> time spent by the child learning his first language and that available for
> learning the second language should not be underestimated. It is not
> difficult to calculate the many thousands more hours which the first
> language learner has in exposure to the language he is learning in com-
> parison with the time spent by second language learners. The second
> language learner is typically a part-time learner. (Kennedy, 1973: 75)

With regard to L2 learning, a widely quoted finding from Carroll's
(1969, 1975) researches is that amount of instruction is *the* most important
predictor of L2 learning success. Burstall *et al.'s* (1974) study yielded a
similar finding. At a more theoretical level, not only Krashen's Input
Hypothesis but all perspectives which foreground the role of input in
language learning also imply that exposure time is crucially important.

The logical conclusion must be that the earlier one starts learning an L2
the better the eventual outcome will be. If there is also some evidence that
younger learners in the long run outperform older learners with equal
exposure, then this ought to be a further argument in favour of early L2
instruction. The difficulty is that in a formal learning situation, as we have
seen, older students' initial learning superiority may for a considerable
period of time mask these long-term effects. Also, in the absence of very
long-term studies, it is impossible at present to be precise about the
magnitude of the eventual advantages of an early start in the formal
learning of an L2. It is thus impossible to weigh in an informed fashion the
benefits of early L2 instruction against the costs thereof. A further question
that arises is whether age effects are likely to be associated with school-
based learning at all, given that such learning is likely to be more conscious
and explicit and thus, according to researchers such as DeKeyser, not
affected by maturational factors (cf. discussion of cognitive developmental
factors in Chapter 5).

If the long-term positive effects of early L2 instruction have not yet been
firmly established, can we at least rely on there being no negative effects
associated with the early introduction of an L2? One way of approaching
this question is to look at research focusing on extreme examples of the phe-

nomenon. One such example is the case of children who grow up acquiring two languages more or less simultaneously. Admittedly, such early bilingualism does not immediately connect with formal educational issues, but if the early mastery of more than one language had deleterious consequences for any aspect of development, one might expect to find evidence of such among early bilinguals. One view is that there are no firm indications of bilingual children being either negatively or positively affected by their condition. This is the conclusion reached by Arnberg (1987: 31) after reviewing research on early bilingualism in relation to intelligence, cognitive development, language development and social development, and is also that of McLaughlin, whom she quotes, after a similar survey:

> . . . almost no general statements are warranted by research on the effects of early bilingualism. It has not been demonstrated that early bilingualism has positive or negative consequences for language development, cognitive functioning or intellectual development. (McLaughlin, 1984: 225)

Another view is that bilinguals may have cognitive advantages as compared with monolinguals. Many of the relevant studies in this connection are focused on language awareness and appear to demonstrate, for example, that bilinguals are more likely than monolinguals to have understood that linguistic signs are arbitrary and that an object and its attributes are to be distinguished from its label (see e.g., Ben Zeev, 1977; Bialystok, 1987; Ianco-Worrall, 1972). However, other cognitive advantages have been found for bilinguals in areas beyond the linguistic domain such as Piagetian conservation tasks and visual-spatial abilities (see, e.g. Diaz & Klingler, 1994) and in the capacity to solve problems based on conflict and attention (such as sorting cards by colour and then re-sorting by shape) (Bialystok, 1999).

A third view, as we have seen from discussion in Chapters 4 and 5, is that there is competition and compromise between competencies in more than one language. For example, a number of studies seem to indicate that bilinguals have representations of phonetic categories which differ from monolingual categories, and which, depending on the particularities of the communicative circumstances, to a greater or lesser extent compromise between the monolingual categories (see e.g. Flege, 1981, 1991; Obler, 1982; Schmidt & Flege, 1996; Zampini & Green, 2001). What this means is that bilinguals' competence in both their languages may differ from that of monolingual users of the languages in question. On the other hand, the differences seem to be typically subtle, and to be detectable only when very detailed analysis is brought to bear.

The other obvious extreme test case with relevance to the effects of early

L2 instruction is that of early L2 immersion programmes. We saw in the previous chapter that Swain and Lapkin, in an evaluation of Canadian immersion programmes published in 1982, found no ill effects on the first language development of immersion programmes. In a 'research update' published two years later they reiterate this point, as well as their earlier finding that general academic development is not impaired by participation in early immersion programmes:

> The English achievement results for students in the early total immersion programme indicate that, although initially behind students in unilingual English programmes in literacy skills, within a year of the introduction of an English Language Arts component into the curriculum, the immersion students perform equivalently on standardized tests of English achievement to students in the English-only programme. This is the case even if English is not introduced until grade 3 or grade 4. (Lapkin & Swain, 1984: 50)

> The results associated with early total-immersion programmes consistently show that, whether in science or mathematics, the immersion students perform as well as their English-instructed comparison groups. (Lapkin & Swain, 1984: 52)[1]

More recent evaluations of the Canadian immersion programmes (e.g. Swain, 1997) essentially repeat the above conclusions.

As we saw in Chapter 5, some researchers argue that such results are to be found only where the students in question are native speakers of the language of the majority community and are being immersed in another language. Where the language of immersion is the majority language and the students are speakers of a minority language, it is claimed, negative results can ensue for both languages – these negative results sometimes being referred to as 'semilingualism'. The explanation commonly advanced for this phenomenon is some version of what Cummins calls the 'interdependence hypothesis' (see above, Chapter 5). That is to say, it is suggested that the more academic aspects of language proficiency are language-independent, but are more likely to flourish if first approached via the language that the child is most at ease in, namely his/her first language. The whole concept of semilingualism has been sharply criticised, notably by Ekstrand. He claims (see e.g. Ekstrand, 1978b, 1978c, 1981a, 1981b, 1983, 1984a, 1984b, 1985) that the Finnish studies which are supposed to provide empirical support for the notion of semilingualism are fatally flawed by a confounding of variables – there being no control for socioeconomic status or IQ – and that they fail to take account of cognitive factors other than language. He further claims that the alleged positive effects of Swedish measures designed to counteract semilingualism – Finnish-medium elementary school programmes for children of Finnish immigrants – are not supported by hard evidence. These views are echoed by other researchers who have examined the Scandinavian data (see e.g. Henrysson, 1981; Bratt Paulston, 1983).

It has been counter-claimed that Ekstrand misrepresents the 'interdependence hypothesis', or 'mother tongue hypothesis', as he calls it (see e.g. Ruotsalainen, 1981). One might argue that one such misrepresentation is Ekstrand's claim (1981a: 29) that the 'mother tongue hypothesis' rests on the assumption that 'language 1 and language 2 must be learned in a certain order, not simultaneously'.[2] The crux of the interdependence hypothesis argument is *not* that there is something wrong with the simultaneous acquisition of two languages. It is that in the situations in question the order of acquisition of the two languages is a *given* – the first language of the minority community children being different from that of the majority community, which they acquire second – and that this given needs to be taken into account by educational planners. One might add that not all of the evidence adduced in support of the notion of semilingualism and the interdependence hypothesis is of Scandinavian origin (see Chapter 5) and that the supporters of the Finnish home language programmes in Sweden were confident enough about the effects of such programmes to have invited Ekstrand to inspect them for himself (see e.g. Hanson, 1981). More recent studies of Finnish-medium classes for Finnish immigrants in Sweden (e.g. Hill, 1995; Peura & Skutnabb-Kangas, 1994 – both reported in Skutnabb-Kangas, 1997) indicate that the provision of such classes yields benefits in respect of both the Finnish and the Swedish proficiency of the children involved. It should be noted that the provision of Finnish-medium classes does not imply the exclusion of Swedish, which is taught as an L2 in the schools in question, and in which those attending such schools are in any case already immersed in their day-to-day lives.

To sum up, early bilingualism does not seem to be associated with any significant negative effects and indeed may well yield metalinguistic and general cognitive benefits. With regard to early L2 immersion, any negative consequences in this case appear to be associated only with situations where members of linguistic minorities receive no formal educational support for their L1. With regard to the teaching of L2s to members of a majority community, it seems that early L2 immersion has no significant long-term deleterious effects either in terms of L1 development or in terms of general academic development. However, even accepting all of this, one can hardly say that the case for early L2 instruction which emerges from an examination of the evidence on the age factor in language learning and the bilingualism and bilingual education literature is irresistible. Given this, it might be interesting to examine the arguments that have been used in support of early L2 programmes in recent years by researchers who are well aware of the unhelpfulness of the empirical evidence.

An example of this kind of advocacy is an article of Ekstrand's (1971) based on a radio talk he gave on the subject of English in the Swedish primary curriculum. As is clear from references to Ekstrand's work in Chapter 4, he was to the fore in casting doubt on the 'younger = better' view of age in L2 learning. And yet, he was also a supporter of early L2 instruction. In justifying his stance in the article in question, he begins with two general educational arguments. First, he argues that all aspects of development are favourably affected by stimulation and that the earlier this stimulation begins the better. His second point is that, given the total amount of knowledge that the modern student has to acquire, it is natural to examine what can be broached early – the implication being that L2s fall into this category. His third argument relates to the rapid internationalisation of the world and suggests that in this context it makes sense for children to make early contact with a language and culture other than their own. Since the particular foreign language he is focusing on is English, he is able to underline his point by referring to the important role of English internationally. He also mentions the evidence that early L2 instruction has no ill effects on general academic development. Finally, with regard to evidence that older learners are better at L2 learning than younger learners, he argues that this is no more a reason to delay the introduction of L2 than the fact that older pupils demonstrate superiority at literacy skills and mathematics is a reason for deferring instruction in reading, writing or arithmetic.

Another researcher who accepts the evidence against the 'younger = better' hypothesis but who has nevertheless written in favour of L2s being learned at primary level is Genesee. In an article published in 1978, Genesee argues that Carroll's and Burstall's findings (see above) concerning the importance of instruction time in L2 learning suggest that an early beginning in this context is a good idea not because of any maturational considerations, but simply because of the additional exposure such an early start affords:

> . . . there is an advantage to early instruction in a second language as perhaps in the case of early instruction in any skill, which derives from the opportunity for more instructional time, rather than from the age factor *per se*. (Genesee, 1978: 150)

A secondary, related argument employed by Genesee is that if basic L2 competence is laid down in the early grades, then this can act as a foundation for the acquisition of more sophisticated skills in later years. Examples he gives (1978: 151) of these are discourse rules and socio-linguistic sensitivity. He claims that a late start may preclude working in such areas because of the heavy timetable demands at more senior levels.

A third researcher, Hatch, presents a somewhat different case, insofar as she does not in a real sense *advocate* early L2 instruction. She does, however, intimate (1983a: 197) that, despite the contradictory nature of the evidence on the age factor in language learning, she would in fact prefer her own children to start learning a L2 'at the early elementary stage rather than later'.[3] The reason she gives for this preference coincides exactly with Genesee's line of argument:

> I don't make that decision on the basis of physiological age. Rather I think the more *exposure* to language learning the better. And the more practice the better. The more interaction in the language the better. (Hatch, 1983a: 197)

Finally in this context, let us examine Titone's approach to justifying the early introduction of L2s into the school curriculum in the context of his direction in the 1980s of the ILSSE Project – a nationwide Italian experiment with foreign language teaching in elementary schools (Insegnamento delle Lingue Straniere nelle Scuole Elementare). In an article appearing in an edition *of L'Educatore* devoted almost entirely to this project, Titone (1986a) puts the emphasis on the broad educative value of beginning L2 learning early rather than on success in terms of L2 proficiency. He describes L2 teaching in the primary school as a way of bringing children to an early understanding and appreciation of different cultures and of thereby sowing the seeds of international understanding and friendship. He also refers to the possibility of using the early-acquired L2 subsequently as a medium of instruction in other subject areas, and thus of enhancing the integration of language education with other dimensions of the curriculum.

It is evident from the foregoing that one does not need to rely on maturational arguments in order to make a case for early L2 instruction. On the other hand, there is at least one question-mark over early L2 instruction which is *also* independent of the age factor issue. This has to do simply with the quality of the experience of learning a L2 in the initial stages of schooling; unless the experience is a positive one it is likely to result in antipathy towards the language and culture in question and in demotivation in respect of subsequent L2 learning experience. Of course, this kind of argument can be applied to any sequence of learning experiences at any stage of life. However, given that second-level schooling – of which L2 learning typically forms a part – is vital to the child's basic formation, it is particularly important that pupils should not arrive at the start of their secondary studies with negative attitudes towards a particular language or to language learning in general. We are obliged to ask, therefore, how probable it is that the experience of learning an L2 at primary school will in fact be positive.

The answer to this question undoubtedly depends on a multitude of factors, each of which is further decomposable. If one were to select, by way of example, just three such factors – course materials, teaching personnel and attitudes towards the language to be taught – one would need to pose a whole series of further questions, including the following:

(1) Are the course materials to be used:
- commercially produced and aimed at no particular age-group?
- commercially produced and aimed at older learners?
- commercially produced with the generality of younger learners in mind?
- locally produced (whether commercially or not) with local younger learners in mind?
- produced by one particular teacher with one particular class of younger learners in mind?
- some combination of the above?
- principally oriented towards the written language?
- principally oriented towards the spoken language?
- oriented towards both the written and the spoken language?
- dependent on a very restricted range of presentation modes and activity-types?
- flexible and varied in the presentation modes and activity-types employed?
- devoid of or replete with content which reflects learners' interests?

(2) Does the teaching personnel consist of:
- primary school teachers with only minimal training and interest in the language to be taught?
- primary school teachers with substantial training but little interest in the language to be taught?
- primary school teachers with substantial training and interest in the language to be taught?
- specialists in / native speakers of the language to be taught with only minimal training in respect of primary level teaching?
- specialists in / native speakers of the language to be taught with substantial training in respect of primary level teaching?
- some combination of the above?

(3) Is the language to be taught widely regarded in the community as:
  - of little cultural or vocational value?
  - of little cultural value but vocationally valuable?
  - of little vocational value but culturally valuable?
  - of high cultural and vocational value?
  - of little importance either nationally or internationally?
  - of little national importance but important internationally?
  - of little international importance but important nationally?
  - of importance both nationally and internationally?
  - representative of a culture which is on the whole congenial?
  - representative of a culture which is on the whole uncongenial?

The above is not intended to be a systematic or exhaustive 'grid', but merely indicative of the range of possibilities that present themselves. Clearly, one would not expect a positive early experience of L2 learning to result if the course materials used were aimed at a different age-group, of a narrowly written orientation, unvaried in their presentational approach and activity-types, and unreflective of learners' interests; if the teachers involved had little formation in or commitment to the language to be taught or on the other hand little training in respect of primary teaching; or if the language itself were popularly regarded as having little value or importance and/or as representing an uncongenial culture. When even some of these negative elements are present, the results can be less than happy in terms of learners' perceptions of the language learning experience. A good illustration of this point is the case of Irish.

In the Republic of Ireland Irish is taught as part of the core primary curriculum from the infant grades onwards. Since only a tiny minority of the population are native speakers of Irish – recent estimates range from 10,000 to 100,000 (Hindley, 1990; Markey, 2003; Ó Murchú, 1984; Salminen, 1993–99), for the vast majority of pupils it is an L2. The course materials are for the most part commercially produced, but with the particular situation of the Irish primary school pupil in mind. A new primary school curriculum, including a new learner-centred syllabus for Irish is currently being implemented (see e.g. Ó Murchú, 2001: 16f.), but from the late 1960s until the end of the 1990s the most widely used instructional materials were the so-called *Nuachúrsaí* ('New Courses'), which were classically audio-visual in nature and based on word and structure frequency research similar to that which underlay the establishment of *le français fundamental* (see, e.g. Ó Domhnalláin, 1967, 1977). They implied a fair range of modes of presentation (book, audio-tape, film-strip, felt-board, etc.), but the equipment requisite for the full exploitation of this range was often not available. Also, the activity-types specified were somewhat limited, much emphasis being placed on repetition and drilling. With regard to the teaching personnel, in order to be eligible for training as a primary teacher, a student has to have good school-leaving qualifications in Irish, and every teacher in training compulsorily attends courses in Irish and language teaching methodology. On the other hand, a large-scale survey among primary school teachers in the 1980s revealed that a substantial minority of such teachers were distinctly cool about Irish; while '73% of respondents [N = 9942] described their attitude to teaching Irish as enthusiastic, 22% described their attitude as indifferent' (INTO, 1985: 7). Public attitudes are in general terms favourable towards the language (see, e.g. CLAR, 1975; Ó Riagáin & Ó Gliasáin, 1984), but time and again surveys have shown that Irish is popularly seen as of cultural rather than vocational value and as bound up with the definition of national identity rather than having any wider role. As Deirdre Davitt (2003), Chief Executive of Bord na Gaeilge (the state board with responsibility for promoting Irish) recently put it:

> We may see little practical use for the language, yet we don't want it to die; we feel little need to use it on our daily lives, yet want our children to learn it. When these attitudes are probed more deeply, it seems that our language has become for us one of the few badges which we have left of a distinctive identity as a People.

The outcome of this particular combination of circumstances in terms of learners' perceptions can be gauged from a study conducted in the 1980s (Little *et al.*, 1984) which was mainly focused on the student population of Trinity College Dublin, thus very much on the academic success stories. It involved the sending of questionnaires to random samples of the undergraduate and graduate students registered at Trinity College. The great majority of these subjects had received all of their education in the Republic of Ireland, and had thus learned Irish at primary school; of these the undergraduate subjects would have been exposed to the *Nuachúrsaí*. Such subjects' reactions to the experience of primary school Irish is indicated in Table 6.1, which summarises, in respect of Irish, English and French,[4] their responses to the questions 'Which language did you enjoy learning most in primary school?' and 'Which language did you enjoy learning least in primary school?'

It is obvious that Irish comes off poorly in the above results. Nor does it fare any better in the follow-up survey which Little *et al.* carried out, using the same questionnaire, among undergraduate students registered at 12 other Irish third-level institutions. Table 6.2 tells its own story.

It would obviously be unwise to assume too much about the consequences of a disappointing experience of learning a L2 at primary school

Table 6.1 Enjoyment of Irish, English and French at primary school as expressed by Little *et al.*'s (1984) undergraduate subjects*

	'Enjoyed most'
Irish	26.7%
English	53.4%
French	39.3%
	'Enjoyed least'
Irish	54.4%
English	13.7%
French	33.9%

*Percentages relate to total number taking each subject at primary school.

Table 6.2 Enjoyment of Irish, English and French at primary school as expressed by Little *et al.*'s (1984) subjects registered at institutions other than Trinity College, Dublin*[5]

	'Enjoyed most'
Irish	23.2%
English	57.9%
French	29.3%
	'Enjoyed least'
Irish	64.7%
English	12.2%
French	22.0%

*Percentages relate to total number taking each subject at primary school.

for later learning and learning choices. However, it would be still less wise to disregard the possibility of such consequences. After all, in all other areas of life, from what we eat to whom we spend our time with, present preferences tend to be heavily influenced by past experience. To return to Little *et al.*'s study, it may be significant that in responses to the question 'Are there any languages you know but would like to know better? – If yes, which languages?', Irish, of all the L2s on the Irish school curriculum, was proportionately least often specified, and by a wide margin (Little *et al.*, 1984, table 158, p. 150, and table A23, p. 256). It is also worth noting that in the most recent census in the Republic of Ireland only 42.8% of responses to the question 'Can the person speak Irish?' were in the affirmative and that nearly two-thirds of persons recorded as being able to speak Irish reported never speaking it or speaking it less often than weekly (Central Statistics Office, 2003: 27f.).

L2s for the 'Young-Old'

There has been much talk in recent years in industrialised countries about the falling birth rate and the implications this has for education. In this connection most attention has been paid to the declining numbers of children in our schools and of young adults in our colleges. However, the question does have another aspect. The death rate is also dropping and, while fewer young people are making demands on educational facilities, more older people, including elderly people, are opting to return to part-time or full-time education.

By way of illustration, the United States and Australia, both of which, because of their histories but also because of their ongoing acceptance of relatively large numbers of youthful immigrants, are thought of as 'young' countries, are both in fact undergoing a major demographic shift in the direction of a significantly older population. With regard to the United States (cf. (Joiner, 1981: 1ff.):

> The trends in the proportions of people under 15 years old and those age 65 and over generally moved in opposite directions during the [20th] century. Every region's proportion of people under age 15 in 2000 declined substantially from its level in 1900, while the proportion of people 65 years and over increased. (Hobbs & Stoops, 2002: 60)

Similarly, in Australia (cf. Brändle, 1986: 17):

> The '20-something' age group is flat-lining: 2.83 million in 1999, 2.84 million in 2000, and expected to be 2.93 million in 2021.... By contrast, the '50-something' age group is growing steadily: 2.04 million in 1999, 2.12 million in 2000 and projected to be 2.96 million in 2021. There will be more people in middle age than people in youth (people in their twenties). (Salt, 2001)

With regard to student numbers, Joiner retails the following statistics for the United States, from Elling (1980) and Hameister and Hickey (1977):

> . . . the participation of part-time [college] students over age 55 increased by 55.2% between 1969 and 1975 in 1973–74, the college-going population over the age of 21 increased by 81% over the previous year . . . ; . . . by 1977 48% of college students were over 21, 10.4% of whom were over 35 years of age . . . (Joiner, 1981: 2)

It is true that college student numbers in the under 25 age-range have recently been increasing and that the current projection in the United States is that numbers in this category will rise by 14% in the period 2000–2010, but it is also true that enrolments of students in the 25 and over age category are still rising fairly dramatically, the expectation being that they will increase by 9% in the same period (Snyder & Hoffman, 2003: 201).

In Europe the same kind of trend emerges. Skilbeck (2001: 43f.) reports that in Iceland, Hungary, Norway and Sweden 'more than 20% of first-time entrants to university are 27 years of age or older'. Even in Ireland, where the birth rate was considerably slower to fall than in many other countries, there have for some considerable time been sizeable minorities of college students from 'non-traditional' age-groups. For example, 12.1% of Little *et al.*'s (1984) respondents from a random sample of undergraduates at Trinity College, Dublin, were aged between 22 and 25 years, and 5.8% were over 25; of their postgraduate respondents 7.3% were over 40 (Little *et al.*, table III, p. 7). More recent figures show that in 1999–2000 31% of the total third-level education population of the Republic of Ireland were aged between 21 and 24 years and that 11% were 25 years or over (Ryan & O'Kelly, 2002).

In addition to institutions that have traditionally catered for young adults, there are of course institutions and organisations specialising in adult or continuing education. These latter have attracted learners from the entire adult age spectrum. Thus, for example, in 1973 Hay reported that at the City Literary Institute, an adult education centre in London, there were approximately equal numbers of students from the age groups under 25, 25–35, 35–45, 45–55, and over 55 (cited in Joiner, 1981: 7). With regard to the national picture in the United Kingdom, recent trends can be summed up as follows: in the period 1996–2002 adult education participation rates increased in all age groups except the 17–19 and the over–75 categories, and the greatest rise in participation rates was among those aged 49–54 (NIACE, 2002: 3).

A particular mature adult grouping which has attracted special comment in America is the so-called 'young-old' category (cf. Neugarten, 1974), which comprises people between 55 and 75 who are more like their juniors than like their seniors and who – in terms of a wide range of attributes and aspirations – depart from the traditional profile of their age-group (Joiner, 1981: 6). A major factor in the evolution of this 'young-old' grouping is that of education. In their discussion of the future prospects for 'senior centers', for example, Martin *et al.* (2002: 22) note that in the United States, whereas in 1950 only 18% of over–65s had finished high school, by 2000 this figure had risen to 67% and that, with regard to possession of an undergraduate degree in this age-group, the rise between 1950 and 2000 had been from 4% to 15%. The 'young-old' are perceived as an extremely promising constituency for late education. Moreover, given that they appear to have a penchant for foreign travel and for exploring other cultures (cf. e.g. Pace & Topini, 2003; Weinstock, 1978) they would seem to offer the possibility of a particularly rich harvest in the domain of foreign languages. On this last point, for example, Grotek (2002a, 2002b: 29), citing Konieczna (1997), notes in relation to Poland that foreign languages are the third most popular area of study in Universities of the Third Age.

In sum, the uptake of late-in-life educational opportunities seems set to increase steadily in many parts of the world. Furthermore, it appears that the particular subsection of the growing middle-aged and elderly population which will probably make most use of such opportunities manifests interests which can be expected to translate into enrolments in foreign language classes. A sensible question to pose in the light of the foregoing is: how successful is the 'young-old' L2 learner likely to be? This is a question which will be in the minds not only of teachers and administrators but also of the potential 'young-old' learners themselves. Unfortunately it is not yet possible to give it anything like the full answer it deserves. L2 acquisition research which, because of its relatively recent beginnings, is not in any case an abundant provider of answers, has to date concentrated almost exclusively on the younger end of the age continuum.

Let us look first at some indirect evidence, that is, evidence from cognitive developmental and memory research in respect of older adults. It appears that healthy elderly people do not uniformly exhibit general cognitive decline and that where such decline occurs it is often a precursor of dementia (Haan *et al.*, 1999; Schaie, 1996). Stability in respect of verbal intelligence seems to be particularly high (Deary, 1998). It has been widely claimed that of the two types of intelligence distinguished by Cattell (1963, 1968), namely fluid intelligence (defined as the innate intellectual functioning which is the basis for mastering new skills) and crystallised intelligence (defined as abilities based on education, life experience and professional expertise) the former declines in older adults, whereas the latter holds up well (Horn, 1982). Another oft-mentioned finding is that ageing appears to affect the ability to focus on relevant information where such information is embedded in a context which also contains irrelevant information (Cavanaugh, 1995: 112f.; Madden *et al.*, 1994; Plude & Doussard-Roosevelt, 1990). This has been interpreted by some researchers not so much as a deficit as an indication that the elderly have difficulty inhibiting irrelevant information, resulting in overload (Hartmann & Hasher, 1991).

With regard to memory, there is some evidence that – perhaps because of expectations generated by folk wisdom – older people's judgements about their own memory capacity is not very reliable (Hertzog & Dunlosky, 1996) and that memory failures may be judged more harshly in the elderly than in other age-groups (Erber *et al.*, 1990). Ageing does appear to have a negative impact on the durability of the retention of newly learned material, but it appears that when older people are offered suggestions regarding the organisation of such material, they perform as well as younger adults (see, e.g. Poon, 1985). It is also worth noting in this connection Grotek's (2002a, 2002b) finding that memory strategy training yielded memory improvements for older adult learners. The main problem seems to lie in the area of working memory, which holds information while that information or other information is being processed. Whereas performance on comfortably paced tests of capacity simply to recall digit-spans and word-spans seems to decline only slightly, if at all, with age, memory tests which require subjects to hold information while engaged in true/false judgements or computation of one kind or another show a marked effect for age (see, e.g. Salthouse & Babcock, 1991; Wingfield *et al.*, 1988). One explanation for this phenomenon (see Salthouse, 1996; Salthouse & Babcock, 1991) is that ageing is associated with a slowing down of processing speed – which is of a piece with a slowing down of all reactions among older adults (Cavanaugh, 1995:114; Papalia & Olds, 1995: 535); this would imply not a specific cognitive deficit but simply that, since the number of elements that can be processed is equal to the number that can be activated before the first has decayed, fewer elements at a time can be processed by older subjects..

Moving on now to more direct evidence relating to L2 learning in later life, there is one area in which adults of middle and advanced years consistently emerge as disadvantaged as compared with their juniors, namely the acquisition of oral-aural skills. This is clearly relatable to the deterioration of auditory acuity in middle-age and senescence, but may also be connected with the above-noted decline in working memory, which may in turn be occasioned by a slowing down of responses in general; phonological working memory has been shown to have considerable importance in the internalisation of new linguistic material (see, e.g. Papagno *et al.*, 1991). In relation to other aspects of L2 learning, as we saw in Chapter 4, there is evidence of a gradual decline in L2 learning capacity throughout adulthood, although this is not a consistent finding. There is certainly no particular point in the ageing of healthy adults where L2 learning becomes impossible. Informal support for the foregoing is provided by the impressions of those with experience of teaching older adult students. Brändle, for instance, speaking out of many years of this kind of experience, confirms that older adult learners have problems with 'auditory imitation and memorising' as well as with 'oral response'. He also notes, however, that in other respects such learners can do well:

> ... in the case of reading skills they invariably set the highest learning goals. They have little difficulty with grammatical principles and storing lexical items ...

> Older students are conscious of their special learning interests and abilities. Some achieve considerable reading skills which permit access to difficult prose tests, poems and plays. Those older learners who have successfully studied foreign languages at school often maintain their learning mechanism, which enables a remarkable growth of the active knowledge of the target language. (Brändle, 1986: 19)

All in all, the evidence summarised above would by no means lead one to think that the older L2 learner faces insuperable difficulties. Given clear speech input, plenty of opportunities and encouragement to rehearse such input, appropriate guidance in respect of memory strategies, a watchful eye over task complexity, and an absence of time pressure, progress ought to be unproblematic for the healthy older adult. It may be worth examining in this context the kinds of characteristics that have classically been associated with successful L2 learning and reflecting on how such characteristics are likely to relate to the older adult learner. Carroll, in his (1977) article on the successful language learner – based on decades of experience and research in the field – mentions the following characteristics:

(i)   phonetic coding ability;
(ii)   grammatical sensitivity;
(iii)   ability to infer grammatical rules from samples of the language;
(iv)   high motivation;
(v)   recognition of the difficulty of the task of language learning;
(vi)   tolerance of ambiguity;
(vii)   outgoing personality;
(viii) concentration on detail;
(ix)   activating approach to passive knowledge;
(x)   use of linguistic knowledge in communicative situations (including imaginary ones);
(xi)   tendency to seek out opportunities to use and practise language;
(xii)   willingness to take risks.

Naiman *et al.* (1995), after investigating the learning strategies of 30 outstanding adult language learners through retrospective interviews, arrive at the following set of optimal strategies:

(i)   an active approach to learning and practice;
(ii) coming to grips with the language as system;
(iii) use of the language in real communication;
(iv) monitoring of output;
(v)   coming to terms with the affective demands of language learning.

There is clearly a high degree of correspondence also between Naiman *et al.*'s and Carroll's proposals. For example, Naiman *et al.*'s 'active approach' can be related to the strategies mentioned by Carroll numbered (viii), (ix) and (xi) above, their reference to coping with the affective demands of the language learning situation can be related to Carroll's suggestions numbers (iv) to (vii), and so on. On the basis of what research and common sense tell us about 'young-old' L2 learners, we can see that there is some bad news but also some good news for such learners in what the above writers have had to say about the characteristics of the successful language learner. The bad news is Carroll's reference to the 'phonetic coding ability' and what Naiman *et al.* say about the affective demands of the learning situation. To take the former first, Carroll glosses 'phonetic coding ability' as follows:

> . . . the ability to listen to L2 sounds or words, to identify them as distinctive, and then to store them in memory so that they can later be recalled accurately on an appropriate occasion. A person with a high degree of this ability finds it easy to imitate accurately a second language utterance of, for example, 10 to 15 syllables, even without knowing the language. (Carroll, 1977: 2)

In view of the findings of studies of older adult L2 learners in respect of oral-aural skills, good 'phonetic coding ability' would have to be excluded from any general characterisation of 'young-old' learners.

As far as the affective dimensions of classroom-based L2 learning are concerned, Stern observes:

> Classroom learning as well as immersion in the target language each entail specific affective problems which have been characterised as language shock and stress, and as culture shock and stress. In spite of these difficulties, good language learners approach the task in a positive frame of mind, develop the necessary energy to overcome frustrations, and persist in their efforts. (Stern, 1983: 411f.)

Given that most middle-aged and elderly learners will have been away from formal education for very many years, it is to be expected that a fair proportion of them will find the return to the classroom hard to cope with, especially in view of the way in which the educational environment has changed over the last three decades:

> Older students who enrol for the first time in a continuing education course are often bewildered by the new learning environment. They may not have experienced a large campus with its profusion of buildings and labyrinthine corridors. The technology of the language laboratory makes some older students apprehensive. (Brändle, 1986: 20)

Also, there may be difficulties in the student–teacher relationship which have to do with the fact that the adult student 'refuses to receive passively the impress which the teacher may conceive to be desirable' (McLeish, 1963: 123). In extreme cases the student may feel entitled virtually to take control:

> Some students held professional positions of power and influence in their working life and they do not hesitate to make demands on the teacher and, indirectly, on the other students. Such demands may have a disruptive effect on the whole class. (Brändle, 1986: 20)

It would appear, then, that many older adults find the readjustment to classroom learning particularly problematic. However, it would be wrong to overemphasise this. At least older learners, in their trepidation, are unlikely to fail to recognise the difficulty of the task before them and this, from Carroll's perspective (see above), would be a point in their favour. Also, if there is a bewilderment factor in re-entering the strange world of formal education, there may well also be a novelty factor. As any adult educator knows, many older students return to the classroom with high motivation levels (cf. Hillage *et al.*, 2000: 63ff.) and take a positive delight in the difference of the experience from their everyday routine. Furthermore, the tendency of the part of some older adults to make demands on the teacher may, in a traditional classroom context, be disruptive, but it does, after all, bespeak an active, autonomous approach to the learning task – one of Naiman *et al.*'s characteristics of the good language learner, and one much emphasised in recent thinking on L2 teaching/learning (see, e.g. Benson, 2001; Little *et al.*, 2002). With regard to other affective aspects of L2 learning, older adult learners would appear to be very well placed. They attend classes because they choose to do so, which clearly has positive implications for their motivation (see above). Choosing to enrol in a language class also implies a fairly outgoing personality.

The remaining characteristics ascribed to the successful language learner do not seem at all incompatible with what we know about the older learner. The question of an active approach to learning has already been touched on in connection with student–teacher relationships. In addition, what has just been said regarding motivation would appear to have some relevance too. Also of interest in this context, and germane to both of the above matters, is the notion of self-direction, which some writers on adult education see as particularly associated with the adult learner:

> Once an adult makes the discovery that he can take responsibility for his learning, as he does for other facets of his life, he experiences a sense of release and exhilaration. He then enters into learning with deep ego-involvement, with results that are frequently startling both to himself and to his teachers. Teachers who have helped their adult students to achieve this breakthrough report repeatedly that it is one of the most rewarding experiences of their lives. (Knowles, 1970; reprint: 57; cf. further discussion below)

Clearly, given the right conditions, adult learners, including presumably older adult learners, can take an extremely active approach to learning. As far as 'young-old' learners' capacity to come to grips with the systemic aspects of their target language is concerned, and their capacity to use such systemic knowledge in self-monitoring, what has been observed about older L2 learners' grammar-acquiring ability (see above) would indicate that they have no particular difficulties in recognising and assimilating system or in making use of systemic knowledge. It is worth noting in this connection Von Elek and Oskarsson's (1973) finding that a teaching approach involving explicit grammatical analysis yielded significantly higher results with adult subjects than an approach from which such analysis was absent. It has often been remarked that adult language learners tend to be extremely interested in system and formal accuracy. Brändle, for example, talks about older adult learners requesting 'learning rules and a schematic grammar' and being obsessed with error analysis right from the start of the foreign language course' (Brändle, 1986: 20). Similarly, Devitt *et al.*'s (1982–83) investigation of reactions to a broadcast Irish course among a group of volunteers whose ages ranged up to 65+ found that one of the most frequent comments on the deficiencies of the course units was that they did not provide enough grammar (1982–83: 82). Whether this interest is excessive and counterproductive in certain instances is a matter of judgement; that it exists in very many older learners is indisputable.

Finally in this context, are older adult learners likely to engage in real communication through their target language? 'Real' communication presumably refers to using the target language to interact in ways similar to those in which one interacts in one's native language, that is to say, using the language for the sake of relationships to be maintained, business to be transacted, information to be exchanged or aesthetic pleasure to be received or given, rather than for the sake of forms to be practised. In this sense, real communication can actually occur within the classroom, as the entire literature on communicative language teaching makes clear (see e.g. Brumfit, 1984b; Galloway, 1993; Little *et al.*, 1985; Lee, 2003; Littlewood, 1981; Sauvignon, 2002). What this implies is that the extent to which the older learner – or any learner – experiences real communication is at least partly a function of instructional approach.

As far as communication outside the classroom is concerned, common sense would suggest that in general the older language learner who has chosen, at some financial cost and almost certainly also some emotional cost, to enrol in a L2 class is at least as likely to make extracurricular use of the language being learned as, say, the adolescent school pupil who is obliged to attend such a class. More specifically, it has already been noted that many older learners read literary works in the target language. This can certainly be seen as real communication in the above sense. Moreover, if it is true that the kind of older adults likely to re-enter formal education are also those who are inclined to travel abroad (cf. above), then one can expect not a few older adult foreign language students to become involved in face-to-face oral communication with native speakers of the target language, indeed to be primarily motivated by a desire to be able to engage in precisely this type of communication. Admittedly, the older adult's difficulties in the oral-aural domain might cause some problems here, but need not be a serious impediment.

In short, of those abilities and strategies isolated by researchers as making for successful L2 learning, only phonetic coding and some affective aspects of classroom learning appear to disfavour the older adult learner. Specific disadvantages associated with the latter area can, moreover, be seen as having positive dimensions, and other aspects of the affective factor can be seen as actually advantaging older learners. With regard to active involvement in learning, internalising and using systemic knowledge, and engaging in real communication, only the oral-aural aspect of the last two appears to present a problem for the older adult learner.

Before ending this section, it may be of interest to consider briefly the conditions under which the older adult learner is to be taught and the teaching approach which is to be used with such learners. It has been argued in recent years by various adult educationalists, notably Knowles (1970, 1975, 1984), that adult students are different enough from their juniors to require their own particular set of learning conditions – *'andragogy'* rather than *pedagogy* (see also e.g. Allman, 1983; Mezirow, 1981). The andragogical perspective, makes five assumptions which depict the adult learner as:

. . . someone who (1) has an independent self-concept and who can direct his or her own learning, (2) has accumulated a reservoir of life experiences that is a rich resource for learning, (3) has learning needs closely related to changing social roles, (4) is problem-centered and interested in immediate application of knowledge, and (5) is motivated to learn by internal rather than external factors. (Merriam, 2001: 5)

On the basis of such assumptions about adult-learner characteristics Knowles argues for the desirability in adult education of a learning climate which is not teacher-dominated, a programme which takes account of the learner's needs and which involves the learner in planning his/her own learning, a role for the teacher which is of a catalysing rather than a strictly instructional nature, and evaluation procedures which rely on self-assessment rather than external judgement. He also proposes a teaching approach which taps experience through participatory experiential techniques, emphasises practicability, and promotes self-analysis. With regard to the curriculum, he suggests that this should be co-ordinated with learners' developmental tasks and that learners should be divided into homogeneous task-related subgroups for certain kinds of teaching. In short, he advocates an approach which is person-centred, problem-centred and needs analysis-based.

Other educationalists have criticised the notion of andragogy, not because they find the principles it incorporates objectionable, but because they do not regard such principles as necessarily peculiar to adult learning and teaching (see e.g. Hanson, 1996; Tennant, 1996). It is certainly true that, with specific reference to L2 teaching, the principles in question are precisely those on which the communicative approach seeks to proceed. In the wake of such criticisms Knowles and his followers moved away from seeing pedagogy and andragogy as dichotomous and increasingly recognised that 'both approaches are appropriate with children and adults' (Merriam, 2001: 6). It seems then that the quest for an andragogy has not in fact yielded principles for the education of adults which are qualitatively distinct from those proposed in recent times for the education of children and adolescents, and that we cannot look to andragogy for guidance about teaching languages to a very specific subset of adults, i.e. the middle-aged and senescent. Such insights as are available relative to this problem are based partly on the research summarised above, and also on experience and common sense.

One aspect of the problem which is easy to overlook is the timing of classes (cf. Joiner, 1981: 18ff.). Among the middle-aged to elderly age-group some prospective students will be still working, others retired or unemployed; among those still working some will have a very rigid work schedule, others a more flexible timetable. Thus, some will be available during (part of) the day, others not. As for evenings, some prospective students will be prepared to commit themselves until quite late, others unable or unwilling to do so. These different patterns of availability clearly have to be taken into consideration when courses are being planned, and decisions about the time-slots to be used will ideally be based on market research of some kind. Self-evidently, the fine-tuning of curriculum, materials and methodology will be to absolutely no avail if would-be learners find no class on offer at a convenient time.

Another question that arises at the course planning stage is whether or not to separate adult learners by age-group. Brändle (1986: 12f.) points out that, unlike students in other age-groups, 'young-old' students are not normally in need of a formal qualification, and do not usually require knowledge of a L2 for professional reasons. Rather, they are attracted to language classes by curiosity, the desire to keep their intellectual faculties alive, social or recreational motives, the wish to be in a position to assist children or grandchildren with their homework, attachment (often based on ethnicity) to a particular language, or an interest in communicating with speakers of the target language – whether in their own community or when travelling abroad. (Obviously, these various motivations are not mutually exclusive; very often, perhaps most often, several will operate in concert). In addition to this motivational difference between younger and older adult learners, there also seem to be differences in capacity. As we have seen, older learners may have memory problems; they also tend to be less successful at coping with the oral-aural aspects of the target language. These differences may be interpreted as arguments for separate classes for the 'young-old'. A counter-argument would be that many older people would undoubtedly find the idea of being placed in a class consisting entirely of their age peers distinctly unappealing, especially if part of their motivation were social.

Another response to the problem would be to introduce a high degree of individualisation into adult classes (cf. Joiner, 1981: 34ff.). Individuali-sation can in any case be readily enough justified on general didactic grounds, and is much referred to in the context of communicative language teaching (see e.g. Benson & Voller, 1997; Brookes & Grundy, 1988; Holec *et al.*, 1996). The point is that any class of learners, even within a particular age- or ability-group, will be marked by some degree of heterogeneity. Individualisation simply recognises that heterogeneity by allowing learn-ers (within the limits set by the situation) to proceed at their own rhythm using materials and activities which are suited to their own tastes, interests, knowledge and capacities. While, then, this is not an approach which is geared uniquely to adult learning, it does seem an ideal way of taking account of older adult learners' particular difficulties without resorting to a strategy of isolation.

A very important aspect of learning conditions for older adults is their physical dimension (cf. Joiner, 1981: 38; Brändle, 1986: 20). Like all other classrooms, the 'young-old' classroom should ideally be pleasantly decorated and comfortably furnished. However, it is particularly important in the case of older adult learners, given their loss of sensory acuity, that lighting be bright, all visual materials easily legible, and all aural input, including the teacher's own speech, loud and clear. With younger learners it may be possible to get away with the odd faint photocopy or poorly recorded tape; with many older learners any attempt to use such materials will be not only entirely unproductive but also have very serious negative consequences in terms of morale.

With regard to an optimal teaching methodology (for full discussion see Joiner, 1981: 24ff.), the picture is really no clearer in respect of older adult language learners than in respect of language learners generally. The best one can do is to try to infer from research on older learners the kinds of teaching procedures that might be particularly helpful to such learners. For example, in view of older adults' memory problems, one would expect them to derive benefits (cf. earlier discussion) from memory strategy training, and, as Joiner suggests (1981: 14), to be helped by the provision of summaries and by frequent review and practice. One might need to be careful, however, about the nature of the practice involved. It is a general finding of memory research that material perceived as meaningless is subject to more rapid decay than material perceived as meaningful (see e.g. Wingfield & Byrnes, 1981: 98f.; 352ff.). This would appear to be a general argument against a heavy emphasis on the rote-learning or drilling of forms with little or no semantic relationship. But this argument may have a special force in the case of older adults who, because of a greater reliance on 'crystallised' rather than 'fluid' intelligence, may be less disposed to make novel mnemonic connections between items.

Older learners' reliance on crystallised intelligence and their slowing reactions (with implications, as we have seen, for working memory) may have further relevance. Normal language processing is apparently associated with crystallised intelligence, but in a formal language learning environment tasks are sometimes set which require more than just language processing operations. In certain quarters of the communicative movement, for example, there is an enthusiasm for games and role-plays which involve the collective solving of quite complicated logical problems – sometimes under conditions of time-pressure. Teachers of older adults who might be inclined to use such techniques would presumably need to bear in mind that if the logical problems in question were highly complex they might leave their students frustrated and demoralised. On the other hand, engagement with *language* problems seems to pose no particular problem for older learners, who, as we have seen, apparently respond well to a cognitive method which allows conscious analysis of 'linguistic phenomena' (Brändle, 1986: 21).

Finally, because of the oral-aural difficulties of older adult learners, it has been suggested (see e.g. Brändle, 1986: 19f.) that teachers of such students should ensure that the input they provide contains plenty of written material, and that teaching should concentrate on less problematic non-oral activities. Such an approach may well suit some learners – such as those who are primarily interested in gaining access to a foreign literature. However, as we have seen, many older adult students are likely to be motivated to learn a L2 by a desire to use it when travelling. Clearly, such persons would be looking for a command of the spoken language rather than a substantial proficiency in the written language, a theoretical knowledge of grammar or translating skills. As Joiner says, '[g]rammar and translation cannot be expected to lead to oral proficiency, and this is precisely what many adults wish to achieve' (Joiner, 1981: 28).

Summary and Conclusions

(1) The 'younger = better' premise on which the case for the early introduction of L2s tended to be made in the past can no longer be accepted in its simple form.

(2) A modified version of the 'younger = better' position may, however, form part of the argument for early L2 instruction. If one takes into account the differences in amount of exposure, there is not necessarily a discrepancy between the finding of naturalistic L2 studies that those who begin learning a L2 in childhood, after initially lagging behind adult beginners, eventually outstrip them and the finding of FLES studies that within the periods investigated older learners learn more quickly than younger learners. Extrapolating from the naturalistic studies, one may plausibly argue that early formal instruction in an L2 is likely to yield advantages after rather longer periods of time than have so far been studied.

(3) Since length of exposure to an L2 is recognised as an important predictor of L2 success, one would expect students who begin to learn an L2 at elementary level to have a considerable advantage over those who begin later. The fact that this advantage does not show up in currently available research findings may have, to do with the blurring effect of mixing FLES and non-FLES students together in the same classes at

secondary level and/or with the masking effect of older learners' initial superiority.

(4) On the other hand, in the absence of hard evidence about the (very) long-term advantages of early L2 instruction, one cannot be sure about their magnitude.

(5) With regard to possible negative effects of early L2 instruction in terms of mother tongue development and general academic progress, research on early bilingualism and early L2 immersion programmes appears to indicate that such negative effects are associated only with instances where the L2 in question is the majority language of the community and the first language of the child is given no educational support.

(6) There being no strong empirical support for early L2 instruction from research on the age factor in L2 acquisition, those who favour such instruction have used other arguments, notably: the desirability of early stimulation generally; the advantage of starting some subjects early in the context of the modern crowded curriculum; the educational merits of early contact with another culture; and the benefits conferred by as long as possible an exposure to the L2.

(7) If there are age factor-independent arguments in favour of early L2 instruction, there is also at least one such argument against the early introduction of L2s into the school curriculum: unless factors such as the focus of learning materials, teacher training and commitment, and public attitudes towards the target language are favourable, the experience of learning an L2 at primary school may be negative – with probable consequences for subsequent contact with that language and language learning generally.

(8) At the other end of the age spectrum, there is a demographic shift occurring in many societies towards an older population and this is being reflected in the student population. A particularly promising source of adult L2 students seems to be the 'young-old' section of the population – middle-aged and elderly people whose circumstances resemble those of their juniors more than those of their elders.

(9) With regard to the likelihood of success of the 'young-old' as learners, research and experience seem to indicate that such learners are at a disadvantage in only a few respects: their general processing of information tends to be slower, they may have problems (unless helped) in respect of durability of memory traces and their handling of oral-aural material is less efficient than that of their juniors.

(10) When examined in the light of abilities and strategies which research and experience have suggested as characterising successful L2 learners, 'young-old' learners come off relatively well. The only char-

acteristics specifically associated with middle age and senescence which, according to this yardstick, point to less successful language learning are problems with phonetic coding and difficulties in re-adjusting to some aspects of classroom learning.

(11) Given what is known about the older adult language learner, it would appear that L2 programmes aiming to attract such learners should:
  (a) take care with the timing of courses;
  (b) take account of older learners' particular needs and difficulties in terms of class organisation;
  (c) pay particular attention to the visibility and audibility of instructional input; and
  (d) promote a teaching approach which assists memorisation in a meaningful manner, avoids setting complex and time-pessured tasks, allows for some degree of linguistic analysis and takes cognisance of older learners' weaknesses in the oral-aural domain.

Notes

1. Adiv (1984) reports an evaluation of kindergarten and elementary programmes in Canadian Jewish Day Schools in which English-speaking students are taught through Hebrew as well as French and English. According to Adiv's report, even this 'double immersion' has not been found to have any adverse affects on English or general academic development.
2. Our translation: 'Språk 1 och språk 2 [. . .] måste läras i en viss ordning, inte samtidigt'.
3. Our translation: 'en aktiv delaktighet i två kulturer'.
4. These were the only languages that emerged as having been taken by meaningful numbers of subjects. Of the 240 undergraduates who sent back questionnaires, 234 reported having taken English at primary school, 195 reported having taken Irish at primary school, and 56 reported having taken French at this level. Cf. Little *et al.*, 1984, Table 40: 41.
5. Of the 382 undergraduate subjects involved in this follow-up survey, 376 reported having taken English at primary school, 354 reported having taken Irish at primary school, and 41 reported having taken French at this level. Cf. Little *et al.*, 1984, Table A17: 251.

Chapter 7
Concluding Remarks

Having now reached the point where some general conclusions need to be drawn from the evidence, counter-evidence, arguments, counter-arguments, likelihoods, possibilities and faint chances set out in the preceding chapters, we are reminded of Oscar Wilde's aphorism about the truth being rarely pure and never simple. What is quite clear from the foregoing discussion is that there are very few simple truths concerning the role of age in language acquisition. Such as there are concern either end of the age continuum. Of the very young acquiring their mother tongue it can be uncomplicatedly asserted that their early major speech milestones occur in a predictable order and, in the case of normal development, within well-defined age-ranges. Of the middle-aged and senescent embarking on the acquisition of an L2 one can say with some degree of confidence that they are likely to experience more difficulties with oral-aural aspects of that language than younger learners and that under pressure their memory work in this context will generally not be so good.

For the rest we must be content with uncertainty and complexity. It seems unlikely, in view of the evidence, that there is a *particular* point in a child's development where language acquisition can be said to truly begin. With regard to the hypothesis that there is a point beyond which one cannot begin to acquire a language with any hope of complete success, no direct evidence can ever be adduced in support of such a hypothesis in relation to L1 development which is not weakened by doubts about the psychological normalcy of the subject(s) observed. It does seem, though, that L1 acquisition normally continues, in some of its aspects at least, right into old age and that a high degree of success in many aspects of L2 acquisition is possible at any age. With specific regard to L2 acquisition, it is no longer possible to accept the view that younger L2 learners are in all respects and at every stage of learning superior to older learners, nor that older learners are in all respects and at every stage of learning superior to younger learners. The question of whether younger L2 learners have an advantage over older learners in terms of context-embedded oral-aural skills and whether older learners have an advantage in terms of context-reduced literacy skills remains to be settled (except insofar as a consistent trend has been found for older adult L2 learners to be weaker than their juniors in the oral-aural domain). The one interpretation of the evidence which does not appear to run into contradictory data is that *in general* those who are naturalistically exposed to an L2 and whose exposure to the L2 in question begins in childhood *eventually* surpass those whose exposure begins in adulthood, even though the latter usually show some initial advantage over the former.

Concerning explanations for age-related effects, it is difficult not to infer that talking about *an* age factor may be misconceived, and that we should rather be thinking in terms of a range of age-related factors. This was in fact the reading of the evidence that was offered 15 years ago in the first edition of this book, the conclusion of which suggested that the various age-related phenomena isolated by language acquisition research probably result from the interaction of a multiplicity of causes and that different phenomena may have different combinations of causes. We see no reason to conclude otherwise in the present volume. Such a perspective can certainly encompass the notion that decreasing cerebral plasticity and/or other changes in the brain may play a role, but the notion that age effects are exclusively a matter of neurological predetermination, that they are associated with absolute, well-defined maturational limits and that they are particular to language looks less and less plausible. In other words, the idea of a critical period specifically for language development may well have had its day.

On the question of educational implications, we have dealt with only two age-related language education issues: the desirability of teaching L2s at primary level and the prospects of L2 learning success for the 'young-old'. With regard to the former, the currently available empirical evidence on the age factor in L2 acquisition is not particularly helpful to those who advocate early L2 instruction. The best one can say on this score is that, *given the right learning conditions*, learners exposed to early L2 instruction may have some advantage in the very long run over those whose exposure begins later. Concerning L2s for the middle-aged and elderly, there is every reason to believe that, again given suitable learning conditions, such learners can in many respects be as successful in acquiring an L2 as their juniors.

Concluding sections of works of this kind traditionally end with a plea for further research. We shall not presume to break with this tradition, if only to avoid the implication that the state of knowledge in this area entitles us to do so. It clearly does not. A great deal more age-focused empirical research is needed in respect of both L1 and L2 acquisition. Because the Critical Period Hypothesis has tended to generate studies of language learning before, during and immediately after puberty, there is a particular dearth of data on L1 and L2 learning *through* adulthood. This imbalance should be remedied. The role of cross-linguistic interaction in relation to age-related effects also warrants a very great deal more investigation than it has received to date. In addition, there is an absence of studies which follow up the effects of earlier and later L2 programmes over very long periods; such studies are essential if the debate about the value of early L2 instruction is ever to be settled. Finally, if theoretical accounts of age-related factors in language acquisition are ever to get beyond the speculative stage, we require research which correlates age-related variables and language gains in a thoroughgoingly detailed manner. What this last point amounts to is an appeal – yet another! – for more longitudinal studies.

Bibliography

Aaronson, D and Rieber, R. (eds) (1975) *Developmental Psycholinguistics and Communication Disorders*. New York: New York Academy of Sciences.

Abutalebi, J., Cappa, S. and Perani, D. (2001) The bilingual brain as revealed by functional neuroimaging. *Bilingualism: Language and Cognition* 4, 179–90.

Adams, C. (1997) Onset of speech after a left hemispherectomy in a 9 year old boy. *Brain* 120, 159–82.

Adams, M. (1978) Methodology for examining second language acquisition. In E. Hatch (ed.) *Second Language Acquisition: A Book of Readings*. Rowley, MA: Newbury House.

Adiv, E. (1980) A comparative evaluation of three French immersion programs: Grades 10 and 11. Paper presented at the Fourth Annual Convention of CAIT. Montreal: The Protestant School Board of Greater Montreal. Cited in B. Harley (1986) *Age in Second Language Acquisition*. Clevedon: Multilingual Matters.

Adiv, E. (1984) An example of double immersion. *Language and Society/Langue et Société* 12, 30–2.

Akhtar, N. (1999) Acquiring basic word order: Evidence for data-driven learning of syntactic structure. *Journal of Child Language* 26, 339–56.

Akhtar, N. and Tomasello, M. (1997) Young children's productivity with word order and verb morphology. *Developmental Psychology* 33, 952–65.

Alajouanine, Th. and L'hermite, F. (1965) Acquired aphasia in children. *Brain* 88, 653–62.

Allman, P. (1983) The nature and process of adult development. In M. Tight (ed.) *Education for Adults. Volume 1. Adult Learning and Education*. London: Croom Helm (in association with the Open University).

Allwright, R. (1984) The analysis of discourse in interlanguage studies: The pedagogical evidence. In A. Davies *et al.* (eds) *Interlanguage*. Edinburgh: Edinburgh University Press.

Andersen, R. (ed.) (1983a) *Pidginization and Creolization as Language Acquisition*. Rowley, MA: Newbury House.

Andersen, R. (1983b) Introduction: A language acquisition interpretation of pidginization and creolization. In R. Andersen (ed.), *Pidginization and Creolization as Language Acquisition*. Rowley, MA: Newbury House.

Andersson, T. (1960) The optimum age for beginning the study of modern languages. *International Review of Education* 6, 298–306.

Aram, D. (1988) Language sequelae of unilateral brain lesions in children. In F. Plum (ed.) *Language, Communication and the Brain*. New York: Raven Press.

Argyle, M. (1967) *The Psychology of Interpersonal Behaviour*. Harmondsworth: Penguin.

Arnberg, L. (1987) _Raising Children Bilingually: The Pre-school Years._ Clevedon: Multilingual Matters.

Arthur, B., Weiner, R., Culver, M., Lee, Y.J., Thomas, D. (1980) The register of impersonal discourse to foreigners: Verbal adjustments to foreign accent. In D. Larsen-Freeman (ed.) _Discourse Analysis in Second Language Research._ Rowley, MA: Newbury House.

Asher, J. (1981) The Total Physical Response: Theory and practice. In H. Winitz (ed.) _Native Language and Foreign Language Acquisition._ New York: The New York Academy of Sciences.

Asher, J. and Garcia, R. (1969) The optimal age to learn a foreign language. _Modern Language Journal_ 53, 334–41. Reprinted in S. Krashen, R. Scarcella and M. Long (eds) (1982) _Child-Adult Differences in Second Language Acquisition._ Rowley, MA: Newbury House.

Asher, J. and Price, B. (1967) The learning strategy of the Total Physical Response: Some age differences. _Child Development_ 38, 1219–27. Reprinted in S. Krashen, R. Scarcella and M. Long (eds) (1982) _Child-Adult Differences in Second Language Acquisition._ Rowley, MA: Newbury House.

Audin, L., Ligozat, M.-A. and Luc, C. (1999) _Enseignement des langues vivantes au CM2._ Paris: Institut National de Recherche Pédagogique.

Ausubel, D. (1964) Adults versus children in second language learning. _Modern Language Journal_ 48, 420–24.

Bailey, K., Long, M. and Peck, S. (eds) (1983) _Second Language Acquisition Studies._ Rowley, MA: Newbury House.

Bailey, N., Madden, C. and Krashen, S. (1974) Is there a 'natural sequence' in adult second language learning? _Language Learning_ 24, 235–43. Reprinted in E. Hatch (ed.) (1978a) _Second Language Acquisition: A Book of Readings._ Rowley, MA: Newbury House.

Baker, C. (1997) Bilingual education in Ireland, Scotland and Wales. In J. Cummins and D. Corson (eds) _Bilingual Education_ (Volume 5 of the _Encyclopedia of Language and Education_). Dordrecht: Kluwer.

Bar-Adon, A. (1959) _Lesonam hameduberet sel hayeladim beyisrael_ (Children's Hebrew in Israel). Doctoral dissertation, Hebrew University of Jerusalem. Cited in M. Braine (1971a) The acquisition of language in infant and child. In C. Reed (ed.) _The Learning of Language._ New York: Appleton-Century-Crofts.

Bar-Adon, A. and Leopold, W. (eds) (1971) _Child Language: A Book of Readings._ Englewood Cliffs, NJ: Prentice-Hall.

Barnes, S., Gutfreund, M. Satterly, D. and Wells, G. (1983) Characteristics of adult speech which predict children's language development. _Journal of Child Language_ 10, 65–84.

Barnet, A., Vincentini, M. and Campos, S. (1974) EEG sensory evoked responses (ERs) in early infancy malnutrition. Paper presented at the Society for Neuroscience, St. Louis, MO. Cited in S. Segalowitz (1983a) _Language Functions and Brain Organization._ New York: Academic Press.

Baron-Cohen, S., Leslie, A.M. and Frith, U. (1985) Does the autistic child have a 'theory of mind'. _Cognition_ 21, 37–46.

Barrett, M. (1995) Early lexical development. In P. Fletcher and B. MacWhinney (eds) _The Handbook of Child Language._ Oxford. Blackwell.

Basilius, H. (1939) Further note concerning quality of work done in evening classes. _Educational Research Bulletin_ 10, 164–5.

Basser, L. (1962) Hemiplegia of early onset and the faculty of speech with special reference to the effects of hemispherectomy. *Brain* 85, 427–60.

Bateman, W. (1914) A child's progress in speech. *Journal of Educational Psychology* 5, 475–93.

Bates, E., Bretherton, I., Snyder, L. (1988) *From First Words to Grammar: Individual Differences and Dissociable Mechanisms*. New York: Cambridge University Press.

Bateson, M. (1975) Mother-infant exchanges: The epigenesis of conversational interaction. In D. Aaronson and R. Rieber (eds) *Developmental Psycholinguistics and Communication Disorders*. New York: New York Academy of Sciences.

Bayley, N. (1933) Mental growth during the first three years. *Genetic Psychology Monographs* 14, 92.

Baynes, K., Kegl, J.A., Brentari, D., Kussmaul, C. and Poizner, H. (1998) Chronic auditory agnosia following Landau-Kleffner syndrome: A 23 year outcome study. *Brain and Language* 63, 381–425

Bellugi, U. (1965) The development of interrogative structures in children's speech. In K. Riegel (ed.) *The Development of Language Functions*. Ann Arbor: Michigan Language Development Program, Report No. 8.

Benedict, H. (1979) Early lexical development: Comprehension and production. *Journal of Child Language* 6, 183–201.

Benson, P. (2001) *Teaching and Researching Autonomy in Language Learning*. London: Longman.

Benson P. and Voller P. (eds) (1997) *Autonomy and Independence in Language Learning*. London: Longman.

Ben Zeev, S. (1977) Mechanisms by which childhood bilingualism affects understanding of language and cognitive structures. In P.A. Hornby (ed.) *Bilingualism: Psychological, Social, and Educational Implications*. New York: Academic Press.

Berndt, R. and Caramazza, A. (1982) Phrase comprehension after brain damage. *Applied Psycholinguistics* 3, 263–78.

Best, C., McRoberts, G. and Sithole, N. (1988) Examination of perceptual reorganization for nonnative speech contrasts: Zulu click discrimination by English-speaking adults and infants. *Journal of Experimental Psychology* 14, 345–60.

Bever, T. (1970) Cognitive basis for linguistic structure. In J. Hayes (ed.) *Cognition and Language*. New York: Wiley.

Bever, T. (1971) The nature of cerebral dominance in speech behavior of the child and adult. In R. Huxley and E. Ingram (eds) *Language Acquisition: Models and Methods*. New York: Academic Press.

Bever, T. (1981) Normal acquisition processes explain the critical period for language learning. In K. Diller (ed.) *Individual Differences and Universals in Language Learning Aptitude*. Rowley, MA: Newbury House.

Bhri, L. and Ammons, P. (1974) Children's comprehension of comparative sentence transformations. *Child Development* 45, 512–16.

Bialystok, E. (1987) Influences of bilingualism on metalinguistic development. *Second Language Research* 3, 154–166.

Bialystok, E. (1997) The structure of age: In search of barriers to second language acquisition. *Second Language Research* 13, 116–37.

Bialystok, E. (1999) Cognitive complexity and attentional control in the bilingual mind. *Child Development* 70, 636–44.

Bialystok, E. (2001) *Bilingualism in Development: Language Literacy and Cognition*. Cambridge: Cambridge University Press.

Bialystok, E. (2002a) On the reliability of robustness: A reply to DeKeyser. *Studies in Second Language Acquisition* 24, 481–88.

Bialystok, E. (2002b) Cognitive processes of L2 users. In V. Cook (ed.) *Portraits of the L2 User*. Clevedon: Multilingual Matters.

Bialystok, E. and Hakuta, K. (1994) *In Other Words: The Science and Psychology of Second Language Acquisition*. New York: Basic Books.

Bialystok, E. and Hakuta, K. (1999) Confounded age: Linguistic and cognitive factors in age differences for second language acquisition. In D. Birdsong (ed.) *Second Language Acquisition and the Critical Period Hypothesis*. Mahwah, NJ: Erlbaum.

Birdsong, D. (1992) Ultimate attainment in second language acquisition. *Language* 68, 706–55.

Birdsong, D. (1999) Introduction: Whys and why nots of the critical period hypothesis for second language acquisition. In D. Birdsong (ed.) *Second Language Acquisition and the Critical Period Hypothesis*. Mahwah, NJ: Erlbaum.

Birdsong, D. (2002) The locus of age effects in L2A: A reconsideration. Paper presented at the 24th annual conference of the Deutsche Gesellschaft für Sprachwissenschaft, Mannheim, February.

Birdsong, D. (2003a) Interpreting age effects in second language acquisition. In J. Kroll and A. de Groot (eds) *Handbook of Bilingualism: Psycholinguistic Perspectives*. Cambridge: Cambridge University Press.

Birdsong, D. (2003b) Authenticité de prononciation en français L2 chez les apprenants tardifs anglophones: Analyses segmentales et globales. *Acquisition et Interaction en Langue Étrangère* 18, 17–36.

Bishop, D. (1997) *Uncommon Understanding: Development and Disorders of Language Comprehension in Children*. Hove: Psychology Press.

Bishop, D., Bishop, S., Bright, P., James, C., Delaney, T. and Tallal, P. (1999) Different origin of auditory and phonological processing in children with language impairment: Evidence from a Twin Study. *Journal of Speech and Hearing Research* 36, 155–168.

Bland, M. and Keislar, E. (1966) A self-controlled audio-lingual program for children. *French Review* 40, 266–76.

Bley-Vroman, R.W. (1989) What is the logical problem of foreign language learning? In S.M. Gass and J. Schachter (eds) *Linguistic Perspectives on Second Language Acquisition*. Cambridge: Cambridge University Press.

Blonder, L., Bowers, D. and Heilman, K. (1991) The role of the right hemisphere in emotional communication. *Brain* 114, 1115–27.

Blondin, G., Candelier, M., Edelenbos, P., Johnstone, R., Kubanek-German, A. and Taeschner, T. (1998) *Les langues étrangères dès l'école maternelle ou primaire. Conditions et resultants*. Paris and Brussels: DeBoeck Université.

Bloom, L. (1970) *Language Development: Form and Function in Emerging Grammars*. Cambridge MA: MIT Press.

Bloom, L. (1991) *Language Development from Two to Three*. Cambridge: Cambridge University Press.

Bloom, P. (1994) Recent controversies in the study of language acquisition. In M. Gernsbacher (ed.) *Handbook of Psycholinguistics*. London: Academic Press.

Bloomfield, L. (1927) Literate and illiterate speech. *American Speech* 2, 423–39.

Blumstein, S. and Cooper, W. (1974) Hemisphere processing of intonation contours. *Cortex* 10, 146–58.

Boden, M. (1979) *Piaget*. London: Fontana.

Bongaerts, T. (1999) Ultimate attainment in L2 pronunciation: The case of very advanced late L2 learners. In D. Birdsong (ed.) *Second Language Acquisition and the Critical Period Hypothesis*. Mahwah, NJ: Lawrence Erlbaum.

Bongaerts, T. (2003) Effets de l'âge sur l'acquisition de la prononciation d'une seconde langue. *Acquisition et Interaction en Langue Étrangère* 18, 79–98.

Bongaerts, T., Planken, B. and Schils, E. (1995) Can late starters attain a native accent in a foreign language: A test of the Critical Period Hypothesis. In D. Singleton and Z. Lengyel (eds) *The Age Factor in Second Language Acquisition*. Clevedon: Multilingual Matters.

Bongaerts, T., Mennen, S. and Van der Slik, F. (2000) Authenticity of pronunciation in naturalistic second language acquisition: The case of very advanced late learners of Dutch as a second language. *Studia Linguistica* 54, 298–308.

Bongaerts, T., van Summeren, C., Planken, B. and Schils, E. (1997) Age and ultimate attainment in the pronunciation of a foreign language. *Studies in Second Language Acquisition* 19, 447–65.

Bonnaterre, P. (1800) *Notice historique sur le sauvage de l'Aveyron et sur quelques autres individus qu'on a trouvés dans les forêts à différentes époques*. Paris: Panckouke.

Bonvillian, J., Nelson, K. and Charrow, V. (1976) Languages and language-related skills in deaf and hearing children. *Sign Language Studies* 12, 211–50.

Boothroyd, A. (1982) *Hearing Impediments in Young Children*. Englewood Cliffs, NJ: Prentice-Hall.

Bowley, A. (1957) *The Natural Development of the Child* (4th edn). Edinburgh: Livingstone.

Bown, L. (1983) Adult education in the Third World. In M. Tight (ed.) *Education for Adults. Volume 1. Adult Learning and Education*. London: Croom Helm (in association with the Open University).

Braidi, S.M. (1999) *The Acquisition of Second Language Syntax*. London: Edward Arnold.

Braine, M. (1971a) The acquisition of language in infant and child. In C. Reed (ed.) *The Learning of Language*. New York: Appleton-Century-Crofts.

Braine, M. (1971b) On two types of models of the internalization of grammars. In D. Slobin (ed.) *The Ontogenesis of Grammar*. New York: Academic Press.

Brändle, M. (1986) Language teaching for the 'young-old'. *Babel* 21 (1), 17–21.

Brasseur, J. and Jimenez, B.C. (1989) Performance of university students on the Fullerton subtest of idioms. *Journal of Communication Disorders* 22, 351–9.

Bratt Paulston, C. (1983) *Swedish Research and Debate about Bilingualism*. Stockholm: National Swedish Board of Education.

Breathnach, C. (1993) Temporal determinants of language acquisition and bilingualism. *Irish Journal of Psychological Medicine* 10 (1), 41–7.

Brega, E. and Newell, J. (1965) Comparison of performance by FLES program students and regular French III students on Modern Language Asssociation tests. *French Review* 39, 433–8.

Brega, E. and Newell, J. (1967) High school performance of FLES and non-FLES students. *Modern Language Journal* 5, 408–11.

Brenner, C. (1957) *An Elementary Textbook of Psychoanalysis*. Garden City, NY: Doubleday.

Brière, E. (1978) Variables affecting native Mexican children's learning Spanish as a second language. *Language Learning* 28, 159–74.

Britton, J. (1970) *Language and Learning*. Harmondsworth: Penguin.

Brookes A. and Grundy, P. (eds) (1988) *Individualization and Autonomy in Language Learning. ELT Documents 131*. London: Modern English Publications and the British Council.

Brooks, N. (1960) *Language and Language Learning*. New York: Harcourt Brace and World.

Brown, A. and Smiley, S. (1977) Rating the importance of structural units of prose passages: A problem of metacognitive development. *Child Development* 48, 1–8.

Brown, A. and Smiley, S (1978) The development of strategies for studying texts. *Child Development* 49, 1076–1088.

Brown, A., Smiley, S. and Lawton, S. (1978) The effect of experience on the selection of suitable retrieval cues for studying texts. *Child Development* 49, 829–35.

Brown, C. (1983) The distinguishing characteristics of the older second language learner. Unpublished PhD. dissertation. University of California. Cited in L. Seright (1985) Age and aural comprehension achievement in Francophone adults learning English. *TESOL Quarterly* 19, 455–73.

Brown, J.A. (1961) *Freud and the Post-Freudians*. London: Cassell.

Brown, J.W. and Hécaen, H. (1976) Lateralization and language representation. *Neurology* 26, 183–9.

Brown, J.W. and Jaffe, J. (1975) Hypothesis on cerebral dominance. *Neuropsychologia* 13, 107–110.

Brown, P. and Levinson, S. (1987) *Politeness: Some Universals in Language Usage*. Cambridge: Cambridge University Press.

Brown, R. (1968) The development of wh-questions in child speech. *Journal of Verbal Learning and Verbal Behavior* 7, 279–90.

Brown, R. (1973) *A First Language: The Early Stages*. London: George, Allen and Unwin.

Brown, R., Cazden, C. and Bellugi, U. (1971) The child's grammar from I to III. In A. Bar-Adon and W. Leopold (eds) *Child Language: A Book of Readings*. Englewood Cliffs, NJ: Prentice-Hall.

Bruhn de Garavito, J. (1999) Adult SLA of *se* constructions in Spanish: Evidence against pattern learning. *Proceedings of the Boston University Conference on Language Development* 23, 112–19.

Brumfit, C. (1984a) Theoretical implications of interlanguage studies for language learning. In A. Davies *et al.* (eds) *Interlanguage*. Edinburgh: Edinburgh University Press.

Brumfit, C. (1984b) *Communicative Methodology in Language Teaching*. Cambridge: Cambridge University Press.

Bruner, J. (1975) The ontogenesis of speech acts. *Journal of Child Language* 2, 1–19.

Bruner, J. (1983) *Child's Talk*. Cambridge: Cambridge University Press.

Buckby, M. (1976) Is primary French in the balance? *Modern Language Journal* 60, 340–6.

Buckley, S. (1985) Attaining basic educational skills: reading, writing and number. In D. Lane and B. Stratford (eds) *Current Approaches to Down Syndrome*. New York: Praeger.

Bühler, C. (1930) *The First Year of Life*. New York: John Day.

Bühler, C. and Hetzer, H. (1928) Das erste Verständnis für Ausdruck im ersten Lebensjahr. *Zeitschrift für Psychologie* 107, 50–61

Bühler, C. and Hetzer, H. (1935) *Testing Children's Development from Birth to School Age*. New York: Farrar and Rinehart.

Bühler, U. (1972) *Empirische und lernpsychologische Beiträge zur Wahl des Zeitpunktes für den Fremdsprachenunterrichtsbeginn*. Zurich: Orell Fussli.

Burstall, C. (1975a) Factors affecting foreign-language learning: A consideration of some recent research findings. *Language Teaching and Linguistics Abstracts* 8, 5–25. Reprinted in V. Kinsella (ed.) (1978) *Language Teaching and Linguistics Surveys*. Cambridge: Cambridge University Press.

Burstall, C. (l975b) Primary French in the balance. *Educational Research* 17, 193–7.

Burstall, C., Jamieson, M., Cohen, S. and Hargreaves, M. (1974) *Primary French in the Balance*. Windsor: NFER Publishing Company.

Burt, M., Dulay, H. and Hernandez, E. (1973) *Bilingual Syntax Measure*. New York: Harcourt Brace Jovanovich.

Burt, M., Dulay, H. and Finocchiaro, M. (eds) (1977) *Viewpoints on English as a Second Language*. New York: Regents.

Calvin, W. (1997) *How Brains Think: Evolving Intelligence, Then and Now*. London: Weidenfeld and Nicolson.

Cancino, H., Rosansky, E. and Schumann, J. (1978) The acquisition of English negatives and interrogatives by native Spanish speakers. In E. Hatch (ed.) *Second Language Acquisition: A Book of Readings*. Rowley, MA: Newbury House.

Candland, D. (1995) *Feral Children and Clever Animals: Reflections on Human Nature*. Oxford: Oxford University Press.

Caparulo, B. and Cohen, D. (1983) Developmental language studies in the neuropsychiatric disorders of childhood. In K. Nelson (ed.) *Children's Language. Volume 4*. Hillsdale, NJ: Lawrence Erlbaum.

Cappa, S., Papagno, C. and Vallar, G. (1990) Language and verbal memory after right hemispheric stroke: A clinical CT scan study. *Neuropsychologia* 28, 503–9.

Caramazza, A. and Yeni-Komshian, G. (1974) Voice onset time in two French dialects. *Journal of Phonetics* 2, 239–45.

Caramazza, A., Yeni-Komshian, G., Zurif, E. and Carbone, E. (1973) The acquisition of a new phonological contrast: The case of stop consonants in French-English bilinguals. *Journal of the Acoustical Society of America* 54, 421–8.

Carmichael, L. (ed.) (1946) *Manual of Child Psychology*. New York: Wiley; London: Chapman and Hall.

Carroll, F. (1980) Neurolinguistic processing of a second language: Experimental evidence. In R. Scarcella and S. Krashen (eds) *Research in Second Language Acquisition*. Rowley, MA: Newbury House.

Carroll, J. (1967) Foreign language proficiency levels attained by language majors near graduation from college. *Foreign Language Annals* 1, 131–51.

Carroll, J. (1969) Psychological and educational research into second language teaching to young children. In H. Stern (ed.) *Languages and the Young School Child*. London: Oxford University Press.

Carroll, J. (1971) Development of native language skills beyond the early years. In C. Reed (ed.) *The Learning of Language*. New York: Appleton-Century-Crofts.

Carroll, J. (1975) *The Teaching of French as a Foreign Language in Eight Countries*. New York: Wiley.

Carroll, J. (1977) Characteristics of a successful language learner. In M. Burt, H. Dulay and M. Finocchiaro (eds) *Viewpoints on English as a Second Language*. New York: Regents.

Carroll, J. and Sapon, S. (1959) *Manual: Modern Language Aptitude Test*. New York: The Psychological Corporation.

Castner, B. (1940) Language development. In A. Gesell (ed.) _The First Five Years of Life: A Guide to the Study of the Preschool Child._ London: Methuen.

Catford, J. (1965) _A Linguistic Theory of Translation._ London: Oxford University Press.

Cattell, P. (1940) _The Measurement of Intelligence of Infants and Young Children._ New York: The Psychological Corporation, Lancaster, PA: The Science Press.

Cattell, R. (1963) Theory of fluid and crystallized intelligence: A critical experiment. _Journal of Educational Psychology_ 54, 1–22.

Cattell, R. (1968) Fluid and crystallized intelligence. _Psychology Today_ 3, 56–62.

Cavanaugh, J. (1995) Ageing. In P. Bryant and A. Colman (eds) _Developmental Psychology._ London: Longman.

Cellerier, G. (1979) Quelques éclaircissements sur l'innéisme et le constructivisme. In M. Piatelli-Palmarini (ed.) _Théories du langage, théories de l'apprentissage: Le débat entre Jean Piaget et Noam Chomsky._ Paris: Editions du Seuil.

Cenoz, J. (2003a) Facteurs déterminant l'acquisition d'une L3: Âge, développement cognitif et milieu. _Acquisition et Interaction en Langues Étrangères_ 18, 37–51.

Cenoz, J. (2003b) The influence of age on the acquisition of English: General proficiency, attitudes and code mixing. In M.P. García Mayo and M.L. García Lecumberri (eds) _Age and the Acquisition of English as a Foreign Language._ Clevedon: Multilingual Matters.

Cenoz, J., Jessner, U. and Hufeisen, B. (eds) (2003) _The Multilingual Lexicon._ Dordrecht: Kluwer.

Central Statistics Office (2003) _Census 2002: Principal Demographic Results._ Dublin: Central Statistics Office, Government of Ireland.

Chapman, R. (1995) Language development in children and adolescents with Down syndrome. In P. Fletcher and B. MacWhinney (eds) _The Handbook of Child Language._ Oxford. Blackwell.

Cheydleur, F. (1932) An experiment in adult learning of French at the Madison, Wisconsin, Vocational School. _Journal of Educational Research_ 4, 259–75.

Chi, J., Dooling, E. and Giles, F. (1977) Left-right asymmeries of the temporal speech areas of the human fetus. _Archives of Neurology_ 34, 346–8.

Chihara, T. and Oller, J. (1978) Attitudes and attained proficiency in EFL: A sociolinguistic study of adult Japanese speakers. _Language Learning_ 28, 55–68.

Chomsky, C. (1969) _The Acquisition of Syntax in Children from 5 to 10._ Cambridge, MA: MIT Press.

Chomsky, N. (1959) Review of Skinner's _Verbal Behavior. Language_ 35, 26–58.

Chomsky, N. (1965) _Aspects of the Theory of Syntax._ Cambridge, MA: MIT Press.

Chomsky, N. (1967) The formal nature of language. In E. Lenneberg, _Biological Foundations of Language._ New York: Wiley. Appendix A.

Chomsky, N. (1972) _Language and Mind._ Enlarged Edition. New York: Harcourt Brace Jovanovich.

Chomsky, N. (1976a) On the biological basis of language capacities. In R. Rieber (ed.) _The Neuropsychology of Language: Essays in Honor of Eric Lenneberg._ New York: Plenum Press.

Chomsky, N. (1976b) _Reflections on Language._ London: Temple Smith.

Chomsky, N. (1978) Noam Chomsky on the genetic gift of tongues [Interview with Brian Magee]. _The Listener,_ April 6, 1978, 434–6.

Chomsky, N. (1980) _Rules and Representations._ New York: Columbia University Press, Oxford: Blackwell.

Chomsky, N. (1981) _Lectures on Government and Binding._ Dordrecht: Foris.

Chomsky, N. (1986) *Knowledge of Language: Its Nature, Origin and Use.* New York: Praeger.

Chomsky, N. (1988) *Language and Problems of Knowledge: The Managua Lectures.* Cambridge, MA: MIT Press.

Chomsky, N. (1989) Some notes on economy of derivation and representation. *MIT Working Papers in Linguistics* 10, 43–74.

Chomsky, N., Atran, S., Piatelli-Palmarini, M., Bateson, G., Danchin, A., Fodor, J., Sperber, D., Cellerier, G., Piaget, J. and Jacob, F. (1979) Discussion of Cellerier (1979). In M. Piatelli-Palmarini (ed.) *Théories du langage, théories de l'apprentissage: Le débat entre Jean Piaget et Noam Chomsky.* Paris: Éditions du Seuil.

Christophersen, P. (1973) *Second Language Learning: Myth and Reality.* Harmondsworth: Penguin.

Clancy, B. and Finlay, B. (2001) Neural correlates of early language learning. In M. Tomasello and E. Bates (eds) *Language Development: The Essential Readings.* Oxford: Blackwell.

CLAR (Committee on Language Attitudes Research) (1975) *Report.* Dublin: Stationery Office.

Clark, H. and Clark, E. (1977) *Psychology and Language: An Introduction to Psycholinguistics.* New York: Harcourt Brace Jovanovich.

Coates, S. and Messer, D. (1996) The influence of parity on children's speech. *Early Child Development and Care* 117, 29–43.

Conrad, R. (1972) The developmental role of vocalizing in short-term memory. *Journal of Verbal Learning and Verbal Behavior* 11, 521–33.

Conti-Ramsden, G. and Windfuhr, K. (2002) Productivity with word order and morphology: A comparative look at children with SLI and normal language abilities. *International Journal of Language and Communication Disorders* 37, 17–30.

Cook, V. (1973) The comparison of language development in native children and foreign adults. *International Review of Applied Linguistics* 11, 13–28.

Cook, V. (1978) Second language learning: A psycholinguistic perspective. *Language Teaching and Linguistics: Abstracts* 11:2, 73–89. Reprinted in V. Kinsella (ed.) (1982) *Surveys 1.* Cambridge: Cambridge University Press.

Cook, V. (1986a) Experimental approaches applied to two areas of second language learning research: Age and listening-based teaching methods. In V. Cook (ed.) (1986b) *Experimental Approaches to Second Language Learning.* Oxford: Pergamon.

Cook, V. (ed.) (1986b) *Experimental Approaches to Second Language Learning.* Oxford: Pergamon.

Cook, V. (1992) Evidence for multicompetence. *Language Learning* 42, 557–91.

Cook, V. (1995) Multicompetence and effects of age. In D. Singleton and Z. Lengyel (eds) *The Age Factor in Second Language Acquisition.* Clevedon: Multilingual Matters.

Cook, V. (2002) Background to the L2 user. In V. Cook (ed.) *Portraits of the L2 User.* Clevedon: Multilingual Matters.

Cook, V. (ed.) (2003) *Effects of the Second Language on the First.* Clevedon: Multilingual Matters.

Cook, V. and Newson, M. (1996) *Chomsky's Universal Grammar: An Introduction.* (2nd edn). Oxford: Blackwell.

Coppetiers, R. (1987) Competence differences between native and fluent non-native speakers. *Language* 63, 544–73.

Corder, S. (1973) *Introducing Applied Linguistics.* Harmondsworth: Penguin.

Cranberg, L., Filley, C., Hart, E. and Alexander, M. (1987) Acquired aphasia in childhood: Clinical and CT investigations. *Neurology* 3, 1165–72.

Cromer, R. (1970) 'Children are nice to understand': Surface structure clues for the recovery of deep structure. *British Journal of Psychology* 61, 397–408.

Cromer, R. (1988) The cognition hypothesis revisited. In F. Kessel (ed.) *The Development of Language and Language Researchers: Essays in Honor of Roger Brown.* Hillsdale, NJ: Laurence Erlbaum Associates.

Cross, P. (1981) *Adults as Learners.* San Francisco: Jossey-Bass.

Crossley, R. (1994) *Facilitated Communication Training.* New York. Teachers College Press.

Crossley, R. (1997) *Speechless: Facilitating Communication for People without Voices.* Caulfield: DEAL Communication Centre.

Crystal, D. (1976) *Child Language, Learning and Linguistics.* London: Edward Arnold.

Crystal, D. (1986) Prosodic development. In P. Fletcher and M. Garman (eds) *Language Acquisition: Studies in First Language Development.* Cambridge: Cambridge University Press.

Crystal, D. (1997) *A Dictionary of Linguistics and Phonetics* (4th edn). Oxford: Blackwell.

Crystal, D. and Fletcher, P. (1979) Profile analysis of language disability. In C. Fillmore, D. Kempler and W. Wang (eds) *Individual Differences in Language Ability and Language Behavior.* New York: Academic Press. Reprinted as Chapter 3 of D. Crystal (ed.) (1981) *Directions* in *Applied Linguistics.* New York: Academic Press, 1981.

Crystal, D., Fletcher, P. and Garman, M. (1976) *The Grammatical Analysis of Language Disability.* First Edition. London: Edward, Arnold (Second Edition. London: Cole and Whurr, 1988).

Cummins, J. (1977) Immersion education in Ireland: A critical review of Macnamara's findings. *Working Papers on Bilingualism* 13, 121–129.

Cummins, J. (1979) Cognitive / academic language proficiency, linguistic interdependence, the optimum age question and some other matters. *Working Papers on Bilingualism* 19, 198–203.

Cummins, J. (1980) The cross-lingual dimensions of language proficiency: Implications for bilingual education and the optimal age issues. *TESOL Quarterly* 14, 175–187.

Cummins, J. (1981) Age on arrival and immigrant second language learning in Canada: A reassessment. *Applied Linguistics* 2, 132–149.

Cummins, J. (1983) Language proficiency and academic achievement. In J. Oller (ed.) *Current Issues in Language Testing Research.* Rowley, MA: Newbury House.

Cummins, J. (1984) *Bilingualism and Special Education: Issues in Assessment and Pedagogy.* Clevedon: Multilingual Matters.

Cummins, J. (1991) Interdependence of first and second language proficiency in bilingual children. In E. Bialystok (ed.) *Language Processing in Bilingual Children.* Cambridge: Cambridge University Press.

Cummins, J. and Swain, M. (1986) *Bilingualism in Education.* London: Longman.

Cummins, J., Swain, M., Nakajima, K., Handscombe, J., Green D. and Tran, C. (1984) Linguistic interdependence among Japanese and Vietnamese immigrant students. In C. Rivera (ed.) *Communicative Competence Approaches to Language Proficiency Assessment: Research and Application.* Clevedon: Multilingual Matters.

Cunningham, C. (1982) *Downs Syndrome: An Introduction for Parents.* London: Souvenir Press.

Cunningham, C. and Mittler, P. (1981) Maturation, development and mental handicap. In K. Connolly and H. Prechtl (eds) *Maturation and Development: Biological and Psychological Perspectives*. London: Heinemann.

Curran, C. (1961) Counselling skills adapted to the learning of foreign languages. *Bulletin of the Menninger Clinic* 25, 78–93.

Curriculum and Examinations Board (1985*) Language in the Curriculum/Teanga sa Churaclam*. Dublin: Curriculum and Examinations Board/An Bord Curaclaim agus Scruduithe.

Curtiss, S. (1977) *Genie: A Psycholinguistic Study of a Modern-day 'Wild Child'*. New York: Academic Press.

Curtiss, S. (1988) Abnormal language acquisition and the modularity of language. In F. Newmeyer (ed.) *Linguistics: The Cambridge Survey: Volume. 2. Linguistic Theory: Extensions and Implications*. Cambridge: Cambridge University Press.

Curtiss, S., Fromkin, V., Rigler, D., Rigler, M. and Krashen, S. (1975) An update on the linguistic development of Genie. In D. Dato (ed.) *Georgetown University Round Table on Languages and Linguistics*. Washington, DC: Georgetown University Press.

Cutler, A. (1994) Segmentation problems, rhythmic solutions. In L. Gleitman and B. Landau (eds) *The Acquisition of the Lexicon*. Cambridge, MA: MIT Press.

D'Anglejan, A., Renaud, C., Arseneault, R. and Lortie, A. (1981) *Difficultés d'apprentissage de la langue seconde chez l'immigrant adulte en situation scolaire: Une étude dans le contexte québecoi*s. Quebec: International Centre for Research on Bilingualism: University of Laval Press.

Danks, J. and Sorce, P. (1973) Imagery and deep structure in the prompted recall of passive sentences. *Journal of Verbal Learning and Verbal Behavior* 12, 114–17.

Darwin, C. (1877) A biographical sketch of an infant. *Mind* 2, 285; 292–4. Reprinted in A. Bar-Adon and W. Leopold (eds) *Child Language: A Book of Readings*. Englewood Cliffs, NJ: Prentice-Hall.

Davies, A., Criper, C. and Howatt, A. (eds) (1984) *Interlanguage*. Edinburgh: Edinburgh University Press.

Davitt, D. (2003) The language. *Inside Ireland* http://www.insideireland.com/sample04.htm.

Deacon, T. (1997) *The Symbolic Species*. London: Penguin.

Deary, I. (1998) Differences in mental abilities. *British Medical Journal* 317, 1701–3.

De Boysson-Bardies, B., Sagart, L. and Durand, C. (1984) Discernible differences in the babbling of infants according to target languages. *Journal of Child Language* 11, 1–15.

Dechert, H. (1995) Some critical remarks concerning Penfield's theory of second language acquisition. In D. Singleton and Z. Lengyel (eds) *The Age Factor in Second Language Acquisition*. Clevedon: Multilingual Matters.

DeKeyser, R. (2000) The robustness of critical period effects in second language acquisition. *Studies in Second Language Acquisition* 22, 499–533.

DeKeyser, R. (2003) Confusion about confounding: The critical period and other age-related aspects of second language learning. Paper presented at ELIA VIII (Encuentros de Linguistica Inglesa Aplicada), El factor edad en la adquisición y enseñanza de L2, Seville.

DeKeyser, R. and Montgomery, J. (2002) How age and aptitude interact in adult second language acquisition. Paper presented at the Second Language Research Forum, Toronto.

Dekydtspotter, L., Sprouse, R.A. and Thyre, R. (1998) Evidence of full UG access in L2 acquisition from the interpretive interface: Quantification at a distance in English-French interlanguage. *Proceedings of the Boston University Conference on Language Development* 22, 141–52.

Delisle, H. (1982) Native speaker judgment and the evaluation of errors in German. *Modern Language Journal* 66, 39–48.

Dennis, M. (1980) Capacity and strategy for syntactic comprehension after left and right hemidecortication. *Brain and Language* 7, 287–317.

Dennis, M. and Whitaker, H. (1977) Hemispheric equipotentiality and language acquisition. In S. Segalowttz and F. Gruber (eds) *Language Development and Neurological Theory*. New York: Academic Press.

De Villiers, J. and De Villiers, P. (1973) A cross-sectional study of the acquisition of grammatical morphemes in child speech. *Journal of Psycholinguistic Research* 2, 267–78.

De Villiers. J. and De Villiers, P. (1978) *Language Acquisition*. Cambridge, MA: Harvard University Press.

DeVilliers, J. and DeVilliers, P. (1999) Linguistic determinism and the understanding of false beliefs. In P. Mitchell and K. Riggs (eds) *Children's Reasoning and the Mind*. Hove: Psychology Press.

Devitt, S., Little, D., Ó Conchuir, S. and Singleton, D. (1982–3) *Learning Irish with Anois is Aris*. CLCS Occasional Paper 6 (published in association with RTÉ). Centre for Language and Communication Studies, Trinity College Dublin. ERIC ED 252 437.

Diaz, E.M. and Klingler, C. (1994) Towards an explanatory model of the interaction between bilingualism and cognitive development. In E. Bialystok (ed.) *Language Processing in Bilingual Children*. Cambridge: Cambridge University Press.

Diggs, C. and Basili, A. (1987) Verbal expression of right cerebrovascular accident patients: Convergent and divergent language. *Brain and Language* 30, 130–46.

Diller, K. (1971) *Generative Grammar, Structural Linguistics and Language Teaching*. Rowley, MA: Newbury House.

Diller, K. (1981a) 'Natural methods' of foreign language teaching: Can they exist? What criteria must they meet? In H. Winitz (ed.) *Native Language and Foreign Language Acquisition*. New York: The New York Academy of Sciences.

Diller, K. (ed.) (1981b) *Individual Differences and Universals in Language Learning Aptitude*. Rowley, MA: Newbury House.

Dittmar, N. (1982) Ich fertig arbeite – nicht mehr spreche Deutsch: Semantische Eigenschaften pidginisierter Lernervarietäten des Deutschen. *Zeitschrift für Literaturwissenschaft und Linguistik* 45, 9–34.

Donoghue, M. (1965) What research tells us about the effects of FLES. *Hispania* 48, 555–9.

Downing, J. (1966) Reading readiness re-examined. In J. Downing (ed.) *The First International Reading Symposium*. London: Cassell, New York: Day.

Draves, W. (1984) *How to Teach Adults*. Kansas: The Learning Resources Network.

Dromi, E. (1987) *Early Lexical Development*. Cambridge: Cambridge University Press.

Dulay, H. and Burt, M. (1973) Should we teach children syntax? *Language Learning* 23, 245–58.

Dulay, H. and Burt, M. (1974a) You can't learn without goofing: An analysis of children's second language errors. In J. Richards (ed.) *Error Analysis: Perspectives in Second Language Acquisition*. London: Longman.

Dulay, H. and Burt, M. (1974b) Errors and strategies in child second language acquisition. *TESOL Quarterly* 8, 129–36.

Dulay, H. and Burt, M. (1974c) Natural sequences in child second language acquisition. *Language Learning* 24, 37–53. Reprinted in E. Hatch (ed.) (1978) *Second Language Acquisition: A Book of Readings*. Rowley, MA: Newbury House.

Dulay, H. and Burt, M. (1974d) A new perspective on the creative construction process in child second language acquisition. *Language Learning* 24, 253–78.

Dulay, H. and Burt, M. (1977) Remarks on creativity in language acquisition. In M. Burt, H. Dulay and M. Finnochiaro (eds) *Viewpoints on English as a Second Language*. New York: Regents.

Duncan, S. and De Avila E. (1979) Bilingualism and cognition: Some recent findings. *NABE Journal* 4, 15–50.

Dunkel, H. (1948) *Second Language Learning*. Boston, MA: Ginn and Company.

Dunkel, H. and Pillet, R. (1957) A second year of French in the elementary school. *Elementary School Journal* 58, 142–51.

Dunkel, H. and Pillet, R. (1962) *French in the Elementary School: Five Years' Experience*. Chicago: University of Chicago Press.

Durette, R. (1972) A five-year FLES report. *Modem Language Journal* 56, 23–4.

Dyson, P. (1986) An evaluation of the year spent abroad by undergraduates in terms of improvement in oral competence. Paper presented at a 'Language and Linguistics' seminar, Centre for Language and Communication Studies, Trinity College, Dublin, October.

Eadie, P., Fey, M., Douglas, J., and Parsons, C. (2002) Profiles of grammatical morphology and sentence imitation in children with specific language impairment and Down's Syndrome. *Journal of Speech, Language and Hearing Research* 45, 720–33.

Eckman, F. and Washabaugh, W. (1983) The Acculturation Model and the problem of variation in second language acquisition. In R. Andersen (ed.) *Pidginization and Creolization as Language Acquisition*. Rowley, MA: Newbury House.

Eilers, R., Wilson, W. and Moore, J. (1979) Speech discrimination in the language innocent and the language wise: A study in the perception of voice onset time. *Journal of Child Language* 6, 1–18.

Eimas, P., Siqueland, E., Jusczyk, P. and Vigorito, J. (1971) Speech perception in infants. *Science* 171, 303–6.

Eisele, J. and Aram, D. (1995) Lexical and grammatical development in children with early hemisphere damage: A cross-sectional view from birth to adolescence. In P. Fletcher and B. MacWhinney (eds) *The Handbook of Child Language*. Oxford: Blackwell.

Ekberg, L. (1998) Regeltillämpning kontra lexikonkunskap in svenskan hos invandrarbarn i Malmö (Rule application versus lexical knowledge in Swedish among immigrant children in Malmö). In J. Møller, P. Quist, A. Holmen and J. Jørgensen (eds) *Nordiske Sprog som andet Sprog. Københavnerstudier i Tosprogethed* 30 (pp. 247–63). Copenhagen: Institut for humanistike fag, Danmarks Lærerhøjskole.

Ekstrand, L. (1959) *Utvärdering av metodik och resultat på grundval av inspelade prov från elever i l:a, 2: a, 3e och 4e klass i Västerås, Linkoping och Hallstahammar. (Evaluation of methodology and results on the basis of recorded tests from pupils in grades 1, 2, 3 and 4 in Västerås, Linköping and Hallstahammar)*. Stencilled. Stockholm: National Swedish Board of Education. Cited in Ekstrand (1976a) Age and length of residence as variables related to the adjustment of migrant children, with special reference to second language learning. In G. Nickel (ed.) _Proceedings of the Fourth International Congress of Applied Linguistics. Volume 3._ Stuttgart: Hochschulverlag.

Ekstrand, L. 1964, _Språkfärdighet och språkmetodik._ _(Language skill and language teaching methodology)._ Licenciate of Philosophy thesis, University of Stockholm. Cited in Ekstrand (1976a) Age and length of residence as variables related to the adjustment of migrant children, with special reference to second language learning. In G. Nickel (ed.) _Proceedings of the Fourth International Congress of Applied Linguistics. Volume 3._ Stuttgart: Hochschulverlag.

Ekstrand, L. (1971) Varför engelska redan in åk 3? (Why begin English as early as grade 3?) In S. Jakobson and L. Mellgren (eds) _Metodik och Praktisk Språkfärdighet 2._ Kristianstad: Hermods.

Ekstrand, L. (1976a) Age and length of residence as variables related to the adjustment of migrant children, with special reference to second language learning. In G. Nickel (ed.) _Proceedings of the Fourth International Congress of Applied Linguistics. Volume 3._ Stuttgart: Hochschulverlag. Reprinted in S. Krashen, R. Scarcella and M. Long (eds) (1982) _Child-Adult Differences in Second Language Acquisition._ Rowley, MA: Newbury House.

Ekstrand, L. (1976b) Adjustment among immigrant pupils in Sweden. _International Review of Applied Psychology_ 25 (3), 167–88.

Ekstrand, L. (1977) Social and individual frame factors in L2 learning: Comparative aspects. In T. Skutnabb-Kangas (ed.) _Papers from the First Nordic Conference on Bilingualism._ Helsingfors: Universitetet.

Ekstrand, L. (1978a) English without a book revisited: The effect of age on second language acquisition in a formal setting. _Didakometry No. 60._ Department of Educational and Psychological Research, School of Education, Malmö. Reprinted in S. Krashen, R. Scarcella and M. Long (eds) (1982) _Child-Adult Differences in Second Language Acquisition._ Rowley, MA: Newbury House.

Ekstrand, L. (1978b) Bilingual and bicultural adaptation. _Educational and Psychological Interactions_ 66. Department of Educational and Psychological Research, School of Education, Malmö.

Ekstrand, L. (l978c) Migrant adaptation: A cross-cultural problem. In R. Freudenstein (ed.) _Teaching the Children of Immigrant._ Brussels: Didier.

Ekstrand, L. (1980) Optimum age, critical period, harmfulness or what, in early bilingualism? Paper presented at the 22nd International Congress of Psychology, Leipzig, July.

Ekstrand, L. (l981a) Språk, identitet och kultur. (Language, identity and, culture). _Forskning om utbildning_ 8 (1), 28–58.

Ekstrand, L. (1981b) Språk, identitet, kultur: Replik till Pirkko Ruotsalainen och Göte Hanson. (Language, identity, culture: Reply to Pirkko Ruotsalainen and Göte Hanson). _Forskning om utbildning_ 8 (3), 50–2.

Ekstrand, L. (1983) Maintenance or transition – or both? A review of Swedish ideologies and empirical research. In T. Husen (ed.) _Multicultural and Multilingual Education in Immigrant Countries._ Oxford: Pergamon.

Ekstrand, L. (1984a) Review of Hugo Baetens Beardsmore's _Bilingualism: Basic Principles. Journal of Language and Social Psychology_ 3, 149–53.

Ekstrand, L. (l984b) Review of Christina Bratt Paulston's _Swedish Research and Debate about Bilingualism. Journal of Language and Social Psychology_ 3, 219–21.

Ekstrand, L. (1985) Immigrant children: Policies for educating. In T. Husen and T. Postlethwaite (eds) _The International Encyclopedia of Education: Research and Studies._ Volume 5. Oxford: Pergamon.

Elbers, L. (1982) Operating principles in repetitive babbling: A cognitive continuity approach. *Cognition* 12, 45–63.

Elkind, D. (1970) *Children and Adolescents: Interpretive Essays on Jean Piaget*, New York: Oxford University Press.

Elling, B. (1980) Special curricula for special needs. In J. Phillips (ed.) *The New Imperative: Expanding the Horizons of Foreign Language Education*. Skokie, IL: National Textbook.

Elliot, A. (1981) *Child Language* . Cambridge: Cambridge University Press.

Ellis, A. and Beattie, G. (1986) *The Psychology of Language and Communication*. London: Weidenfeld and Nicholson.

Ellis, A., Weismer, S., Evans, J. and Hesketh, L. (1999) An examination of verbal working memory capacity in children with specific language impairment. *Journal of Speech, Language and Hearing Research* 41, 1136–46.

Ellis, R. (1984) The role of instruction in second language acquisition. In D. Singleton and D. Little (eds) *Language Learning in Formal and Informal Contexts*. Dublin: Irish Association for Applied Linguistics.

Ellis, R. (1985) *Understanding Second Language Acquisition*. Oxford: Oxford University Press.

Emerick, L. and Hatten, J. (1974) *Diagnosis and Evaluation in Speech Pathology*. Englewood Cliffs, NJ: Prentice-Hall.

Emmorey, K. (2002) The Critical Period Hypothesis and the effects of late language acquisition. In K. Emmorey (ed.) *Language, Cognition and the Brain*. Mahwah, NJ: Laurence Erlbaum Associates.

Emmorey, K., Bellugi, U., Friederici, A. and Horn, P. (1995) Effects of age of acquisition on grammatical sensitivity: Evidence from on-line and off-line tasks. *Applied Psycholinguistics* 16, 1–23.

Entus, A. (1977) Hemispheric asymmetry in processing of dichotically presented speech and nonspeech stimuli by infants. In S. Segalowitz and E. Gruber (eds) *Language Development and Neurological Theory*. New York: Academic Press.

Erber, J., Szuchman, L. and Rothberg, S. (1990) Everyday memory failure: Age differences in appraisal and attribution. *Psychology and Aging* 5, 236–41.

Ervin-Tripp, S. (1974) Is second language learning like the first? *TESOL Quarterly* 8, 111–27.

Eubank, L. and Gregg, K. (1999) Critical periods and (second) language acquisition: divide et impera. In D. Birdsong (ed.) *Second Language Acquisition and the Critical Period Hypothesis*. Mahwah, NJ: Erlbaum.

Fabbro, F. (1999) *The Neurolinguistics of Bilingualism: An Introduction*. Hove: Psychology Press.

Fabbro. F. (2002) The neurolinguistics of L2 users. In V. Cook (ed.) *Portraits of the L2 User*. Clevedon: Multilingual Matters.

Faerch, C., Haastrup, K. and Phillipson, R. (1984) *Learner Language and Language Learning*. Clevedon: Multilingual Matters.

Fathman, A. (1975a) The relationship between age and second language productive ability. *Language Learning* 25, 245–53.

Fathman, A. (1975b) Language background, age and the order of acquisition of English structures. In H. Dulay and M. Burt (eds) *On TESOL 75: New Directions in Second Language Learning, Teaching and Bilingual Education*. Washington, DC: TESOL.

Fathman, A. (1979) The value of morpheme order studies for second language learning. *Working Papers on Bilingualism* 18, 179–99.

Fathman, A. and Precup, L. (1983) Influences of age and setting on second language oral proficiency. In K. Bailey, M. Long and S. Peck (eds) _Second Language Acquisition Studies_. Rowley, MA: Newbury House.

Favard, J. (1993) Apprentissage précoce. En France ... Trois ans après ... _Le Français dans le Monde_ 257, 37–9.

Felix, S. (1981) Competing cognitive structures in second language acquisition. Paper presented at the European-North American Workshop on Cross-Linguistic Second Language Acquisition Research, Lake Arrowhead CA, September. Cited in B. Harley (1986) _Age in Second Language Acquisition_. Clevedon: Multilingual Matters.

Fenson, L., Dale, P.S., Reznick, J.S., Bates, E., Hartnung, J., Pethick, S. and Reilly, J. (1993) _The MacArthur Communicative Development Inventories: User's Guide and Technical Manual_. San Diego: Singular Publishing Group.

Fenson, L., Dale, P., Reznick, J., Bates, E., Thal, D. and Pethick, S. (1994) _Variability in Early Communicative Development. Monographs of the Society for Research in Child Development_ 59 (5).

Feofanov, M. (1960) Oshibki v postroenii predlozhenii kak pokazatel' stepeni usvoeniya grammmaticheskogo stroya yazyka. (Errors in sentence construction as an indicator of the degree of mastery of the grammatical structure of the language). _Doklady Akad. Pedag. Nauk RSFR1_, pp. 37–8. Abstracted by D. Slobin in E. Smith and G. Miller (eds) (1966) _The Genesis of Language: A Psycholinguistic Approach_. Cambridge, MA: MIT Press.

Ferguson, C. (1975) Towards a characterization of English foreigner talk. _Anthropological Linguistics_ 17, 1–14.

Ferris, M. and Politzer, R. (1981) Effects of early and delayed second language acquisition: English composition skills of Spanish-speaking junior high school students. _TESOL Quarterly_ 15, 263–74.

Flege, J. (1981) The phonological basis of foreign accent: A hypothesis. _TESOL Quarterly_ 15, 443–55.

Flege, J. (1991) Age of learning affects the authenticity of voice onset time in stop consonants produced in a second language. _Journal of the Acoustical Society of America_ 89, 395–411.

Flege, J. (1995) Second-language speech learning: Theory, findings and problems. In W. Strange (ed.) _Speech Perception and Linguistic Experience: Theoretical and Methodological Issues_. Timonium, MD: York Press.

Flege, J. (1999) Age of learning and second language speech. In D. Birdsong (ed.) _Second Language Acquisition and the Critical Period Hypothesis_. Mahwah, NJ: Lawrence Erlbaum.

Flege, J. (2002) Interactions between the native and second-language phonetic systems. In P. Burmeister, T. Piske and A. Rohde (eds) _An Integrated View of Language Development_. Trier: Wissenschaftlicher Verlag Trier.

Flege, J., Frieda, E. and Nozawa, T. (1997) Amount of native language (L1) use affects the pronunciation of an L2. _Journal of Phonetics_ 25, 169–86.

Flege, J., MacKay, I. and Meador, D. (1999) Native Italian speakers' production and perception of English vowels. _Journal of the Acoustical Society of America_ 106, 2973–87.

Flege, J., Munro, M. and McKay, I. (1995) Factors affecting degree of perceived foreign accent in a second language. _Journal of the Acoustical Society of America_ 97, 3125–34.

Flege, J., Yeni-Komshian, S. and Liu, S. (1999) Age constraints on second-language acquisition. *Journal of Memory and Language* 41, 78–104.

Fletcher, P. and Garman, M. (eds) (1986) *Language Acquisition: Studies in First Language Development.* Cambridge: Cambridge University Press.

Florander, J. and Jensen, M. (1969) *Skoleforsøg i engelsk* 1959–1965. (*School experiments in English* 1959–1965). Stencilled. Denmark's Institute of Education. Cited in Ekstrand (1976a) Age and length of residence as variables related to the adjustment of migrant children, with special reference to second language learning. In G. Nickel (ed.) *Proceedings of the Fourth International Congress of Applied Linguistics. Volume 3.* Stuttgart: Hochschulverlag. Reprinted in S. Krashen, R. Scarcella and M. Long (eds) (1982) *Child-Adult Differences in Second Language Acquisition.* Rowley, MA: Newbury House.

Flynn, S. (1987) *A Parameter-Setting Model of L2 Acquisition: Experimental Studies in Anaphora.* Dordrecht: Reidel.

Foss, D. and Hakes, D. (1978) *Psycholinguistics: An Introduction to the Psychology of Language.* Englewood Cliffs, NJ: Prentice-Hall.

Foster-Cohen, S.H. (1999) *An Introduction to Child Language Development.* London: Longman.

Fowler, A. (1990) Language abilities in children with Down syndrome: Evidence for a specific syntactic delay. In D. Cichetti and M. Beeghley (eds) *Children with Down Syndrome: A Developmental Perspectiv*e. Cambridge: Cambridge University Press.

Freedman, P. and Carpenter, R. (1976) Semantic relations used by normal and language-impaired children at Stage I. *Journal of Speech and Hearing Research* 19, 784–95.

Freeman, R., Malkin, S. and Hastings, J. (1975) Psychological problems or deaf children and their families: A comparative study. *American Annals of the Deaf* 120, 391–405.

Freeman, R., Carbin, C. and Boese, R. (1981) *Can't Your Child Hear? A Guide for Those who Care about Deaf Children.* Baltimore, MD: University Park Press.

Freud, S. (1964) *New Introductory Lectures on Psychoanalysis.* Translated by J. Strachey. First published in *The Standard Edition of the Complete Psychological Works of Sigmund Freud. Volume 22.* London: Hogarth Press. Reprinted Harmondsworth: Penguin, 1973.

Freud, S. (1968) *Infantile Cerebral Paralysis.* Translated by L. Russin. Coral Gables: University of Miami Press.

Friederici, A. (2003) The brain basis of language learning: Insights from natural and artificial grammar acquisition. Contribution to the *Language Learning* Round-table on the Cognitive Neuroscience of Second Language Acquisition, 13th Annual Conference of the European Second Language Assocation (EUROSLA), Edinburgh.

Frisina, D., Frisina, R., Snell, K., Burkard, R., Walton, J. and Ison, J. (2000) Auditory temporal acuity during aging. In P. Hof and C. Mobbs (eds) *Functional Neurobiology of Aging.* San Diego: Academic Press.

Fromkin, V., Krashen, S., Curtiss, S., Rigler, D. and Rigler, M. (1974) The development of language in Genie: A case of language acquisition beyond the 'critical period'. *Brain and Language* 1, 81–107.

Gainotti, G., Caltagirone, C., Miceli, G. and Masullo, C. (1981) Selective semantic lexical impairment of language comprehension in right brain damaged patients. *Brain and Language* 13, 201–211.

Gallagher, T. and Darnton, B. (1977) Revision behaviors in the speech of language disordered children. Paper presented to the American Speech and Hearing Association, Chicago. Cited in M. Harris and M. Coltheart (1986) _Language Processing in Children and Adults: An Introduction_. London: Routledge and Kegan Paul.

Galloway, A. (1993) Communicative language teaching: An introduction and sample activities. _ERIC Digests_, June 1993, ED357642.

Galloway, L. (1981) The convolutions of second language: A theoretical article with a critical review and some hypotheses towards a neuropsychological model of bilingualism and second language performance. _Language Learning_ 31, 439–64.

Galloway, L. and Krashen, S. (1980) Cerebral organization in bilingualism and second language. In R. Scarcella and S. Krashen (eds.), _Research in Second Language Acquisition_. Rowley, MA: Newbury House.

García Lecumberri, M.L. and Gallardo, F. (2003) English FL sounds in school learners of different ages. In M.P. García Mayo and M.L. García Lecumberri (eds) _Age and the Acquisition of English as a Foreign Language_. Clevedon: Multilingual Matters.

García Mayo M.P. (2003) Age, length of exposure and grammaticality judgments in the acquisition of English as a foreign language. In M.P. García Mayo and M.L. García Lecumberri (eds) _Age and the Acquisition of English as a Foreign Language_. Clevedon: Multilingual Matters.

Gardiner, M. and Walter, D. (1977) Evidence of hemispheric specialization from infant EEG. In S. Harnad, R. Doty, L. Goldstein, J. Jaynes and G. Kranthamer (eds) _Lateralization in the Nervous System_. New York: Academic Press.

Gardner, R. (1968) Attitudes and motivation: their role in second language acquisition, _TESOL Quarterly_ 2, 141–50. Reprinted in J. Oller and J. Richards (eds) (1973) _Focus on the Learner: Pragmatic Perspectives for the Language Teacher_. Rowley, MA: Newbury House.

Gardner, R. (1979) Social psychological aspects of second language acquisition. In H. Giles and R. St. Clair (eds) _Language and Social Psychology_. Oxford: Blackwell.

Gardner, R. (1980) On the validity of affective variables in second language acquisition: Conceptual, contextual and statistical considerations. _Language Learning_ 30, 255–70.

Gardner, R. (1985) _Social Psychology and Second Language Learning: The Role of Attitudes and Motivation_. London: Edward Arnold.

Gardner, R. (2001) Integrative motivation and second language acquisition. In Z. Dörnyei and R. Schmidt (eds) _Motivation and Second Language Acquisition_. Honolulu: University of Hawai'i Press.

Gardner, R. and Lalonde, R. (1983) The socio-educational model of second language acquisition: An investigation using Lisrel causal modeling. _Journal of Language and Social Psychology_ 2, 1–15.

Gardner, R. and Lambert, W. (1972) _Attitudes and Motivation in Second Language Learning_. Rowley, MA: Newbury House.

Gardner, R. and Smythe, P. (1975) Motivation and second language acquisition. _Canadian Modern Language Review_ 31, 218–30.

Gardner, R., Lalonde, R. and Macpherson, J. (1985) Social factors in second language attrition. _Language Learning_ 35, 519–40.

Gardner, R., Smythe, P. and Clement, R. (1979) Intensive second language language study in a bicultural milieu: An investigation of attitudes, motivation and language proficiency. _Language Learning_ 29, 305–20.

Gardner, R., Smythe, P., Kirkby, D. and Bramwell J. (1974) *Second Language Acquisition: A Social Psychological Approach.* Final Report. London, Ontario: Ontario Ministry of Education.

Gardner, R., Smythe, P., Clement, R. and Glicksman, L. 1976, Second language learning: a social psychological perspective. *Canadian Modern Language Review* 32, 198–213.

Gazzaniga, M. (1970) *The Bisected Brain.* New York: Appleton-Century-Crofts.

Gazzaniga, M. (1983) Right hemisphere language following brain bisection: A 20 year perspective. *American Psychologist* 38, 342–6.

Gazzaniga, M.S. (1992) *Nature's Mind: The Biological Roots of Thinking, Emotions, Sexuality, Language, and Intelligence.* New York: Basic Books.

Genesee, F. (1976) The role of intelligence in second language learning. *Language Learning* 26, 267–80.

Genesee, F. (1978) Is there an optimal age for starting second language instruction? *McGill Journal of Education* 13, 145–54.

Genesee, F. (1978/9) Scholastic effects of French immersion: An overview after ten years. *Interchange* 9, 20–9.

Genesee, F. (1979) A *Comparison of Early and Late Immersion Programs.* McGill University, Montreal. Mimeo. Cited in B. Harley (1986) *Age in Second Language Acquisition.* Clevedon: Multilingual Matters.

Genesee, F. (1982) Experimental neuropsychological research on second language processing. *TESOL Quarterly* 16, 315–21.

Geschwind, N. (1983) Comments on Zaidel (1983). In M. Studdert-KIennedy (ed.) *Psychobiology of Language.* Cambridge, MA: MIT Press.

Gesell, A. (1925) *The Mental Growth of the Pre-School Child: A Psychological Outline of Normal Development From Birth to the Sixth Year, Including a System of Developmental Diagnosis.* New York: Macmillan.

Gesell, A. (ed.) (1940a) *The First Five Years of Life: A Guide to the Study of the Preschool Child.* London: Methuen.

Gesell, A. (1940b) The first year of life. In A. Gesell (ed.) *The First Five Years of Life: A Guide to the Study of the Preschool Child.* London: Methuen.

Gesell, A. (1940c) From one to five. In A. Gesell (ed.) *The First Five Years of Life: A Guide to the Study of the Preschool Child.* London: Methuen.

Gesell, A. and Thompson, H. (1934) *Infant Behavior: Its Genesis and Growth.* New York: McGraw-Hill.

Gesell, A., Thompson, H. and Amatruda, C. (1938) *The Psychology of Early Growth.* New York: Macmillan.

Ghenghea, V. (1984) Relationships between mother tongue (Romanian) and a foreign language (German) in developing rational reading skills in German. Paper presented at the 7th International Congress of Applied Linguistics, Vrije Universiteit Brussel, August. Abstract in J. Den Haese and J. Nivette (eds) *AILA Brussels 84: Proceedings. Volume 2.* Brussels: ITO/VUB, 1984. Cited in Titone (1985a) Measurement and evaluation of bilingualism and bilingual education: A psycholinguistic perspective. *Rassegna Italiana di Linguistica Applicata* 17: 2–3, 19–30.

Gibbs, E. and Carswell, L. (1988) Early use of total communication with a young Down syndrome child: A procedure for evaluating effectiveness. *66th Annual Convention of the Council for Exceptional Children,* 1–26.

Gilbert, J. and Climan, I. (1974) Dichotic studies in 2 and 3 year-olds: A preliminary report. *Speech Communication Seminar, Stockholm. Volume 2.* Uppsala: Almqvist and Wiksell.

Gilbert, J., Mitchell, G., Brown, L. and Chow, P. (1985) Long term consequences of traumatic head injury in childhood and adolescence. Paper presented at the Boston University Child Language Conference, Boston.

Gillham, B. (1986) Mental handicap. In B. Gillham (ed.) *Handicapping Conditions in Children.* London: Croom Helm.

Glanville, B., Best, C. and Levinson, R. (1977) A cardiac measure of cerebral asymmetries in infant auditory perception. *Developmental Psychology* 13, 54–9.

Goldfield, B. and Reznick, J. (1990) Early lexical acquisition: rate, content and the vocabulary spurt. *Journal of Child Language* 17, 171–83.

Goldin-Meadow, S. and Feldman, H. (1975) The creation of a communication system: A study of deaf children of hearing parents. *Sign Language Studies* 8, 221–36.

Goldin-Meadow, S. and Mylander, C. (1990) Beyond the input given: The child's role in the acquisition of language. *Language* 66, 323–55.

Goodluck, H. (1991) *Language Acquisition: A Linguistic Introduction.* Oxford: Blackwell.

Gould, J. (1976) Language development and non-verbal skills in severely mentally retarded children: An epidemiological study. *Journal of Mental Deficiency Research* 20, 129–46.

Green, D. (2003) Exploring the convergence hypothesis: Processing and representational implications. Contribution to the *Language Learning* Roundtable on the Cognitive Neuroscience of Second Language Acquisition, 13th Annual Conference of the European Second Language Assocation (EUROSLA), Edinburgh.

Green, P. (ed.) (1975) *The Language Laboratory in School.* Edinburgh: Oliver and Boyd.

Griffiths, P. (1986) Early vocabulary. In P. Fletcher and M. Garman (eds) *Language Acquisition: Studies in First Language Development.* Cambridge: Cambridge University Press.

Grinder, R., Otomo, A. and Toyota, W. (1961) *Comparisons between 2nd, 3rd and 4th Grade Children in the Audio-Lingual Learning of Japanese as a Second Language.* Honolulu: Psychological Research Center, University of Hawaii.

Grinder, R.E. (1973) *Adolescence.* New York: Wiley.

Grosjean, F. (1992) *Life with Two Languages.* Cambridge, MA: Harvard University Press.

Grotek, M. (2002a) Learning a foreign language in late adulthood – overcoming memory problems. Paper presented at the 15th International Conference on Second/Foreign Language Learning. Szczyrk, May.

Grotek, M. (2002b) *Foreign Language Learning in Late Adulthood: Memory Strategy Training.* Unpublished MA dissertation, University of Silesia.

Gruber, H. and Vonèche, J. (1982) Introduction. In H. Gruber and J. Vonèche (eds) *The Essential Piaget: An Interpretive Reference and Guide.* London: Routledge and Kegan Paul.

Guion, S., Flege, J. and Loftin, J. (2000) The effect of L1 use on pronunciation in Quichua-Spanish bilinguals. *Journal of Phonetics* 28, 27–42.

Guiora, A. (1972) Construct validity and transpositional research: Toward an empirical study of psychoanalytic concepts. *Comprehensive Psychiatry* 13, 139–50.

Guiora, A. (1992) Notes on the psychology of language – the Gent lectures. *Scientia Paedogogica Experimentalis* 29 (Supplement), vii–62.

Guiora, A., Acton, W., Erard, R. and Strickland, F. (1980) The effects of benzodiaz-epine (Valium) on permeability of language ego boundaries. *Language Learning* 30, 351–63.

Guiora, A., Beit-Hallahmi, B., Brannon, R., Dull, C. and Scovel, T. (1972) The effects of experimentally induced changes in ego states on pronunciation ability in a second language: An exploratory study. *Comprehensive Psychiatry* 13, 421–28.

Guiora, A., Brannon, R. and Dull, C. (1972) Empathy and second language learning. *Language Learning* 22, 111–30.

Guiora, A., Lane, H. and Bosworth, L. (1967) An exploration of some personality variables in authentic pronunciation of a second language. *Studies in Language and Language Behavior* 4, 510–514.

Guttmann, E. (1942) Aphasia in children. *Brain* 65, 205–19.

Haan, M., Shemanski, L., Jagust, W., Manolio, T. and Kuller, L. (1999) The role of APOE ε4 in modulating effects of other risk factors for cognitive decline in elderly persons. *The Journal of the American Medical Association* 282, 40–6.

Hakuta, K. (1975) *Becoming Bilingual at Five: The Story of Uguisu*. Unpublished undergraduate thesis. Harvard University. Cited in J. Schumann (1978a) *The Pidginization Process: A Model for Second Language Acquisition*. Rowley, MA: Newbury House.

Hakuta K. and Diaz R. (1984) The relationship between degree of bilingualism and cognitive ability: A critical discussion and some longitudinal data. In K. Nelson (ed.) *Children's Language*. Volume 5. Hillsdale, NJ: Erlbaum.

Hakuta, K., Bialystok, E. and Wiley, E. (2003) Critical evidence: A test of the Critical Period Hypothesis for second-language acquisition. *Psychological Science* 14, 31–8.

Hale, T. and Budar, E. (1970) Are TESOL classes the only answer? *Modern Language Journal* 54, 487–92.

Halladay, L. (1970) *A Study of the Effects of Age on Achievement in Adults Studying English in an Intensive Course*. Unpublished Ph.D. dissertation, University of Michigan. Cited in L. Seright (1985) Age and aural comprehension: Achievement in Francophone adults learning English. *TESOL Quarterly* 19, 455–73.

Halliday, M. (1975) *Learning How to Mean: Explorations in the Development of Language*. London: Edward Arnold.

Hameister, D. and Hickey, T. (1977) Traditional and adult students: A dichotomy. *Lifelong Learning* 1 (4), 6–8.

Hamers, J. and Blanc, M. (2000) *Bilinguality and Bilingualism*. (2nd edn). Cambridge: Cambridge University Press.

Hammer, M. (1977) Lateral differences in the newborn infant's response to speech and noise stimuli. Ph.D. dissertation, New York University. *Dissertation Abstracts International* 38, 1439-B. Cited in Segalowitz (1983b) Cerebral asymmetries for speech in infancy. In S. Segalowitz (ed.) *Language Function and Brain Organization*. New York: Academic Press.

Hampson, J. and Nelson, K. (1993) The relation of maternal language to variation in rate and style of acquisition. *Journal of Child Language* 20, 313–42.

Hand, S. (1973) What it means to teach older adults. In A. Hendrickson (ed.) *A Manual on Planning Educational Programs For Older Adults*. Tallahassee, FL: Florida State University.

Hanson, A. (1996) The search for separate theories of adult learning: Does anyone really need andragogy? In R. Edwards, A. Hanson and P. Raggatt (eds) *Adult Learning, Adult Learners Education and Training. Volume 1.* London: Routledge.

Hanson, G. (1981) Kan man lita på Lars Henric Ekstrand? (Can one rely on Lars Henric Ekstrand?). *Forskning om utbildning* 8 (3), 48–50.

Harley, B. (1986) *Age in Second Language Acquisition.* Clevedon: Multilingual Matters.

Harley, B. and Hart, D. (1997) Language aptitude and second language proficiency in classroom learners of different starting ages. *Studies in Second Language Acquisition* 19, 379–400.

Harley, B. and Hart, D. (2002) Age, aptitude and second language learning on a bilingual exchange. In P. Robinson (ed.) *Individual Differences and Instructed Language Learning.* Amsterdam: John Benjamins.

Harley, B., Howard, J. and Hart, D. (1995) Second language processing at different ages: Do younger learners pay more attention to prosodic cues to sentence structure? *Language Learning* 45, 43–71.

Harley, B. and Wang, W. (1997) The critical period hypothesis. Where are we now? In A. de Groot and J. Kroll (eds) *Tutorials in Bilingualism: Psycholinguistic Perspectives.* Mahwah, NJ: Lawrence Erlbaum.

Harris, J. (1984) *Spoken Irish in Primary Schools: An Analysis of Achievement.* Dublin: Institiúid Teangeolaíochta Éireann.

Harris, J. and Conway, M. (2003) *Modern Languages in Irish Primary Schools: An Evaluation of the National Pilot Project.* Institiúid Teangeolaíochta Éireann.

Harris, M. (1992) *Language Experience and Early Language Development: From Input to Uptake.* Hove and Hillsdale, NJ: Lawrence Erlbaum.

Harris, M., Jones, D. and Grant, J. (1983) The non-verbal context of mothers' speech to children. *First Language* 4, 21–30.

Harris, R. (1980) *The Language-makers.* London: Duckworth.

Hartmann, M. and Hasher, L. (1991) Aging and suppression: Memory for previously relevant information. *Psychology and Aging* 6, 587–94.

Hatch, E. (ed.) (1978a) *Second Language Acquisition: A Book of Readings.* Rowley, MA: Newbury House.

Hatch, E. (1978b) Discourse analysis and second language acquisition. In E. Hatch (ed.) *Second Language Acquisition: A Book of Readings.* Rowley, MA: Newbury House.

Hatch, E. (1978c) Discourse analysis, speech acts, and second language acquisition. In W. Ritchie (ed.) *Second Language Acquisition Research: Issues and Implications.* New York: Academic Press.

Hatch, E. (1980) Second language acquisition – Avoiding the question. In S. Felix (ed.) *Second Language Development.* Tubingen: Gunther Narr.

Hatch, E. (1983a) *Psycholinguistics: A Second Language Perspective.* Rowley, MA: Newbury House.

Hatch, E. (1983b) First and second language acquisition – A bit of magic. *Bulletin de l'ACLA/ Bulletin of the CAAL* 5 (2), 29–50.

Hatch, E. (1983c) Simplified input and second language acquisition. In R. Andersen (ed.) *Pidginization and Creolization as Language Acquisition.* Rowley, MA: Newbury House.

Hawkins, R. (2001) *Second Language Syntax: A Generative Introduction.* Oxford: Blackwell.

Hay, M. (1973) *Languages for Adults.* Bristol: Longman.

Haynes, C. (1982) Vocabulary acquisition problems in language disordered children. Unpublished M.Sc. thesis, Guy's Hospital Medical School, University of London. Cited in J. Harris and M. Coltheart (1986) *Language Processing in Children and Adults: An Introduction*. London: Routledge and Kegan Paul.

Heilman, K., Scholes, R. and Watson, R. (1975) Auditory affective agnosia. *Journal of Neurology, Neurosurgery and Psychiatry* 38, 69–72.

Henrysson, S. (1981) Tvåspråkigshetsdebatten (The bilingualism debate). *Forskning om utbildning* 8 (4), 35–6.

Henzl, V. (1973) Linguistic register of foreign language instruction. *Language Learning* 23, 207–22.

Herdina, P. and Jessner, U. (2002) *A Dynamic Model of Multilingualism: Perspectives of Change in Psycholinguistics*. Clevedon: Multilingual Matters.

Hermelin, B. and O'Connor, N. (1970) *Psychological Experiments with Children*. New York: Pergamon.

Hertzog, C. and Dunlosky, J. (1996) The aging of practical memory: An overview. In D. Herrmann, C. McEvoy, C. Hertzog, P. Hertel, P. and M. Johnson (eds) *Basic and Applied Memory Research: Volume 1: Theory in Context*. Hillsdale, NJ: Lawrence Erlbaum.

Heyman, A.G. (1973) *Invandrarbarn: Slutrapport (Immigrant children: Final report)*. Stockholm: Invandrarnamd.

Hier, D. and Kaplan, J. (1980) Verbal comprehension deficits after right hemisphere damage. *Applied Psycholinguistics* 1, 279–94.

Hill, J. (1970) Foreign accents, language acquisition and cerebral dominance revisited. *Language Learning* 20, 237–48.

Hill, M. (1995) *Invandrarbarns möjligsheter. Om kanskapsutveckling och språkutveckling I förskola och skola (Immigrant Children's Prospects. On Development of Knowledge and Language in Preschool and School)*. Göteborg: Institutionen för Pedagogik: Göteborgs Universitet.

Hillage, J., Uden, T., Aldridge, F. and Eccles, J. (2000) *Adult Learning in England: A Review*. Brighton: Institute for Employment Studies.

Hindley, R. (1990) *The Death of the Irish Language: A Qualified Obituary*. London: Routledge.

Hirsch-Pasek, K. and Golinkoff, R. (1996) *The Origins of Grammar: Evidence from Early Language Comprehension*. Cambridge, MA: MIT Press.

Hoar, N. (1977) Paraphrase capabilities of language impaired children. Paper presented to the Boston University Conference on Language Development. Cited in J. Harris and M. Coltheart (1986) *Language Processing in Children and Adults: An Introduction*. London: Routledge and Kegan Paul.

Hobbs, F. and Stoops, N. (2002) *Demographic Trends in the 20th Century*. Washington, DC: US Government Printing Office.

Hoff-Ginsberg, E. (1991) Mother-child conversation in different social classes and communicative settings. *Child Development* 62, 782–96.

Hoff-Ginsberg, E. (1998) The relationship of birth order and socioeconomic status to children's language experience and language development. *Applied Psycholinguistics* 19, 603–29.

Holec, H., Little, D. and Richterich, R. (eds) (1996). *Strategies in Language Learning and Use. Studies Towards a Common European Framework of Reference for Language Learning and Teaching*. Strasbourg: Council of Europe.

Holland, T. (1997) Ageing and its consequences for people with Down's syndrome. *Down's Syndrome Association Newsletter*, July 1997.

Holmgren, K., Lindblom, B., Aurelius, G., Jalling, B. and Zetterstrom, R. (1986) On the phonetics of infant vocalization. In B. Lindblom and R. Zetterstrom (eds) *Precursors of Early Speech*. New York: Stockton Press.

Holobow, N., Genesee, F. and Lambert, W. (1991) The effectiveness of a foreign language immersion program for children from different ethnic and social class backgrounds: Report 2. *Applied Psycholinguistics* 12, 179–98.

Holtzmann, J., Sidtis, J., Volpe, B., Wilson, D. and Gazzaniga, M. (1981) Dissociation of spatial information for stimulus localization and the control of attention. *Brain* 104, 861–72.

Horn, J.L. (1982) The aging of human abilities. In B. Wolman (ed.) *Handbook of Developmental Psychology*. Englewood Cliffs, NJ: Prentice-Hall.

Horwitz, E.K. (1983) The relationship between conceptual level and communicative competence in French. *Studies in Second Language Acquisition*, 65–73.

Howe, H. and Hillman, D. (1973) The acquisition of semantic restrictions in children. *Journal of Verbal Learning and Verbal Behavior* 12, 132–9.

Hughes, C. and Russel, J. (1993) Autistic children's difficulty with mental disengagement from an object: Its implications for theories of autism. *Developmental Psychology* 29, 498–510.

Hughes, S. and Walsh, J. (1971) Effects of syntactical mediation. Age and modes of representation in paired associate learning. *Child Development* 42, 1827–36.

Hunt, C. (1966) Language choice in a multilingual society. *International Journal of American Linguistics* 33 (2), 112–25.

Hunt, D. (1971) *Matching Models in Education: The Coordination of Teaching Methods with Student Characteristics*. Toronto: The Ontario Institute for Studies in Education.

Hunt, D., Butler, L., Noy, J. and Rosser, M. (1978) *Assessing Conceptual Level by the Paragraph Completion Method*. Toronto: The Ontario Institute for Studies in Education.

Hurley, E. (1986) French for young beginners: Why and how. Paper presented at a forum for primary teachers on the theme 'French for Young Beginners', Carysfort College, Blackrock, Co. Dublin, February.

Hyltenstam, K. (1992) Non-native features of near-native speakers: On the ultimate attainment of childhood L2 learners. In R. Harris (ed.) *Cognitive Processing in Bilinguals*. Amsterdam: Elsevier.

Hyltenstam, K. and Abrahamsson, N. (2000) Who can become native-like in a second language? All, some or none? On the maturational contraints controversy in second language acquisition. *Studia Linguistica* 54, 150–66.

Hyltenstam, K. and Abrahammson, N. (2003) Âge de l'exposition initiale et niveau terminal chez les locuteurs du suédois L2. *Acquisition et Interaction en Langue Étrangère* 18, 99–127.

Hymes, D. (1974) *Foundations of Sociolinguistics*. Philadelphia: University of Pennsylvania Press.

Iacono, T.A. and Duncan, J.E. (1995) Comparison of sign language alone and in combination with an electronic communication device in early language intervention. *Augmentative and Alternative Communication* 11 (4), 249–59.

Ianco-Worrall, A. (1972) Bilingualism and cognitive development. *Child Development* 43, 1390–1400.

Ingram, D. (1975) Cerebral speech lateralization in young children. *Neuropsychologia* 13, 103–5.

Ingram, D. (1989) *First Language Acquisition: Method, Description and Explanation.* Cambridge: Cambridge University Press.

Inhelder, B. (1979) Langage et connaissance dans le cadre constructiviste. In M. Piatelli-Palmarini (ed.) *Théories du langage, théories de l'apprentissage: Le débat entre Jean Piaget et Noam Chomsky.* Paris: Editions du Seuil.

Inhelder, B. and Piaget, J. (1958) *The Growth of Logical Thinking from Childhood to Adolescence.* Translated by A. Parsons and S. Milgram. London: Routledge and Kegan Paul.

Inhelder, B. and Sinclair-De-Zwart, H. (1969) Learning cognitive structures. In P. Mussen, J. Langer and M. Covington (eds) *Trends and Issues in Developmental Psychology.* New York: Holt Rinehart and Winston.

INTO (1985) *The Irish Language in Primary Education.* Dublin: Irish National Teachers' Organisation.

Ioup, G. (1995) Evaluating the need for input enhancement in post-critical period language acquisition. In D. Singleton and Z. Lengyel (eds) *The Age Factor in Second Language Acquisition.* Clevedon: Multilingual Matters.

Ioup, G., Boustagui, E., Tigi, M. and Moselle, M. (1994) Reexamining the critical period hypothesis: A case of successful adult SLA in a naturalistic environment. *Studies in Second Language Acquisition* 16, 73–98.

Itard, J. (1801) *De L'éducation d'un homme sauvage ou des premiers développements physiques et moraux du jeune sauvage de l'Aveyron.* Paris: Gouyon.

Itard, J. (1807) *Rapport fait à S.E. le Minstre de L'Intérieur sur les nouveaux développements et l'état actuel du sauvage de l'Aveyron.* Paris: Imprimerie Impériale.

Jakobovits, L. (1970) *Foreign Language Learning: A Psycholinguistic Analysis of the Issues.* Rowley, MA: Newbury House.

Jakobson, R. (1942) Kindersprache, Aphasie und Allgemeine Lautgesetze. *Uppsala Universitets Årsskrift* 9, 1–83.

Jakobson, R. (1968) *Child Language: Aphasia and Phonological Universals.* The Hague: Mouton.

Jia, G., and Aaronson, D. (1999) Age differences in second language acquisition: The Dominant Language Switch and Maintenance Hypothesis. *Proceedings of the Boston University Conference on Language Development* 23, 301–12.

Joanette, Y. and Goulet, P. (1994) Right hemisphere and verbal communication: conceptual, methodological and clinical issues. *Clinical Aphasiology* 22, 1–23.

Johnson, J. and Newport, E. (1989). Critical period effects in second language learning: The influence of maturational state on the acquisition of ESL. *Cognitive Psychology* 21, 60–99.

Johnson, R. and Swain, M. (1997) *Immersion Education: International Perspectives.* Cambridge: Cambridge University Press.

Johnston, J. and Schery, T. (1976) The use of grammatical morphemes by children with communication disorders. In D. Morehead and A. Morehead (eds) *Normal and Deficient Child Language.* Baltimore, MD: University Park Press.

Johnstone, R. (1996) The Scottish initiatives. In E. Hawkins (ed.) *30 Years of Language Teaching.* London: CILT.

Joiner, E. (1981) *The Older Language Learner: A Challenge for Colleges and Universities.* Washington, DC: Center for Applied Linguistics.

Jusczyk, P. (1997) *The Discovery of Spoken Language.* Cambridge, MA: MIT Press.

Jusczyk, P. (2001) Finding and remembering words: Some beginnings by English learning infants. In M. Tomasello and E. Bates (eds) *Language Development: The Essential Readings.* Oxford: Blackwell.

Justman, J. and Nass, M. (1956) The high school achievement of pupils who were and were not introduced to a foreign language in elementary school. *Modern Language Journal* 40, 120–3.

Kamhi, A.G. (1987) Normal Language Development: Ages 9 to 19. Short course presented at the Annual Convention of the American Speech-Language-Hearing Association. New Orleans, LA.

Kanner, L. (1943) Autistic disturbances of affective contact. *Nervous Child 2*, 217–50. Reprinted in L. Kanner (ed.) (1973) *Childhood Psychosis: Initial Studies and New Insights*. Washington, DC: Winston.

Kecskes, I. and Papp, T. (2000) *Foreign Language and Mother Tongue*. Hillsdale, NJ: Lawrence Erlbaum.

Keenan, E. (1974) Conversational competence in children. *Journal of Child Language* 1, 163–83.

Kegl, J., Senghas, A. and Coppola, M. (1999) Creation through contact: Sign language emergence and sign language change in Nicaragua. In M. DeGraff (ed.) *Language Creation and Language Change: Creolization, Diachrony and Development*. Cambridge, MA: MIT Press.

Kellerman, E. (1977) Towards a characterization of the strategy of transfer in second language learning. *Interlanguage Studies Bulletin* 2, 58–145.

Kellerman, E. (1979) Transfer and non-transfer: Where are we now? *Studies in Second Language Acquisition* 2, 37–57.

Kellerman, E. (1995) Age before beauty: Johnson and Newport revisited. In L. Eubank, L. Selinker and M. Sharwood Smith (eds) *The Current State of Interlanguage: Studies in Honor of William E. Rutherford*. Amsterdam: John Benjamins.

Kennedy, G. (1973) Conditions for language learning. In J. Oller and J. Richards (eds) *Focus on the Learner: Pragmatic Perspectives for the Language Teacher*. Rowley, MA: Newbury House.

Kent, R.D. and Miolo, G. (1995) Phonetic abilities in the first year of life. In P. Fletcher and B. MacWhinney (eds) *The Handbook of Child Language*. Oxford: Blackwell.

Kessler, C. and Idar, I. (1979) Acquisition of English by a Vietnamese mother and child. *Working Papers on Bilingualism* 18, 65–79.

Kim, K.H.S., Relkin, N.R., Kyoung-Min, L. and Hirsch, J. (1997) Distinct cortical areas associated with native and second languages. *Nature* 388, 171–4.

Kinsbourne, M. (1975) The ontogeny of cerebral dominance. In D. Aaronson and R. Rieber (eds) *Developmental Psycholinguistics and Communication Disorders*. New York: New York Academy of Sciences.

Kinsbourne, M. (1981) Neuropsychological aspects of bilingualism. In H. Winitz (ed.) *Native Language and Foreign Language Acquisition*. New York: The New York Academy of Sciences.

Kinsbourne, M. and Hiscock, M. (1977) Does cerebral dominance develop? In S. Segalowttz and F. Gruber (eds) *Language Development and Neurological Theory*. New York: Academic Press.

Kirch, M. (1956) At what age elementary school language teaching? *Modern Language Journal* 40, 399–400.

Kleim, J., Swain, R., Czerlanis, C., Kelly, J., Pipitone, M. and Greenough, W. (1997) Learning-dependent dendritic hypertrophy of cerebellarstellate neurons: Plasticity of local circuit neurons. *Neurobiology of Learning and Memory* 67, 29–33.

Klein, W. (1981) Some rules of regular ellipsis in German. In W. Klein and W. Levelt (eds) *Crossing the Boundaries in Linguistics: Studies Presented to Manfred Bierwisch*. Dordrecht: Reidel.

Klein, W. (1986) *Second Language Acquisition*. Cambridge: Cambridge University Press.

Klein, W. and Dittmar, N. (1979) *Developing Grammars: The Acquisition of German Syntax by Foreign Workers*. Berlin: Springer.

Klima, E. and Bellugi, U. (1966) Syntactic regularities in the speech of children. In J. Lyons and R. Wales (eds) *Psycholinguistic Papers*. Edinburgh: Edinburgh University Press.

Knowles, M. (1970) *The Modern Practice of Adult Education*. New York: Association Press. Cited extract reprinted as Andragogy: An emerging technology for adult learning. In M. Tight (ed.) (1983) *Education for Adults. Volume 1. Adult Learning and Education*. London: Croom Helm (in association with the Open University).

Knowles, M. (1975). *Self-Directed Learning*. New York: Association Press.

Knowles, M. (1984). *The Adult Learner: A Neglected Species*. Houston: Gulf Publishing.

Knox, A. (1978) *Adult Development and Learning*. San Francisco: Jossey-Bass.

Kolb, B. and Whishaw, I. (1996) *Human Neuropsychology*. (4th edn). New York: Worth Publishers

Konieczna, R. (1997) Znaczenie Uniwersytetów Trzeciego Wieku w życiu ludistarszych (The importance of the Universities of the Third Age in the life of elderly people). *Edukacja Dorosłych* 4 (19), 58–66.

Kosslyn, S. and Bower, G. (1974) The role of imagery in sentence menory: A developmental study. *Child Development* 45, 30–8.

Kowalski, C. and Cangemi, J. (1978) Characteristics of older adults and the aging: Some new evidence. *Education* 99, 203–7.

Krashen, S. (1973) Lateralization, language learning and the critical period: Some new evidence. *Language Learning* 23, 63–74.

Krashen, S. (1975) The critical period for language acquisition and its possible bases. In D. Aaronson and R. Rieber (eds) *Developmental Psycholingulstics and Communication Disorders*. New York: New York Academy of Sciences.

Krashen, S. (1976) Formal and informal linguistic environments in language acquisition and language learning. *TESOL Quarterly* 10, 157–68.

Krashen, S. (1981a) *Second Language Acquisition and Second Language Learning*. Oxford: Pergamon.

Krashen, S. (1981b) The 'Fundamental Pedagogical Principle' in second language teaching *Studia Linguistica* 35/*AILA* 81 *Proceedings* II, 50–70,

Krashen, S. (1982a) *Principles and Practice in Second Language Acquisition*. Oxford: Perganon.

Krashen, S. (1982b) Accounting for child-adult differences in second language rate and attainment. In S. Krashen, R. Scarcella and M. Long (eds) *Child-Adult Differences in Second Language Acquisition*. Rowley, MA: Newbury House.

Krashen, S. (1985) *The Input Hypothesis: Issues and Implications*. London: Longman.

Krashen, S. and Harshman, R. (1972) Lateralization and the critical period. *UCLA Working Papers in Phonetics* 23, 13–21.

Krashen, S. and Seliger, H. (1976) The role of formal and informal linguistic environments in adult second language learning. *International Journal of Psycholinguistics* 3, 15–21.

Krashen S., Long, M. and Scarcella, R. (1979) Age, rate and eventual attainment in second language acquisition. *TESOL Quarterly* 13, 573–82 Reprinted in S. Krashen, R., Scarcella and M. Long (eds) (1982) *Child-Adult Differences in Second Language Acquisition*, Rowley, MA: Newbury House.

Krashen, S., Scarcella, R. and Long, M. (eds) (1982) *Child-Adult Differences in Second Language Acquisition*. Rowley, MA: Newbury House.

Krashen, S., Seliger, H. and Hartnett, D. (1974) Two studies in adult second language learning. *Kritikon Litterarum* 213, 220–8.

Krashen, S., Sferlazza, V. and Fathman, A. (1976) Adult performance on the SLOPE test. More evidence for a natural sequence in adult language acquisition. *Language Learning* 26, 145–51.

Krashen, S., Butler, J., Birnbaum, R. and Robertson, J. (1978a) Two studies in language acquisition and language learning. *ITL: Review of Applied Linguistics* 39/40, 73–92.

Krashen, S., Zelinski, S., Jones, C. and Uprich, C. (1978b) How important is instruction? *English Language Teaching Journal* 32, 257–61.

Kris, E. (1952) *Psychoanalytic Explorations in Art.* New York: International University Press.

Kuusinen, J. and Salin, E. (1971) Children's learning of unfamiliar phonological sequences. *Perceptual and Motor Skills* 33, 559–62. Cited in Cook (1986a) Experimental approaches applied to two areas of second language learning research: Age and listening-based teaching methods. In V. Cook (ed.) (1986b) *Experimental Approaches to Second Language Learning.* Oxford: Pergamon.

Kuusinen, J., Lasonen, K. and Särkelä, T. (1977) *Research Reports,* No. 53, Department of Education, University of Jyväskylä. Cited in Ekstrand (1981a) Språk, identitet och kultur. (Language, identity and, culture;). *Forskning om utbildning* 8 (1), 28–58.

Labov, W. (1966) *The Social Stratification of English in New York City.* Washington, DC: Center for Applied Linguistics.

Labov, W. (1970) *The Study of Non-Standard English.* Urbana, IL: National Council of Teachers of English.

Lackner, J. (1976) A developmental study of language behavior in retarded children. In D. Morehead and A. Morehead (eds) *Normal and Deficient Child Language.* Baltimore, MD: University Park Press.

Lambert, W. (1975) Culture and language as factors in learning and education. In A. Wolfgang (ed.) *Education of Immigrant Students.* Toronto: The Ontario Institute for Studies in Education.

Lambert, W. and Klineberg, O. (1967) *Children's Views of Foreign Peoples: A Crossnational Study.* New York: Appleton.

Lambert, W., Gardner, R., Olton, R. and Tunstall, K. (1970) A study of the roles of attitudes and motivation in second language learning. In J. Fishman (ed.) *Readings in the Sociology of Language.* The Hague: Mouton.

Lamberts, F. (1980) Developmental auditory agnosia in the severely retarded: A further investigation. *Brain and Language* 11, 106–18.

Lamendella, J. (1977) General principles of neurofunctional organisation and their manifestation in primary and non-primary language acquisition. *Language Learning* 27, 155–96.

Lane, H. (1976) *The Wild Boy of Aveyron.* Cambridge, MA: Harvard University Press.

Langabaster, D. and Doiz, A. (2003) Maturational constraints on foreign language written production. In M.P. García Mayo and M.L. García Lecumberri (eds) *Age and the Acquisition of English as a Foreign Language*. Clevedon: Multilingual Matters.

Lapkin, S. and Swain, M. (1984) Research update. *Language and Society/Langue et Société* 12, 48–54.

Lapkin, S. and Swain, M. (1990) French immersion research agenda for the 90s. *Canadian Modern Language Review* 46, 638–74.

Larsen, D. and Smalley, W. (1972) *Becoming Bilingual: A Guide to Language Learning*. New Canaan, CT: Practical Anthropology.

Larsen-Freeman, D. (1975) The acquisition of grammatical morphemes by adult ESL students. *TESOL Quarterly* 9, 409–20.

Larsen-Freeman, D. (1976) An explanation for the morpheme acquisition order of second language learners. *Language Learning* 26, 125–34.

Larsen-Freeman, D. and Long, M. (1991) *An Introduction to Second Language Acquisition Research*. London: Longman.

Lasonen, K. (1978) *Research Reports, No 66*. Department of Education, University of Jyväskylä. Cited in C. Bratt Paulston (1983) *Swedish Research and Debate about Bilingualism*. Stockholm: National Swedish Board of Education.

Leadholm, B. and Miller, J. (1992) *Language Sample Analysis: The Wisconsin Guide*. Madison, WI: Waismen Center Language Analysis Laboratory.

Lee, J. (2003) *Making Communicative Language Teaching Happen*. New York: McGraw-Hill.

Lees, J. (1993) *Children with Acquired Aphasias*. London: Whurr Publishers.

Lemmon, C. and Goggin, J. (1989) The measurement of bilingualism and its relationship to cognitive ability. *Applied Psycholinguistics* 10, 133–55.

Lengyel, Z. (1995) Some critical remarks on the phonological component. In D. Singleton and Z. Lengyel (eds) *The Age Factor in Second Language Acquisition*. Clevedon: Multilingual Matters.

Lenneberg, E. (1964) A biological perspective of language. In E. Lenneberg (ed.) *New Directions in the Study of Language*. Cambridge, MA: MIT Press. Reprinted in R. Oldfield and J. Marshall (eds) (1968) *Language: Selected Readings*. Harmondsworth: Penguin.

Lenneberg, E. (1966) The natural history of language. In F. Smith and G. Miller (eds) *The Genesis of Language: A Psycholinguistic Approach*. Cambridge, MA: MIT Press.

Lenneberg, E. (1967) *Biological Foundations of Language*. New York: Wiley.

Lenneberg, E., Nichols, I. and Rosenberger, E. (1964) Primitive stages of language development in mongolism. *Disorders of Communication* 42, 119–37.

Leona, M.H. (1978) An examination of adolescent clique language in a suburban secondary school. *Adolescence* 13, 495–502.

Leonard, L. (1979) Language impairment in children. *Merrill-Palmer Quarterly* 25, 205–32.

Leonard, L. (1998) *Children with Specific Language Impairment*. Cambridge, MA: MIT Press.

Leonard, L., Steckol, K. and Schwartz, R. (1978) Semantic relations and utterance length in child language. In F. Peng and W. Von Raffler (eds) *Language Acquisition and Developmental Kinesics*. Tokyo: Bunka Hyoren.

Leonard, L., Camarata, S., Rowan, L. and Chapman, K. (1982) The communicative functions of lexical usage by language impaired children. *Applied Linguistics* 3, 109–25.

Leopold, W. (1939) *Speech Development of a Bilingual Child: A Linguist's Record. Volume 1.* Evanston, IL: Northwestern University Press.

Leopold, W. (1947) *Speech Development of a Bilingual Child: Sound-learning in the First Two Years. Volume 2.* Evanston IL: Northwestern University Press.

Leopold, W. (1948) The study of child language and infant bilingualism. *Word* 4, 1–17. Reprinted in A. Bar-Adon and W. Leopold (eds) (1971) *Child Language: A Book of Readings.* Englewood Cliffs, NJ: Prentice-Hall.

Leopold, W. (1949) Original invention in language. *Symposium* 3, 66–75.

Levy, J., Nebes, R. and Sperry, R. (1971) Expressive language in the surgically separated minor hemisphere. *Cortex* 7, 49–58.

Lewis, M. (1936, 1951) *Infant Speech: A Study of the Beginnings of Language.* London: Routledge and Kegan Paul. References are to the Second Edition.

Lieven, E., Pine, J. and Dressner-Barnes, H. (1992) Individual differences in early vocabulary development: Refining the referential-expressive distinction. *Journal of Child Language* 19, 287–310.

Little, D., Ridley, J., and Ushioda, E. (2002) *Towards Greater Autonomy in the Foreign Language Classroom.* Dublin: Authentik.

Little, D., Singleton, D. and Silvius, W. (1984) *Learning Second Languages in Ireland: Experience, Attitudes and Needs.* Dublin: Centre for Language and Communication Studies, Trinity College. ERIC ED 246 670.

Little, D., Ó Murchú, H. and Singleton, D. (1985) *Towards a Communicative Curriculum for Irish.* Dublin: Centre for Language and Communication Studies, Trinity College (in association with Bord na Gaeilge).

Littlewood, W. (1981) *Communicative Language Teaching.* Cambridge: Cambridge University Press.

Littlewood, W. (1984) *Foreign and Second Language Learning: Language-Acquisition Research and its Implications for the Classroom.* Cambridge: Cambridge University Press.

Liu, H., Bates, E. and Li, P. (1992) Sentence interpretation in bilingual speakers of English and Chinese. *Applied Psycholinguistics* 12, 451–84.

Locke, J. (1969) Experimentally elicited articulatory behaviour. *Language and Speech* 12, 187–91. Cited in V. Cook (1986a) Experimental approaches applied to two areas of second language learning research: Age and listening-based teaching methods. In V. Cook (ed.) (1986b) *Experimental Approaches to Second Language Learning.* Oxford: Pergamon.

Locke, J. (1988) The sound shape of early lexical representations. In M. Smith and J. Locke (eds) *The Emergent Lexicon.* New York: Academic Press.

Long, H. (1978) Presidential letter. *Lifelong Learning* 1 (7), 13, 31.

Long, M. (1983) Does second language instruction make a difference? A review of research. *TESOL Quarterly* 17, 359–82.

Long, M. (1990) Maturational constraints on language development. *Studies in Second Language Acquisition* 12, 251–85.

Lorenz, K.Z. (1958) The evolution of behavior. *Scientific American* 119 (6), December, 67–78.

Lundy, J.E.B. (1999) Theory of mind: Development in deaf children. *Perspectives in Education and Deafness* 18 (1), 1–5.

McCandless, B. and Coop, R. (1979) *Adolescents: Behavior and Development.* (2nd edn). New York: Holt, Rinehart and Winston.

McCarthy, D. (1930) *The Language Development of the Preschool Child.* Minneapolis: University of Minnesota Press.

McCarthy, D. (1946) Language development in children. In L. Carmichael (ed.) *Manual of Child Psychology.* New York: Wiley; London: Chapman and Hall.

McDonald, J. (2000) Grammaticality judgments in a second language: Influences of age of acquisition and native language. *Applied Psycholinguistics* 21, 395–423.

McDonough, S. (1981) *Psychology in Foreign Language Teaching.* London: George Allen and Unwin.

McGhee-Bidlack, B. (1991) The development of noun definitions: A metalinguistic analysis. *Journal of Child Language* 18, 417–34.

MacKay, I., Meador, D. and Flege, J., (2001) The identification of English consonants by native speakers of Italian. *Phonetica* 58, 103–25.

Maclaran, R. and Singleton, D. (1984a) Native speaker clarifications and the notion of simplicity. Paper presented at the Seventh International Congress of Applied Linguistics, Vrije Universiteit Brussel, August. Abstract in J. Den Haese and J. Nivette (eds), *AILA Brussels 84: Proceedings. Volume 3.* Brussels: ITO/FUB.

Maclaran, R. and Singleton, D. (1984b) Foreigner register. In D. Singleton and D. Little (eds) (1984) *Language Learning in Formal and Informal Contexts.* Dublin: Irish Association for Applied Linguistics.

McLaughlin, B. (1978, 1984) *Second Language Acquisition in Childhood. Volume I. Preschool Children.* Hillsdale, NJ: Lawrence Erlbaum. 1984 references are to the Second Edition.

McLaughlin, B. (1981) *A cognitive process approach to second language learning.* Santa Cruz: University of California. Mimeo. Cited in B. Harley (1986) *Age in Second Language Acquisition.* Clevedon: Multilingual Matters.

McLaughlin, B. (1987) *Theories of Second Language Learning.* London: Edward Arnold.

McLeish, J. (1963) *The Science of Behaviour.* London: Barrie and Rockcliff.

Mac Mathúna, L. (1988) Can the gap between 'lesser used and 'less widely taught' languages be bridged: a status challenge for Irish. In L. Mac Mathúna, N. French, E. Murphy and D. Singleton (eds) *The Less Widely Taught Languages of Europe.* Dublin: Irish Association for Applied Linguistics.

Macnamara, J. (1966) *Bilingualism and Primary Education: A Study of Irish Experience.* Edinburgh: Edinburgh University Press.

Macnamara, J. (1973a) The cognitive strategies of language learning. In J. Oller and J. Richards (eds) *Focus on the Learner: Pragmatic Perspectives for the Language Teacher.* Rowley, MA: Newbury House.

Macnamara, J. (1973b) Nurseries, streets and classrooms: Some comparisons and deductions. *Modern Language Journal* 57, 250–4.

McShane, J. (1991) *Cognitive Development: An Information Processing Account.* Oxford: Blackwell.

MacWhinney, B. and Snow, C. (1985) The child language data exchange system. *Journal of Child Language* 12, 271–96.

MacWhinney, B. and Snow, C. (1990) The child language data exchange system: An update. *Journal of Child Language* 17, 457–72.

Madden, D., Connelly, S. and Pierce, T. (1994) Adult age differences in shifting focused attention. *Psychology and Aging* 9, 529–38.

Mägiste (1987) Further evidence for the optimal age hypothesis in second language learning. In J. Lantolf and A. Labarca (eds) *Language Learning: Focus on the Classroom.* Norwood, NJ: Ablex.

Magnan, S. (1983) Age and sensitivity to gender in French. *Studies in Second Language Acquisition* 5, 194–212.

Major, R. (1977) Phonological differentiation of a bilingual child. _Ohio State University Working Papers in Linguistics_ 22, 88–122.

Mandell, D.R., Jusczyk, P.W., Pisoni, D. (1995) Infants' recognition of the sound patterns of their own names. _Psychological Science_ 6, 314–7.

Marinova-Todd, S., Marshall, D. and Snow, C. (2000) Three misconceptions about age and L2 learning. _TESOL Quarterly_ 34, 9–34.

Markey, S. (2003) Rural Irish speakers fight influx of English. _National Geographic News_   http://news.nationalgeographic.com/news/2003/02/0225_030225_irishlanguage.html#main.

Martin, C., Johnson, S. and Teaford, M. (2002) _Senior Centers: Ohio's Blueprint for the Future_. Columbus, OH: Ohio Department of the Aging.

Martohardjono, G. (1993) _Wh-movement in the Acquisition of a Second Language: A Cross-linguistic Study of Three Languages with and without Syntactic Movement_. Unpublished Ph.D. thesis, Cornell University.

Martohardjono, G. and Flynn, S. (1995) Is there an age factor for Universal Grammar? In D. Singleton and Z. Lengyel (eds) _The Age Factor in Second Language Acquisition_. Clevedon: Multilingual Matters.

Mason, C. (1971) The relevance of intensive training in English as a foreign language for university students. _Language Learning_ 21, 197–204.

Mateer, C. and Ojemann, G. (1983) Thalamic mechanisms in language and memory. In S. Segalowitz (ed.) _Language Functions and Brain Organization_. New York: Academic Press.

Matthews, P., Adcock, J., Chen, Y., Fu, S., Devlin, J., Rushworth, M., Smith, S., Beckmann, C. and Iversen, S. (2003) Towards understanding language organisation in the brain using fMRI. _Human Brain Imaging_ 18, 239–47.

Mayberry, R. (1993) First language acquisition after childhood differs from second language acquisition: The case of ASL. _Journal of Speech and Hearing Research_ 36, 1258–70.

Mayberry, R. and Eichen, E. (1991) The long-lasting advantage of learning sign language in childhood: Another look at the critical period for language acquisition. _Journal of Memory and Language_ 30, 486–512.

Mayberry, R. and Fischer, S. (1989) Looking through phonological shape to lexical meaning: The bottleneck of non-native sign language processing. _Memory and Cognition_ 17, 740–54.

Mayberry, R., Fischer, S. and Hatfield, N. (1983) Sentence repetition in American Sign Language. In J. Kyle and B. Woll (eds) _Language in Sign: International Perspectives on Sign Language_. London: Croom Helm.

Meier, R.P. (1991) Language acquisition by deaf children. _American Scientist_ 79 (10), 60–70.

Meier, R.P. (2001) Review of D. Birdsong (ed.) _Second Language Acquisition and the Critical Period Hypothesis. Journal of Child Language_ 28, 222–8.

Meisel, J. (1983) Strategies of second language acquisition: More than one kind of simplification. In R. Andersen (ed.) _Pidginization and Creolization as Language Acquisition_. Rowley, MA: Newbury House.

Menyuk, P. (1975) The language-impaired child: Linguistic or cognitive impairment? In D. Aaronson and R. Rieber (eds) _Developmental Psycholinguistics and Communication Disorders_. New York: New York Academy of Sciences.

Menyuk, P. (1977) _Language and Maturation_. Cambridge, MA: MIT Press.

Menyuk, P. (1978) Linguistic problems in children with developmental dysphasia. In M. Wyke (ed.) _Developmental Dysphasia_. London: Academic Press.

Merriam, S. (2001) Andragogy and self-directed learning: Pillars of adult learning theory. *New Directions for Adult and Continuing Education* 89, 3–13

Messer, D. (1978) The integration of mothers' referential speech with joint play. *Child Development* 49, 781–7.

Messer, D. (1980) The episodic structure of maternal speech to young children. *Journal of Child Language* 7, 29–40.

Mezirow, J. (1981) A critical theory of adult learning and education. *Adult Education* 32, 3–24. Reprinted in M. Tight (ed.), 1983, *Education for Adults. Volume 1. Adult Learning and Education.* London: Croom Helm (in association with the Open University).

Millar, J. and Whitaker, H. (1983) The right hemisphere's contribution to language: A review of the evidence from brain-damaged subjects. In S. Segalowitz (ed.) *Language Functions and Brain Organization.* New York: Academic Press.

Mitchell R. and Myles, F. (1998) *Second Language Learning Theories.* London: Edward Arnold.

Moeser, S. and Bregman, A. (1972) The role of reference in the acquisition of a miniature artificial language. *Journal of Verbal Learning and Verbal Behavior* 11, 759–69.

Moeser, S. and Bregman, A. (1973) Imagery and language acquisition. *Journal of Verbal Learning and Verbal Behavior* 12, 91–8.

Molfese, D. (1977) Infant cerebral asymmetry. In S. Segalowitz and F. Gruber (eds) *Language Development and Neurological Theory.* New York: Academic Press.

Molfese, D., Freeman, R. and Palermo, D. (1975) The ontogeny of brain lateralization for speech and nonspeech stimuli. *Brain and Language* 2, 356–68.

Morehead, D. and Morehead, A. (eds) (1976) *Normal and Deficient Child Language.* Baltimore, MD: University Park Press.

Morford, J. and Mayberry, R. (2000) A reexamination of 'early exposure' and its implications for language acquisition by eye. In C. Chamberlain, J. Morford and R. Mayberry (eds) *Language Acquisition by Eye.* Mahwah, NJ: Lawrence Erlbaum.

Morley, M. (1957) *The Development and Disorders of Speech in Childhood.* Edinburgh: Livingstone.

Moscovitch, M. (1973) Language and the cerebral hemispheres: Reaction time studies and their implications for models of cerebral dominance. In P. Pliner, L. Krames and T. Alloway (eds) *Communication and Affect: Language and Thought.* New York: Academic Press.

Moscovitch, M. (1977) The development of lateralization of language functions and its relation to cognitive and linguistic development: A review and some theoretical speculations. In S. Segalowitz and F. Gruber (eds) *Language Development and Neurological Theory.* New York: Academic Press.

Moscovitch, M. (1979) Information processing and the cerebral hemispheres. In M. Gazzaniga (ed.) *Handbook of Behavioral Neurobiology. Volume 2.* New York: Plenum Press.

Moscovitsch, M. (1983a) The linguistic and emotional functions of the normal right hemisphere. In E. Perecman (ed.) *Cognitive Processing in the Right Hemisphere.* New York: Academic Press.

Moscovitch, M. (1983b) Stages of processing and hemispheric differences in language in the normal subject. In M. Studdert-Kennedy (ed.) *Psychobiology of Language.* Cambridge, MA: MIT Press.

Mowrer, O. (1960) *Learning Theory and Symbolic Processes.* New York: Wiley.

Moyer, A. (1999) Ultimate attainment in L2 phonology: The critical factors of age, motivation and instruction. *Studies in Second Language Acquisition* 21, 81–108.

Muñoz, C. (2003a) Le rythme d'acquisition des savoirs communicationels chez des apprenants guidés. L'influence de l'âge. *Acquisition et Interaction en Langue Étrangère* 18, 53–76.

Muñoz, C. (2003b) Variation in oral skills development and age of onset. In M.P. García Mayo and M.L. García Lecumberri (eds) *Age and the Acquisition of English as a Foreign Language*. Clevedon: Multilingual Matters.

Munro, M. and Derwing, T. (1995) Foreign accent, comprehensibility and intelligibility in the speech of second language learners. *Language Learning* 45, 73–97.

Murrell, H. and Humphries, S. (1978) Age, experience and short-term memory. In M. Gruneberg, P. Morris and R. Sykes (eds) *Practical Aspects of Memory*. New York: Academic Press.

Myers, P. (1994) Communication disorders associated with right-hemisphere brain damage. In R. Chapey (ed.) *Language Intervention Strategies in Adult Aphasia*. Baltimore, MD: Williams and Wilkins.

Myers P. (1999) *Right Hemisphere Damage: Disorders of Communication and Cognition*. San Diego, CA: Singular Publishing Group.

Mylov, P. (1972) *Skoleforsøg i Engelsk (School Experiments in English)*. Copenhagen: Munksgaar.

Naiman, N., Fröhlich, M., Stern, H. and Todesco, A. (1995) *The Good Language Learner*. Second Edition. Clevedon: Multilingual Matters.

Nakazima, S. (1980) The organisation process of babbling. In T. Murry and J. Murry (eds) *Infant Communication: Cry and Early Speech*. Houston, TX: College-Hill Press.

Nelson, E. and Rosenbaum, E. (1968) Sociolinguistic dimensions of youth culture. Paper presented at the meeting of the American Educational Research Association, Chicago.

Nelson, E. and Rosenbaum, E. (1972) Language patterns within the youth subculture: Development of slang vocabularies. *Merrill-Palmer Quarterly* 18, 273–85.

Nelson, K. (1973) Structure and strategy in learning to talk. *Monographs of the Society for Research in Child Development* 38 (1–2). Series No. 149.

Neufeld, G. (1977) Language learning ability in adults: A study on the acquisition of prosodic and articulatory features. *Working Papers on Bilingualism* 12, 45–60.

Neufeld, G. (1979) Towards a theory of language learning ability. *Language Learning* 29, 227–41.

Neugarten, B. (1974) Age groups in American society and the rise of the young-old. *Annals of the American Academy of Political and Social Science* 415, 187–98.

Neville, H., Coffey, S., Lawson, D., Fischer, A. Emmorey, K. and Bellugi, U. (1997) Neural systems mediating American Sign Language: Effects of sensory experiences and age of acquisition. *Brain and Language* 57, 285–308.

Newmark, L. and Reibel, D. (1968) Necessity and sufficiency in language learning. *International Review of Applied Linguistics* 6, 145–64.

Newport, E. (1984) Constraints on learning: Studies in the acquisition of American Sign Language. *Papers and Reports on Child Language Development* 23, 1–22.

Newport, E. (1990) Maturational constraints on language learning. *Cognitive Science* 14, 11–28.

Newport, E. and Supalla, T. (1987) *Critical Period Effects in the Acquisition of a Primary Language*. Unpublished manuscript.

Newton, M. (2002) *Savage Girls and Wild Boys: A History of Feral Children*. London: Faber and Faber.

NIACE [National Institute of Adult Continuing Education] (2002) *Older People and Learning: Some Key Statistics*. *NIACE Briefing Sheet* 32.

Nida, E. (1957–58) Some psychological problems in second language learning. *Language Learning* 8, 7–15.

Niemeier, S. (2003) The need for lexical, syntactic and conceptual integration: 'Bilingual' teaching in Germany. Paper presented at the 8th International Cognitive Linguistics Conference, Logroño.

Nippold, M.A. (1988) *Later Language Development: The School-Age and Adolescent Years*. Second Edition. Austin: Pro-Ed.

Nippold, M.A. and Rudzinski, M (1993) Familiarity and transparency in idiom explanation: A developmental study of children and adolescents. *Journal of Speech, Language and Hearing Research* 40, 245–53.

Nippold, M., Uhden, L., Schwarz, I. (1997) Proverb explanation through the lifespan: A developmental study of adolescence and adults. *Journal of Speech, Language and Hearing Research* 36, 728–37.

Nique, C. (1974) *Initiation méthodique à la grammaire générative*. Paris: Armand Colin.

Nolan, M. and Tucker, I. (1981) *The Hearing Impaired Child and the Family*. London: Souvenir Press.

Obler, L. (1981) Right hemisphere participation in second language acquisition. In K. Diller (ed.) *Individual Differences and Universals in Language Learning Aptitude*. Rowley, MA: Newbury House.

Obler, L. (1982) The parsimonious bilingual. In L. Obler and L. Menn (eds) *Exceptional Language and Linguistics*. New York: Academic Press.

Obler, L. and Gjerlow, K. (1999) *Language and the Brain*. Cambridge: Cambridge University Press.

Ó Domhnalláin, T. (1967) Language teaching research in Ireland. In P. Strevens (ed.) *Modem Languages in Great Britain and Ireland*. Strasbourg: AIDELA; London: Harrap.

Ó Domhnalláin, T. (1977) Ireland: The Irish language in education. *Language Problems and Language Planning* 1, 83–96.

Olguin, R. and Tomasello, M. (1993) Twenty-five-month-old children do not have a grammatical category of verb. *Cognitive Development* 8, 245–72.

Oller, D. (1976) Analysis of Infant Vocalizations: A Linguistic and Speech Scientific Perspective. Invited miniseminar given at the American Speech and Hearing Convention, Houston. Cited in R. Stark (1986) Prespeech segmental feature development. In P. Fletcher and M. Garman (eds) *Language Acquisition: Studies in First Language Development*. Cambridge: Cambridge University Press.

Oller, D. (1978) Infant vocalizations and the development of speech. *Allied Health and Behavioral Science* 1, 523–49.

Oller, J. and Nagato, N. (1974) The long-term effect of FLES: An experiment. *Modern Language Journal* 58, 15–19.

Oller, J. and Richards, J. (eds) (1973) *Focus on the Learner: Pragmatic Perspectives for the Language Teacher*. Rowley, MA: Newbury House.

Olson, L. and Samuels, S. (1973) The relationship between age and accuracy of foreign language pronunciation. *Journal of Educational Research* 66, 263–7. Reprinted in S. Krashen, R. Scarcella and M. Long (eds) (1982) *Child-Adult Differences in Second Language Acquisition*. Rowley, MA: Newbury House.

Ó Murchú, H. (2001) *The Irish Language in Education in the Republic of Ireland.* Ljouwert/Leeuwarden: Mercator-Education.

Ó Murchú, M. (1984) Irish and English now. *Ireland Today: Bulletin of the Department of Foreign Affairs* 1101, 11–13.

Ó Riagáin, P. and Ó Gliasáin, M. (1984) *The Irish Language in the Republic of Ireland: Preliminary Report of a National Survey.* Dublin: Institiúid Teangeolaíochta Eireann.

Oyama, S. (1976) A sensitive period for the acquisition of a non-native phonological system. *Journal of Psycholinguistic Research* 5, 261–84.

Oyama, S. (1978) The sensitive period and comprehension of speech. *Working Papers on Bilingualism* 16, 1–17. Reprinted in M. Krashen, R. Scarcella and M. Long (eds) (1982) *Child-Adult Differences in Second Language Acquisition.* Rowley, MA: Newbury House.

Pace, C. and Topini, A. (2003) Analysis of the age-related physical and psychological changes in learners over 60: Implications for the learning of L2 Italian and suggestions on suitable teaching techniques and syllabus design. Paper presented at ELIA VIII (Encuentros de Linguistica Inglesa Aplicada), 'El factor edad en la adquisición y enseñanza de L2', Seville.

Palmen, M.-J., Bongaerts, T. and Schils, E. (1997) L'authenticité de la prononciation dans l'acquisition d'une langue étrangère au-delà de la période critique: Des apprenants néerlandais parvenus à un niveau très avancé en français. *Acquisition et Interaction en Langue Étrangère* 9, 173–91.

Papagno, C., Valentine, T. and Baddeley, A. (1991) Phonological short-term memory and foreign-language vocabulary learning. *Journal of Memory and Language* 30, 331–47.

Papalia, D. and Olds, S. (1995) *Human Development.* New York: McGraw-Hill.

Paquier, P. and Van Dongen, H. (1993) Acquired child aphasia: An introduction. *Aphasiology* 7, 421–40.

Paris, S. and Mahoney, G. (1974) Cognitive integration in children's memory for sentences and pictures. *Child Development* 45, 633–42.

Parker, R. and Davis, F. (eds) (1983) *Developing Literacy: Young Children's Use of Language.* Newark, DE: International Reading Association.

Patkowski, M. (1980) The sensitive period for the acquisition of syntax in a second language. *Language Learning* 30, 449–72.

Patkowski, M. (1990) Accent in a second language: A reply to James Emil Flege. *Applied Linguistics* 11, 73–89.

Peal, E. and Lambert, W. (1962) The relation of bilingualism to intelligence. *Psychological Monographs* 76, 1–23.

Penfield, W. (1958) *The Excitable Cortex in Conscious Man.* Liverpool: Liverpool University Press.

Penfield, W. and Roberts, L. (1959) *Speech and Brain Mechanisms.* Princeton, NJ: Princeton University Press.

Perecman, E. (ed.) (1983) *Cognitive Processing in the Right Hemisphere.* New York: Academic Press.

Pertz, D. and Bever, T. (1975) Sensitivity to phonological universals in children and adults. *Language* 51, 149–62.

Peterson, C. and Siegal, M. (1995) Deafness, conversation, and theory of mind. *Journal of Child Psychology and Psychiatry* 36, 459–74.

Peura, M. and Skutnabb-Kangas, T. (eds) (1994) *'Man kan vara tvåländare också.' Den sverigefinska minoriteten väg från tystnad till kamp.* (*'You can be Bicontrial too.' The Road of the Swedish-Finnish Minority from Silence to Struggle*). Stockholm: Sverigefinländarnas Arkiv.

Piaget, J. (1926) *The Language and Thought of the Child.* Translated by M. and R. Gabain. London: Routledge and Kegan Paul.

Piaget, J. (1962) *Play, Dreams and Imitation in Childhood.* Translated by C. Gattegno and F. Hodgson. London: Routledge and Kegan Paul.

Piaget, J. and Inhelder, B. (1969) *The Psychology of the Child.* London : Routledge & Kegan Paul.

Piattelli-Palmarini, M. (ed.) (1979) *Théories du langage, théories de L'apprentissage: Le débat entre Jean Piaget et Noam Chomsky.* Paris: Éditions du Seuil.

Pimsleur, P. (1966) Testing foreign language learning. In A. Valdman (ed.) *Trends in Language Teaching.* New York: McGraw-Hill.

Pinker, S. (1989) *Learnability and Cognition: The Acquisition of Argument Structure.* Cambridge, MA: MIT Press.

Pinker, S. (1994) *The Language Instinct: How the Mind Creates Language.* New York: HarperPerennial.

Piper, T. and Cansin, D. (1988) Factors influencing the foreign accent. *Canadian Modern Language Review* 44, 334–42.

Piske, T., MacKay, I. and Flege, J. (2001) Factors affecting degree of foreign accent in an L2: A review. *Journal of Phonetics* 29, 191–215.

Pitchford, N. (2000) Spoken language correlates of reading impairments acquired in childhood. *Brain and Language* 72, 129–49.

Plude, D. and Doussard-Roosevelt, J. (1990) Aging and attention: Selectivity, capacity and arousal. In E. Lovelace (ed.) *Aging and Cognition: Mental Processes, Self-Awareness and Interventions.* Amsterdam: North Holland.

Politzer, R. (1978) Errors of English speakers of German as perceived and evaluated by German natives. *Modern Language Journal* 62, 253–61.

Politzer, R. and Weiss, L. (1969) Developmental aspects of auditory discrimination, echo response and recall. *Modern Language Journal* 53, 75–85.

Poon, L.W. (1985). Differences in human memory with aging: Nature, causes and clinical implications. In J. Birren and K. Schaie (eds) *Handbook of the Psychology of Aging.* New York: Van Nostrand Reinhold.

Posner, M. and Pavese, A. (1998) Anatomy of word and sentence meaning. *Proceedings of the National Academy of Sciences* 95, 899–905.

Potter, G., Hoy, P., Hawkins, E., Lewis, M., Maddox, J., Robinson, J., Spicer, A. and Wigram, M. (1977) *The Early Teaching of Modern Languages.* London: The Nuffield Foundation.

Preyer, W. (1889) Abstract of B. Sigismund's *Kind und Welt* (Brunswick 1856). In W. Preyer, *The Mind of the Child. Volume 2.* Translated by H. Brown. New York: Appleton-Century-Crofts. Reprinted in A. Bar-Adon and W. Leopold (eds) (1971) *Child Language: A Book of Readings.* Englewood Cliffs, NJ: Prentice-Hall.

Prior, M. (1977) Psycholinguistic disabilities of autistic and retarded children. *Journal of Mental Deficiency Research* 21, 37–45.

Pulvermüller, F. and Schumann, J. (1994) Neurobiological mechanisms of language acquisition. *Language Learning* 44, 681–734.

Pusey, E. (Translator) (1907) *The Confessions of St. Augustine.* London: Dent; New York: Dutton.

Radford, A. (1990) _Syntactic Theory and the Acquisition of English Syntax: The Nature of Early Child Grammars in English._ Oxford: Blackwell.

Ramsey, C. and Wright, C. (1974) Age and second language learning. _Journal of Social Psychology_ 94, 115–21.

Ramus, F., Hauser, M.D., Miller, C., Morris, D. and Mehler, J. (2001) Language discrimination by human newborns and cotton-top tamarin monkeys. In M. Tomasello and E. Bates (eds) _Language Development: The Essential Readings._ Oxford: Blackwell.

Ramus, F., Nespor, M. and Mehler, J. (1999) Correlates of linguistic rhythm in the speech signal. _Cognition_ 73, 265–92.

Ravem, R. (1968) Language acquisition in a second language environment. _International Review of Applied Linguistics_ 6 (2), 175–85. Reprinted in J. Richards (ed.) _Error Analysis: Perspectives in Second Language Acquisition._ London: Longman, 1974.

Ravem, R. (1970) The development of wh-questions in first and second language learners. Occasional Paper, University of Essex. Reprinted in J. Richards (ed.) _Error Analysis: Perspectives in Second Language Acquisition._ London: Longman, 1974.

Ravem, R. (1978) Two Norwegian children's acquisition of English syntax. In E. Hatch (ed.) _Second Language Acquisition: A Book of Readings._ Rowley, MA: Newbury House.

Redlinger, W. and Park, T. (1980) Language mixing in young bilinguals. _Journal of Child Language_ 7, 337–52.

Reed, C. (ed.) (1971) _The Learning of Language._ New York: Appleton-Century-Crofts.

Reznick, J. and Goldfield, B. (1992) Rapid change in lexical development in comprehension and production. _Developmental Psychology_ 28, 406–13.

Richards, J. (ed.) (1974) _Error Analysis: Perspectives in Second Language Acquisition._ London: Longman.

Rickford, J. (1983) What happens in decreolization. In R. Andersen (ed.), _Pidginization and Creolization as Language Acquisition._ Rowley, MA: Newbury House.

Ricks, D. and Wing, L. (1975) Language, communication and the use of symbols in normal and autistic children. _Journal of Autism and Childhood Schizophrenia_ 5, 191–21.

Riney, T. and Flege, J. (1998) Changes over time in global foreign accent and liquid identifiability and accuracy. _Studies in Second Language Acquisition_ 20, 213–43.

Ringbom, H. (1987) _The Role of the First Language in Foreign Language Learning._ Clevedon: Multilingual Matters.

Ritchie, W. (ed.) (1978a) _Second Language Acquisition Research: Issues and Implications._ New York: Academic Press.

Ritchie, W. (1978b) The right roof constraint in an adult acquired language. In W. Ritchie (ed.) _Second Language Acquisition Research: Issues and Implications._ New York: Academic Press.

Rivers, D.L. and Love, R.J. (1980) Language performance on visual processing tasks in right hemisphere lesion cases. _Brain and Language_ 42, 203–17.

Roberts, K. (1983) Comprehension and production of word order in stage I. _Child Development_ 54, 443–4.

Robertson, I. (1999) _Mind Sculpture._ London: Bantam.

Robinson, J. (1967) The development of certain pronunciation skills in the case of suffixed words. Unpublished Ph.D. dissertation, Harvard Graduate School of Education. Cited in Carroll (1971) Development of native language skills beyond the early years. In C. Reed (ed.) _The Learning of Language._ New York: Appleton-Century-Crofts.

Robinson, R. (1981) Equal recovery in child and adult brain? *Developmental Medicine and Child Neurology* 23, 379–82.

Rondal, J. (1998) Cases of exceptional language in mental retardation and Down syndrome. *Down Syndrome Research and Practice* 5 (1), 1–15.

Rosansky, E. (1975) The critical period for the acquisition of language: Some cognitive developmental considerations. *Working Papers on Bilingualism* 6, 93–100.

Rosansky, E. (1976) Methods and morphemes in second language acquisition research. *Language Learning* 26, 409–25.

Rosier, P. and Farella, M. (1976) Bilingual education at Rock Point – Some early results. *TESOL Quarterly* 10, 379–88.

Rosin, M., Swift, E., Bless, D. and Vetter, D. (1988) Communication profiles of adolescents with Down syndrome. *Journal of Childhood Communication Disorders* 12, 49–64.

Ross, E. (1981) The aprosodias. *Archives of Neurology* 38, 561–69.

Ruotsalainen, P. (1981) Språk, identitet och kultur: Några reflexioner kring Lars Henric Ekstrands artikel (Language, identity and culture: Some reflections concerning Lars Henric Ekstrand's article). *Forskning om utbildning* 8 (2), 40–2.

Russell, W. and Espir, M. (1961) *Traumatic Aphasia*. Oxford: Oxford University Press.

Ryan, L. and O'Kelly, C. (2002) *Euro Student Survey 2000: Irish Report: Social and Living Conditions of Higher Education Students*. Dublin: Higher Education Authority.

Salisbury, R. (1962) Notes on bilingualism and linguistic change in New Guinea. *Anthropological Linguistics* 4 (7), 1–13.

Salminen, T. (1993–1999) *UNESCO Red Book of Endangered Languages: Europe*. http://www.helsinki.fi/~tasalmin/europe_report.html.

Salt, B. (2001) Emerging Australian demographic trends. *On Line Opinion* http://www.onlineopinion.com.au/2001/May01/Salt.htm.

Salthouse, T. (1996) The processing-speed theory of adult age differences in cognition. *Psychological Review* 103, 403–28.

Salthouse, T. and Babcock, T. (1991) Decomposing adult age differences in working memory. *Developmental Psychology* 27, 763–76.

Satz, P. and Bullard-Bates, P.C. (1981) Acquired childhood aphasis. In M.T. Sarno (ed.) *Acquired Aphasia*. San Diego: Academic Press.

Satz, P., Strauss, E. and Whitaker, H. (1990) The ontogeny of hemispheric specialization: Some old hypotheses revisited. *Brain and Language* 38, 596–614.

Sauvignon, S. (ed.) (2002) *Interpreting Communicative Language Teaching: Contexts and Concerns in Teacher Education*. New Haven, CT: Yale University Press.

Scarcella, R. and Higa, C. (1982) Input and age differences in second language acquisition. In S. Krashen, R. Scarcella and M. Long (eds) *Child-Adult Differences in Second Language Acquisition*. Rowley, MA: Newbury House.

Scarcella, R. and Krashen, S. (eds.) (1980) *Research in Second Language Acquisition*. Rowley, MA: Newbury House.

Schachter, J. (1988) Second language acquisition and its relationship to Universal Grammar. *Applied Linguistics* 9, 219–35.

Schaffer, H., Hepburn, A. and Collis, G. (1983) Verbal and non-verbal aspects of mothers' directives. *Journal of Child Language* 10, 337–55.

Schaie, K. and Geiwitz, J. (1982) *Adult Development and Aging*. Toronto: Little, Brown.

Schaie, K. (1996) *Intellectual Development in Adulthood: The Seattle Longitudinal Study.* New York: Cambridge University Press.

Schildroth, A. (1976) The relationship of non-verbal intelligence test scores to selected characteristics of hearing impaired. In C. Williams (ed.) *Proceedings of the Third Gallaudet Symposium on Research in Deafness: Emotional Development Research Programs.* Washington, DC: Gallaudet University Press.

Schleppegrell, M. (1987) The older language learner. *ERIC Digests* ED287313, http://www.ed.gov/databases/ERIC_Digests/ed287313.html.

Schmidt, A. and Flege, J. (1996) Speaking rate effects on stops produced by Spanish and English monolinguals and Spanish/English bilinguals. *Phonetica* 53, 162–9.

Schmidt, R. (1983) Interaction, acculturation, and the acquisition of communicative competence: A case study of an adult. In N. Wolfson and E. Judd (eds) *Sociolinguistics and Second Language Acquisition.* Rowley, MA: Newbury House.

Schneidermann, E. and Saddy, J. (1988) A linguistic deficit resulting from right-hemisphere damage. *Brain and Language* 34, 38–53.

Schumann, J. (1975a) Affective factors and the problem of age in second language acquisition. *Language Learning* 25, 209–35.

Schumann, J. (1975b) Second language acquisition: Getting a more global look at the learner. In H. Brown (ed.) *Papers in Second Language Acquisition.* Ann Arbor, MI: University of Michigan Press.

Schumann, J. (1975c) Implications of pidginization and creolization for the study of adult second language acquisition. In J. Schumann and N. Stenson (eds) *New Frontiers in Second Language Learning.* Rowley, MA: Newbury House.

Schumann, J. (1976a) Social distance as a factor in second language acquisition. *Language Learning* 26, 135–43.

Schumann, J. (1976b) Second language acquisition: The Pidginization Hypothesis. *Language Learning* 26, 391–408. Reprinted in E. Hatch (ed.) (1978a) *Second Language Acquisition: A Book of Readings.* Rowley, MA: Newbury House.

Schumann, J. (1978a) *The Pidginization Process: A Model for Second Language Acquisition.* Rowley, MA: Newbury House.

Schumann, J. (1978b) The Acculturation Model for second language acquisition. In R. Gingras (ed.) *Second Language Acquisition and Foreign Language Teaching.* Arlington, VA: Center for Applied Linguistics.

Schumann, J. (1983) Reaction to Eckman and Washabaugh (1983). In R. Andersen (ed.) *Pidginization and Creolization as Language Acquisition.* Rowley, MA: Newbury House.

Schumann, J. (1997) *The Neurobiology of Affect in Language.* Oxford: Blackwell.

Schumann, J. (2001a) Appraisal psychology, neurobiology, and language. *Annual Review of Applied Linguistics* 21, 23–42.

Schumann, J. (2001b) Learning as foraging. In Z. Dörnyei and R. Schmidt (eds) *Motivation and Second Language Acquisition.* Honolulu: University of Hawai'i Press.

Schumann, J. and Stauble, A.M. (1983a) A discussion of second language acquisition and decreolization. In R. Andersen (ed.) *Pidginization and Creolization as Language Acquisition.* Rowley, MA: Newbury House.

Schumann, J. and Stauble, A.M. (1983b) Reply to J. Rickford (1983). In R. Andersen (ed.) *Pidginization and Creolization as Language Acquisition.* Rowley, MA: Newbury House.

Schumann, J., Holroyd J., Campbell, N. and Ward, F. (1978) Improvement of foreign language pronunciation under hypnosis: A preliminary study. *Language Learning* 28, 143–8.

Schwartz, G. and Merten, D. (1967) The language of adolescence: An anthropological approach to the youth culture. *The American Journal of Anthropology* 72, 453–68.

Scollon, R. (1974) One child's language from one to two: The origins of construction. Unpublished Ph.D. dissertation, University of Hawaii. Cited in E. Hatch (1978b). Discourse analysis and second language acquisition. In E. Hatch (ed.) *Second Language Acquisition: A Book of Readings*. Rowley, MA: Newbury House.

Scollon, R. (1979) A real early stage: An unzippered condensation of a dissertation on child language. In E. Ochs and B. Schieffelin (eds) *Developmental Pragmatics*. New York: Academic Press.

Scott, C. (1988) Spoken and written syntax. In M.A. Nippold (ed.) *Later Language Development: Ages Nine through Nineteen*. Austin: Pro-Ed.

Scott, C. and Stokes, S. (1995) Measures of syntax in school-age children and adolescents. *Language, Speech and Hearing Services in Schools* 26, 309–19.

Scott, L. (1967) *Child Development: An Individual Longitudinal Approach*. New York: Holt Rinehart and Winston.

Scott, S., Blank, C., Rosen, S. and Wise, R. (2000) Identification of a pathway for intelligible speech in the left temporal lobe. *Brain* 123, 2400–6.

Scottish Education Department (1969) *French in the Primary School*. Edinburgh: Her Majesty's Stationery Office.

Scovel, T. (1969) Foreign accents, language acquisition and cerebral dominance. *Language Learning* 19, 245–53.

Scovel, T. (1988) *A Time to Speak: A Psycholinguistic Inquiry into the Critical Period for Human Language*. Rowley, MA: Newbury House.

Scovel, T. (2000) A critical review of the Critical Period Hypothesis. *Annual Review of Applied Linguistics* 20, 213–23.

Seagoe, M. (1964) *Yesterday was Tuesday, All Day and All Night: The Story of a Unique Education*. Boston: Little Brown.

Segalowitz, S. (ed.) (1983a) *Language Functions and Brain Organization*. New York: Academic Press.

Segalowitz, S. (1983b) Cerebral asymmetries for speech in infancy. In S. Segalowitz (ed.) *Language Function and Brain Organization*. New York: Academic Press.

Segalowitz, S. and Chapman, J. (1980) Cerebral asymmetry for speech in neonates: A behavioral measure. *Brain and Language* 9, 281–8.

Segalowitz, S. and Gruber, F. (eds) (1977) *Language Development and Neurological Theory*. New York: Academic Press.

Seliger, H. (1978) Implications of a multiple critical periods hypothesis for second language learning. In W. Ritchie (ed.) *Second Language Acquisition Research: Issues and Implications*. New York: Academic Press.

Seliger, H. (1982) On the possible role of the right hemisphere in second language acquisition. *TESOL Quarterly* 16, 307–14.

Seliger, H., Krashen, S. and Ladefoged, P. (1975) Maturational constraints in the acquisition of second language accent. *Language Sciences* 36, 20–2.

Selinker, L., Swain, M. and Dumas, G. (1975) The interlanguage hypothesis extended to children. *Language Learning* 25, 139–52.

Seright, L. (1985) Age and aural comprehension achievement in Francophone adults learning English. *TESOL Quarterly* 19, 455–73.

Shattuck, R. (1980) *The Forbidden Experiment. The Story of the Wild Boy of Aveyron*. New York: Farrar Straus Giroux.

Shatz, M. (1982) On mechanisms of language acquisition: Can features of the communicative environment account for development? In L. Gleitman and E. Wanner, E. (eds) *Language Acquisition: The State of the Art*. New York. Cambridge University Press.

Shields, J. (1991) Semantic-pragmatic disorder: A right hemisphere syndrome? *British Journal of Disorders of Communication* 26, 383–92.

Shirley, M. (1933) *The First Two Years: A Study of Twenty-five Babies*. Minneapolis: University of Minnesota Press.

Shore, C. (1995) *Individual Differences in Language Development*. London: Sage Publications.

Sidtis, J. and Gazzaniga, M. (1983) Competence vs. performance after callosal section: Looks can be deceiving. In J. Hellige (ed.) *Cerebral Hemisphere Asymmetry*. New York: Praeger.

Simmonds, R. and Scheibel, A. (1989) The postnatal development of the motor speech area: A preliminary study. *Brain and Language* 37, 42–58.

Simons-Derr, J. (1983) Signing vs silence. *The Exceptional Parent* 13 (6), 49–52.

Sinclair, H. and Bronckart, J.-P. (1971) S.V.O. A linguistic universal? A study in developmental psycholinguistics. *Journal of Experimental Child Psychology* 14, 329–48.

Singleton, D. (1981) Age as a factor in second language acquisition: A review of some recent research. *CLCS Occasional Paper* 3. Dublin: Centre for Language and Communication Studies, Trinity College. ERIC ED 217 712.

Singleton, D. (1987a) The fall and rise of language transfer. In J. Coleman and R. Towell (eds) *The Advanced Language Learner*. London: Centre for Information on Language Teaching and Research.

Singleton, D. (1987b) Mother and other tongue influence on learner French: A case study. *Studies in Second Language Acquisition* 9, 327–45.

Singleton, D. (1995) Second languages in the primary school: The age factor dimension. *Teanga: The Irish Yearbook of Applied Linguistics* 15, 155–66.

Singleton, D. (1998) Age and the second language lexicon. *Studia Anglica Posnaniensia* 23, 365–76.

Singleton, D. (1999) *Exploring the Second Language Mental Lexicon*. Cambridge: Cambridge Universitry Press.

Singleton, D. and Little, D. (eds) (1984) *Language Learning in Formal and Informal Contexts*. Dublin: Irish Association for Applied Linguistics.

Singleton, J. (1989) *Restructuring of Language from Impoverished Input: Evidence for Linguistic Compensation*. Unpublished Ph.D. thesis. University of Illinois at Urbana-Champaign.

Skehan, P. (1984) On the non-magical nature of second and foreign language acquisition. *Polyglot* 5:1, A3-B14.

Skehan, P. (2002) Theorizing and updating aptitude. In P. Robinson (ed.) *Individual Differences and Instructed Language Learning*. Amsterdam: John Benjamins.

Skilbeck, M. (2001) *The University Challenged: A Review of International Trends and Issues with Particular Reference to Ireland*. Dublin: Higher Education Authority.

Skinner, B. (1957) *Verbal Behavior*. New York: Appleton-Century-Crofts.

Skipp, A., Windfuhr, K.L. and Conti-Ramsden, G. (2001) *Children's Grammatical Categories of Verb and Noun: A Comparative Look at Children with SLI and Normal Language*. Unpublished study.

Skutnabb-Kangas, T. (1984) *Bilingualism or Not. The Education of Minorities*. Clevedon: Multilingual Matters.

Skutnabb-Kangas, T. (1997) Bilingual education for Finnish minority students in Sweden. In J. Cummins and D. Corson (eds) *Bilingual Education* (Volume 5 of the *Encyclopedia of Language and Education*). Dordrecht: Kluwer.

Skutnabb-Kangas, T. and Toukomaa, P. (1976) Teaching migrant children's mother tongue and learning the language of the host country in the context of the sociocultural situation of the migrant family. Helsinki: The Finnish National Commission for UNESCO. Cited in B. Harley (1986) *Age in Second Language Acquisition*. Clevedon: Multilingual Matters.

Slavoff, G. and Johnson, J. (1995) The effects of age on the rate of learning a second language. *Studies in Second Language Acquisition* 17, 1–16.

Smedts, W. (1988) De beheersing van de nederlandse woordvorming tussen 7 en 17 (The mastering of Dutch word formation between 7 and 17). In F. van Besien (ed.) *First Language Acquisition*. Antwerp: Association Belge de Linguistique Appliquée/Universitaire Instelling Antwerpen (*ABLA Papers* No. 12).

Smith, A. (1968) *The Body*. London: George Allen and Unwin. Pelican Edition, Harmondsworth: Penguin, 1970.

Smith, F. and Miller, G. (eds) (1966) *The Genesis of Language: A Psycholinguistic Approach*. Cambridge MA: MIT Press.

Smith, K. and Braine, M. (1972) Miniature languages and the problem of language acquisition. In T. Bever and W. Weksel (eds) *The Structure and Psychology of Language*, Volume 2. New York: Holt, Rinehart and Winston.

Smith, M. (1926) An investigation of the development of the sentence and the extent of vocabulary in young children. *University of Iowa Studies in Child Welfare* 3 (5), 92.

Smith, N. and Wilson, D. (1979) *Modern Linguistics: The Results of Chomsky's Revolution*. Harmondsworth: Penguin.

Smythe, P., Stennet, R. and Gardner, R. (1975) The best age for foreign language training: Issues, options and facts. *Canadian Modern Language Review* 32, 10–23.

Snow, C. (1977) The development of conversation between mothers and babies. *Journal of Child Language* 4, 1–22.

Snow, C. (1979) The role of social interaction in language acquisition. In W. Collins (ed.) *Children's Language and Communication*. Hillsdale, NJ. Laurence Erlbaum Associates.

Snow, C. (1981) English speakers' acquisition of Dutch syntax. In H. Winitz (ed.) *Native Language and Foreign Language Acquisition*. New York: New York Academy of Sciences.

Snow, C. (1983) Age differences in second language acquisition: Research findings and folk psychology. In K. Bailey, M. Long and S. Peck (eds) *Second Language Acquisition Studies*. Rowley, MA: Newbury House.

Snow, C. (1986) Conversations with children. In P. Fletcher and M. Garman (eds) *Language Acquisition: Studies in First Language Development*. Cambridge: Cambridge University Press.

Snow, C. (1987) Relevance of the notion of a critical period to language acquisition. In M. Bornstein (ed.) *Sensitive Periods in Development*. Hillsdale, NJ: Laurence Erlbaum Associates.

Snow, C. and Hoefnagel-Höhle, M. (1977) Age differences in the pronunciation of foreign sounds. *Language and Speech* 20, 357–65.

Snow, C. and Hoefnagel-Höhle, M. (1978a) Age differences in second language acquisition. In G. Nickel (ed.) *Applied Linguistics: Psycholinguistics*. Stuttgart: Hochschulverlag.

Snow, C. and Hoefnagel-Höhle, M. (1978b) The critical period for language acquisition: Evidence from second language learning. *Child Development* 49, 1114–28. Reprinted in S. Krashen, R. Scarcella and M. Long (eds) (1982) *Child-Adult Differences in Second Language Acquisition*. Rowley, MA: Newbury House.

Snow, C. and Hoefnagel-Höhle, M. (1979) Individual differences in second language ability: A factor analytic study. *Language and Speech* 22, 151–62.

Snyder, T. and Hoffman C. (2003) *Digest of Education Statistics 2002*. Washington, DC: National Center for Educational Statistics.

Sorenson, A. (1967) Multilingualism in the Northwest Amazon. *American Anthropologist* 69, 670–84.

Spence, J., Walton, W., Miller, F. and Court, S. (1954) A *Thousand Families in Newcastle-upon-Tyne*. London: Oxford University Press.

Sperry, R. and Gazzaniga, M. (1967) Language after section of the cerebral commissures. *Brain* 90, 131–48.

Sperry, R., Gazzaniga, M. and Bogen, J. (1969) Interhemispheric relationship: The neocortical commissures; syndromes of hemispheric disconnection. In P. Vinken and G. Bruyn (eds), *Handbook of Clinical Neurology. Volume 4*. Amsterdam: North Holland.

Spiker, D. (1990) Early intervention: A developmental perspective. In D. Cichetti and M. Beeghly (eds) *Children with Down Syndrome: A Developmental Perspective*. Cambridge. Cambridge University Press.

Spiker, D. and Hopmann, M. (1997) The effectiveness of early intervention for children with Down syndrome. In M. Guralnick (ed.) *The Effectiveness of Early Intervention*. Baltimore, MD: Paul H. Brookes Publishing Company.

Springer, S. and Deutsch, G. (1985) *Left Brain, Right Brain*. Revised Edition. New York: W.H. Freeman.

Stafford-Clark, D. (1965) *What Freud Really Said*. London: Macdonald.

Stankowski Gratton, R. (1980) Una ricerca sperimentale sull' insegnamento del tedesco dalla prima classe elementare (An experimental study on the teaching of German from the first elementary grade). *Rassegna Italiana di Linguistica Applicata* 12 (3), 119–41.

Stapp, Y. (1999) Neural plasticity and the issue of mimicry tasks in L2 pronunciation studies. *TESL-EJ: Teaching English as a Second or Foreign Language* 3 (4), A1, 1–24, http://www-writing.berkeley.edu/TESL-EJ/ej12/a1.html.

Stark, R. (1986) Prespeech segmental feature development. In P. Fletcher and M. Garman (eds) *Language Acquisition: Studies in First Language Development*. Cambridge: Cambridge University Press.

Steckol, K. and Leonard, L. (1979) The use of grammatical morphemes by normal and language-impaired children. *Journal of Communication Disorders* 12, 291–301.

Steinberg, D. (1993) *An Introduction to Psycholinguistics*. London: Longman.

Stengel, E. (1939) On learning a new language. *International Journal of Psycho-Analysis* 20, 471–9.

Stern, C. and Stern, W. (1928) *Die Kindersprache: Eine psychologische und sprachtheoretische Untersuchung*. Fourth Edition. Leipzig: Barth.

Stern, H. (1976) Optimal age: Myth or reality? *Canadian Modern Language Review* 32:3, 283–94.

Stern, H. (1983) *Fundamental Concepts of Language Teaching*. Oxford: Oxford University Press.

Stern, W. (1930) *Psychology of Early Childhood.* (2nd edn). London: George Allen and Unwin. Extract reprinted in A. Bar-Adon and W. Leopold (eds) (1971) *Child Language: A Book of Readings.* Englewood Cliffs NJ: Prentice-Hall.

Stevenson, J. and Richman, N. (1976) The prevalence of language delay in a population of three-year-old children and its association with general retardation. *Developmental Medicine and Child Neurology* 18, 433–41.

Stiles, J., Bates, E, Thal, D., Traumer, D. and Reilly, J. (2002) Linguistic and spatial cognitive development in children with pre- and perinatal focal brain injury: A ten year overview from the San Diego Longitudinal Project. In M. Johnson, Y. Munakata and R. Gilmore (eds) *Brain Development and Cognition: A Reader.* Oxford: Blackwell.

Streiter, L. (1976) Language perception of two-month old infants shows effects of both innate mechanisms and experience. *Nature* 1, 39–41.

Studdert-Kennedy, M. (ed.) (1983) *Psychobiology of Language.* Cambridge MA: M.I.T. Press.

Swain, M. (1978) Home-school language switching. In J. Richards (ed.) *Understanding Second and Foreign Language Learning.* Rowley, MA: Newbury House.

Swain, M. (1981a) Time and timing in bilingual education. *Language Learning* 31, 1–15.

Swain, M. (1981b) Bilingual education for majority and minority language children. *Studia Linguistica* 35, 15–32.

Swain, M. (1997) French immersion programs in Canada. In J. Cummins and D. Corson (eds) *Bilingual Education* (Volume 5 of the *Encyclopedia of Language and Education*). Dordrecht: Kluwer.

Swain, M. and Lapkin, S. (1982) *Evaluating Bilingual Education: A Canadian Case-Study.* Clevedon: Multilingual Matters.

Taft, R. and Cahill, D. (1981) Education of immigrants in Australia. In J. Bhatnagar (ed.) *Educating Immigrants.* London: Croom Helm.

Tager-Flusberg, H. (1994) *Constraints on Language Acquisition: Studies of Atypical Children.* Hillsdale, NJ: Laurence Erlbaum Associates.

Tahta, S., Wood, M. and Loewenthal, K. (1981a) Foreign accents: Factors relating to transfer of accent from the first language to a second language. *Language and Speech* 24, 265–72.

Tahta, S., Wood, M. and Loewenthal, K. (1981b) Age changes in the ability to replicate foreign pronunciation and intonation. *Language and Speech* 24, 363–72.

Taine, H. (1877) Acquisition of language by children. *Mind* 2, 252–59. Reprinted in A. Bar-Adon and W. Leopold (eds) (1971) *Child Language: A Book of Readings.* Englewood Cliffs NJ: Prentice-Hall.

Taylor, B. (1974) Toward a theory of language acquisition. *Language Learning* 24, 23–35.

Taylor, J. (ed.) (1958) *Selected Writings of John Hughlings Jackson.* New York: Basic Books.

Taylor, L., Guiora, A., Catford, J. and Lane, H. (1969) The role of personality variables in second language behavior. *Comprehensive Psychiatry* 10, 463–74.

Tennant, M. (1996) *Psychology and Adult Learning.* London: Routledge.

Tervoort, B. (1979) Foreign language awareness in a five-to nine-year-old lexicographer. *Journal of Child Language* 61, 159–66.

Thal, D. and Bates, E. (1990) Continuity and variation in early language development. In J. Colombo and J. Fagen (eds) *Individual Differences in Infancy: Reliability, Stability, Prediction.* Hillsdale, NJ: Laurence Erlbaum.

Thompson, I. (1991) Foreign accents revisited: The English pronunciation of Russian immigrants. *Language Learning* 41, 177–204.

Thorndike, E.L. (1928) *Adult Learning*. New York: Macmillan.

Thurstone, L. (1955) *The Differential Growth of Mental Abilities*. Chapel Hill, NC: University of North Carolina Press.

Tiedemann, D. (1787) Observations on the development of the mental faculties of children. Translated by C. Murchison and S. Langer in their article: Tiedemann's observations on the development of the mental faculties of children. *Pedagogical Seminary* 34, 205–30. Reprinted in abridged form in A. Bar-Adon and W. Leopold (eds) (1971) *Child Language: A Book of Readings*. Englewood Cliffs, NJ: Prentice-Hall. First published as Über die Entwicklung der Seelenfähigkeiten bei Kindern, *Hessische Beiträge zur Gelehrsamheit und Kunst*, 1787.

Tight, M. (ed.) (1983) *Education for Adults. Volume 1. Adult Learning and Education*. London: Croom Helm (in association with the Open University).

Titone, R. (1985a) Measurement and evaluation of bilingualism and bilingual education: A psycholinguistic perspective. *Rassegna Italiana di Linguistica Applicata* 17 (2–3), 19–30.

Titone, R. (1985b) Research trends in applied psycholinguistics: An introduction report. *Rassegna Italiana di Linguistica Applicata* 17 (2–3), 75–84.

Titone, R. (1986a) Un passaporto per il futuro (A passport for the future). *L'Educatore* 34 (6), 4–9.

Titone, R. (1986b) Evaluating bilingual education: The Italian 'FLES' experience. Paper presented at a seminar on the theme Bilingual Education in Italy and Ireland organized by the Irish Committee of the European Bureau for Lesser Used Languages, Italian Cultural Institute, Dublin.

Tomasello, M. (1992) *First Verbs: A Case Study of Early Grammatical Development*. Cambridge: Cambridge University Press.

Tomasello, M. (2000) Acquiring syntax is not what you think. In D. Bishop and L. Leonard (eds) *Speech and Language Impairments in Children: Causes, Characteristics, Intervention and Outcome*. Hove: Psychology Press.

Tomasello, M. and Bates, E. (2001) Introduction to Part 1: Speech perception. In M. Tomasello and E. Bates (eds) *Language Development: The Essential Readings*. Oxford: Blackwell.

Tomasello, M. and Todd, J. (1983) Joint attention and lexical acquisition style. *First Language* 4, 197–212.

Tomb J.W. (1925) On the intuitive capacity of children to understand spoken languages. *British Journal of Psychology* 16, 53–4.

Tomblin, J., Freese, P. and Records, N. (1992) Diagnosing specific language impairment in adults for the purposes of pedigree analysis. *Journal of Speech and Hearing Research* 35, 832–43.

Toukomaa, P. (1972) Om finska invandrarelevernas utvecklingsförhållanden in den svenska skolan (On Finnish immigrant pupils' development prospects in the Swedish school). University of Uleaborg. Cited in T. Skutnabb-Kangas (1984) *Bilingualism or Not: The Education of Minorities*. Clevedon: Multilingual Matters.

Towell, R. (1987) *An Analysis of the Oral Language Development of British Undergraduate Learners of French*. Unpublished Ph.D. dissertation, University of Salford.

Towell, R. and Hawkins, R. (1994) *Approaches to Second Language Acquisition*. Clevedon: Multilingual Matters.

Trechmann, E. (Translator) (n.d.). *The Essays of Montaigne*. New York and London: Oxford University Press.

Tremaine, R. (1975) *Syntax and Piagetian Operational Thought: A Developmental Study of Bilingual Children.* Washington, DC: Georgetown University Press.

Tuchman, R., Rapin, I. and Shinnar, S. (1991) Autistic and dysphasic children I: Clinical characteristics. *Paediatrics* 88, 1211–18.

Tucker, D., Watson, R. and Heilman, K. (1977) Discrimination and evocation of effectively intoned speech in patients with right parietal disease. *Neurology* 27, 947–50.

Turnbull, M., Lapkin, S., Hart, D. and Swain M. (1998) Time on task and immersion graduates' French proficiency. In S. Lapkin (ed.) *French Second Language Education in Canada: Empirical Studies.* Toronto: University of Toronto Press.

Ullman, M. (2003) A neurocognitive perspective on second language acquisition and processing: The Declarative/Procedural Model. Contribution to the *Language Learning* Roundtable on the Cognitive Neuroscience of Second Language Acquisition, 13th Annual Conference of the European Second Language Assocation (EUROSLA), Edinburgh.

Upshur, J. (1968) Four experiments on the relation between foreign language teaching and learning. *Language Learning* 21, 111–24.

Vaid, J. (1983) Bilingualism and brain lateralization. In S. Segalowitz (ed.) *Language Function and Brain Organization.* New York: Academic Press.

Valdman, A. (1983) Creolization and second language acquisition. In R. Andersen (ed.) *Pidginization and Creolization as Language Acquisition.* Rowley, MA: Newbury House.

Valentine, C. (1942) *The Psychology of Early Childhood.* London: Methuen.

Valette, R. (1964) Some reflections on second-language learning in young children. *Language Learning* 14, 91–98.

Van Boxtel, S., Bongaerts, T. and Coppen, P.-A. (2003) Native-like attainment in L2 syntax. *EUROSLA Yearbook* 3, 157–81.

Van Dongen, H., Loonen, M. and Van Dongen, K. (1985) Anatomical basis for acquired fluent aphasia in children. *Annals of Neurology* 17, 306–9.

Van Els, T., Bongaerts, T., Extra, G., Van Os, C. and Janssen-Van Dieten, A.-M. (1984) *Applied Linguistics and the Teaching of Foreign Languages.* Translated by R. Van Oirsouw. London: Edward Arnold.

Vanevery, A. and Rosenberg, S. (1970) Semantics, phrase structure and age as variables in sentence recall. *Child Development* 41, 853–9.

Van Hout, A., Evrard, P. and Lyon, G. (1985) On the positive semiology of acquired aphasia in children. *Developmental Medicine and Child Neurology* 27, 231–41.

Vargha-Khadem, F. and Corballis, M. (1979) Cerebral asymmetry in infants. *Brain and Language* 8, 1–9.

Vernon, M. (1969) Sociological and psychological factors associated with hearing loss. *Journal of Speech and Hearing Research* 12, 541–63.

Vihman, M., Ferguson, C. and Elbert, M. (1986) Phonological development: from babbling to speech: common tendencies and individual differences. *Applied Psycholinguistics* 7, 3–40.

Virey, J.J. (1800) *Histoire naturelle du genre humain (avec une dissertation sur le sauvage de L'Aveyron).* Paris: Dufart.

Vollmer, J. (1962) *Evaluation of the Effect of Foreign Language Study in the Elementary School upon Achievement in the High School* U.S. Office of Education Contract SAE 9516. Sornerville: Public Schools.

Von Elek, T. and Oskarsson, M. (1973) *Teaching Foreign Language Grammar to Adults: A Comparative Study.* Stockholm: Almqvist and Wiksell.

Wada, J., Clark, R. and Hamm, A. (1975) Cerebral hemispheric asymmetry in humans. *Archives of Neurology* 32, 239–46.

Walberg, H., Hase, K. and Pinzur Rasher, S. (1978) English acquisition as a diminishing function of experience rather than age. *TESOL Quarterly* 12, 427–37.

Wallace, C. and Macaskie, J. (1984) Stop the Monitor I want to get off: Or looking for a way forward in language teaching. In D. Singleton and D. Little (eds) *Language Learning in Formal and Informal Contexts*. Dublin: Irish Association for Applied Linguistics.

Walsh, T. and Diller, K. (1981) Neurological considerations on the optimum age for second language learning. In K. Diller (ed.) *Individual Differences and Universals in Language Learning Aptitude*. Rowley, MA: Newbury House.

Walz, H. (1976) The human brain as the source of linguistic behaviour. In G. Nickel (ed.) *Proceedings of the Fourth International Congress of Applied Linguistics. Volume 1*. Stuttgart: Hochschulverlag.

Warner-Gough, J. and Hatch, E. (1975) The importance of input data in second language acquisition studies. *Language Learning* 25, 297–308.

Wattendorf, E., Westermann, B., Zappatore, D., Franceschini, R., Lüdi, G., Radü, E.-W. and Nitsch, C. (2001) Different languages activate different subfields in Broca's area. *NeuroImage* 13, 624.

Weinstock, R. (1978) *The Graying of the Campus*. New York: Educational Facilities Laboratories.

Wells, G. (1979) Describing children's linguistic development at home and at school. *British Educational Research Journal* 5, 75–89.

Wells, G. (1985) *Language Development in the Pre-school Years*. Cambridge: Cambridge University Press.

Werker, J. and Tees, R. (1983) Developmental changes across childhood in the perception of non-native sounds. *Canadian Journal of Psychology* 37, 278–86.

Whitaker, H., Bub, D. and Leventer, S. (1981) Neurolinguistic aspects of language acquisition and bilingualism. In H. Winitz (ed.) *Native Language and Foreign Language Acquisition*. New York: The New York Academy of Sciences.

White, L. and Genesee, F. (1996) How native is near-native? The issue of ultimate attainment in adult second language acquisition. *Second Language Research* 12, 238–65.

Wieczerkowski, W. (1971) *Erwerb einer zweiten Sprache im Unterricht*. Hamburg: Schroedelverlag.

Wingfield, A. and Byrnes, D. (1981) *The Psychology of Human Memory*. New York: Academic Press.

Wingfield, A., Stine, E., Lahar, C. and Aberdeen, J. (1988) Does the capacity of working memory change with age? *Experimental Aging Research* 14, 103–7.

Winitz, H. (ed.) (1981) *Native Language and Foreign Language Acquisition*. New York: The New York Academy of Sciences.

Witelson, S. (1977) Early hemisphere specialization and interhemispheric plasticity: An empirical and theoretical review. In S. Segalowitz and F. Gruber (eds) *Language Development and Neurological Theory*. New York: Academic Press.

Witelson, S. (1983) Bumps on the brain: Right-left anatomic asymmetry as a key to functional lateralization. In S. Segalowitz (ed.) *Language Function and Brain Organization*. New York: Academic Press.

Wode, H. (1976) Developmental sequences in naturalistic L2 acquisition. *Working Papers on Bilingualism* 11, 1–31. Reprinted in E. Hatch (ed.) (1978a) *Second Language Acquisition: A Book of Readings*. Rowley, MA: Newbury House.

Woll, B. and Grove, N. (1996) On language deficits and modality in children with Down syndrome: A case study of twins bilingual in BSL and English. *Journal of Deaf Studies and Deaf Education* 1 (4), 271–78.

Wong-Fillmore, L. (1976) The second time around: Cognitive and social structures in second language acquisition. Unpublished Ph.D. dissertation, University of California, Berkeley. Cited in B. Harley (1986) *Age in Second Language Acquisition*. Clevedon: Multilingual Matters.

Woods, B. (1980) The restricted effects of right-hemisphere lesions after age nine: Wechsler Test data. *Neuropsychologia* 18, 65–70.

Woods, B. and Teuber, H. (1978) Changing patterns of childhood aphasia. *Annals of Neurology* 6, 405–9.

Woodward, J.C. (1973) Some characteristics of pidgin sign English. *Sign Language Studies* 3, 39–59.

Wuillemin, D. and Richardson, B. (1994) Right hemisphere involvement in processing later-learned languages in multilinguals. *Brain and Language* 46, 620–36.

Yamada, J., Takatsuka, S., Kotake, N. and Kurusu, J. (1980) On the optimum age for teaching foreign vocabulary to children. *International Review of Applied Linguistics in Language Teaching* 18, 245–47.

Zaidel, E. (1983) On multiple representations of the lexicon in the brain – The case of two hemispheres. In M. Studdert-Kennedy (ed.) *Psychobiology of Language*. Cambridge, MA: MIT Press.

Zampini, M.L. and Green, K.P. (2001) The voicing contrast in English and Spanish: the relationship between perception and production. In J. Nicol (ed.) *One Mind, Two Languages: Bilingual Language Processing*. Oxford: Blackwell.

Zidonis, F. (1965) Generative grammar: A report on research. *English Journal* 54, 405–9.

Index